There's Something About Mary

There's Something About Mary

Essays on Phenomenal Consciousness and Frank Jackson's Knowledge Argument

edited by Peter Ludlow, Yujin Nagasawa, and Daniel Stoljar

A Bradford Book
The MIT Press
Cambridge, Massachusetts
London, England

MIT Press books may be purchased at special quantity discounts for business or sales promotional use. For information, please email special_sales@mitpress.mit.edu.

This book was set in Stone serif and Stone sans on 3B2 by Asco Typesetters, Hong Kong. Printed and bound in the United States of America.

Library of Congress Cataloging-in-Publication Data

There's something about Mary : essays on Frank Jackson's knowledge argument /
edited by Peter Ludlow, Yujin Nagasawa, Daniel Stoljar.
   p. cm.
"A Bradford Book."
Includes bibliographical references and index.
ISBN 978-0-262-12272-6 (hc : alk. paper) — ISBN 978-0-262-62189-2 (pbk. : alk. paper)
1. Consciousness. 2. Jackson, Frank, 1943– . 3. Knowledge, Theory of. I. Ludlow,
Peter, 1957– . II. Nagasawa, Yujin, 1975– . III. Stoljar, Daniel, 1967– .
BF311.T455   2004
126—dc22   2004042586

10 9 8 7 6 5 4 3 2

Contents

Acknowledgments

Torin Alter, Benj Hellie, Frank Jackson, and Paul Raymont read a draft of the introduction and provided useful comments and suggestions. John Bigelow and Howard Robinson furnished important historical information. Martin Davies and Michael Smith gave us guidance about the overall direction of the work. David Chalmers did all three things, and in addition gave good advice about essay selection. We are grateful to all of them. We would also like to thank those authors and publishers who let us reprint the essays collected here and those authors who wrote new essays for the volume: David Chalmers, Benj Hellie, Philip Pettit, and Robert Van Gulick. We are grateful also to Judy Feldmann, Jessica Lawrence-Hurt, and Tom Stone of The MIT Press. Finally, further thanks to Frank Jackson for the foreword, and of course for his splendid creation, Mary.

Sources

Frank Jackson, "Epiphenomenal Qualia," *Philosophical Quarterly* 32 (1982): 127–136. Reprinted by permission of the author and publisher.

Frank Jackson, "What Mary Didn't Know," *Journal of Philosophy* 83 (1986): 291–295. Reprinted by permission of the author and publisher.

Daniel C. Dennett, "'Epiphenomenal' Qualia?" from his *Consciousness Explained* (New York: Little, Brown, 1991), 398–406. Reprinted by permission of the author and publisher.

Howard Robinson, "Dennett on the Knowledge Argument," *Analysis* 53 (1993): 174–177. Reprinted by permission of the author and publisher.

David Lewis, "What Experience Teaches," from J. Copley-Coltheart, ed., *Proceedings of the Russellian Society* 13 (1988): 29–57. Reprinted by permission of Stephanie R. Lewis and the publisher.

Michael Tye, "Knowing What It Is Like: The Ability Hypothesis and the Knowledge Argument," from his *Consciousness, Color, and Content* (Cambridge, Mass.: The MIT Press, 2000), 3–20. Reprinted by permission of the author and publisher.

John Bigelow and Robert Pargetter, "Acquaintance with Qualia," *Theoria* 61 (1990): 129–147. Reprinted by permission of the author and publisher.

Paul M. Churchland, "Knowing Qualia: A Reply to Jackson," from his *A Neurocomputational Perspective* (Cambridge, Mass.: The MIT Press, 1989), 67–76. Reprinted by permission of the author and publisher.

Paul M. Churchland, "Postscript: 1997," from P. M. Churchland and P. S. Churchland, *On the Contrary: Critical Essays, 1987–1997* (Cambridge, Mass.: The MIT Press, 1998), 153–157. Reprinted by permission of the author and publisher.

Earl Conee, "Phenomenal Knowledge," *Australasian Journal of Philosophy* 72 (1994): 136–150. Reprinted by permission of the author and publisher.

Brian Loar, "Phenomenal States (Revised Version)," excerpted from J. E. Tomberlin, ed., *Philosophical Perspectives 4: Action Theory and Philosophy of Mind* (Atascadero, Calif.: Ridgeview, 1990), 81–108. Reprinted by permission of the author and publisher. (Revised version in N. Block, O. Flanagan, and G. Güzeldere, eds., *The Nature of Consciousness: Philosophical Debates*, Cambridge, Mass.: The MIT Press, 1997, 597–608.)

Martine Nida-Rümelin, "What Mary Couldn't Know: Belief About Phenomenal States," from T. Metzinger, ed., *Conscious Experience* (Exeter, U.K.: Imprint Academic, 1995), 219–241. Reprinted by permission of the author and publisher.

Terence Horgan, "Jackson on Physical Information and *Qualia*," *Philosophical Quarterly* 34 (1984): 147–152. Reprinted by permission of the author and publisher.

Daniel Stoljar, "Two Conceptions of the Physical," excerpted from *Philosophy and Phenomenological Research* 62 (2001): 253–270. Reprinted by permission of the author and publisher.

Frank Jackson, "Postscript," from P. Moser and J. Trout, eds., *Contemporary Materialism* (London: Routledge, 1995), 184–189. Reprinted by permission of the author and publisher.

Frank Jackson, "Postscript on Qualia," from his *Mind, Method, and Conditionals* (London: Routledge, 1998), 76–79. Reprinted by permission of the author and publisher.

Frank Jackson, "Mind and Illusion," by permission of the author and the Royal Institute of Philosophy.

Contributors

John Bigelow is Professor of Philosophy at Monash University, Australia.

David J. Chalmers is Professor of Philosophy and Director of the Center for Consciousness Studies at University of Arizona.

Paul M. Churchland is Professor of Philosophy at University of California, San Diego.

Earl Conee is Professor of Philosophy at University of Rochester.

Daniel C. Dennett is University Professor and Austin B. Fletcher Professor of Philosophy and Director of the Center for Cognitive Studies at Tufts University.

Benj Hellie is Assistant Professor in the Sage School of Philosophy at Cornell University.

Terence Horgan is Professor of Philosophy at University of Arizona.

Frank Jackson is Distinguished Professor of Philosophy and Director of the Research School of Social Sciences at Australian National University, Australia.

David Lewis was Class of 1943 University Professor of Philosophy at Princeton University.

Brian Loar is Professor of Philosophy at Rutgers University.

Peter Ludlow is Professor of Philosophy and Linguistics at University of Michigan.

Yujin Nagasawa is Research Fellow at the Australian Research Council Special Research Centre for Applied Philosophy and Public Ethics at Australian National University, Australia, and Izaak Walton Killam Memorial

Postdoctoral Fellow in the Department of Philosophy at University of Alberta, Canada.

Martine Nida-Rümelin is Professor of Philosophy at University of Fribourg, Switzerland.

Robert Pargetter is Professor of Philosophy at Monash University, Australia, and Principal of Haileybury College, Australia.

Philip Pettit is William Nelson Cromwell Professor of Politics at Princeton University.

Howard Robinson is Professor of Philosophy at Central European University, Hungary.

Daniel Stoljar is Senior Fellow in the Philosophy Program, the Research School of Social Sciences at Australian National University, Australia.

Michael Tye is Professor of Philosophy at University of Texas at Austin.

Robert Van Gulick is Professor of Philosophy and Director of the Cognitive Science Program at Syracuse University.

Foreword
Looking Back on the Knowledge Argument

Frank Jackson

1. I think we should be realists about the theories we accept. To the extent that we accept one or another theory, we should hold that its entities exist and its properties and relations are instantiated. This requires us to take ontologically seriously the pictures our theories paint of what our world is like. To accept the kinetic theory of gases is to accept *inter alia* that gases are literally made up of the particles the theory is framed in terms of, and that these particles have the properties the theory uses in its explanations. It follows that it is always a good question to ask of the picture painted by one theory we accept how it relates to the picture painted by another theory we accept. A special case of this good question is the relation between the physical sciences and psychology. The physical sciences, by which I mean roughly physics, chemistry, and biology, tell us that human beings are very complex aggregations of molecules that make up the cells, neurons, blood, and so on that biology talks of, and that these molecules are in turn made up of the smaller particles that atomic and subatomic physics talks of. These aggregations interact with an environment that is itself a vast aggregation of the entities that the physical sciences talk of, set in a spacetime whose nature itself is the subject of the physical sciences, physics in particular. Where, if anywhere, in this picture do we find the entities and properties of psychology? Where are the pains, the sensings of red, the pangs of conscience, the hope that there will not be a war next year, and so on and so forth?

The question is especially pressing in the case of the pangs, the pains and the sensings of red. On the face of it, no amount of aggregating of elements with the kinds of properties the physical sciences talk of can make up the phenomenal, conscious side of our psychology. That side of things is, in

one way or another, an extra; a part of the account of what our world is like
that is left out by the physical sciences—or so it seems. The kinetic theory
of gases tells us how to get pressure and temperature out of a certain kind of
aggregation of purely physical elements obeying purely physical laws. Perhaps functionalism and information theory tell us how to get intentionality and the propositional attitudes out of certain kinds of aggregations
of purely physical elements obeying purely physical laws, but nothing like
that would, on the face of it, seem possible for pain or sensing red or consciousness in general.

That was and is my view, and the view of many others. *On the face of it,*
physicalism about the mind across the board cannot be right. Any purely
physical account of what goes on in us and of how we relate to our surroundings leaves out the phenomenal and conscious side of psychology.
Accordingly, the knowledge argument was never an attempt to settle the
question for myself, or indeed, for the many others who found it obvious
that physicalism left something out. It was an attempt to find an argument
that might convince those who had, somehow or other, been able to overlook the fact that the physical account of what our world is like had a big
gap in it. The account left out consciousness and mental phenomenology.

I now think that what is, on the face of it, true is, on reflection, false. I
now think that we have no choice but to embrace some version or other
of physicalism. We are nothing over and above a very complex aggregation
of purely physical elements interacting with, and carrying information
about, a vast complex of purely physical elements. And as I have no intention of embracing eliminativism about phenomenal consciousness (or
about the propositional attitudes, if it comes to that), I think that, somewhere or other, in the vast, complex, purely physical aggregation that
makes up our world, there is phenomenal consciousness. I give my reasons
for this change of heart in the "Postscript on Qualia" reprinted in this volume. The key point is that we now know enough to know that were there
anything nonphysical about our psychology, it would be *screened out* by
our physical natures in the sense that no indicative traces of it would survive in memory, in reports, in articles called "Epiphenomenal Qualia" and
so on. This creates an insurmountable epistemic problem for the views of
my former self. As I now see matters, the challenge is to say where the
knowledge argument goes wrong. I say a bit about this in "Postscript on
Qualia" and give a fuller answer in "Mind and Illusion" reprinted in this

volume. Here I will confine myself to saying a little about how the solution I favor relates to some of the replies to the knowledge argument in the literature.

2. There are two main parts to the knowledge argument (in the form in which I advanced it; there have been many versions of it): the part that says that complete physical knowledge is not complete knowledge *tout court* (or anyway not as far as the mind is concerned), and the part that says that if physicalism is true, it is. The final step is then modus tollens. The first part is the part supported by the plausibility of the contention that Mary would learn something about what the world is like on her release. As we might put it, she would acquire an enlarged view of the available dimensions of similarity in our world. Before her release, runs the first part, she knew a lot about how different people looking at ripe tomatoes typically were alike, both in themselves and in their relations to the tomatoes. She knew, for example, how the ripe tomatoes typically induced a tendency to use the word 'red' in such people, provided they were English speakers. After her release, she would realize that there was another dimension altogether to how they are alike, and to how they differ from people looking at, say, grass. The second part of the knowledge argument is the part where it is observed that because she knows all there is to know physically, this means that were physicalism true, there would be no dimensions of similarity instantiated in our world other than those she knows about in the room before her release. Therefore, physicalism is false.

There have been many objections to both parts of the argument. My impression (I have not been counting) is that it is the second part that has attracted the most dissension. Those who object to the second part urge that it is consistent to hold that Mary's knowledge is incomplete while insisting that physicalism is true. However, I think, for the reasons I give in "Mind and Illusion" (and in "Finding the Mind in the Natural World," reprinted in *The Nature of Consciousness*, ed. Ned Block, Owen Flanagan, and Güven Güzeldere, Cambridge, Mass.: The MIT Press, 1997, pp. 483–491, where the emphasis is on the role of two-dimensionalism about the necessary a posteriori in the argument) that it is the first part that should be rejected. Mary's knowledge about what our world is like is not incomplete, or if it is, it is because she has failed to think things through aright or to put them together aright. She learns nothing about what her and our world is like that is not available to her in principle while in the black and white room. Here I will mention my concerns about two ways some justify rejecting the second part, two ways I do not discuss in "Mind and Illusion."

3. Some critics of the second part point out that no amount of knowledge of what one's world is like amounts to knowledge of, for example, who one is in one's world, or of what one's own part of one's world is like. A way of seeing this (as many have noted) is to reflect on the fact that information about what one's world is like can be represented by a division of the possible worlds into those that agree with one's own in the respect in question, and those that do not. However, such a division makes no discrimination *internal* to the possible worlds—any possible world is either, in its entirety, on one side or on the other side of the division. Such a division, therefore, cannot represent how things are in parts of worlds, and that is what we need to represent information about who or where one is in one's world. Analogy: a division of countries into the democratic and nondemocratic cannot represent the distribution of democracy within countries except to extent that it impacts on countries' overall ratings. These critics of the second part of the knowledge argument then point out, rightly, (i) that Mary will acquire perspectival knowledge, as we might put it, on her release; (ii) that this is a kind of knowledge *that*; and (iii) that the fact that it cannot be deduced by her from the nonperspectival (and perspectival) knowledge she has while in the black and white room is no objection to physicalism, for it simply reflects the point that perspectival knowledge is not reducible to nonperspectival knowledge. They conclude that we can allow that Mary lacks knowledge that without raising a problem for physicalism.

However, the first part of the knowledge argument was always a contention about Mary's lack of knowledge about what her *world* was like. It was not about her lack of certain perspectival knowledge. The appealing claim, as we put it above, was that after her release, she learns about certain similarities *between* the people she had been observing on her black and white monitor. The range of similarities that can hold between entities in her world is, she learns, bigger than she realizes, or could realize, while inside the black-and-white room. No doubt she would acquire perspectival knowledge as well—for example, that she herself was here and now instantiating one of the striking similarities—but, ran the argument, she would also acquire knowledge about the classification her world (that is, her world in its entirety) fell into: it is one of the ones where the respects of similarity that she did not know about before are exemplified.

4. Some critics of the second part of the knowledge argument point out that physical facts, or states of affairs, or events, or happenings, and so on, can be known under many aspects, or modes of presentation, or *qua* things falling under one or another concept, and that you can know something under one aspect, mode of presentation, or conceptual categorization without knowing of it under another. They infer from this that allowing that Mary's knowledge of what her world is like is incomplete—allowing, that is, the contention of the first part of the knowledge argument—does not mean that what is not known is not physical. Her lack of knowledge is a result of there being aspects, or modes, or conceptual categorizations that are unavailable to her while she is inside the room. Their suggestion is that when Mary leaves the room she acquires knowledge by knowing about the very same physical facts, states of affairs, events, and so on, but under different aspects, modes, or conceptual categorizations. The problem with this line of reply, it seems to me, is that these aspects, modes, or conceptual categorizations had better all be physical ones (in the wide sense operating in discussions of the knowledge argument that counts, e.g., functional and topic-neutral properties as physical) if physicalism is true. But then she could have known about them when inside the room. For example, I cannot see how there is a way of grouping things into categories that is, in principle, unavailable to her while in the room.

5. Enough. I have already abused my "foreword" privileges. Although I no longer agree with the knowledge argument, I do think it has been, and continues to be, a major impetus to many important debates that have cast a great deal of light on some very hard problems in the philosophy of mind. In many ways, I wish I could still accept it.

Introduction

Daniel Stoljar and Yujin Nagasawa

Mary is confined to a black-and-white room, is educated through black-and-white books and through lectures relayed on black-and-white television. In this way she learns everything there is to know about the physical nature of the world. She knows all the physical facts about us and our environment, in a wide sense of 'physical' that includes everything in *completed* physics, chemistry, and neurophysiology, and all there is to know about the causal and relational facts consequent upon all this, including of course functional roles. If physicalism is true, she knows all there is to know. For to suppose otherwise is to suppose that there is more to know than every physical fact, and that is just what physicalism denies.... It seems, however, that Mary does not know all there is to know. For when she is let out of the black-and-white room or given a color television, she will learn what it is like to see something red, say. This is rightly described as *learning*—she will not say "ho, hum." Hence, physicalism is false. (Jackson 1986, p. 291, reprinted as chap. 2, this vol.)

Frank Jackson's knowledge argument is one of the most discussed, important, and controversial arguments in contemporary philosophy and in the debates about consciousness to which philosophers make a contribution.[1] On its face, the argument purports to show that physicalism—the doctrine that everything is physical or supervenes on the physical—is false or at least is incompatible with the existence of consciousness. And it does so on the basis of easily understood premises and by employing an apparently impeccable argumentative structure.

The argument has implications for questions wider than simply that of physicalism. For one thing, even those philosophers who think of physicalism as not up for serious debate regard the knowledge argument as zeroing in on that aspect of conscious experience which is most puzzling, and most challenging for their view. Moreover, for many the real lesson of the argument is not the falsity of physicalism, but rather the possibility that conscious experience lies quite beyond our comprehension, and perhaps beyond the limits of rational inquiry generally.

It is therefore important to achieve a deeper understanding of the argument. That is the impetus behind the present volume. Its purpose is to gather together the main essays in which Jackson has presented—and later rejected[2]—his argument, plus some classic and more recent essays in which the argument is discussed and debated.[3] In turn, the purpose of this introduction is to set out the main themes of the discussion and explain the relations between them.

1   The Knowledge Intuition

Many arguments in philosophy of mind, and in other areas of philosophy, are based on intuitions that are extremely persistent and widespread, intuitions that (it is natural to speculate) have their sources in deep aspects of human psychology. Perhaps the best-known such intuition is the inverted spectrum, the idea, as Locke put it, that "the same Object should produce in several Men's Minds different Ideas at the same time; v.g. the Idea, that a Violet produces in one Man's Mind by his Eyes, were the same that a Marigold produced in another Man's and vice versa".[4] The inverted spectrum seems so compelling that one suspects that it is to some extent 'latent' in human thinking—that the contingent structure of the mind is such that we are prone to find the inverted spectrum possible (see Block 1990).

Something similar is plausible in the case of the knowledge argument. At the beginning of "Epiphenomenal Qualia," (chap. 1, this vol.), Jackson describes the intuition that he says lies behind the argument:

Tell me everything physical there is to tell about what is going on in a living brain, the kind of states, their functional role, their relation to what goes on at other times and in other brains, and so on and so forth, and be I as clever as can be in fitting it all together, you won't have told me about the hurtfulness of pains, the itchiness of itches, pangs of jealousy, or about the characteristic experience of tasting a lemon, smelling a rose, hearing a loud noise or seeing the sky. (1982, p. 127)

The intuition that Jackson is pointing to here concerns knowledge: no matter how it is put together, no amount of knowledge of a certain sort—a physical sort—is going by itself to suffice for knowledge of a different sort,

namely, a phenomenal sort. This intuition is not yet the knowledge argument, but it is an intuition on which that argument is based. Let us call it
the *knowledge intuition.*

The knowledge intuition is properly called an *intuition* in this sense: it
presents us with a prima facie modal truth, a truth about what is possible.
What it says is that it is possible for someone to know all the physical
truths about, say, smelling a rose, without knowing what it is like to smell
a rose.[5] The issue is not about what in fact anybody *does* know; perhaps
nobody knows *all* the physical truths about smelling roses. And the issue is
not whether it is psychologically possible to know all the physical truths of
this sort without knowing the phenomenal truths; perhaps this is not psychologically possible. The issue is, rather, logical: knowledge of the physical
sort does not suffice logically for knowledge of the phenomenal sort.

If the knowledge intuition is something that is present in ordinary
thought, it could scarcely be original with Jackson, and he certainly doesn't
say that it is. In fact, not only is it easy to find examples of the knowledge
intuition in the literature prior to Jackson, it is also easy to find the intuition being discussed in a context that is quite distinct from the one in
which he discusses it. To illustrate, consider the following passage from
Bertrand Russell's *The Problems of Philosophy*:

Physical science, more or less unconsciously, has drifted into the view that all natural
phenomena ought to be reduced to motions. Light and heat and sound are all due to
wave-motions, which travel from the body emitting them to the person who sees
light or feels heat or hears sound. That which has the wave-motion is either ether or
'gross matter' but in either case is what the philosopher would call matter. The only
properties which science assigns to it are position in space, and the power of motion
according to the laws of motion. Science does not deny that it *may* have other properties; but if so, such other properties are not useful to the man of science, and in no
way assist him in explaining the phenomena.

It is sometimes said that 'light *is* a form of wave-motion', but this is misleading, for
the light which we immediately see, which we know directly by means of our senses,
is not a form of wave-motion, but something quite different—something we all
know if we are not blind, though we cannot describe it so as to convey our knowledge to a man who is blind. A wave-motion, on the contrary, could quite well be
described to a blind man, since he can acquire a knowledge of space by the sense of
touch; and he can experience a wave-motion by a sea voyage almost as well as we
can. But this, which a blind man can understand, is not what we mean by light: we
mean by light just that which a blind man can never understand, and which we can
never describe to him. (1967 [1912], pp. 27–28)

Russell regards a certain sort of empiricism to be obvious, namely, that experience is necessary for the sort of phenomenal knowledge of light usually available to the sighted. It follows from this that a blind person—someone who by definition has not had the relevant experiences—cannot attain that sort of knowledge. On the other hand, Russell regards it as equally obvious that physical knowledge *is* in principle available to a blind person. Russell therefore endorses the knowledge intuition: no amount of knowledge of a physical sort is by itself sufficient for phenomenal knowledge. Nevertheless, Russell is concerned here not with metaphysics or physicalism, but with epistemology. In particular, he wants to argue that our epistemic position with respect to physical objects is analogous to the blind person's epistemic position with respect to light: "physical objects remain unknown in their intrinsic nature, at least as far as discovered by means of the senses" (ibid., p. 34).

The knowledge intuition is also present in discussion of a question that is related to Russell's but different from it, the question, in philosophy of perception, of what makes a psychological faculty one of sensory perception rather than simply a way of registering information about the world.[6] An interesting example is provided by British engineer J. W. Dunne. Along with a rather odd theory of time and dreaming, Dunne provides the following thought experiment in his *An Experience with Time*:[7]

Let us suppose that you are entertaining a visitor from some country where the inhabitants are all born blind; and that you are trying to make your guest understand what you mean by 'seeing'. You discover, we will further assume, that the pair of you have, fortunately, this much in common: You are both thoroughly conversant with the meaning of all the technical expressions employed in the physical sciences.

Using this ground of mutual understanding, you endeavour to explain your point. You describe how, in that little camera which we call the 'eye', certain electromagnetic waves radiating from a distant object are focused on to the retina, and there produce physical changes over the area affected; how these changes are associated with currents of 'nervous energy' in the criss-cross of nerves leading to the brain-centres, and how molecular or atomic changes at those centres suffice to provide the 'seer' with a registration of the distant object's outline.

All this your visitor could appreciate perfectly.

Now, the point to be noticed is this. Here is a piece of knowledge concerning which the blind man had no previous conception. It is knowledge which he cannot, as you can, acquire for himself by the ordinary process of personal experiment. In substitution, you have offered him a *description*, framed in the language of physical science. And that substitute has served the purpose of conveying the knowledge in question from yourself to him.

But in 'seeing' there is, of course, a great deal more than mere registration of outline. There is, for example—colour. ... Physical description cannot here provide the information which experience could have given. (1958 [1927], pp. 13–15)

Dunne's example is reminiscent both of Russell's example in the passage quoted above, and also to H. G. Wells' story, "The Country of Blind" (1904), in which a sighted stranger tries to convince the blind locals that he has one more sense than them. (Jackson mentions the story in the 1982 essay.)[8] Dunne takes it for granted that you would need to be able to see to have the concept of seeing, and on that basis he endorses (something like) the knowledge intuition. But since he is apparently primarily concerned with the nature of sight rather than the falsity of physicalism, we again have a use of the knowledge intuition that is different from Jackson's.

Unlike Russell and Dunne, the bearing of the knowledge intuition on epistemology or philosophy of perception is not important for Jackson. What is important for him is its bearing on the metaphysical thesis of physicalism, the doctrine, as he puts it, that "all (correct) information is physical information" (1982, p. 127). But what exactly *is* the connection between the knowledge intuition and physicalism?

2 From Intuition to Argument

In the 1982 essay, Jackson notes the simplest way in which the connection between the knowledge intuition and physicalism might be forged:

Nothing you could tell me of a physical sort captures the smell of a rose, for instance. Therefore, Physicalism is false. (1982, p. 127)

He continues:

By [my] lights this is a perfectly good argument. It is obviously not to the point to question its validity, and the premise is intuitively obviously true ... to me. I must, however, admit that it is weak from a polemical point of view. There are ... many who do not find the premise intuitively obvious. The task then is to present an argument whose premises are obvious to all, or at least to as many as possible. (Ibid., pp. 127–128)

Suppose we say that any argument whose premises constitute or contain the knowledge intuition, and whose conclusion is that physicalism is false, is properly called *a knowledge argument*. It would then appear that the simplest form of a knowledge argument is the one that Jackson presents in the first of these two passages. And, as he goes on to say in the second passage, the goal of the 1982 essay is to find a version of the argument that improves on the dialectical weakness of this simplest version. In a moment we will consider how the argument that Jackson develops differs from the simplest version that he begins with, and we will also take up the question of whether "it is obviously not to the point to question [the argument's] validity" (pp. 127–128). But first we should note that, if we define a knowledge argument in these terms, it is not hard to find examples of it in the literature.[9]

One example can be found in C. D. Broad's *The Mind and Its Place in Nature* (1925), and in particular in the chapter "Mechanism and Its Alternatives."[10] In that chapter, Broad is concerned with "the logical distinction between mechanism and emergence" (p. 70). The problem with mechanism, as he conceives of it, is that "a mathematical archangel"—that is, a being who is both logically omniscient and who knows all the mechanistic truths about various chemical compounds—would know all the truths if mechanism is true. But it appears that the archangel would not know all the truths (pp. 71–72):

Take any ordinary statement, such as we find in chemistry books; e.g. "Nitrogen and Hydrogen combine when an electric discharge is passed through a mixture of the two. The resulting compound contains three atoms of Hydrogen to one of Nitrogen; it is a gas readily soluble in water, and possessed of a pungent and characteristic smell." If the mechanistic theory be true, the archangel could deduce from his knowledge of the microscopic structure of atoms all these facts but the last. He would know exactly what the microscopic structure of ammonia must be; but he would be totally unable to predict that a substance with this structure must smell as ammonia does when it gets into the human nose. The utmost that he could predict on this subject would be that certain changes would take place in the mucous membrane, the olfactory nerves and so on. But he could not possibly know that these changes would be accompanied by the appearance of a smell in general, or of the peculiar smell of ammonia in particular unless someone told him so or he had smelled it for himself. If the existence of the so-called secondary qualities, or the fact of the their appearance, depends on the microscopic movements and arrangements of material particles which do not have these qualities themselves, then the laws of this dependence are certainly of the emergent type.

In this passage, Broad is endorsing a version of a knowledge argument in the sense we have introduced: Broad takes the knowledge intuition as his premise, and draws from this premise the conclusion that physicalism ("mechanism") is false.

A different presentation of the knowledge argument is in B. A. Farrell's essay "Experience":

Suppose we had obtained from our Martian visitor all the information that we, as psychologists and physiologists, could obtain about his sensory faculties. We should probably still want to say: "I wonder what it would be like to be a Martian—with his pseudo-radio sense, able, for example, to listen to whatever wave length he chooses. Extraordinary!". This seems to be a perfectly sensible remark. But if there was nothing more to be discovered about the Martian than his actual and possible responses, then this would *not* be a sensible remark. We would know what it would be like to be a Martian and there would be no point wondering about it. So there is something more to be learnt about the Martian, and that is what his experience is like. (1950, p. 183)

Farrell's exposition is somewhat less straightforward than Broad's; in part he is picking up on themes already present in the passages from Russell and Dunne. Yet it is obvious from his article that Farrell is interested in a line of thought that takes us from the knowledge intuition to the falsity of physicalism—a knowledge argument in our sense. His intriguing response is that this line of thought presupposes a mistaken conception of experience, a conception that forgets that experience is, as he puts it, featureless.[11]

Still further versions of the argument can be found in the debates over the identity theory in the 1950s, particularly in the discussion between Paul E. Meehl and Herbert Feigl. Here is Feigl:

Let us assume that a complete explanation of animal and human behavior can be achieved by reduction to the basic physical laws, and that the structures (initial and boundary conditions) of organisms can be described in purely ... [physical] ... terms; then there is no need for the phenomenal terms—just as there would be no need for typically biological or physiological concepts. They would all be "reduced" to whatever are the concepts of the "ultimate" physics (e.g., something like the concepts of current atomic, quantum and field physics). The Martian's repertory—if he has a repertory of qualities of immediate experience at all (i.e., if he is not a "mere robot")—may not in any way overlap with that of us earthlings. In that case he would lack altogether any "acquaintance" with the qualities of our "raw feels." He would consequently also lack the sort of "empathy" that humans can have for each other. The physicalist would formulate this, of course, by pointing to essential differences between the Martian and the human central states and processes. The Martian would thus not know "what colors look like"; "what musical tones sound like."

Nevertheless he would be able to explain—and possibly also predict—all of human behavior on the basis of his micro-theories. His theories may be expressed in a notation (reflecting concept formation) utterly different from our basic physics—but his physics would be completely translatable into ours and vice versa.

Now, the question arises: Is there something about human beings that the Martian does not (and never could) "know"? (1967, pp. 139–140)[12]

Feigl himself goes on to answer this question in the negative—"I maintain that, given enough time and intelligence, the Martian ... would in principle arrive at a complete explanation of the behavior of earthlings" (ibid., p. 140)—but it is clear that in raising the question he thinks that a positive answer is at least possible, and that such a positive answer, if it could be defended, would defeat physicalism. In short, he thinks that the knowledge intuition is false, but that if it were true it would defeat physicalism.

Unlike Feigl, Meehl regards the knowledge intuition as undoubtedly true:

Suppose that knowers K1 and K2 share knowledge of the Utopian scientific network, including of course the psychophysiology of vision and the psycholinguistics of color language. However, K2 is congenitally blind and although he has recently undergone a corneal transplant, it is very shortly postsurgery and he has not as yet experienced any visual raw feels. Does K1 know anything K2 does not know?

I have put this question to a number of "plain men" as well as to some not so plain. The natural tendency is to say that K1 knows something that K2 does not know, to wit, "what red looks like." Without taking vulgar speech or the theories it embodies as criteria of truth, I must confess that my own instincts in this matter are very like those of the plain man. (1966, p. 151)

However, while Meehl thinks the intuition is true, he does not think the inference from the knowledge intuition to the conclusion that physicalism is false is a reasonable one—a point noted in the last footnote of Jackson 1982. Meehl writes:

Some have felt that this line of thought is adverse to the identity theory. But I am unable to see why.... Can anything be inferred about ontological identity from the admission that a knower is historically acquainted "by direct experience" with raw-feel quality Q can, by virtue of that acquaintance, recognize a new instance of it and token it appropriately, whereas a knower who lacks such acquaintance "by direct acquaintance" cannot do so? (1966, pp. 157–158)

For Meehl, the knowledge intuition only shows something epistemological, namely, that a person who has no experience of red does not understand or does not fully understand the meaning of the term 'red', or the concept of red. But he insists that it does not follow from this that anything ontological—like the denial of physicalism or the identity theory—is true. As we will see later on, Meehl's suggestion here—that there is something illicit in the knowledge argument since it apparently moves from an epistemological premise to an ontological conclusion—is something that has been taken up by many of the contemporary critics of Jackson's argument.

Indeed, in Broad, Farrell, Meehl, and Feigl, we see four distinct responses to the argument, responses that are still very much alive today: Broad accepts the argument as sound; Farrell rejects the argument on the grounds that it rests on a mistaken view of experience; Feigl accepts the argument as valid, but insists that the premise—the knowledge intuition—is false; finally, Meehl rejects the argument as invalid.[13]

3   The Argument Itself

If the knowledge intuition and the knowledge argument were widespread in philosophical literature prior to his papers, what is distinctive about Jackson's contribution? What is the difference between the knowledge argument of (e.g.) Broad and the knowledge argument of Jackson?

3.1   The Thought Experiment

The first difference is that the thought experiment with which Jackson operates provides a much better illustration of the knowledge intuition than other thought experiments. As is of course well known, Jackson's thought experiment introduces Mary, a famous neuroscientist. (A concise statement of this example is to be found in the passage we quoted at the outset.)[14] The central fact about the Mary example is that reflection on it supports two quite separate claims. First, there is the claim that, before her release, Mary knows everything there is to know about the physical nature of the world. Second, there is the claim that, on coming out of her room, Mary learns something. If you grant these two claims you cannot but agree with the knowledge intuition. It is simply part of the notion of learning that if S learns p at t, then there is a previous time t^* such that S did not know p at t^*. Thus if you agree both that Mary knows everything physical in her room *and* that she learns something when she comes out, you cannot but agree that she did not know everything in her room. So we might say that the polemical importance of the Mary example derives from the

fact that it factors the knowledge intuition into two quite distinct claims—
the complete physical knowledge claim, and the learning claim—and that
acceptance of both of these claims amounts to acceptance of the knowledge intuition.

3.2   The Thought Experiment Contrasted

It is instructive in this regard to compare the example of Mary with other
examples that also support the knowledge intuition, but which are less
successful from a polemical point of view.

3.2.1   Broad's archangel
Broad says that it is obvious that the archangel
did not know something about the physical world. But suppose a mechanist responds by challenging or denying the intuition. Broad would then
be in the weak position of insisting that his intuitions go one way, while
the mechanist's intuitions go the other way, and matters would quickly
degenerate into a stalemate. What the Mary case does, however, is break
the stalemate in favor of a proponent of the argument. Suppose a physicalist suggests that Mary *does* know what the smell of roses is like. Then
they would be faced with the problem that Mary apparently learns this on
coming out. And, if she learns this on coming out, logic alone dictates that
she did not know it previously. In a sense, then, Jackson's version of the
argument might properly be called *the learning argument*, and it is precisely
this that makes it an improvement on Broad's version.

3.2.2   Feigl's Martian super-scientist
Feigl discusses the possibility that a
Martian super-scientist, if he had a "totally different repertory of raw feels,"
might not know everything about human beings. However, this example
does not improve on that of the archangel. For we can easily imagine
someone insisting that the Martian might be able to figure everything
out—indeed Feigl himself insists just this. And it is unclear how the argument might be developed beyond this rather unsatisfying point. The difference between Mary and the Martian is that Mary learns something
phenomenal—in Feigl's terminology, she becomes acquainted with a new
raw feel—but this is precisely what the Martian does not and cannot do.

3.2.3   Nagel's bat
This is an example that has figured prominently in the
recent literature—more prominently perhaps even than Mary. Nagel (1974)

says that we can never know what the experiences of bats are like because we are too dissimilar from them, and thus we will never know what it is like to be a bat. Something that is at least strongly suggested[15] by Nagel's discussion is the following consideration. In principle, I could know all the physical truths about bats, and yet I could not know about their experiences. So here too we have the knowledge intuition, and the suggestion that the falsity of physicalism follows from the intuition.

However, even if one were to appeal to Nagel's example to establish a knowledge intuition and argue that physicalism is false, it is still not clear that this is to advance on the simplest knowledge argument. The reason this time is that the bat example relies on the fact that we are so different from bats that it is unlikely we could so much as conceive of or imagine their experiences. But this invites the response that the reason that physical knowledge doesn't yield phenomenal knowledge in this case is that is that is impossible for us to attain the concepts to formulate the relevant phenomenal knowledge in the first place. On the other hand, if this is the explanation for the knowledge intuition, it is difficult see that it places physicalism under threat. After all, physicalism does not entail that we humans must be able to imagine or conceive the experiences of bats.[16]

3.2.4 Robinson's deaf scientist Mary made her first appearance in 1982. That same year, Howard Robinson produced a version of the knowledge argument founded on the following example:

Imagine that a deaf scientist should become the world's leading expert on the neurology of hearing. Thus, if we suppose neurology more advanced than the present, we can imagine that he knows everything that there is to know about the physical processes involved in hearing, from the ear-drum in. It remains intuitively obvious that there is something which this scientist will not know, namely what it is like to hear. (1982, p. 4)

Robinson's deaf scientist is obviously a close cousin of the Russell's blind man, though unlike Russell and like Jackson, Robinson is focused on physicalism, not empiricism. In addition, like Mary, the Martian, and the archangel, Robinson's protagonist is an omniscient scientist who is experientially challenged. But Robinson's example still is not an advance on that of the archangel. Suppose again that a physicalist responded to Robinson by challenging the intuition; we would then reach a stalemate. But with Mary the stalemate is broken.

Of course, one can imagine a development of Robinson's case in which the deaf scientist is suddenly made to hear again—perhaps this is in fact what Robinson had in mind, though he does not say so. Then one would be able to appeal to the concept of learning in just the way that one can in the Mary case.[17] However, while this version of the case is no doubt an improvement, there would then be the independent problem that a person who was deaf and who is now made to hear would change intrinsically in a way that Mary does not change intrinsically when she comes out of her room. Intrinsic changes of this sort are difficult to adjudicate—what happens *exactly* when someone who was deaf is now made to hear?—and so the Mary example is an advantage even over that case.

3.2.5 Jackson's Fred   When Mary makes her first appearance, it is almost as an afterthought.[18] The main example in the section of the paper that introduces the argument is not Mary but Fred:

Fred has better colour vision than anyone else on record; he makes every discrimination that anyone has ever made, and moreover he makes one that we cannot ever begin to make.... Fred can see, really see, at least one more colour than we can: red1 is a different colour from red2.... What is the new colour ... like? We would dearly like to know but do not; and it seems that no amount of physical information about Fred's brain and optical system tells us.... We have all the physical information. Therefore, knowing all this is not knowing everything about Fred. It follows that Physicalism leaves something out. (1982, pp. 128–129)

Clearly it is possible to develop a knowledge argument on the basis of Fred rather than Mary. What then is the comparison between the two? The most natural thing to say is that Fred is similar to Nagel's bat—he has an experience that, because of various features of our psychological and neural makeup, we cannot have. But then we might be tempted to say that the reason we cannot know the phenomenal facts about Fred is that it is impossible for us to attain the relevant concepts required to formulate this knowledge. If that is so, however, a knowledge argument that relies on Fred would suffer from the same problem as a knowledge argument that relies on the bat.

Although the case of Fred is similar in this respect to the case of the bat, there is still a further respect in which Fred and Mary are similar, while the issues raised by Nagel are different from both. Unlike Nagel, Jackson is not concerned with the issue of knowing what it is like to *be* something other than oneself. Jackson contrasts the Nagel example with Fred in the following terms:

> When I complained that all the physical knowledge about Fred was not enough to tell us what his special colour experience was like, I was not complaining that we weren't finding out what it is like to *be* Fred. I was complaining that there is something *about* his experience, a property of it, of which we were left ignorant. And if and when we come to know what this property is we still will not know what it is like to *be* Fred, but we will know more about him. No amount of knowledge about Fred, be it physical or not, amounts to knowledge "from the inside" concerning Fred. We are not Fred. There is thus a whole set of items of knowledge expressed by forms of words like 'that it is *I myself* who is ...' which Fred has and we simply cannot have because we are not him. (1982, p. 132)

This point is connected to one that often comes up in discussions of the knowledge argument: the suggestion that the questions about experience that are raised by the argument are at root identical to questions about indexicals and demonstratives that have been widely discussed in philosophy of language. This issue is still very much a live one in the literature. Lewis (1988) (chap. 5, this vol.) refers to the idea as "the third way to miss the point," but the view is defended at length in Loar 1990, 1997 (chap. 11, this vol.), McMullen 1985, Bigelow and Pargetter 1990 (chap. 9, this vol.), and Perry 2001.

3.3 The Structure of the Argument

So far we have concentrated on one difference between Jackson's version and the other versions of the argument:[19] the thought experiment on which his argument is based. The other important differentiating feature of Jackson's version concerns his defense of the inference, that is, his defense of the step from the knowledge intuition to the falsity of physicalism.

We may approach the issue by noting three points about what Jackson says is a "convenient and accurate way" (1986, p. 293) to present the structure of the argument:

(1) Mary (before her release) knows everything physical there is to know about other people.

(2) Mary (before her release) does not know everything there is to know about other people (because she learns something about them on being released).

(3) Therefore, there are truths about other people (and herself) that escape the physicalist story.

The first point is that we can clearly see here the two claims identified previously as being the ones prompted by reflection on the Mary example: (1) tells us that Mary knows all physical truths; (2) tells us that she does not know all truths because she learns something. So in setting out the argument in this way, Jackson is making explicit the idea that the knowledge intuition is best factored into two.

Second, it is important to notice that the argument—at least in its conclusion—quite explicitly quantifies over truths. Thus the logical form of the argument might be better rendered as:

(4) Every physical truth is such that Mary (before her release) knows that truth.

(5) It is not the case that every truth is such that Mary (before her release) knows that truth.

(6) Therefore, there is at least one truth that is nonphysical.

So understood, it is quite clear that the argument is a valid argument. It is as if someone had reasoned as follows: I have examined all the oranges in the box, but I have not examined all the fruit in the box; therefore there must be in the box some pieces of fruit that are not oranges.

However, and this the third point, even if the argument from (4) and (5) to (6) is valid, one might still question whether the conclusion of this argument—and so of the previous argument also—entails the falsity of physicalism, and in that sense one might still question the validity of the knowledge argument against physicalism. For it is reasonable to wonder whether physicalism is consistent with the existence of nonphysical truths. To illustrate this issue, we need to say a little more about physicalism than we have so far.

3.4 Supervenience and the Psychophysical Conditional

We noted earlier that, in contemporary philosophy, physicalism is usually construed in terms of what is called a supervenience thesis. A simple way to express the idea is as follows. Suppose we gather together all the physical truths of the world into one megatruth, P. And suppose we do the same with all the psychological truths to produce one psychological megatruth, Q. Now consider the conditional formed from P and Q—if P then Q—and call this conditional *the psychophysical conditional*. To say that the psychological nature of the world supervenes on its physical nature is to say or imply that the psychophysical conditional is necessarily true. Given the supervenience account of physicalism, therefore, the following conditional is true: if physicalism is true, the psychophysical conditional is necessarily true.

Now, the question of whether the conclusion (6) of the argument above entails the falsity of physicalism turns on the question of whether the necessity of the psychophysical conditional is compatible with there being nonphysical truths. On the face of it, however, it is difficult to see why these are not compatible. For, as Kripke (1980) famously pointed out, being necessary is not coextensive with being a priori. So it is possible that the psychophysical conditional is a necessary and a posteriori truth. If it is a posteriori, however, it would be reasonable to say that Q is a distinct truth from P, even if they are necessarily connected. But if Q is a distinct truth from P, and P includes all physical truths, then Q is not a physical truth.

In light of the shadow cast by the necessary a posteriori on the validity of the knowledge argument, we should assume that, in both the 1982 and 1986 essays, Jackson was supposing not only that:

if physicalism is true the psychophysical conditional is necessary,

but also that:

if physicalism is true, the psychophysical conditional is a priori.

And indeed, in subsequent work, this is an assumption he has spent considerable time explaining and defending (see Jackson 1998, chap. 19, this vol.).[20] The key idea is that although Kripke is of course right that there are examples of the necessary a posteriori, it is unreasonable to suppose that the psychophysical conditional is one of them, at least if physicalism is true. According to Jackson, if a statement is necessary and a posteriori, it can be derived a priori from some further contingent statement. In turn, if the psychophysical conditional is a posteriori it too must be derived from some further contingent statement. On the other hand, if physicalism is true, there is *no* other contingent truth from which the psychophysical conditional can be derived. For physicalism aims at completeness—any contingent truth must already be included in the antecedent of the psychophysical conditional. Conclusion: if physicalism is true, the psychophysical conditional is not only necessary but also a priori.

Whether Jackson is right in this account of the necessary a posteriori is a large issue. Many will question his assumption that any necessary a posteriori statement follows a priori from something contingent. But for our purposes the important points are these: (i) Jackson's claim that the psychophysical conditional is a priori is not ad hoc but is supported by independent premises; and (ii) if that claim is true, the knowledge argument is a valid argument against physicalism. Putting these two points together, we arrive at the second respect in which Jackson's knowledge argument is an improvement on earlier versions: his defense of the inference.

4 Responses to the Argument

We have already taken note of some of the ways in which one might respond to the argument. However, a more detailed assessment of these responses can be arrived at if we adopt the policy, first instituted by Van Gulick (1993, chap. 17, this vol.), of organizing the responses around a series of questions.[21]

Question 1: Does Mary Learn Anything New?

Everyone agrees that something happens when Mary comes out of her room. Jackson says that what happens is rightly described as learning, and initially this is certainly the natural thing to say. However, not everyone agrees on reflection that Mary *does* learn something.

This issue is the topic of part II of the book. In Dennett 1991 (chap. 3, this vol.) we find the suggestion that if we really think about what it is to know everything physical then Mary can know everything before she comes out. Similarly, in his 1998a (chap. 19, this vol.),[22] Jackson suggests that the idea that Mary learns something when she comes out is an illusion induced by the fact that the new information is presented as information concerning an intrinsic property, rather than a relational property.

If Mary does not learn anything new then the argument need proceed no further. The Mary example is no advance on Broad's archangel. On the other hand, if we agree that Mary does learn something and thus we answer "yes" to Question 1, we can proceed to other questions.[23]

Question 2: Is Her Learning Factual or Nonfactual?

We have already noted one sense in which 'learn' is closely related to 'know' —if S learns that p at time t, then there is a time t^* prior to t such that it is not the case that S knows that p at t^*. But the connections are even closer than this. For example, as is evident from the following, both 'learn' and 'know' can take both 'that'-clauses *and* 'wh'-clauses in the object position:

(7) Bill knows/learns that the cat is not on the mat.

(8) Bill knows/learns how to darn socks.

(9) Bill knows/learns what black holes are.

(10) Bill knows/learns who the president is.

(11) Bill knows/learns where the good clubs are.

(12) Bill knows/learns when the election starts.

According to a tradition instigated by Ryle (1949), there is an important difference between (7) and (8) construed as statements about knowledge. Statement (7) reports a case of genuine factual or propositional knowledge, but (8) reports the presence only of a certain sort of skill or ability—knowledge how versus knowledge that, as Ryle put it. This basic point can be generalized in two ways. First, the point has an obvious application to learning—one might equally distinguish learning how and learning that. Second, knowing how seems to group naturally with knowing who, what, when, and where, and so on, that is, with cases in which the object of the verb is a 'wh'-clause rather than a 'that'-clause. So we might distinguish more generally between factual learning and knowledge, and nonfactual learning and knowledge.

This distinction opens up the possibility—discussed in parts III and IV of this volume—that the learning Mary undergoes when she comes out of her room is not factual learning. But if that is so, the knowledge argument fails. For as we saw above, the argument relies on the idea that we can quantify over truths known, and this is precisely to rely on a factual account of learning.

Question 3: Does She Gain Only Know-How?

Suppose that what Mary learns is not factual. The question remains as to what sort of nonfactual knowledge she does acquire. The essays in part III discuss the ability hypothesis, according to which what Mary learns is know-how.[24] According to Lewis (1988, chap. 5, this vol.) for example, while it is true that she learns something, it is false that there is some new truth about the world—all she learns is how to imagine, identify, and recollect certain experiences.

There are a number of controversial aspects of the ability hypothesis. One is that it is not clear that this is *all* Mary learns (Jackson 1986, chap. 2, this vol.). A related point (Loar 1990; 1997, chap. 11, this vol.) says that since we can embed what Mary learns in the antecedent of a conditional, it cannot be that she learns mere know-how. A third objection focuses more directly on whether there is in fact the sort of distinction between knowledge how and knowledge that that is required by the ability hypothesis.[25]

Question 4: Does She Merely Get Acquainted?

The ability hypothesis is not the only position according to which Mary's learning is nonfactual. Another is the acquaintance hypothesis, discussed in part IV. The acquaintance hypothesis says that what happens when Mary is released from her room is that she becomes acquainted with a new property, the property of being red.[26] There are a number of different ideas doing business under the label 'acquaintance', but the core idea can perhaps be formulated as follows: to be acquainted with the property of being red is to know what red is. The general idea of the acquaintance hypothesis is that one can come to know what red is without knowing any further truths, and that this is precisely what happens to Mary.

The acquaintance hypothesis is much less discussed than the ability hypothesis, but it is likely that similar sorts of problems will arise for both views. First, it is not clear that this is all Mary learns; second, it is not clear that there is a distinction between knowing which and knowing that in the relevant sense. Also, there is here the additional problem that the notion of acquaintance is an extraordinarily slippery one. Sometimes it is used to denote a certain sort of knowledge, as we have noted. But it is also used to denote experience. On this interpretation, however, the acquaintance hypothesis does not move beyond the truism that Mary comes to have a new experience when she comes out of her room.

Question 5: If the Learning Is Factual, Is It Learning of a Genuinely New Fact or of an Old Fact in Disguise?

Suppose one is persuaded by these criticisms of the acquaintance and ability hypotheses and therefore rejects the idea that the factual–nonfactual distinction is the key to the knowledge argument. There is still the question of whether Mary learns what might be called a genuinely new fact or whether what she learns is an old fact in disguise. The essays in part V explore the possibility that the latter is the correct way to respond to the argument.[27]

This sort of position comes in either of two varieties. One version—stated most clearly in Loar (1990; 1997, chap. 11, this vol.), Van Gulick (chap. 17, this vol.), and Horgan (1984, chap. 14, this vol.)—appeals directly to the necessary a posteriori. Earlier we pointed out that Jackson is assuming that the psychophysical conditional is a priori, or at least that if it is a posteriori then this is irrelevant to the argument. What we find in the essays by Loar, Van Gulick, and Horgan are considerations to the effect that he is mistaken in supposing this, and that it is reasonable to view the psychophysical conditional as necessary and a posteriori. Jackson (2002, chap. 20, this vol.), Chalmers (chap. 13, this vol.), and Stoljar (2000) present criticisms of this position.

The other version of the new facts view—presented here in Tye (2000, chap. 7, this vol.) but also in Loar (1990; 1997, chap. 11, this vol.)—focuses not so much on whether the psychophysical conditional is a posteriori, but rather on the idea that Mary gains a new 'phenomenal' concept when she comes out of her room. If Mary gains a new concept, then there is a straightforward response to the argument: the reason that she does not know the relevant phenomenal truths is because she does not so much as understand them. In effect, this position makes the charge against Jackson's version of the knowledge argument that we noted when discussing Nagel's bat: the objection that the knowledge intuition can be explained psychologically, and if so, there is no threat here to physicalism.

The appeal to phenomenal concepts raises a number of issues of quite independent interest—what phenomenal concepts are, for example, and what it takes to possess them. It also invites a reconsideration of some of the themes already covered. For example: (i) It is sometimes suggested that, at least given the sort of creatures we are, one can have a phenomenal concept only if one has had the relevant sort of perceptual or imaginative experience—this connects with the issue of empiricism and the knowledge intuition noted at the outset. (ii) It is sometimes thought that to possess a phenomenal concept is to have certain sorts of abilities or to be acquainted in the right sort of way with a property—this connects with the ability and acquaintance hypotheses. (iii) It is sometimes said that it is part of the nature of phenomenal concepts that they pick out various properties directly, and not via any mode of presentation—this connects the issue

to the question of the necessary and a posteriori. The connections between phenomenal concepts and the knowledge argument are explored
in Nida-Rümelin (1995, chap. 12, this vol.), Hellie (chap. 16, this vol.), and
Chalmers (chap. 13, this vol.).

Question 6: Did She Know All the Physical Facts Prior to Release?

In questions 2 through 4 we explored the possibility that Mary does not
learn any (genuinely) new facts, either because she did not learn any facts
at all, or else because the facts learned are not genuinely new. But suppose
we agree that she *does* learn some new facts. At this point we might shift
focus and consider the other aspect of the Mary example we have distinguished, the claim that she knows everything physical prior to her release. Of course, according to the usual description of the case, she does
know everything. But one might argue that this is a misdescription.

This is a possibility explored in different ways in part VI. Horgan (1984,
chap. 14, this vol.), Stoljar (2001a, chap. 15, this vol.), and Hellie (chap. 16,
this vol.) present arguments that there is a sense in which Mary might be
said to fail to know all the physical facts. If that can be made good, there is
no argument here against physicalism, this time for the simple reason that
the first premise of the knowledge argument can be denied.[28]

Question 7: Is Physicalism False?

The final question is simply whether physicalism is false, or rather, whether
this is the correct position to adopt in the face of the knowledge argument.
This is the position advocated by Jackson in the essays in part I of the book.
In the 1982 essay, for example, the argument is presented as "a knowledge
argument for qualia," and in turn qualia are defined as properties of experiences that are nonphysical. The upshot is that physicalism is denied and a
version of nonphysicalism—epiphenomenalism—is advocated.[29]

But is dualism really the right conclusion to draw from the knowledge
argument? Several philosophers have argued that the argument is so strong
that, if successful, it would refute not just physicalism, but antiphysicalism
also. For example, Churchland (1985a,b; 1989b, chap. 8, this vol.) argues
that *if* the knowledge argument defeated physicalism it would defeat substance dualism as well.[30] To take another example, Nagasawa (2002) argues
that if the knowledge argument were cogent it would defeat Chalmers'
"panprotopsychism" to the exact extent that it would defeat physicalism.

Jackson's different view (1986, chap. 2, this vol.) is that the sort of dualism under discussion is such that no parity of reasons objection is plausible.[31]

5   Some Further Questions

So far we have concentrated on what the knowledge argument is, and how one might respond to it. However, as we noted at the outset, much of what is interesting here concerns topics the argument raises rather than simply the thesis it attacks. Some of these further topics—the connection to modal epistemology and semantics, empiricism, and phenomenal concepts—have already been canvased. In this section we will briefly indicate some other topics that are raised by the argument.

5.1   The Scientific Study of Consciousness

Block (1995) famously distinguishes between two concepts of consciousness: access consciousness and phenomenal consciousness. He goes on to say that the hard part of the problem of consciousness is the phenomenal notion rather than the access notion. A problem with this suggestion is that the phenomenal aspect of consciousness is notoriously hard to pin down. Here, however, it is natural to appeal to the knowledge argument. Whatever it is Mary does not know about before she comes out of her room, and whatever it is that she learns about when she comes out, is phenomenal consciousness, or at least is intimately connected to phenomenal consciousness. To put the point another way, regardless of whether the knowledge argument and the intuition it is based on ultimately defeat physicalism, they are nevertheless important because they provide a very clear account of what needs to be explained in the study of consciousness.

5.2   The Scope of Scientific Understanding

While the knowledge argument focuses our attention on what a scientific theory of consciousness needs to explain, it also raises the possibility that explaining it will be beyond us. This theme is raised by Jackson himself in the closing passages of the 1982 essay (p. 135):

Physicalists typically emphasize that we are a part of nature on their view, which is fair enough. But if we are a part of nature, we are as nature left us after however many years of evolution it is, and each step in that evolutionary progression has been a matter of chance constrained just by the need to preserve or increase survival value. The wonder is that we understand as much as we do, and there is no wonder that there should be matters which fall quite outside our comprehension. Perhaps exactly how epiphenomenal qualia fit into the scheme of things is one such.

Jackson himself mentions this simply as a possibility, as an antidote to "excessive optimism" (ibid., p. 136). But some philosophers have gone further, suggesting that the nature of the case is such that we could decide now that the explanation of experience is beyond our ken. This theme has been taken up and defended by McGinn (1989).

5.3   The Definition of Physicalism

The issues of the target of a possible scientific explanation of consciousness and of whether we will be able to carry out the project both seem real enough. But a number of writers have questioned whether these issues should be approached via the thesis of physicalism, and perhaps more broadly whether at root they are philosophical issues at all. An example is provided by Noam Chomsky. Chomsky does not discuss the knowledge argument as such, but it is clear that his remarks apply to it:

The mind–body problem can be posed sensibly only insofar as we have a definite conception of body. If we have no such definite and fixed conception, we cannot ask whether some phenomena fall beyond its range. The Cartesians offered a fairly definite conception of body in terms of their contact mechanics, which in many respects reflects commonsense understanding. Therefore they could sensibly formulate the mind–body problem.... (1988a, p. 142)

Chomsky goes on to argue that while the concept of body made sense against the particular historical background of the mid-seventeenth-century ("the Cartesians"), in later work—particularly the work of Newton and others—those presuppositions were rejected. Chomsky of course does not deny that there might be a commonsensical conception of body or of the physical; nor does he deny that the knowledge argument might be useful in separating out the ordinary conception of the physical from that of the experiential. His position is rather that modern science after Newton has no use for that notion, and that it operates instead with a conception according to which 'physical' in 'physical world' has only an emphatic use, much like 'true' in 'true fact'.

Now, in the 1982 essay, Jackson makes it clear where he stands on the question of the definition of the physical: "It is well known that there are problems with giving a precise definition of these notions, and so of the thesis of physicalism. But—unlike some—I take the central problems of definition to cut across the central problems I want to discuss ..." (p. 127; see also Jackson 1998, chap. 19, this vol.). Jackson is surely correct in supposing that to understand the basic intuition behind the knowledge argument we do not need a definition of the notion of the physical—indeed, one might instead view the knowledge intuition as data that any proposed definition would explain. On the other hand, it would surely be strange if the issue of how to understand the concept of the physical had no role to play in the final assessment of the argument. This too, then, is an issue raised by the argument.[32]

6 Jackson's Current View

In 1993 Jackson thought that physicalism was "contrary to fact"; by 1996, he had changed his mind: the argument, he said, contained no obvious fallacy, and yet its conclusion—that physicalism is false—must be mistaken. This is one of the more remarkable turnarounds in contemporary philosophy.[33] We will close by making some remarks about Jackson's current view.

In *From Metaphysics to Ethics* (1998), Jackson sets out a vision of how metaphysics should proceed, and then raises some problem cases for it. He begins with the assumption that modern science has within it a certain picture of the world, a picture that is best distilled as the thesis of physicalism. He then notices that physicalism apparently finds no place for a number of items we ordinarily assume to exist—persons, values, free will, experience. The basic problem that metaphysics sets out to solve is therefore "the location problem"—the problem of stating what the location of persons (etc.) is in the world presented to us by science. Now, the most interesting versions of this problem emerge when we are presented with arguments apparently showing that the placement problem cannot be solved—that is, when it is suggested that persons or values as we currently conceive them cannot find a place in the physical world. Thus for example, Moore's (cf. Jackson 1998b, pp. 150–151) open-question argument reveals something about our concept of value that shows that values-as-Moore-thought-of-them cannot find a place in the natural world. Similarly, van Inwagen's (1983; cf. Jackson 1998b, p. 44) consequence argument reveals something about the concept of free will that shows that free-will-as-we-ordinarily-think-of-it cannot find a place in the natural world. In such cases, Jackson says, we have no choice but to settle for something less—to articulate a replacement concept of value or freedom that can take the place of the old. Of course, in both cases, one can imagine also the response that what is needed here is not a replacement notion, but rather a rejection of physicalism, or at least a different approach to the picture of the world implicit in modern science. To this Jackson responds that it is a methodological mistake to suppose that philosophy itself should revise science. That would be to give philosophy and metaphysics an overly "immodest" (1998b, pp. 42–43) role.

In this context, it is perhaps not too difficult to see the motivation behind Jackson's change of mind with respect to the knowledge argument. Like the open-question argument and the consequence argument, the interest of the knowledge argument lies in the apparent inconsistency it finds between an item on the troubling list and physicalism. But to adopt dualism in response to this argument would be to let philosophy play an immodest role, and this is something that Jackson rejects in parallel cases. In short, there seems to be a pattern in Jackson's thinking on these topics, and his earlier position represents an important departure from this pattern.

There are many questions to be discussed here about Jackson's change of mind and his conception of philosophy, some of which are taken up in this book. Is it really true that there is a pattern in the questions that Jackson is interested in? Is it really true that the necessary a posteriori is to be analyzed in the way that he says? Is it really true that physicalism is the picture of the world implicit in modern science? What exactly are the commitments of physicalism, anyway? What are the replacement notions that Jackson articulates, and to what extent can they play the role of the original notions? What does it mean for one notion to play the role of another? And—what is most important for this book—if there is a mistake in the knowledge argument, where exactly does it lie? All of these fascinating questions—including of course the question of what the scientific explanation of consciousness is—bubble to the surface when one discusses the knowledge argument.

Notes

1. The knowledge argument is popular beyond the philosophy community. It plays a crucial role in David Lodge's (2001) novel, *Thinks . . .* , in which a cognitive scientist

at the "University of Gloucester" has an affair with a widowed novelist. The knowledge argument is also discussed in the recent series *Brainspotting*, which showed on the U.K. on channel 4 in 1996. Thanks to Martin Davies and Michael Smith for bringing these to our attention.

2. For his reasons see section 6 below, the foreword, and chapters 18 and 19 of this volume.

3. The literature on the knowledge argument is voluminous. We have tried to include the key papers from each of the many responses to the argument. But inevitably there are fine papers we have not been able to include and there are papers that someone else putting together a similar volume would have preferred to some of those we have included.

4. Locke 1975 (originally 1689), p. 389, bk. II, ch. 32, sec. 15. The classic contemporary discussion is Shoemaker 1982.

5. The prominence in contemporary philosophy of the phrase 'what it is like' is owing to Nagel (1974), but as far as we are able to judge, the phrase was originally used, in the context of phenomenal consciousness, in Wittgenstein's *Remarks on the Philosophy of Psychology*, vol. 1, which dates from 1946–1947. (A comparable usage is Farrell 1950.) At §91, Wittgenstein writes: "The 'content' of experience, of experiencing: I know what tooth-aches are like, I am acquainted with them, *I know what it's like to see red, green, blue, yellow, I know what it's like to feel sorrow, hope, fear, joy, affection ...". (It is interesting to note that the material following the asterisk was written by Wittgenstein in English rather than German.)

6. This question was of course posed and discussed by Grice (1962).

7. We are indebted to John Bigelow for bringing this passage to our attention.

8. Indeed, discussion of the blind is standard in the literature from at least the seventeenth century. See the quotation from Locke in Van Gulick (chap. 17, this vol.).

9. What follows are examples of the knowledge argument from the twentieth century. So far as we can judge, it is difficult to find clear examples of the argument prior to this, though of course there are many close cousins of the argument in the literature, e.g., Leibniz's Mill argument, and Descartes's conceivability argument.

10. Thanks to David Chalmers for bringing this passage to our attention.

11. What Farrell means by 'featurelessness' is very closely related to the phenomenon of the transparency of experience, much discussed by contemporary philosophers, including Jackson in chapter 20, this volume.

12. Original publication: 1956.

13. Nicholas Maxwell (2000, 2001) suggests that he introduced the knowledge argument in the 1960s in Maxwell 1966, 1968. However, it is not obvious that Maxwell's

argument *is* a clear example of a knowledge argument in the sense we intend. Maxwell certainly provides a clear formulation of the knowledge intuition—like Russell, Dunne, and Meehl he uses the example of a blind person—but it is not clear that he infers from this the falsity of physicalism.

14. Thought experiments in philosophy are often based on logically possible but not necessarily realistic scenarios. The Mary case is usually taken as a thought experiment of this sort. However, the case might not be as unrealistic as one may initially think. For there is a Norwegian vision scientist, Knut Nordby, who is completely achromatic. See Nordby 1996. Nordby visited, with Oliver Sacks, the Micronesian island of Pingelap where at least 6 percent of the population is achromatic, and the island of Pohnpei, which has two enclaves populated by Pingelapese, many of whom are achromatic. (Compare H. G. Well's story mentioned earlier.) Their journey is introduced in a book by Oliver Sacks (1996), and a TV documentary film, both of which are entitled *The Island of the Colorblind*. See also "The Case of the Colorblind Painter" in Sacks 1985.

15. Suggested, because, as Jackson (1982) notes, by the end of Nagel's paper, he renounces any attempt to refute physicalism: "[i]t would be mistake to conclude that physicalism must be false" (1974, p. 446). Despite this, many philosophers (e.g. Lewis 1983; McMullen 1985; Pereboom 1994) claim that Nagel's argument is, at its root, identical to Jackson's knowledge argument, and some even call this style of antiphysicalist argument the "Nagel–Jackson knowledge argument" (e.g., Pereboom 1994). Jackson himself disagrees: "[i]t is important to distinguish [Nagel's] argument from the knowledge argument" (1982, p. 132).

16. Of course, one might argue that Mary too lacks a concept while in her room—some philosophers do in fact argue in this way, as we will see. The point at this stage is that it is plausible to suppose that it is psychologically impossible for us to attain the relevant concepts of the experience of bats. Presumably, it is not psychologically impossible for Mary to attain the relevant concepts—on the contrary, after coming out, there is no question but that she does possess them.

17. One sometimes hears the suggestion that Robinson's case would be an improvement on Jackson's, because in the Mary case we have the problem that while in her room, she might cut herself, rub her eyes to experience phosphenes (Thompson 1992) or see colorful dreams, whereas the deaf will presumably hear no sounds at all. But in response to this, it is not too difficult to imagine away the various possibilities, and in fact, in most presentations of the argument this is taken as implied. See, e.g., Chalmers 1996, p. 369, n. 7.

18. Indeed, it is fair to say that philosophers had largely overlooked the significance of the Mary case until two important critical papers, Horgan 1984 (chap. 14, this vol.) and Churchland 1985a. Jackson's 1986 essay (chap. 2, this vol.), which focuses solely on the Mary case, was written as a reply to Churchland's essay.

19. It is sometimes suggested that arguments in other areas of philosophy exhibit the same structure as the knowledge argument. For instance, Delmas Kiernan-Lewis (1991) suggests that an argument against the tenseless account of reality that A. N. Prior provides in "Thank Goodness That's Over" (1959) is structurally parallel to the knowledge argument.

20. Another response at this point is that it is a mistake to assume that the a posteriori account, even if it can be made out, would be of help in the knowledge argument. For an early discussion of this point, see Jackson 1980.

21. See also Alter 1999.

22. See also Jackson 2000.

23. For arguments for the claim that Mary does not learn anything new upon her release, see Churchland 1985a, Dennett 1991 (chap. 3, this vol.), Foss 1989, Hardin 1988, Jackson 1998a (chap. 18, this vol.), 2002, (chap. 20, this vol.). For arguments against this claim see Jacquette 1995, McConnell 1995, and Robinson 1993c (chap. 4, this vol.).

24. The ability hypothesis was originally proposed in Nemirow 1980 as a response to Nagel 1974.

25. For arguments for the ability hypothesis see Dennett 1991 (chap. 3, this vol.), Lewis 1983, 1988 (chap. 5, this vol.), Nemirow 1980, 1990, Mellor 1993, Meyer 2001, and Pettit (chap. 6, this vol.). For arguments against, see Alter 1998, 2001, 2002, Bigelow and Pargetter 1990 (chap. 9, this vol.), Chalmers 1996, Conee 1985, 1994 (chap. 10, this vol.), Braddon-Mitchell and Jackson 1996, Furash 1989, Gertler 1999, Levin 1986, Loar 1990, 1997 (chap. 11, this vol.), Lycan 1995, 1996, McConnell 1995, Nida-Rümelin 1995 (chap. 12, this vol.), Noordhof 2003, Perry 2001, Raymont 1999, Robinson 1993b, and Tye 2000 (chap. 7, this vol.). For arguments against the know-that/know-how distinction, see Alter 2001, 2002, Chomsky 1975, 1980, 1988a,b, 1992, Dretske 1988, Lycan 1996, Perry 2001, Stanley and Williamson 2001, and White 1982.

26. For arguments for the acquaintance hypothesis, see Bigelow and Pargetter 1990 (chap. 9, this vol.), Churchland 1985a 1989b, 1998 (chap. 8, this vol.), Conee 1994 (chap. 10, this vol.), Dretske 1999, Hellie (chap. 16, this vol.), Papineau 1993, and Perry 2001. For arguments against, see Alter 1998, Chalmers 1996, Gertler 1999, and Lewis 1988 (chap. 5, this vol.).

27. For arguments in favor of the "old facts, new modes" view, see Bachrach 1990, Bealer 1994, Bigelow and Pargetter 1990 (chap. 9, this vol.), Churchland 1985a, 1989b, 1998 (chap. 8, this vol.), Conee 1985, Horgan 1984 (chap. 14, this vol.), Lycan 1990, 1995, 1996, Loar 1990, 1997 (chap. 11, this vol.), McConnell 1995, McMullen 1985, Pereboom 1994, Papineau 1993, Tye 1986, 2000 (chap. 7, this vol.), Van Gulick 1993 (chap. 17, this vol.). For arguments against, see Alter 1995, 1998,

Braddon-Mitchell and Jackson 1996, Chalmers 1996 (chap. 13, this vol.), Furash 1989, Jackson 1986 (chap. 2, this vol.), Newton 1986, Nida-Rümelin 1995 (chap. 12, this vol.), 1998, Raymont 1995, Robinson 1993b, Stoljar 2000, and Zemach 1990.

28. For arguments for the claim that Mary does not know all the physical facts prior to her release, see Alter 1998, Flanagan 1992, Horgan 1984 (chap. 14, this vol.), Searle 1992, Stoljar 2001a (chap. 15, this vol.), and Strawson 1994.

29. Chalmers (1996), Foster (1991), and Robinson (1982, 1993b) also subscribe to dualism based on the antiphysicalist conclusion of the knowledge argument, though not all of these philosophers embrace epiphenomenalism.

30. For a similar claim see Lewis 1988 (chap. 5, this vol.). Churchland (1985b) notes that he owes "this point to correspondence with David Lewis" (p. 120).

31. For arguments in favor of the view that even dualists should not accept the knowledge argument, see Churchland 1985a,b, 1989b (chap. 8, this vol.), Endicott 1995, Lewis 1988 (chap. 5, this vol.), McGeer forthcoming, Nagasawa 2002, Stjernberg 1999, Vierkant 2002, and Watkins 1989. For arguments against, see Jackson 1986 (chap. 2, this vol.) and Robinson 1993.

32. On defining physicalism, see Hempel 1969, Crane 1993, Crane and Mellor 1990, Pettit 1993, Stoljar 2001a (chap. 15, this vol.), 2001b.

33. His conversion became big news in the philosophy community, and was reported in the Philosophy News Service with the headline "Frank Jackson Changes His Mind": "Frank Jackson is now a physicalist. Yes, the same Frank Jackson who used to call himself a 'qualia freak' now claims that qualia (the visual sensation of red, the feeling of pain, and other sensory experiences) can be given a complete physical explanation. After more than a decade of defending his anti-physicalist views, Jackson has come around to the other side: physicalism, he now claims, is true" (Montero 1999).

References

Alter, Torin. 1995. "Mary's New Perspective." *Australasian Journal of Philosophy* 73: 582–584.

———. 1998. "A Limited Defence of the Knowledge Argument." *Philosophical Studies* 90: 35–56.

———. 1999. "The Knowledge Argument (A Field Guide to the Philosophy of Mind)." Available at http://host.uniroma3.it/progetti/kant/field/ka.html.

———. 2001. "Know-How, Ability, and the Ability Hypothesis." *Theoria* 67: 229–239.

———. 2002. "Implicit Phenomenal Knowledge and the Lewis–Nemirow Ability Hypothesis." Available at http://www.bama.ua.edu/~talter/Implicit.htm.

Bachrach, J. E. 1990. "Qualia and Theory of Reduction: A Criticism of Paul Church-land." *Iyyun* 39: 281–294.

Beakley, Brian, and Peter Ludlow, eds. 1994. *Philosophy of Mind: Classical Problems and Contempoary Issues*. Cambridge, Mass.: The MIT Press.

Bealer, George. 1994. "Mental Properties." *Journal of Philosophy* 91: 185–208.

Bigelow, John, and Robert Paragetter. 1990. "Acquaintance with Qualia." *Theoria* 61: 129–147. Reprinted as chapter 9, this volume.

Block, Ned. 1990. "Inverted Earth," in *Philosophical Perspectives*, vol. 4, 52–79, ed. James Tomberlin. Atascadero: Ridgeview. Reprinted in Block, Flanagan, and Güzeldere 1997.

———. 1995. "On a Confusion About a Function of Consciousness." *Behavioral and Brain Sciences* 18: 227–247. Reprinted in Block, Flanagan, and Güzeldere 1997.

Block, Ned, Owen Flanagan, and Güven Güzeldere, eds. 1997. *The Nature of Consciousness: Philosophical Debates*. Cambridge, Mass.: The MIT Press.

Braddon-Mitchell, David, and Frank Jackson. 1996. *Philosophy of Mind and Cognition*. Oxford: Blackwell.

Broad, C. D. 1925. *The Mind and Its Place in Nature*. London: Routledge and Kegan Paul.

Chalmers, David J. 1996. *The Conscious Mind: In Search of a Fundamental Theory*. New York: Oxford University Press.

———, ed. 2002. *Philosophy of Mind: Classical and Contemporary Readings*. Oxford: Oxford University Press.

———. 2003. "Phenomenal Concepts and the Knowledge Argument." Chapter 13, this volume.

Chomsky, Noam. 1975. "Knowledge of Language," in *Minnesota Studies in the Philosophy of Science*, vol. 7: *Language, Mind, and Knowledge*, ed. Keith Gunderson, 299–320. Minneapolis: University of Minnesota Press.

———. 1980. *Rules and Representations*. New York: Columbia University Press.

———. 1988a. *Language and Problem of Knowledge: The Managua Lectures*. Cambridge, Mass.: The MIT Press. Excerpt reprinted in Beakley and Ludlow 1994.

———. 1988b. "Language and Problems of Knowledge." *Synthesis Philosophica* 5: 1–25.

————. 1992. "Language and Interpretation: Philosophical Reflections and Empirical Inquiry," in *Inference, Explanation, and Other Frustrations: Essays in the Philosophy of Science*, ed. John Earman, 99–128. Berkeley: University of California Press.

————. 1994. "Naturalism and Dualism." *International Journal of Philosophical Studies* 2: 181–209.

Churchland, Paul M. 1985a. "Reduction, Qualia, and the Direct Introspection of Brain States." *Journal of Philosophy* 82: 8–28. Reprinted in Churchland 1989a.

————. 1985b. "Book Review: *Matter and Sense* by Howard Robinson." *Philosophical Review* 94: 117–120.

————. 1989a. *A Nerocomputational Perspective*. Cambridge, Mass.: The MIT Press.

————. 1989b. "Knowing Qualia: A Reply to Jackson," in his 1989a, 67–76. Reprinted in Block, Flanagan, and Güzeldere 1997; chapter 8, this volume.

————. 1998. "Postscript: 1997," in his *On the Contrary: Critical Essays, 1987–1997*, 153–157. Cambridge, Mass.: The MIT Press. Chapter 8, this volume.

Conee, Earl. 1985. "Physicalism and Phenomenal Properties." *Philosophical Quarterly* 35: 296–302.

————. 1994. "Phenomenal Knowledge." *Australasian Journal of Philosophy* 72: 136–150. Reprinted as chapter 10, this volume.

Crane, Tim. 1993. "A Definition of Physicalism: Reply to Pettit." *Analysis* 53: 224–227.

Crane, Tim, and D. H. Mellor. 1990. "There Is No Question of Physicalism." *Mind* 99: 185–206.

Dennett, Daniel C. 1991. *Consciousness Explained*. Boston: Little, Brown. Excerpt reprinted in this volume (chapter 3).

Dretske, Fred. 1988. *Explaining Behavior: Reasons in a World of Causes*. Cambridge, Mass.: The MIT Press.

————. 1999. "The Mind's Awareness of Itself." *Philosophical Studies* 95: 103–124. Reprinted in Dretske 2000.

————. 2000. *Perception, Knowledge, and Belief*. Cambridge: Cambridge University Press.

Dunne, J. W. 1958 (originally 1927). *An Experiment with Time*. London: Farber and Farber.

Endicott, Ronald P. 1995. "The Refutation by Analogous Ectoqualia." *Southern Journal of Philosophy* 33: 19–30.

Farrell, B. A. 1950. "Experience." *Mind* 59: 170–198.

Feigl, Herbert. 1958. "The 'Mental' and the 'Physical'," in *Concepts, Theories, and the Mind–Body Problem*, ed. Herbert Feigl, Michael Scriven, and Grover Maxwell, 370–497. Minneapolis: University of Minnesota Press.

———. 1967. *The 'Mental' and the 'Physical': The Essay and a Postscript.* Minneapolis: University of Minnesota Press.

Flanagan, Owen. 1992. *Consciousness Reconsidered.* Cambridge, Mass.: The MIT Press.

Foss, Jeff. 1989. "On the Logic of What It Is Like to Be a Conscious Subject." *Australasian Journal of Philosophy* 67: 205–220.

Foster, John. 1991. *Immaterial Self.* London: Routledge.

Furash, Gary. 1989. "Frank Jackson's Knowledge Argument Against Materialism." *Dialogue* 32: 1–6.

Gertler, Brie. 1999. "A Defence of the Knowledge Argument." *Philosophical Studies* 93: 317–336.

Grice, H. Paul. 1962. "Some Remarks About the Senses," in *Analytical Philosophy, Series I,* ed. R. J. Butler. Oxford: Oxford University Press.

Hardin, C. L. 1988. *Color for Philosophers.* Indianapolis: Hackett.

Hellie, Benj. 2003. "Inexpressible Truths and the Allure of the Knowledge Argument," Chapter 16, this volume.

Hempel, Carl Gustav. 1969. "Reduction: Ontological and Linguistic Facets," in *Essays in Honor of Ernest Nagel,* ed. S. Morgenbesser, P. Suppies, and M. White, 179–199. New York: St. Martin's Press.

Horgan, Terence. 1984. "Jackson on Physical Information and *Qualia.*" *Philosophical Quarterly* 34: 147–152. Reprinted as chapter 14, this volume.

Jackson, Frank. 1980. "A Note on Physicalism and Heat." *Australasian Journal of Philosophy* 58: 26–34.

———. 1982. "Epiphenomenal Qualia." *Philosophical Quarterly* 32: 127–136. Reprinted in Lycan 1999; Chalmers 2002; chapter 1, this volume.

———. 1986. "What Mary Didn't Know." *Journal of Philosophy* 83: 291–295. Reprinted in Block, Flanagan, and Güzeldere 1997; Moser and Trout 1995; chapter 2, this volume.

———. 1994. "Armchair Metaphysics," in *Philosophy in Mind,* ed. John O'Leary Hawthorne and Michaelis Michael, 23–42. Dordrecht: Kluwer.

———. 1995. "Postscript," in *Contemporary Materialism,* ed. Paul K. Moser and J. D. Trout, 184–189. New York: Routledge. Reprinted as chapter 18, this volume.

———. 1998a. "Postscript on Qualia," in his *Mind, Method, and Conditionals*, 76–79. London: Routledge. Reprinted as chapter 19, this volume.

———. 1998b. *From Metaphysics to Ethics*. Oxford: Oxford University Press.

———. 2000. "Some Reflections on Representationalism." Available at http://www. nyu.edu/gsas/dept/philo/courses/consciousness/papers/RepresentationalismNYU5 April00.PDF.

———. 2002. "Mind and Illusion," paper presented at the Royal Institute of Philosophy. Chapter 20, this volume.

———. 2004. "Looking Back on the Knowledge Argument." Foreword, this volume.

Jacquette, Dale. 1995. "The Blue Banana Trick: Dennett on Jackson's Color Scientist." *Theoria* 61: 217–230.

Kiernan-Lewis, Delmas. 1991. "Not Over Yet: Prior's 'Thank Goodness' Argument." *Philosophy* 66: 241–243.

Kripke, Saul A. 1972. *Naming and Necessity*. Cambridge, Mass.: Harvard University Press.

Lewis, David. 1983. "Postscript to 'Mad Pain and Martian Pain'," in his *Philosophical Papers*, vol. 1, 130–132. New York: Oxford University Press.

———. 1988. "What Experience Teaches," in *Proceedings of Russellian Society* 13: 29–57. Reprinted in Lycan 1999; Block, Flanagan, and Güzeldere 1997; Chalmers 2002; chapter 5, this volume.

Levin, Janet. 1986. "Could Love Be Like a Heatwave? Physicalism and the Subjective Character of Experience." *Philosophical Studies* 49: 245–261. Reprinted in Lycan 1990.

Loar, Brian. 1990. "Phenomenal States," in *Philosophical Perspectives IV: Action Theory and the Philosophy of Mind*, ed. James Tomberlin, 81–108. Atascadero: Ridgeview.

———. 1997. "Phenomenal States (Revised Version)," in Block, Flanagan, and Güzeldere 1997, 597–616. Reprinted in Chalmers 2002; excerpt reprinted in this volume (chapter 11).

Locke, John. 1975 (originally 1689). *An Essay Concerning Human Understanding*. New York: Oxford.

Lodge, David. 2001. *Thinks . . .* London: Secker and Warburg Random House.

Lycan, William G., ed. 1990. *Mind and Cognition: A Reader*. Oxford: Blackwell.

———. 1995. "A Limited Defence of Phenomenal Information," in *Conscious Experience*, ed. Thomas Metzinger, 243–258. Exeter: Imprint Academic.

————. 1996. *Consciousness and Experiences*. Cambridge, Mass.: The MIT Press.

————, ed. 1999. *Mind and Cognition: An Anthology*. Oxford: Blackwell.

Maxwell, Nicholas. 1966. "Physics and Common Sense." *British Journal for the Philosophy of Science* 16: 295–311.

————. 1968. "Understanding Sensations." *Australasian Journal of Philosophy* 46: 127–145.

————. 2000. "The Mind–body Problem and Explanatory Dualism." *Philosophy* 75: 49–71.

————. 2001. *The Human World in the Physical Universe*. Lanham, Maryland: Rowman and Littlefield.

————. "Three Philosophical Problems About Consciousness and Their Possible Solution." Unpublished manuscript.

McConnell, Jeff. 1995. "In Defence of the Knowledge Argument." *Philosophical Topics* 22: 157–187.

McGeer, Victoria. 2003. "The Trouble with Mary." *Pacific Philosophical Quarterly* 84: 384–393.

McGinn, C. 1989. "Can We Solve the Mind–body Problem?" *Mind* 98: 349–366.

McMullen, Carolyn. 1985. "'Knowing What It's Like' and the Essential Indexicals." *Philosophical Studies* 48: 211–233.

Meehl, Paul E. 1966. "The Complete Autocerebroscopist," in *Mind, Matter, and Method: Essays in Philosophy and Science in Honor of Herbert Feigl*, ed. Paul Feyerabend and Grover Maxwell, 103–180. Minneapolis: University of Minnesota Press.

Mellor, D. H. 1993. "Nothing Like Experience." *Proceeding of the Aristotelian Society* 93: 1–16.

Meyer, Uwe. 2001. "The Knowledge Argument, Abilities, and Metalinguistic Beliefs." *Erkenntnis* 55: 325–347.

Montero, Barbara. 1999. "Frank Jackson Changed His Mind." *Philosophy News Service*.

Moser, Pual K., and J. D. Trout, eds. 1995. *Contemporary Materialism*. London: Routledge.

Nagasawa, Yujin. 2002. "The Knowledge Argument Against Dualism." *Theoria* 68: 205–223.

Nagel, Thomas. 1974. "What Is It Like to Be a Bat?" *Philosophical Review* 83: 435–450. Reprinted in his 1979; Block, Flanagan, and Güzeldere 1997.

————. 1979. *Mortal Questions*. Cambridge: Cambridge University Press.

Nemirow, Lawrence. 1980. "Review of *Mortal Questions* by Thomas Nagel." *Philosophical Review* 89: 473–477.

———. 1990. "Physicalism and the Cognitive Role of Acquaintance," in *Mind and Cognition: A Reader*, ed. William G. Lycan, 490–499. Oxford: Blackwell.

Newton, Natika. 1986. "Churchland on Direct Introspection of Brain States." *Analysis* 46: 97–102.

Nida-Rümelin, Martine. 1995. "What Mary Couldn't Know: Belief About Phenomenal States," in *Conscious Experience*, ed. Thomas Metzinger, 219–241. Exeter: Imprint Academic. Chapter 12, this volume.

———. 1998. "On Belief About Experiences: An Epistemological Distinction Applied to the Knowledge Argument Against Physicalism." *Philosophy and Phenomenological Research* 58: 51–73.

Noordhof, Paul. 2003. "Something Like Ability." *Australasian Journal of Philosophy* 81: 21–40.

Nordby, Knut. 1996. "Vision in a Complete Achromat: A Personal Account." Available at http://www.u.arizona.edu/~chalmers/misc/achromat.html.

Papineau, David. 1993. *Philosophical Naturalism*. Oxford: Blackwell.

Pereboom, Derk. 1994. "Bats, Brain Scientists, and the Limitations of Introspection." *Philosophy and Phenomenological Research* 54: 315–329.

Perry, John. 2001. *Knowledge, Possibility, and Consciousness*. Cambridge, Mass.: The MIT Press.

Pettit, Philip. 1993. "A Definition of Physicalism." *Analysis* 53: 213–223.

———. 2003. "Motion Blindness and the Knowledge Argument." Chapter 6, this volume.

Prior, A. N. 1959. "Thank Goodness That's Over." *Philosophy* 34: 12–17.

———. 1962. "The Formalities of Omniscience." *Philosophy* 37: 114–149.

Raymont, Paul. 1995. "Tye's Criticism of the Knowledge Argument." *Dialogue* 34: 713–726.

———. 1999. "The Know-how Response to Jackson's Knowledge Argument." *Journal of Philosophical Research* 24: 113–126.

Robinson, Howard. 1982. *Matter and Sense*. Cambridge: Cambridge University Press.

———, ed. 1993a. *Objections to Physicalism*. Oxford: Oxford University Press.

———. 1993b. "The Anti-materialist Strategy and the 'Knowledge Argument'," in his 1993a, 159–183.

———. 1993c. "Dennett on the Knowledge Argument." *Analysis* 53: 174–177. Reprinted as chapter 4, this volume.

Ryle, Gilbert. 1949. *The Concept of Mind*. London: Hutchinson.

Russell, Bertrand. 1967 (originally 1912). *The Problems of Philosophy*. Oxford: Oxford University Press.

Sacks, Oliver. 1985. *An Anthropologist on Mars*. New York: Alfred K. Knopf.

———. 1996. *The Island of the Colorblind*. New York: Alfred K. Knopf.

Searle, John R. 1992. *The Rediscovery of the Mind*. Cambridge, Mass.: The MIT Press.

Shoemaker, Sydney. 1982. "The Inverted Spectrum." *Journal of Philosophy* 79: 357–381. Reprinted in Block, Flanagan, and Güzeldere 1997.

Stanley, Jason, and Timothy Williamson. 2001. "Knowing How." *Journal of Philosophy* 98: 411–444.

Stjernberg, Fredrik. 1999. "Not So Epiphenomenal Qualia or, How Much of a Mystery is the Mind?" Available at http://www.lucs.lu.se/spinning/categories/language/Stjernberg/index.html.

Stoljar, Daniel. 2000. "Physicalism and the Necessary A Posteriori." *Journal of Philosophy* 97: 33–54.

———. 2001a. "Two Conceptions of the Physical." *Philosophy and Phenomenological Research* 62: 253–281. Reprinted in Chalmers 2002; excerpt reprinted in this volume (chapter 15).

———. 2001b. "Physicalism" (entry in *Stanford Encyclopedia of Philosophy*). Available at http://plato.stanford.edu/entries/physicalism/.

———. "Physicalism and Phenomenal Concepts." Unpublished manuscript.

Strawson, Galen. 1994. *Mental Reality*. Cambridge, Mass.: The MIT Press.

Thompson, Evan. 1992. "Novel Colors." *Philosophical Studies* 68: 321–349.

Tye, Michael. 1986. "The Subjective Qualities of Experience." *Mind* 95: 1–17. Reprinted in his (1989).

———. 1989. *The Metaphysics of Mind*. Cambridge: Cambridge University Press.

———. 1998. "Knowing What It Is Like: The Ability Hypothesis and the Knowledge Argument," in *Reality and Humean Supervenience: Essays on the Philosophy of David Lewis*, ed. Gerhard Preyer and Frank Siebelt. Frankfurt: Proto Sociology. Reprinted in his 2000; chapter 7, this volume.

———. 2000. *Consciousness, Color, and Content*. Cambridge, Mass.: The MIT Press. Excerpt reprinted in this volume (chapter 7).

Van Gulick, Robert. 1993. "Understanding the Phenomenal Mind: Are We All just Armadillos?" in *Consciousness: Psychological and Philosophical Essays*, ed. Martin Davies and Glyn W. Humphreys, Oxford: Balckwell, 137–154. Reprinted in Lycan 1999; Block, Flanagan, and Güzeldere 1997.

van Inwagen, Peter. 1983. *An Essay on Free Will*. Oxford: Clarendon Press.

———. 2003. "So Many Ways of Saying No to Mary." Chapter 17, this volume.

Vierkant, Tillmann. 2002. "Zombie-Mary and the Blue Banana: On the Compatibility of the 'Knowledge Argument' with the Argument from Modality." *Psyche* 8. Available at http://psyche.cs.monash.edu.au/v8/psyche-8-19-vierkant.html.

Watkins, Michael. 1989. "The Knowledge Argument Against the Knowledge Argument." *Analysis* 49: 158–160.

Wells, H. G. 2000 (originally written in 1904 and published in 1911). *The Country of the Blind*. London: Travelman.

White, Alan R. 1982. *The Nature of Knowledge*. Totowa, N.J.: Rowman and Littlefield.

Wittgenstein, Ludwig. 1980. *Remarks on the Philosophy of Psychology*, vol. 1. Chicago: University of Chicago Press.

Zemach, Eddy. 1990. "Churchland, Introspection, and Dualism." *Philosophia* 20: 3–13.

Part I Black-and-White Mary

1   Epiphenomenal Qualia

Frank Jackson

It is undeniable that the physical, chemical and biological sciences have provided a great deal of information about the world we live in and about ourselves. I will use the label 'physical information' for this kind of information, and also for information that automatically comes along with it. For example, if a medical scientist tells me enough about the processes that go on in my nervous system, and about how they relate to happenings in the world around me, to what has happened in the past and is likely to happen in the future, to what happens to other similar and dissimilar organisms, and the like, he or she tells me—if I am clever enough to fit it together appropriately—about what is often called the functional role of those states in me (and in organisms in general in similar cases). This information, and its kin, I also label 'physical'.

I do not mean these sketchy remarks to constitute a definition of 'physical information', and of the correlative notions of physical property, process, and so on, but to indicate what I have in mind here. It is well known that there are problems with giving a precise definition of these notions, and so of the thesis of physicalism that all (correct) information is physical information.[1] But—unlike some—I take the question of definition to cut across the central problems I want to discuss in this paper.

I am what is sometimes known as a "qualia freak." I think that there are certain features of the bodily sensations especially, but also of certain perceptual experiences, which no amount of purely physical information includes. Tell me everything physical there is to tell about what is going on in a living brain, the kind of states, their functional role, their relation to what goes on at other times and in other brains, and so on and so forth, and be I as clever as can be in fitting it all together, you won't have told me about the hurtfulness of pains, the itchiness of itches, pangs of jealousy, or about the characteristic experience of tasting a lemon, smelling a rose, hearing a loud noise or seeing the sky.

There are many qualia freaks, and some of them say that their rejection of physicalism is an unargued intuition.[2] I think that they are being unfair to themselves. They have the following argument. Nothing you could tell of a physical sort captures the smell of a rose, for instance. Therefore, physicalism is false. By our lights this is a perfectly good argument. It is obviously not to the point to question its validity, and the premise is intuitively obviously true both to them and to me.

I must, however, admit that it is weak from a polemical point of view. There are, unfortunately for us, many who do not find the premise intuitively obvious. The task then is to present an argument whose premises are obvious to all, or at least to as many as possible. This I try to do in §I with what I will call "the knowledge argument." In §II I contrast the knowledge argument with the modal argument and in §III with the "What is it like to be" argument. In §IV I tackle the question of the causal role of qualia. The major factor in stopping people from admitting qualia is the belief that they would have to be given a causal role with respect to the physical world and especially the brain;[3] and it is hard to do this without sounding like someone who believes in fairies. I seek in §IV to turn this objection by arguing that the view that qualia are epiphenomenal is a perfectly possible one.

I The Knowledge Argument for Qualia

People vary considerably in their ability to discriminate colors. Suppose that in an experiment to catalogue this variation Fred is discovered. Fred has better color vision than anyone else on record; he makes every discrimination that anyone has ever made, and moreover he makes one that we cannot even begin to make. Show him a batch of ripe tomatoes and he sorts them into two roughly equal groups and does so with complete consistency. That is, if you blindfold him, shuffle the tomatoes up, and then remove the blindfold and ask him to sort them out again, he sorts them into exactly the same two groups.

We ask Fred how he does it. He explains that all ripe tomatoes do not look the same color to him, and in fact that this is true of a great many objects that we classify together as red. He sees two colors where we see one, and he has in consequence developed for his own use two words 'red$_1$' and 'red$_2$' to mark the difference. Perhaps he tells us that he has often tried to teach the difference between red$_1$ and red$_2$ to his friends but has got nowhere and has concluded that the rest of the world is red$_1$-red$_2$ color-blind—or perhaps he has had partial success with his children, it doesn't matter. In any case he explains to us that it would be quite wrong to think that because 'red' appears in both 'red$_1$' and 'red$_2$' that the two colors are shades of the one color. He only uses the common term 'red' to fit more easily into our restricted usage. To him red$_1$ and red$_2$ are as different from each other and all the other colors as yellow is from blue. And his discriminatory behavior bears this out: he sorts red$_1$ from red$_2$ tomatoes with the greatest of ease in a wide variety of viewing circumstances. Moreover, an investigation of the physiological basis of Fred's exceptional ability reveals that Fred's optical system is able to separate out two groups of wavelengths in the red spectrum as sharply as we are able to sort out yellow from blue.[4]

I think that we should admit that Fred can see, really see, at least one more color than we can; red$_1$ is a different color from red$_2$. We are to Fred as a totally red-green color-blind person is to us. H. G. Wells's story "The Country of the Blind" is about a sighted person in a totally blind community.[5] This person never manages to convince them that he can see, that he has an extra sense. They ridicule this sense as quite inconceivable, and treat his capacity to avoid falling into ditches, to win fights and so on as precisely that capacity and nothing more. We would be making their mistake if we refused to allow that Fred can see one more color than we can.

What kind of experience does Fred have when he sees red$_1$ and red$_2$? What is the new color or colors like? We would dearly like to know but do not; and it seems that no amount of physical information about Fred's brain and optical system tells us. We find out perhaps that Fred's cones respond differentially to certain light waves in the red section of the spectrum that make no difference to ours (or perhaps he has an extra cone) and that this leads in Fred to a wider range of those brain states responsible for visual discriminatory behavior. But none of this tells us what we really want to know about his color experience. There is something about it we don't know. But we know, we may suppose, everything about Fred's body, his behavior and dispositions to behavior and about his internal physiology, and everything about his history and relation to others that can be given in physical accounts of persons. We have all the physical information. Therefore, knowing all this is *not* knowing everything about Fred. It follows that physicalism leaves something out.

To reinforce this conclusion, imagine that as a result of our investigations into the internal workings of Fred we find out how to make everyone's physiology like Fred's in the relevant respects; or perhaps Fred donates his body to science and on his death we are able to transplant his optical system into someone else—again the fine detail doesn't matter. The important point is that such a happening would create enormous interest. People would say, "At last we will know what it is like to see the extra color, at last we will know how Fred has differed from us in the way he has struggled to tell us about for so long." Then it cannot be that we knew all along all about Fred. But *ex hypothesi* we did know all along everything about Fred that features in the physicalist scheme; hence the physicalist scheme leaves something out.

Put it this way. *After* the operation, we will know *more* about Fred and especially about his colour experiences. But beforehand we had all the physical information we could desire about his body and brain, and indeed everything that has ever featured in physicalist accounts of mind and consciousness. Hence there is more to know than all that. Hence physicalism is incomplete.

Fred and the new color(s) are of course essentially rhetorical devices. The same point can be made with normal people and familiar colors. Mary is a brilliant scientist who is, for whatever reason, forced to investigate the world from a black-and-white room via a black-and-white television monitor. She specialises in the neurophysiology of vision and acquires, let us suppose, all the physical information there is to obtain about what goes on when we see ripe tomatoes, or the sky, and use terms like 'red', 'blue', and so on. She discovers, for example, just which wave-length combinations from the sky stimulate the retina, and exactly how this produces via the central nervous system the contraction of the vocal chords and expulsion of air from the lungs that results in the uttering of the sentence 'The sky is blue'. (It can hardly be denied that it is in principle possible to obtain all this physical information from black-and-white television, otherwise the Open University would *of necessity* need to use color television.)

What will happen when Mary is released from her black-and-white room or is given a color television monitor? Will she *learn* anything or not? It seems just obvious that she will learn something about the world and our visual experience of it. But then it is inescapable that her previous knowledge was incomplete. But she had *all* the physical information. *Ergo* there is more to have than that, and physicalism is false.

Clearly the same style of knowledge argument could be deployed for taste, hearing, the bodily sensations and generally speaking for the various mental states which are said to have (as it is variously put) raw feels, phenomenal features or qualia. The conclusion in each case is that the qualia are left out of the physicalist story. And the polemical strength of the knowledge argument is that it is so hard to deny the central claim that one can have all the physical information without having all the information there is to have.

II   The Modal Argument

By the modal argument I mean an argument of the following style.[6] Sceptics about other minds are not making a mistake in deductive logic, whatever else may be wrong with their position. No amount of physical information about another *logically entails* that he or she is conscious or feels anything at all. Consequently there is a possible world with organisms exactly like us in every physical respect (and remember that includes functional states, physical history, et al.) but which differ from us profoundly in that they have no conscious mental life at all. But then what is it that we have and they lack? Not anything physical *ex hypothesi*. In all physical regards we and they are exactly alike. Consequently there is more to us than the purely physical. Thus physicalism is false.[7]

It is sometimes objected that the modal argument misconceives physicalism on the ground that that doctrine is advanced as a *contingent* truth.[8] But to say this is only to say that physicalists restrict their claim to *some* possible worlds, including especially ours; and the modal argument is only directed against this lesser claim. If we in *our* world, let alone beings in any others, have features additional to those of our physical replicas in other possible worlds, then we have nonphysical features or qualia.

The trouble rather with the modal argument is that it rests on a disputable modal intuition. Disputable because it is disputed. Some sincerely deny that there can be physical replicas of us in other possible worlds which nevertheless lack consciousness. Moreover, at least one person who once had the intuition now has doubts.[9]

Head-counting may seem a poor approach to a discussion of the modal argument. But frequently we can do no better when modal intuitions are in question, and remember our initial goal was to find the argument with the greatest polemical utility.

Of course, *qua* protagonists of the knowledge argument we may well accept the modal intuition in question; but this will be a *consequence* of our already having an argument to the conclusion that qualia are left out of the physicalist story, not our ground for that conclusion. Moreover, the matter is complicated by the possibility that the connection between matters physical and qualia is like that sometimes held to obtain between aesthetic qualities and natural ones. Two possible worlds which agree in all "natural" respects (including the experiences of sentient creatures) must agree in all aesthetic qualities also, but it is plausibly held that the aesthetic qualities cannot be reduced to the natural.

III The "What Is It Like to Be" Argument

In "What is it like to be a bat?" Thomas Nagel argues that no amount of physical information can tell us what it is like to be a bat, and indeed that we, human beings, cannot imagine what it is like to be a bat.[10] His reason is that what this is like can only be understood from a bat's point of view, which is not our point of view and is not something capturable in physical terms which are essentially terms understandable equally from many points of view.

It is important to distinguish this argument from the knowledge argument. When I complained that all the physical knowledge about Fred was not enough to tell us what his special colour experience was like, I was not complaining that we weren't finding out what it is like to *be* Fred. I was complaining that there is something *about* his experience, a property of it, of which we were left ignorant. And if and when we come to know what this property is we still will not know what it is like to *be* Fred, but we will know more *about* him. No amount of knowledge about Fred, be it physical or not, amounts to knowledge "from the inside" concerning Fred. We are not Fred. There is thus a whole set of items of knowledge expressed by forms of words like 'that it is *I myself* who is ...' which Fred has and we simply cannot have because we are not him.[11]

When Fred sees the colour he alone can see, one thing he knows is the way his experience of it differs from his experience of seeing red and so on, *another* is that he himself is seeing it. Physicalist and qualia freaks alike should acknowledge that no amount of information of whatever kind that *others* have *about* Fred amounts to knowledge of the second. My complaint though concerned the first and was that the special quality of his experience is certainly a fact about it, and one which physicalism leaves out because no amount of physical information told us what it is.

Nagel speaks as if the problem he is raising is one of extrapolating from knowledge of one experience to another, of imagining what an unfamiliar experience would be like on the basis of familiar ones. In terms of Hume's example, from knowledge of some shades of blue we can work out what it would be like to see other shades of blue. Nagel argues that the trouble with bats et al. is that they are too unlike us. It is hard to see an objection to physicalism here. Physicalism makes no special claims about the imaginative or extrapolative powers of human beings, and it is hard to see why it need do so.[12]

Anyway, our knowledge argument makes no assumptions on this point. If physicalism were true, enough physical information about Fred would obviate any need to extrapolate or to perform special feats of imagination or understanding in order to know all about his special color experience. *The information would already be in our possession.* But it clearly isn't. That was the nub of the argument.

IV   The Bogey of Epiphenomenalism

Is there any really *good* reason for refusing to countenance the idea that qualia are causally impotent with respect to the physical world? I will argue for the answer no, but in doing this I will say nothing about two views associated with the classical epiphenomenalist position. The first is that mental *states* are inefficacious with respect to the physical world. All I will be concerned to defend is that it is possible to hold that certain *properties* of certain mental states, namely those I've called qualia, are such that their possession or absence makes no difference to the physical world. The second is that the mental is *totally* causally inefficacious. For all I will say it may be that you have to hold that the instantiation of *qualia* makes a difference to *other mental states* though not to anything physical. Indeed general considerations to do with how you could come to be aware of the instantiation of qualia suggest such a position.[13]

Three reasons are standardly given for holding that a quale like the hurtfulness of a pain must be causally efficacious in the physical world, and so, for instance, that its instantiation must sometimes make a difference to what happens in the brain. None, I will argue, has any real force. (I am much indebted to Alec Hyslop and John Lucas for convincing me of this.)

(i) It is supposed to be just obvious that the hurtfulness of pain is partly responsible for the subject seeking to avoid pain, saying 'It hurts' and so on. But, to reverse Hume, anything can fail to cause anything. No matter how often B follows A, and no matter how initially obvious the causality of the connection seems, the hypothesis that A causes B can be overturned by an overarching theory which shows the two as distinct effects of a common underlying causal process.

To the untutored the image on the screen of Lee Marvin's fist moving from left to right immediately followed by the image of John Wayne's head moving in the same general direction looks as causal as anything.[14] And of course throughout countless Westerns images similar to the first are followed by images similar to the second. All this counts for precisely nothing when we know the overarching theory concerning how the relevant images are both effects of an underlying causal process involving the projector and the film. The epiphenomenalist can say exactly the same about the connection between, for example, hurtfulness and behavior. It is simply a consequence of the fact that certain happenings in the brain cause both.

(ii) The second objection relates to Darwin's theory of evolution. According to natural selection the traits that evolve over time are those conducive to physical survival. We may assume that qualia evolved over time—we have them, the earliest forms of life do not—and so we should expect qualia to be conducive to survival. The objection is that they could hardly help us to survive if they do nothing to the physical world.

The appeal of this argument is undeniable, but there is a good reply to it. Polar bears have particularly thick, warm coats. The theory of evolution explains this (we suppose) by pointing out that having a thick, warm coat is conducive to survival in the Arctic. But having a thick coat goes along with having a heavy coat, and having a heavy coat is *not* conducive to survival. It slows the animal down.

Does this mean that we have refuted Darwin because we have found an evolved trait—having a heavy coat—which is not conducive to survival? Clearly not. Having a heavy coat is an unavoidable concomitant of having a warm coat (in the context, modern insulation was not available), and the advantages for survival of having a warm coat outweighed the disadvantages of having a heavy one. The point is that all we can extract from Darwin's theory is that we should expect any evolved characteristic to be *either* conducive to survival *or* a by-product of one that is so conducive. The epiphenomenalist holds that qualia fall into the latter category. They are a by-product of certain brain processes that are highly conducive to survival.

(iii) The third objection is based on a point about how we come to know about other minds. We know about other minds by knowing about other behavior, at least in part. The nature of the inference is a matter of some controversy, but it is not a matter of controversy that it proceeds from behavior. That is why we think that stones do not feel and dogs do feel. But, runs the objection, how can a person's behavior provide any reason for believing he has qualia like mine, or indeed any qualia at all, unless this behavior can be regarded as the *outcome* of the qualia. Man Friday's footprint was evidence of Man Friday because footprints are causal outcomes of feet attached to people. And an epiphenomenalist cannot regard behavior, or indeed anything physical, as an outcome of qualia.

But consider my reading in *The Times* that Spurs won. This provides excellent evidence that *The Telegraph* has also reported that Spurs won, despite the fact that (I trust) *The Telegraph* does not get the results from *The Times*. They each send their own reporters to the game. *The Telegraph*'s report is in no sense an outcome of *The Times*', but the latter provides good evidence for the former nevertheless.

The reasoning involved can be reconstructed thus. I read in *The Times* that Spurs won. This gives me reason to think that Spurs won because I know that Spurs' winning is the most likely candidate to be what caused the report in *The Times*. But I also know that Spurs' winning would have had many effects, including almost certainly a report in *The Telegraph*.

I am arguing from one effect back to its cause and out again to another effect. The fact that neither effect causes the other is irrelevant. Now the epiphenomenalist allows that qualia are effects of what goes on in the brain. Qualia cause nothing physical but are caused by something physical. Hence the epiphenomenalist can argue from the behaviour of others to the qualia of others by arguing from the behavior of others back to its causes in the brains of others and out again to their qualia.

You may well feel for one reason or another that this is a more dubious chain of reasoning than its model in the case of newspaper reports. You are right. The problem of other minds is a major philosophical problem, the problem of other newspaper reports is not. But there is no special problem of epiphenomenalism as opposed to, say, interactionism here.

There is a very understandable response to the three replies I have just made. "All right, there is no knockdown refutation of the existence of epiphenomenal qualia. But the fact remains that they are an excrescence. They *do* nothing, they *explain* nothing, they serve merely to soothe the intuitions of dualists, and it is left a total mystery how they fit into the world view of science. In short we do not and cannot understand the how and why of them."

This is perfectly true; but is no objection to qualia, for it rests on an overly optimistic view of the human animal, and its powers. We are the products of evolution. We understand and sense what we need to understand and sense in order to survive. Epiphenomenal qualia are totally irrelevant to survival. At no stage of our evolution did natural selection favour those who could make sense of how they are caused and the laws governing them, or in fact why they exist at all. And that is why we can't.

It is not sufficiently appreciated that physicalism is an extremely optimistic view of our powers. If it is true, we have, in very broad outline admittedly, a grasp of our place in the scheme of things. Certain matters of sheer complexity defeat us—there are an awful lot of neurons—but in principle we have it all. But consider the antecedent probability that everything in the universe be of a kind that is relevant in some way or other to the survival of *Homo sapiens*. It is very low surely. But then one must admit that it is very likely that there is a part of the whole scheme of things, maybe a big part, which no amount of evolution will ever bring us near to knowledge about or understanding. For the simple reason that such knowledge and understanding is irrelevant to survival.

Physicalists typically emphasize that we are a part of nature on their view, which is fair enough. But if we are a part of nature, we are as nature has left us after however many years of evolution it is, and each step in that evolutionary progression has been a matter of chance constrained just by the need to preserve or increase survival value. The wonder is that we understand as much as we do, and there is no wonder that there should be matters which fall quite outside our comprehension. Perhaps exactly how epiphenomenal qualia fit into the scheme of things is one such.

This may seem an unduly pessimistic view of our capacity to articulate a truly comprehensive picture of our world and our place in it. But suppose we discovered living on the bottom of the deepest oceans a sort of sea slug which manifested intelligence. Perhaps survival in the conditions required rational powers. Despite their intelligence, these sea slugs have only a very restricted conception of the world by comparison with ours, the explanation for this being the nature of their immediate environment. Nevertheless they have developed sciences which work surprisingly well in these restricted terms. They also have philosophers, called slugists. Some call themselves tough-minded slugists, others confess to being soft-minded slugists.

The tough-minded slugists hold that the restricted terms (or ones pretty like them which may be introduced as their sciences progress) suffice in principle to describe everything without remainder. These tough-minded slugists admit in moments of weakness to a feeling that their theory leaves something out. They resist this feeling and their opponents, the soft-minded slugists, by pointing out—absolutely correctly—that no slugist has ever succeeded in spelling out how this mysterious residue fits into the highly successful view that their sciences have and are developing of how their world works.

Our sea slugs don't exist, but they might. And there might also exist super beings which stand to us as we stand to the sea slugs. We cannot adopt the perspective of these super beings, because we are not them, but the possibility of such a perspective is, I think, an antidote to excessive optimism.[15]

Notes

1. See, e.g., D. H. Mellor, "Materialism and Phenomenal Qualities," *Aristotelian Society Supp. Vol.* 47 (1973), 107–119; and J. W. Cornman, *Materialism and Sensations* (New Haven and London, 1971).

2. Particularly in discussion, but see, e.g., Keith Campbell, *Metaphysics* (Belmont, 1976), p. 67.

3. See, e.g., D. C. Dennett, "Current Issues in the Philosophy of Mind," *American Philosophical Quarterly* 15 (1978), 249–261.

4. Put this, and similar simplifications below, in terms of Land's theory if you prefer. See, e.g., Edwin H. Land, "Experiments in Color Vision," *Scientific American* 200 (5 May 1959), 84–99.

5. H. G. Wells, *The Country of the Blind and Other Stories* (London, n.d.).

6. See, e.g., Keith Campbell, *Body and Mind* (New York, 1970); and Robert Kirk, "Sentience and Behaviour," *Mind* 83 (1974), 43–60.

7. I have presented the argument in an inter-world rather than the more usual intra-world fashion to avoid inessential complications to do with supervenience, causal anomalies and the like.

8. See, e.g., W. G. Lycan, "A New Lilliputian Argument Against Machine Function-alism," *Philosophical Studies* 35 (1979), 279–287, p. 280; and Don Locke, "Zombies, Schizophrenics and Purely Physical Objects," *Mind* 85 (1976), 97–99.

9. See R. Kirk, "From Physical Explicability to Full-Blooded Materialism," *Philosophical Quarterly* 29 (1979), 229–237. See also the arguments against the modal intuition in, e.g., Sydney Shoemaker, "Functionalism and Qualia," *Philosophical Studies* 27 (1975), 291–315.

10. *Philosophical Review* 83 (1974), 435–450. Two things need to be said about this article. One is that, despite my dissociations to come, I am much indebted to it. The other is that the emphasis changes through the article, and by the end Nagel is objecting not so much to physicalism as to all extant theories of mind for ignoring points of view, including those that admit (irreducible) qualia.

11. Knowledge *de se* in the terms of David Lewis, "Attitudes De Dicto and De Se," *Philosophical Review* 88 (1979), 513–543.

12. See Laurence Nemirow's comments on "What is it ..." in his review of T. Nagel, *Mortal Questions*, in *Philosophical Review* 89 (1980), 473–477. I am indebted here in particular to a discussion with David Lewis.

13. See my review of K. Campbell, *Body and Mind*, in *Australasian Journal of Philosophy* 50 (1972), 77–80.

14. Cf. Jean Piaget, "The Child's Conception of Physical Causality," reprinted in *The Essential Piaget* (London, 1977).

15. I am indebted to Robert Pargetter for a number of comments and, despite his dissent, to §IV of Paul E. Meehl, "The Compleat Autocerebroscopist" in *Mind, Matter, and Method*, ed. Paul Feyerabend and Grover Maxwell (Minneapolis, 1966).

2 What Mary Didn't Know

Frank Jackson

Mary is confined to a black-and-white room, is educated through black-and-white books and through lectures relayed on black-and-white television. In this way she learns everything there is to know about the physical nature of the world. She knows all the physical facts about us and our environment, in a wide sense of 'physical' which includes everything in *completed* physics, chemistry, and neurophysiology, and all there is to know about the causal and relational facts consequent upon all this, including of course functional roles. If physicalism is true, she knows all there is to know. For to suppose otherwise is to suppose that there is more to know than every physical fact, and that is just what physicalism denies.

Physicalism is not the noncontroversial thesis that the actual world is largely physical, but the challenging thesis that it is entirely physical. This is why physicalists must hold that complete physical knowledge is complete knowledge simpliciter. For suppose it is not complete: then our world must differ from a world, $W(P)$, for which it is complete, and the difference must be in nonphysical facts; for our world and $W(P)$ agree in all matters physical. Hence, physicalism would be false at our world (though contingently so, for it would be true at $W(P)$).[1]

It seems, however, that Mary does not know all there is to know. For when she is let out of the black-and-white room or given a color television, she will learn what it is like to see something red, say. This is rightly described as *learning*—she will not say "ho, hum." Hence, physicalism is false. This is the knowledge argument against physicalism in one of its manifestations.[2] This note is a reply to three objections to it mounted by Paul M. Churchland.[3]

I Three Clarifications

The knowledge argument does not rest on the dubious claim that logically you cannot imagine what sensing red is like unless you have sensed red. Powers of imagination are not to the point. The contention about Mary is not that, despite her fantastic grasp of neurophysiology and everything else physical, she *could not imagine* what it is like to sense red; it is that, as a matter of fact, she *would not know*. But if physicalism is true, she would know; and no great powers of imagination would be called for. Imagination is a faculty that those who *lack* knowledge need to fall back on.

Second, the intensionality of knowledge is not to the point. The argument does not rest on assuming falsely that, if S knows that a is F and if a = b, then S knows that b is F. It is concerned with the nature of Mary's total body of knowledge before she is released: is it complete, or do some facts escape it? What is to the point is that S may know that a is F and *know* that a = b, yet arguably not know that b is F, by virtue of not being sufficiently logically alert to follow the consequences through. If Mary's lack of knowledge were at all like this, there would be no threat to physicalism in it. But it is very hard to believe that her lack of knowledge could be remedied merely by her explicitly following through enough logical consequences of her vast physical knowledge. Endowing her with great logical acumen and persistence is not in itself enough to fill in the gaps in her knowledge. On being let out, she will not say "I could have worked all this out before by making some more purely logical inferences."

Third, the knowledge Mary lacked which is of particular point for the knowledge argument against physicalism is *knowledge about the experiences of others*, not about her own. When she is let out, she has new experiences, color experiences she has never had before. It is not, therefore, an objection to physicalism that she learns *something* on being let out. Before she was let out, she could not have known facts about her experience of red, for there were no such facts to know. That physicalist and nonphysicalist alike can agree on. After she is let out, things change; and physicalism can happily admit that she learns this; after all, some physical things will change, for instance, her brain states and their functional roles. The trouble for physicalism is that, after Mary sees her first ripe tomato, she will realize how impoverished her conception of the mental life of *others* has been *all along*. She will realize that there was, all the time she was carrying out her laborious investigations into the neurophysiologies of others and into the functional roles of their internal states, something about these people she was quite unaware of. All along their experiences (or many of them, those got from tomatoes, the sky,...) had a feature conspicuous to them but until now hidden from her (in fact, not in logic). But she knew all the physical facts about them all along; hence, what are did not know until her release is not a physical fact about their experiences. But it is a fact about them. That is the trouble for physicalism.

II Churchland's Three Objections

(i) Churchland's first objection is that the knowledge argument contains a defect that "is simplicity itself" (23). The argument equivocates on the sense of 'knows about'. How so? Churchland suggests that the following is "a conveniently tightened version" of the knowledge argument:

(1) Mary knows everything there is to know about brain states and their properties.

(2) It is not the case that Mary knows everything there is to know about sensations and their properties.

Therefore, by Leibniz's law,

(3) Sensations and their properties ≠ brain states and their properties (23).

Churchland observes, plausibly enough, that the type or kind of knowledge involved in premise 1 is distinct from the kind of knowledge involved in premise 2. We might follow his lead and tag the first 'knowledge by description', and the second 'knowledge by acquaintance'; but, whatever the tags, he is right that the displayed argument involves a highly dubious use of Leibniz's law.

My reply is that the displayed argument may be convenient, but it is not accurate. It is not the knowledge argument. Take, for instance, premise 1. The whole thrust of the knowledge argument is that Mary (before her release) does *not* know everything there is to know about brain states and their properties, because she does not know about certain qualia associated with them. What is complete, according to the argument, is her knowledge of matters physical. A convenient and accurate way of displaying the argument is:

(1)′   Mary (before her release) knows everything physical there is to know about other people.

(2)′   Mary (before her release) does not know everything there is to know about other people (because she *learns* something about them on her release).

Therefore,

(3)′   There are truths about other people (and herself) which escape the physicalist story.

What is immediately to the point is not the kind, manner, or type of knowledge Mary has, but *what* she knows. What she knows beforehand is ex hypothesi everything physical there is to know, but is it everything there is to know? That is the crucial question.

There is, though, a relevant challenge involving questions about kinds of knowledge. It concerns the *support* for premise 2′. The case for premise 2′ is that Mary learns something on her release, she acquires knowledge, and that entails that her knowledge beforehand (*what* she knew, never mind whether by description, acquaintance, or whatever) was incomplete. The challenge, mounted by David Lewis and Laurence Nemirow, is that on her release Mary does *not* learn something or acquire knowledge in the relevant sense. What Mary acquires when she is released is a certain representational or imaginative ability; it is knowledge how rather than knowledge that. Hence, a physicalist can admit that Mary acquires something very significant of a knowledge kind—which can hardly be denied—without admitting that this shows that her earlier factual knowledge is defective. She knew all *that* there was to know about the experiences of others beforehand, but lacked an ability until after her release.[4]

Now it is certainly true that Mary will acquire abilities of various kinds after her release. She will, for instance, be able to imagine what seeing red is like, be able to remember what it is like, and be able to understand why her friends regarded her as so deprived (something which, until her release, had always mystified her). But is it plausible that that is *all* she will acquire? Suppose she received a lecture on skepticism about other minds while she was incarcerated. On her release she sees a ripe tomato in normal conditions, and so has a sensation of red. Her first reaction is to say that she now knows more about the kind of experiences others have when looking at ripe tomatoes. She then remembers the lecture and starts to worry. Does

she really know more about what their experiences are like, or is she in-
dulging in a wild generalization from one case? In the end she decides she
does know, and that skepticism is mistaken (even if, like so many of us,
she is not sure how to demonstrate its errors). What was she to-ing and
fro-ing about—her abilities? Surely not; her representational abilities were a
known constant throughout. What else then was she agonizing about than
whether or not she had gained factual knowledge of others? There would
be nothing to agonize about if ability was *all* she acquired on her release.

I grant that I have no *proof* that Mary acquires on her release, as well as
abilities, factual knowledge about the experiences of others—and not just
because I have no disproof of skepticism. My claim is that the knowledge
argument is a valid argument from highly plausible, though admittedly
not demonstrable, premises to the conclusion that physicalism is false. And
that, after all, is about as good an objection as one could expect in this area
of philosophy.

(ii) Churchland's second objection (24/5) is that there must be something wrong with the argument, for it proves too much. Suppose Mary
received a special series of lectures over her black-and-white television
from a full-blown dualist, explaining the "laws" governing the behavior of
"ectoplasm" and telling her about qualia. This would not affect the plausibility of the claim that on her release she learns something. So if the argument works against physicalism, it works against dualism too.

My reply is that lectures about qualia over black-and-white television do
not tell Mary all there is to know about qualia. They may tell her some
things about qualia, for instance, that they do not appear in the physicalist's story, and that the quale we use 'yellow' for is nearly as different
from the one we use 'blue' for as is white from black. But why should it
be supposed that they tell her everything about qualia? On the other hand,
it is plausible that lectures over black-and-white television might in principle tell Mary everything in the physicalist's story. You do not need color
television to learn physics or functionalist psychology. To obtain a good
argument against dualism (attribute dualism; ectoplasm is a bit of fun), the
premise in the knowledge argument that Mary has the full story according
to physicalism before her release, has to be replaced by a premise that she
has the full story according to dualism. The former is plausible; the latter is
not. Hence, there is no "parity of reasons" trouble for dualists who use the
knowledge argument.

(iii) Churchland's third objection is that the knowledge argument claims "that Mary could not even *imagine* what the relevant experience would be like, despite her exhaustive neuroscientific knowledge, and hence must still be missing certain crucial information" (25), a claim he goes on to argue against.

But, as we emphasized earlier, the knowledge argument claims that Mary would not know what the relevant experience is like. What she could imagine is another matter. If her knowledge is defective, despite being all there is to know according to physicalism, then physicalism is false, whatever her powers of imagination.

Acknowledgment

I am much indebted to discussions with David Lewis and with Robert Pargetter.

Notes

1. The claim here is not that, if physicalism is true, only what is expressed in explicitly physical language is an item of knowledge. It is that, if physicalism is true, then if you know everything expressed or expressible in explicitly physical language, you know everything. *Pace* Terence Horgan, "Jackson on Physical Information and Qualia," *Philosophical Quarterly* 34, 135 (April 1984): 147–152.

2. Namely, that in my "Epiphenomenal Qualia," *Philosophical Quarterly* 34, 127 (April 1982): 127–136. See also Thomas Nagel, "What Is It Like to Be a Bat?", *Philosophical Review* 83, 4 (October 1974): 435–450, and Howard Robinson, *Matter and Sense* (New York: Cambridge, 1982).

3. "Reduction, Qualia, and the Direct Introspection of Brain States," *Journal of Philosophy* 82, 1 (January 1985): 8–28. Unless otherwise stated, future page references are to this paper.

4. See Laurence Nemirow, review of Thomas Nagel, *Mortal Questions, Philosophical Review* 89, 3 (July 1980): 473–477, and David Lewis, "Postscript to 'Mad Pain and Martian Pain'," *Philosophical Papers*, vol. i (New York: Oxford, 1983). Churchland mentions both Nemirow and Lewis, and it may be that he intended his objection to be essentially the one I have just given. However, he says quite explicitly (bottom of p. 23) that his objection does not need an "ability" analysis of the relevant knowledge.

Part II Does She Learn Anything?

3 "Epiphenomenal" Qualia?

Daniel C. Dennett

There is another philosophical thought experiment about our experience of color that has proven irresistible: Frank Jackson's (1982) much-discussed case of Mary, the color scientist who has never seen colors. Like a good thought experiment, its point is immediately evident to even the uninitiated. In fact it is a bad thought experiment, an intuition pump that actually encourages us to misunderstand its premises!

Mary is a brilliant scientist who is, for whatever reason, forced to investigate the world from a black-and-white room *via* a black-and-white television monitor. She specializes in the neurophysiology of vision and acquires, let us suppose, all the physical information there is to obtain about what goes on when we see ripe tomatoes, or the sky, and use terms like *red*, *blue*, and so on. She discovers, for example, just which wavelength combinations from the sky stimulate the retina, and exactly how this produces *via* the central nervous system the contraction of the vocal chords and expulsion of air from the lungs that results in the uttering of the sentence 'The sky is blue'.... What will happen when Mary is released from her black-and-white room or is given a color television monitor? Will she *learn* anything or not? It seems just obvious that she will learn something about the world and our visual experience of it. But then it is inescapable that her previous knowledge was incomplete. But she had *all* the physical information. *Ergo* there is more to have than that, and physicalism is false.... (pp. 42–43, this vol.)

The point could hardly be clearer. Mary has had *no* experience of color at all (there are no mirrors to look at her face in, she's obliged to wear black gloves, etc., etc.), and so, at that special moment when her captors finally let her come out into the colored world which she knows only by description (and black-and-white diagrams), "it seems just obvious," as Jackson says, that she will learn something. Indeed, we can all vividly imagine her, seeing a red rose for the first time and exclaiming, "So *that's* what red looks like!" And it may also occur to us that if the first colored things she is shown are, say, unlabeled wooden blocks, and she is told only that one of them is red and the other blue, she won't have the faintest idea which is which until she somehow learns which color words go with her newfound experiences.

That is how almost everyone imagines this thought experiment—not just the uninitiated, but the shrewdest, most battle-hardened philosophers (Tye 1986; Lewis 1988; Loar 1990; Lycan 1990; Nemirov 1990; Harman 1990; Block 1990; Van Gulick 1990). Only Paul Churchland (1985, 1990) has offered any serious resistance to the *image*, so vividly conjured up by the thought experiment, of Mary's dramatic discovery. The image is wrong; if that is the way you imagine the case, you are simply not following directions! The reason no one follows directions is because what they ask you to imagine is so preposterously immense, you can't even try. The crucial premise is that "She has *all* the physical information." That is not readily imaginable, so no one bothers. They just imagine that she knows lots and lots—perhaps they imagine that she knows everything that anyone knows *today* about the neurophysiology of color vision. But that's just a drop in the bucket, and it's not surprising that Mary would learn something if *that* were all she knew.

To bring out the illusion of imagination here, let me continue the story in a surprising—but legitimate—way:

And so, one day, Mary's captors decided it was time for her to see colors. As a trick, they prepared a bright blue banana to present as her first color experience ever. Mary took one look at it and said "Hey! You tried to trick me! Bananas are yellow, but this one is blue!" Her captors were dumfounded. How did she do it? "Simple," she replied. "You have to remember that I know *everything*—absolutely everything—that could ever be known about the physical causes and effects of color vision. So of course before you brought the banana in, I had already written down, in exquisite detail, exactly what physical impression a yellow object or a blue object (or a green object, etc.) would make on my nervous system. So I already knew exactly what *thoughts* I would have (because, after all, the 'mere disposition' to think about this or that is not one of your famous qualia, is it?). I was not in the slightest surprised by my experience of blue (what surprised me was that you would try such a second-rate trick on me). I realize it is *hard for you to imagine* that I could know so much about my reactive dispositions that the way blue affected me came as no surprise. Of course it's hard for you to imagine. It's hard for anyone to imagine the consequences of someone knowing absolutely everything physical about anything!"

Surely I've cheated, you think. I must be hiding some impossibility behind the veil of Mary's remarks. Can you prove it? My point is not that my way of telling the rest of the story proves that Mary *doesn't* learn anything, but that the usual way of imagining the story doesn't *prove* that she *does*. It doesn't prove anything; it simply pumps the intuition that she does ("it seems just obvious") by lulling you into imagining something other than what the premises require.

It is of course true that in any realistic, readily imaginable version of the story, Mary would come to learn something, but in any realistic, readily imaginable version she might know a lot, but she would not know everything physical. Simply imagining that Mary knows a lot, and leaving it at that, is not a good way to figure out the implications of her having "all the physical information"—any more than imagining she is filthy rich would be a good way to figure out the implications of the hypothesis that she owned everything. It may help us imagine the extent of the powers her knowledge gives her if we begin by enumerating a few of the things she obviously knows in advance. She knows black and white and shades of gray, and she knows the difference between the color of any object and such surface properties as glossiness versus matte, and she knows all about the difference between luminance boundaries and color boundaries (luminance boundaries are those that show up on black-and-white television, to put it roughly). And she knows precisely which effects—described in neurophysiological terms—each particular color will have on her nervous system. So the only task that remains is for her to figure out a way of identifying those neurophysiological effects "from the inside." You may find you can readily imagine her making *a little* progress on this—for instance, figuring out tricky ways in which she would be able to tell that some color, whatever it is, is *not* yellow, or *not* red. How? By noting some salient and specific reaction that her brain would have only for yellow or only for red. But if you allow her even a little entry into her color space in this way, you should conclude that she can leverage her way to complete advance knowledge, because she doesn't just know the *salient* reactions, she knows them all.

Recall Julius and Ethel Rosenberg's Jell-O box, which they turned into an *M*-detector. Now imagine their surprise if an impostor were to show up with a "matching" piece that was not the original. "Impossible!" they cry. "Not impossible," says the impostor, "just difficult. I had *all the information* required to reconstruct an *M*-detector, and to make another thing with shape-property *M*." Mary had enough information (in the original case, if correctly imagined) to figure out just what her red-detectors and blue-detectors were, and hence to identify them in advance. Not the usual way of coming to learn about colors, but Mary is not your usual person.

I know that this will not satisfy many of Mary's philosophical fans, and that there is a lot more to be said, but—and this is my main point—the actual proving must go on in an arena far removed from Jackson's example, which is a classic provoker of Philosophers' Syndrome: mistaking a failure of imagination for an insight into necessity. Some of the philosophers who have dealt with the case of Mary may not care that they have imagined it wrong, since they have simply used it as a springboard into discussions that shed light on various independently interesting and important issues. I will not pursue those issues here, since I am interested in directly considering the conclusion that Jackson himself draws from his example: visual experiences have qualia that are "epiphenomenal."

The term "epiphenomena" is in common use today by both philosophers and psychologists (and other cognitive scientists). It is used with the presumption that its meaning is familiar and agreed upon, when in fact, philosophers and cognitive scientists use the term with *entirely* different meanings—a strange fact made even stranger to me by the fact that although I have pointed this out time and again, no one seems to care. Since "epiphenomenalism" often seems to be the last remaining safe haven for qualia, and since this appearance of safety is due entirely to the confusion between these two meanings, I must become a scold, and put those who use the term on the defensive.

According to the *Shorter Oxford English Dictionary*, the term "epiphenomenon" first appears in 1706 as a term in pathology, "a secondary appearance or symptom." The evolutionary biologist Thomas Huxley (1874) was probably the writer who extended the term to its current use in psychology, where it means a *nonfunctional* property or by-product. Huxley used the term in his discussion of the evolution of consciousness and his claim that epiphenomenal properties (like the "whistle of the steam engine") could not be explained by natural selection.

Here is a clear instance of this use of the word:

Why do people who are thinking hard bite their lips and tap their feet? Are these actions just epiphenomena that accompany the core processes of feeling and thinking or might they themselves be integral parts of these processes? (Zajonc and Markus 1984, p. 74)

Notice that the authors mean to assert that these actions, while perfectly detectable, play no enabling role, no designed role, in the processes of feeling and thinking; they are nonfunctional. In the same spirit, the hum of the computer is epiphenomenal, as is your shadow when you make yourself a cup of tea. Epiphenomena are mere by-products, but as such they are products with lots of effects in the world: tapping your feet makes a recordable noise, and your shadow has its effects on photographic film, not to mention the slight cooling of the surfaces it spreads itself over.

The standard philosophical meaning is different: "x is epiphenomenal" means "x is an effect but itself has no effects in the physical world whatever." (See Broad 1925, p. 118, for the definition that inaugurates, or at any rate establishes, the philosophical usage.) Are these meanings really so different? Yes, as different as the meanings of *murder* and *death*. The philosophical meaning is stronger: Anything that has no effects whatever in the physical world surely has no effects on the function of anything, but the converse doesn't follow, as the example from Zajonc and Markus makes obvious.

In fact, the philosophical meaning is too strong; it yields a concept of no utility whatsoever (Harman 1990; Fox 1989). Since x has no physical effects (according to this definition), no instrument can detect the presence of x directly or indirectly; the way the world goes is not modulated in the slightest by the presence or absence of x. How then, could there ever be any empirical reason to assert the presence of x? Suppose, for instance, that Otto insists that he (for one) has epiphenomenal qualia. Why does he say this? Not because they have some effect on him, somehow guiding him or alerting him as he makes his avowals. By the very definition of epiphenomena (in the philosophical sense). Otto's heartfelt avowals that he has epiphenomena *could not* be evidence for himself or anyone else that he does have them, since he would be saying exactly the same thing even if he didn't have them. But perhaps Otto has some "internal" evidence?

Here there's a loophole, but not an attractive one. Epiphenomena, remember, are defined as having no effect in the *physical* world. If Otto wants to embrace out-and-out dualism, he can claim that his epiphenomenal qualia have no effects in the physical world, but do have effects in his (nonphysical) mental world (Broad 1925 closed this loophole by definition, but it's free for the asking). For instance, they *cause some of his (nonphysical) beliefs*, such as his belief that he has epiphenomenal qualia. But this is just a temporary escape from embarrassment. For now on pain of contradiction, his beliefs, in turn, can have no effect in the physical world. If he suddenly lost his epiphenomenal qualia, he would no longer believe he had them, but he'd still go right on *saying* he did. He just wouldn't believe what he was saying! (Nor could he tell you that he didn't believe what he was saying, or do anything at all that revealed that he no longer believed what he was saying.) So the only way Otto could "justify" his belief in epiphenomena would be by retreating into a solipsistic world where there is only himself, his beliefs and his qualia, cut off from all effects in the world. Far from being a "safe" way of being a materialist and having your qualia too, this is at best a way of endorsing the most radical solipsism, by cutting off your mind—your beliefs and your experiences—from any commerce with the material world.

If qualia are epiphenomenal in the standard philosophical sense, their occurrence can't explain the way things happen (in the material world) since, by definition, things would happen exactly the same without them. There could not be an empirical reason, then, for believing in epiphenomena. Could there be another sort of reason for asserting their existence? What sort of reason? An *a priori* reason, presumably. But what? No one has ever offered one—good, bad, or indifferent—that I have seen. If someone wants to object that I am being a "verificationist" about these epiphenomena, I reply: Isn't everyone a verificationist about *this* sort of assertion? Consider, for instance, the hypothesis that there are fourteen epiphenomenal gremlins in each cylinder of an internal combustion engine. These gremlins have no mass, no energy, no physical properties; they do not make the engine run smoother or rougher, faster or slower. There is *and could be* no empirical evidence of their presence, and no empirical way in principle of distinguishing this hypothesis from its rivals: there are twelve or thirteen or fifteen ... gremlins. By what principle does one defend one's wholesale dismissal of such nonsense? A verificationist principle, or just plain common sense?

Ah, but there's a difference! (says Otto.) There is no independent motivation for taking the hypothesis of these gremlins seriously. You just made them up on the spur of the moment. Qualia, in contrast, have been around for a long time, playing a major role in our conceptual scheme!

And what if some benighted people have been thinking for generations that gremlins made their cars go, and by now have been pushed back by the march of science into the forlorn claim that the gremlins are there, all right, but are epiphenomenal? Is it a mistake for us to dismiss their "hypothesis" out of hand? Whatever the principle is that we rely on when we give the back of our hand to such nonsense, it suffices to dismiss the doctrine that qualia are epiphenomenal in this philosophical sense. These are not views that deserve to be discussed with a straight face.

It's hard to believe that the philosophers who have recently described their views as epiphenomenalism can be making such a woebegone mistake. Are they, perhaps, just asserting that qualia are epiphenomenal in Huxley's sense? Qualia, on this reading, *are* physical effects and *have* physical effects; they just aren't functional. Any materialist should be happy to admit that this hypothesis is true—if we identify qualia with reactive dispositions, for instance. As we noted in the discussion of enjoyment, even though some bulges or biases in our quality spaces are functional—or used to be functional—others are just brute happenstance. Why don't I like broccoli? Probably for no reason at all; my negative reactive disposition is purely epiphenomenal, a by-product of my wiring with no significance. It has no function, but has plenty of effects. In any designed system, some properties are crucial while others are more or less revisable *ad lib*. Everything has to be some way or another, but often the ways don't matter. The gear shift lever on a car may have to be a certain length and a certain strength, but whether it is round or square or oval in cross section is an epiphenomenal property, in Huxley's sense. In the CADBLIND systems ..., the particular color-by-number coding scheme was epiphenomenal. We could "invert" it (by using negative numbers, or multiplying all the values by some constant) without making any *functional* difference to its information-processing prowess. Such an inversion might be undetectable to casual inspection, and might be undetectable *by the system*, but it would not be epiphenomenal in the philosophical sense. There would be lots of tiny voltage differences in the memory registers that held the different numbers, for instance.

If we think of all the properties of our nervous systems that enable us to see, hear, smell, taste, and touch things, we can divide them, roughly, into the properties that play truly crucial roles in mediating the information processing, and the epiphenomal properties that are more or less revisable *ad lib*, like the color-coding system in the CADBLIND system. When a philosopher surmises that qualia are epiphenomenal properties of brain states, this might mean that qualia could turn out to be local variations in the heat generated by neuronal metabolism. That cannot be what epiphenomenalists have in mind, can it? If it is, then qualia as epiphenomena are no challenge to materialism.

The time has come to put the burden of proof squarely on those who persist in using the term. The philosophical sense of the term is simply ridiculous; Huxley's sense is relatively clear and unproblematic—and irrelevant to the philosophical arguments. No other sense of the term has any currency. So if anyone claims to uphold a variety of epiphenomenalism, try to be polite, but ask: What *are* you talking about?

Notice, by the way, that this equivocation between two senses of "epiphenomenal" also infects the discussion of zombies. A philosopher's zombie, you will recall, is behaviorally indistinguishable from a normal human being, but is not conscious. There is nothing it is like to be a zombie; it just seems that way to observers (including itself, as we saw in the previous chapter). Now this can be given a strong or weak interpretation, depending on how we treat this indistinguishability to observers. If we were to declare that *in principle*, a zombie is indistinguishable from a conscious person, then we would be saying that genuine consciousness is epiphenomenal *in the ridiculous sense*. That is just silly. So we could say instead that consciousness might be epiphenomenal in the Huxley sense: although there was some way of distinguishing zombies from real people (who knows, maybe zombies have green brains), the difference doesn't show up as a functional difference *to observers*. Equivalently, human bodies with green brains don't harbor observers, while other human bodies do. On this hypothesis, we would be able in principle to distinguish the inhabited bodies from the uninhabited bodies by checking for brain color. This is also silly, of course, and dangerously silly, for it echoes the sort of utterly unmotivated prejudices that have denied full personhood to people on the basis of the color of their skin. It is time to recognize the idea of the possibility of zombies for what it is: not a serious philosophical idea but a preposterous and ignoble relic of ancient prejudices. Maybe women aren't really conscious! Maybe Jews! What pernicious nonsense. As Shylock says, drawing our attention, quite properly, to "merely behavioral" criteria:

Hath not a Jew eyes? Hath not a Jew hands, organs, dimensions, senses, affections, passions; fed with the same food, hurt with the same weapons, subject to the same diseases, heal'd by the same means, warm'd and cool'd by the same winter and summer, as a Christian is? If you prick us, do we not bleed? If you tickle us, do we not laugh? If you poison us, do we not die?

There is another way to address the possibility of zombies, and in some regards I think it is more satisfying. Are zombies possible? They're not just possible, they're actual. We're all zombies.[1] Nobody is conscious—not in the systematically mysterious way that supports such doctrines as epiphenomenalism! I can't prove that no such sort of consciousness exists. I also cannot prove that gremlins don't exist. The best I can do is show that there is no respectable motivation for believing in it.

Note

1. It would be an act of desperate intellectual dishonesty to quote this assertion out of context!

References

Block, N. 1990. "Inverted Earth" in J. E. Tomberlin 1990, pp. 53–79.

Broad, C. D. 1925. *Mind and Its Place in Nature*. London: Routledge and Kegan Paul.

Churchland, P. M. 1985. "Reduction, Qualia, and the Direct Introspection of Brain States." *Journal of Philosophy* 82: 8–28.

Churchland, P. M. 1990. "Knowing Qualia: A Reply to Jackson," pp. 67–76 in Churchland, P. M., *A Neurocomputational Perspective: The Nature of Mind and the Structure of Science*. Cambridge, Mass.: MIT Press/A Bradford Book.

Fox, I. 1989. "On the Nature and Cognitive Function of Phenomenal Content—Part One." *Philosophical Topics* 17: 81–117.

Harman, G. 1990. "The Intrinsic Quality of Experience," in J. E. Tomberlin 1990, pp. 31–52.

Jackson, F. 1982. "Epiphenomenal Qualia." *Philosophical Quarterly* 32: 127–136.

Lewis, D. 1988, "What Experience Teaches," *Proceedings of the Russellian Society of the University of Sydney*, reprinted in W. Lycan, ed., *Mind and Cognition: A Reader*. Oxford: Blackwell, 1990.

Loar, B. 1990. "Phenomenal States" in J. E. Tomberlin 1990, pp. 81–108.

Lycan, W. 1990. "What Is the Subjectivity of the Mental?" in J. E. Tomberlin 1990, pp. 109–130.

Nemirow, L. 1990. "Physicalism and the Cognitive Role of Acquaintance," in W. Lycan, ed., *Mind and Cognition: A Reader*. Oxford: Blackwell, pp. 490–499.

Tomberlin, J. E. ed., 1990. *Philosophical Perspectives, 4: Action Theory and Philosophy of Mind.* Atascadero, Calif.: Ridgeview.

Tye, M. 1986. "The Subjective Qualities of Experience." *Mind* 95: 1–17.

Van Gulick, R. 1990. "Understanding the Phenomenal Mind: Are We All Just Armadillos?" presented at the conference "The Phenomenal Mind—How Is It Possible and Why Is It Necessary?" Zentrum für Interdisziplinäre Forschung, Bielefeld, Germany, May 14–17.

Zajonc, R., and Markus, H. 1984. "Affect and Cognition: The Hard Interface" in C. Izard, J. Kagan, and R. Zajonc, eds., *Emotion, Cognition and Behavior.* Cambridge: Cambridge University Press, pp. 73–102.

4 Dennett on the Knowledge Argument

Howard Robinson

Daniel Dennett's philosophical method in *Consciousness Explained* could be described as the *Jericho method*. He believes that if he marches around a philosophical problem often enough, proclaiming what are, plausibly, relevant scientific truths, the problem will dissolve before our eyes. Insofar as he is inviting us to adopt a new way of looking at things, this method is quite appropriate. It does mean, however, that moments of direct philosophical argument are rare, and are to be cherished when found. The knowledge argument for the existence of qualia is one strategy which condenses the issue of physicalism and consciousness sufficiently precisely to force Dennett to face his opponent directly. When he does face this argument head on his response is unconvincing. This matters, because if he cannot cope with the knowledge argument then his more indirect ways of "deconstructing" our notion of consciousness must be futile.

Dennett considers the argument in Jackson's famous "what Mary didn't know" form. Mary knows everything that a completed physical science could tell her about the physical processes involved in visual perception, including color perception, but has never been allowed to perceive color, only black and white. If she is finally allowed to perceive colours she will discover something she previously did not know, namely what color and seeing color are like. As she previously knew everything physical and relevant, the new knowledge must relate to something nonphysical.

Dennett's response is that if we take seriously the premiss that Mary knew *everything* there was to know about the physical processes, then the conclusion that she would gain new knowledge on being allowed to see color does not follow. He continues the story as follows.

And so, one day, Mary's captors decided it was time for her to see colors. As a trick they prepared a bright blue banana to present as her first color experience ever. Mary took one look at it and said "Hey! You tried to trick me! Bananas are yellow but this one is blue!" Her captors were dumfounded. How did she do it? "Simple," she replied. "You have to remember that I know everything—absolutely everything—that could ever be known about the causes and effects of color vision. So of course before you brought the banana in, I had already written down, in exquisite detail exactly what physical impression a yellow object or a blue object ... would make on my nervous system. So I already knew exactly what thoughts I would have (because, after all, the 'mere disposition' to think about this or that is not one of your famous qualia is it?). I was not in the slightest surprised by my experience of blue ... I realize that it is *hard for you to imagine* that I could know so much about my reactive dispositions that the way blue affected me came as no surprise. Of course it's hard for you to imagine. It's hard for anyone to imagine the consequences of someone knowing absolutely everything about anything!" ([3], pp. 399–400)

The message of Dennett's story is that Mary could know what a color was like because she could work out, on the basis of her physical information, what thoughts she would have, given a *physical* color stimulus—that is, given a certain input of light waves. This is possible because the qualia argument does not deny that a physicalist account of thought could be correct, and so from the physical effects of the light on the eyes she could follow up its consequences in the brain, including in those aspects that constitute her thinking. But if one understands the thought 'that's blue'— which she can because it is just a functional state—then one knows what blue is like.

The first objection to Dennett's argument is that it contains a confusion, resting on an ambiguity. He talks as if Mary could, on the basis of her physical knowledge, recognize the stimulus just by looking at it ("Mary took one look ..."). But she will not know by looking at the banana what *physical* color impression—that is, what input of light waves—it is giving her unless she already has some way of relating how it experientially feels and her current physical states. It might be argued that she knows what the physical stimulus is as part of knowing 'all the physical information', but here the ambiguity enters. This expression should not be taken to mean that she knows every particular physical thing that is going on, only that she knows all the relevant physical science. It is the general scientific knowledge, the antimaterialist says, that ought to be enough to give knowledge of the nature of experience, if physicalism is correct, and this is consistent with not being omniscient about particular physical goings-on, such as what is happening to the rods and cones in one's own eyes at a given moment. Her perfection as a scientist will not tell her—especially not immediately and directly—about current particulars. She may have "written down in exquisite detail, exactly what effect a yellow object ... would have" on her nervous system, but she could not tell by looking at an object whether it was having *that* effect, so would not know that *that* look was the yellow—or the blue—one. Dennett's implication that Mary could, through physical knowledge, acquire the ability for direct recognition of colors is mistaken.[1]

Nevertheless, there is an argument in the vicinity, and it is very close to Shoemaker's ([7] and [8]) argument that if there are qualia then functionalism accommodates them. Dennett is arguing that from knowing the physical stimulus Mary could work out the thought, physicalistically conceived, and, as the possibility of a physicalist account of thought is not being disputed, she therefore knows the thought-proper: so she understands it and so knows what is involved in knowing its contents, which, in this case means knowing the nature of the phenomenal color of which this thought is the recognition. No role is played in this argument by making Mary the subject of the experience. Even while deprived of color experience herself she could work out the functionally defined thoughts that physical stimuli would give others and should, for the same reasons as in her own case, be able to grasp their content.

There is a truth hidden here but it is not the one Dennett thinks it is. A thought, on his account, is a kind of functional state. It is, roughly, a disposition toward a verbal response, plus other bits of sophisticated behaviour. Knowledge of how someone is disposed to react, verbally or otherwise, does not tell you what it is like to possess a mental state, if there is such a thing as what it is like, which it is *ex hypothesi* there is, otherwise the question is begged. All Mary could know is *what one would say and how one would react* to a certain color stimulus. So when she sees the banana, if she also knows the nature of the physical stimulus, she will be able to work out (not know spontaneously) that this is the sort of stimulus that prompts 'that's blue', but it will be a revelation that the sort of physical stimulus that she knew was called 'blue' and led to 'blue appropriate' behavior *looked like that*, and this phenomenal fact is what she comes to know. It is, therefore, not true that she was 'not in the slightest surprised' by the nature of the experience.

It follows that the functional account of the demonstrative thought 'that's blue' does not capture its full content, for Mary can understand the functionally defined recognitional thought without grasping the nature of the phenomenon recognized. The situation is quite different if one is allowed a nonreductive account of thought. Then, provided that the meaning of color names is essentially ostensive, knowing what blue was like would be part of understanding 'that's blue'.

The important truth hidden in Dennett's (and Shoemaker's) argument is that it is not possible to combine a reductively physicalist account of thought with a nonreductive account of experience, because recognitional thoughts essentially involve the qualia. If the functionally defined thought is really all there is to thinking about blue and, hence, to knowing what blue is like, then the functionally defined thought should be adequate to the cognitive state of recognizing blue and the qualia become irrelevant, like the beetle in the box. Once it has been demonstrated that the qualia are not irrelevant, because coming to discover what a quale is like is a new piece of knowledge, then one is obliged to adopt an account of thought that can assimilate this fact. Those who like Jackson (or Ayer and many traditional empiricists) think that physicalism can be correct for everything but qualia are in an inconsistent position.[2] The knowledge argument should not be cast in the form 'physicalism can work for all other mental states but not for qualia', but in the form 'even if it might look as if functionalism will work for less clearly introspectible states, such as thoughts, Mary's case shows that it will not work for qualia, and we can see from this that it does not work for thought—at least, a certain category of thought, namely those involved in simple recognition—either'.

Notes

1. Paul Churchland ([2], pp. 54 ff.) claims that we could be taught to respond to stimuli with scientific descriptions and that we would thus be 'directly aware' of microphysical processes. I have argued ([6], p. 169–170) that there are general problems with this. But even if there are no general problems, this idea cannot be used to justify Dennett's attribution to Mary of immediate recognition of physical inputs, for such teaching is available only to those who have the appropriate experiences. Mary has not previously experienced color, so she could not yet have learned how to respond spontaneously to color experiences with scientific descriptions.

2. Jackson's belief that qualia are epiphenomenal is based on his belief that the physical system is closed and can accommodate everything other than qualia. Dennett's ([3], pp. 401–406) criticism of Jackson's epiphenomenalism is, I think, power-

ful. Ayer combines qualia with behaviorism for other states in [1], pp. 173–179. I discuss Ayer's position in [5], pp. 105–107.

References

[1] A. J. Ayer, *Origins of Pragmatism* (London: Macmillan, 1968).

[2] Paul Churchland, *A Neurocomputational Perspective* (Cambridge, Mass.: MIT Press, 1989).

[3] Daniel Dennett, *Consciousness Explained* (Harmondsworth: Penguin Books, 1991).

[4] Frank Jackson, "Epiphenomenal Qualia," *Philosophical Quarterly* 32, (1982), 127–136.

[5] Howard Robinson, *Matter and Sense* (Cambridge: Cambridge University Press, 1982).

[6] Howard Robinson, "The Anti-Materialist Strategy and the Knowledge Argument," in *Objections to Physicalism*, edited by H. Robinson (Oxford: Oxford University Press, 1993), 159–183.

[7] Sydney Shoemaker, "Functionalism and Qualia," in his *Identity, Cause and Mind*, (Cambridge: Cambridge University Press, 1984), 184–205.

[8] Sydney Shoemaker, "Absent Qualia Are Impossible: A Reply to Ned Block," in same volume as [7], 309–326.

Part III   The Ability Hypothesis

5 What Experience Teaches

David Lewis

Experience the Best Teacher

They say that experience is the best teacher, and the classroom is no substitute for Real Life. There's truth to this. If you want to know what some new and different experience is like, you can learn it by going out and really *having* that experience. You can't learn it by being told about the experience, however thorough your lessons may be.

Does this prove much of anything about the metaphysics of mind and the limits of science? I think not.

Example: Skunks and Vegemite. I have smelled skunks, so I know what it's like to smell skunks. But skunks live only in some parts of the world, so you may never have smelled a skunk. If you haven't smelled a skunk, then you don't know what it's like. You never will, unless someday you smell a skunk for yourself. On the other hand, you may have tasted Vegemite, that famous Australian substance; and I never have. So you may know what it's like to taste Vegemite. I don't, and unless I taste Vegemite (what, and spoil a good example!), I never will. It won't help at all to take lessons on the chemical composition of skunk scent or Vegemite, the physiology of the nostrils or the taste-buds, and the neurophysiology of the sensory nerves and the brain.

Example: The Captive Scientist.[1] Mary, a brilliant scientist, has lived from birth in a cell where everything is black or white. (Even she herself is painted all over.) She views the world on black-and-white television. By television she reads books, she joins in discussion, she watches the results of experiments done under her direction. In this way she becomes the world's leading expert on color and color vision and the brain states produced by exposure to colors. But she doesn't know what it's like to see color. And she never will, unless she escapes from her cell.

Example: The Bat.[2]   The bat is an alien creature, with a sonar sense quite unlike any sense of ours. We can never have the experiences of a bat; because we could not become bat-like enough to have those experiences and still be ourselves. We will never know what it's like to be a bat. Not even if we come to know all the facts there are about the bat's behavior and behavioral dispositions, about the bat's physical structure and processes, about the bat's functional organization. Not even if we come to know all the same sort of physical facts about all the other bats, or about other creatures, or about ourselves. Not even if we come to possess all physical facts whatever. Not even if we become able to recognize all the mathematical and logical implications of all these facts, no matter how complicated and how far beyond the reach of finite deduction.

Experience is the best teacher, in this sense: having an experience is the best way or perhaps the only way, of coming to know what that experience is like. No amount of scientific information about the stimuli that produce that experience and the process that goes on in you when you have that experience will enable you to know what it's like to have the experience.

... But Not Necessarily

Having an experience is surely one good way, and surely the only practical way, of coming to know what that experience is like. Can we say, flatly, that it is the only *possible* way? Probably not. There is a change that takes place in you when you have the experience and thereby come to know what it's like. Perhaps the exact same change could in principle be produced in you by precise neurosurgery, very far beyond the limits of present-day technique. Or it could possibly be produced in you by magic. If we ignore the laws of nature, which are after all contingent, then there is no necessary connection between cause and effect: anything could cause anything. For instance, the casting of a spell could do to you exactly what your first smell of skunk would do. We might quibble about whether a state produced in this artificial fashion would deserve the *name* 'knowing what it's like to smell a skunk', but we can imagine that so far as what goes on within you is concerned, it would differ not at all.[3]

Just as we can imagine that a spell might produce the same change as a smell, so likewise we can imagine that science lessons might cause that same change. Even that is possible, in the broadest sense of the word. If we ignored all we know about how the world really works, we could not say what might happen to someone if he were taught about the chemistry of scent and the physiology of the nose. There might have been a causal mechanism that transforms science lessons into whatever it is that experience gives us. But there isn't. It is not an absolutely necessary truth that experience is the best teacher about what a new experience is like. It's a contingent truth. But we have good reason to think it's true.

We have good reason to think that something of this kind is true, anyway, but less reason to be sure exactly what. Maybe some way of giving the lessons that hasn't yet been invented, and some way of taking them in that hasn't yet been practiced, could give us a big surprise. Consider sight-reading: a trained musician can read the score and know what it would be like to hear the music. If I'd never heard that some people can sight-read, I would never have thought it humanly possible. Of course the moral is that new music isn't altogether new—the big new experience is a rearrangement of lots of little old experiences. It just might turn out the same for new smells and tastes *vis-à-vis* old ones; or even for color vision *vis-à-vis* black and white;[4] or even for sonar sense experience *vis-à-vis* the sort we enjoy. The thing we can say with some confidence is that we have no faculty for knowing on the basis of mere science lessons what some *new enough* experience would be like. But how new is "new enough"?—There, we just might be in for surprises.

Three Ways to Miss the Point

The First Way.   A literalist might see the phrase 'know what it's like' and take that to mean: 'know what it resembles'. Then he might ask: what's so hard about that? Why can't you just be told which experiences resemble one another? You needn't have had the experiences—all you need, to be taught your lessons, is some way of referring to them. You could be told: the smell of skunk somewhat resembles the smell of burning rubber. I have been told: the taste of Vegemite somewhat resembles that of Marmite. Black-and-white Mary might know more than most of us about the resemblances among color-experiences. She might know which ones are spontaneously called 'similar' by subjects who have them; which gradual changes from one to another tend to escape notice; which ones get conflated with which in memory; which ones involve roughly the same neurons firing in similar rhythms; and so forth. We could even know what the bat's sonar experiences resemble just by knowing that they do not at all resemble any experiences of humans, but do resemble—as it might be—certain experiences that occur in certain fish. This misses the point. *Pace* the literalist, 'know what it's like' does not mean 'know what it resembles'. The most that's true is that knowing what it resembles *may* help you to know what it's like. If you are taught that experience A resembles B and C closely, D less, E not at all, that will help you know what A is like—*if* you know already what B and C and D and E are like. Otherwise, it helps you not at all. I don't know any better what it's like to taste Vegemite when I'm told that it tastes like Marmite, because I don't know what Marmite tastes like either. (Nor do I know any better what Marmite tastes like for being told it tastes like Vegemite.) Maybe Mary knows enough to triangulate each color experience exactly in a network of resemblances, or in many networks of resemblance in different respects, while never knowing what any node of any network is like. Maybe we could do the same for bat experiences. But no amount of information about resemblances, just by itself, does anything to help us know what an experience is like.

The Second Way.   Insofar as I don't know what it would be like to drive a steam locomotive fast on a cold, stormy night, part of my problem is just that I don't know what experiences I would have. The firebox puts out a lot of heat, especially when the fireman opens the door to throw on more coal; on the other hand, the cab is drafty and gives poor protection from the weather. Would I be too hot or too cold? Or both by turns? Or would it be chilled face and scorched legs? If I knew the answers to such questions, I'd know much better what it would be like to drive the locomotive. So maybe 'know what it's like' just means 'know what experiences one has'. Then again: what's the problem? Why can't you just be told what experiences you would have if, say, you tasted Vegemite? Again, you needn't have had the experiences—all you need, to be taught your lessons, is some way of referring to them. We have ways to refer to experiences we haven't had. We can refer to them in terms of their causes: the experience one has upon tasting Vegemite, the experience one has upon tasting a substance of such-and-such chemical composition. Or we can refer to them in terms of their effects: the experience that just caused Fred to say "Yeeuch!" Or we can refer to them in terms of the physical states of the nervous system that mediate between those causes and effects: the experience one has when one's nerves are firing in such-and-such pattern. (According to some materialists, I myself for one, this means the experience which is identical with such-and-such firing pattern. According to other materialists it means the experience which is realized by such-and-such firing pattern. According to many dualists, it means the experience which is merely the lawful companion of such-and-such firing pattern. But whichever it is, we get a way of referring to the experience.) Black-and-white Mary is in a position to refer to color-experiences in all these ways. Therefore you should have no problem in telling her exactly what experiences one has upon seeing the colors. Or rather, your only problem is that you'd be telling her what she knows very well already! In general, to know what is the X is to know that the X is the Y, where it's not too obvious that the X is the Y. (Just knowing that the X is the X won't do, of course, because it is too obvious.) If Mary knows that the experience of seeing green is the experience associated with such-and-such pattern of nerve firings, then she knows the right sort of unobvious identity. So she knows what experience one has upon seeing green.

(Sometimes it's suggested that you need a 'rigid designator': you know what is the X by knowing that the X is the Y only if 'the Y' is a term whose referent does not depend on any contingent matter of fact. In the first place, this suggestion is false. You can know who is the man on the balcony by knowing that the man on the balcony is the Prime Minister even if neither 'the Prime Minister' nor any other phrase available to you rigidly designates the man who is, in fact, the Prime Minister. In the second place, according to one version of Materialism [the one I accept] a description of the form 'the state of having nerves firing in such-and-such a pattern' *is* a rigid designator, and what it designates is in fact an experience; and according to another version of Materialism, a description of the form 'having some or other state which occupies so-and-so functional role' is a rigid designator of an experience. So even if the false suggestion were granted, still it hasn't been shown, without begging the question against Material-ism, that Mary could not know what experience one has upon seeing red.)

Since Mary *does* know what experiences she would have if she saw the colors, but she *doesn't* know what it would be like to see the colors, we'd better conclude that 'know what it's like' does not after all mean 'know what experiences one has'. The locomotive example was misleading. Yes, by learning what experiences the driver would have, I can know what driving the locomotive would be like; but only because I already know what those experiences are like. (It matters that I know what they're like under the appropriate descriptions—as it might be, the description 'chilled face and scorched legs'. This is something we'll return to later.) Mary may know as well as I do that when the driver leans out into the storm to watch the signals, he will have the experience of seeing sometimes green lights and sometimes red. She knows better than I what experiences he has when signals come into view. She can give many more unobviously equivalent descriptions of those experiences than I can. But knowing what color-experiences the driver has won't help Mary to know what his job is like. It will help me.

The Third Way. Until Mary sees green, here is one thing she will never know: she will never know that she is seeing green. The reason why is just that until she sees green, it will never be true that she is seeing green. Some knowledge is irreducibly egocentric, or *de se*.[5] It is not just knowledge about what goes on in the world; it is knowledge of who and when in the world one is. Knowledge of what goes on in the world will be true alike for all who live in that world; whereas egocentric knowledge may be true for one and false for another, or true for one at one time and false for the same one at another time. Maybe Mary knows in advance, as she plots her escape, that 9 A.M. on the 13th of May, 1997, is the moment when someone pre-viously confined in a black-and-white cell sees color for the first time. But until that moment comes, she will never know that she herself is then see-ing color—because she isn't. What isn't true isn't knowledge. This goes as much for egocentric knowledge as for the rest. So only those of whom an egocentric proposition is true can know it, and only at times when it is true of them can they know it. That one is then seeing color is an egocentric proposition. So we've found a proposition which Mary can never know until she sees color—which, as it happens, is the very moment when she will first know what it's like to see color! Have we discovered the reason why experience is the best teacher? And not contingently after all, but as a necessary consequence of the logic of egocentric knowledge?

No; we have two separate phenomena here, and only some bewitchment about the 'first-person perspective' could make us miss the difference. In the first place, Mary will probably go on knowing what it's like to see green after she stops knowing the egocentric proposition that she's then seeing green. Since what isn't true isn't known she must stop knowing that proposition the moment she stops seeing green. (Does that only mean that we should have taken a different egocentric proposition: that one *has* seen green? No; for in that case Mary could go on knowing the proposition even after she forgets what it's like to see green, as might happen if she were soon recaptured.) In the second place, Mary might come to know what it's like to see green even if she didn't know the egocentric proposition. She might not have known in advance that her escape route would take her across a green meadow, and it might take her a little while to recognize grass by its shape. So at first she might know only that she was seeing some colors or other, and thereby finding out what some color-experiences or other were like, without being able to put a name either to the colors or to the experiences. She would then know what it was like to see green, though not under that description, indeed not under any description more useful than 'the color-experience I'm having now'; but she would not know the egocentric proposition that she is then seeing green, since she wouldn't know which color she was seeing. In the third place, the gaining of egocentric knowledge may have prerequisites that have nothing to do with experience. Just as mary can't know she's seeing green until she *does* see green, she can't know she's turning 50 until she *does* turn 50. But—I hope!—turning 50 does not involve some special experience. In short, though indeed one can gain egocentric knowledge that one is in some situation only when one is in it, that is not the same as finding out what an experience is like only when one has that experience.

We've just rejected two suggestions that don't work separately, and we may note that they don't work any better when put together. One knows what is the X by knowing that the X is the Y, where the identity is not too obvious; and 'the Y' might be an egocentric description. So knowledge that the X is the Y might be irreducibly egocentric knowledge, therefore knowledge that cannot be had until it is true of one that the X is the Y. So one way of knowing what is the X will remain unavailable until it comes true of one that the X is the Y. One way that I could gain an unobvious identity concerning the taste of Vegemite would be for it to come true that the taste of Vegemite was the taste I was having at that very moment—and that would come true at the very moment I tasted Vegemite and found out what it was like! Is this why experience is the best teacher?—No; cases of gaining an unobvious egocentric identity are a dime a dozen, and most of them do not result in finding out what an experience is like. Suppose I plan ahead that I will finally break down and taste Vegemite next Thursday noon. Then on Wednesday noon, if I watch the clock, I first gain the unobvious egocentric knowledge that the taste of Vegemite is the taste I shall be having in exactly 24 hours, and thereby I have a new way of knowing what is the taste of Vegemite. But on Wednesday noon I don't yet know what it's like. Another example: from time to time I find myself next to a Vegemite-taster. On those occasions, and only those, I know what is the taste of Vegemite by knowing that it is the taste being had by the person next to me. But on no such occasion has it ever yet happened that I knew what it was like to taste Vegemite.

The Hypothesis of Phenomenal Information

No amount of the physical information that black-and-white Mary gathers could help her know what it was like to see colors; no amount of the physical information that we might gather about bats could help us know what it's like to have their experiences; and likewise in other cases. There is a natural and tempting explanation of why physical information does not help. That is the hypothesis that besides physical information there is an irreducibly different kind of information to be had: *phenomenal information*. The two are independent. Two possible cases might be exactly alike physically, yet differ phenomenally. When we get physical information we narrow down the physical possibilities, and perhaps we narrow them down all the way to one, but we leave open a range of phenomenal possibilities. When we have an experience, on the other hand, we acquire phenomenal information; possibilities previously open are eliminated; and that is what it is to learn what the experience is like.

(Analogy. Suppose the question concerned the location of a point within a certain region of the x-y plane. We might be told that its x-coordinate lies in certain intervals, and outside certain others. We might even get enough of this information to fix the x-coordinate exactly. But no amount of x-information would tell us anything about the y-coordinate; any amount of x-information leaves open all the y-possibilities. But when at last we make a y-measurement, we acquire a new kind of information; possibilities previously open are eliminated; and that is how we learn where the point is in the y-direction.)

What might the subject matter of phenomenal information be? *If* the hypothesis of phenomenal information is true, then you have an easy answer: it is information about experience. More specifically, it is information about a certain part or aspect or feature of experience. But if the hypothesis is false, then there is still experience (complete with all its parts and aspects and features) and yet no information about experience is phenomenal information. So it cannot be said in a neutral way, without presupposing the hypothesis, that information about experience is phenomenal information. For if the hypothesis is false and materialism is true, it may be that all the information there is about experience is physical information, and can very well be presented in lessons for the inexperienced.

It makes no difference to put some fashionable new phrase in place of 'experience'. If instead of 'experience' you say 'raw feel' (or just 'feeling'), or 'way it feels', or 'what it's like', then I submit that you mean nothing different. Is there anything it's like to be this robot? Does this robot have experiences?—I can tell no difference between the new question and the old. Does sunburn feel the same way to you that it does to me? Do we have the same raw feel? Do we have the same experience when sunburned?—Again, same question. 'Know the feeling', 'know what it's like'—interchangeable. (Except that the former may hint at an alternative to the hypothesis of phenomenal information.) So if the friend of phenomenal information says that its subject matter is raw feels, or ways to feel, or what it's like, then I respond just as I do if he says that the subject matter is experience. Maybe so, *if* the hypothesis of phenomenal information is true; but if the hypothesis is false and materialism is true, nevertheless there is still information about raw feels, ways to feel or what it's like; but in that case it is physical information and can be conveyed in lessons.

We might get a candidate for the subject matter of phenomenal information that is not just experience renamed, but is still tendentious. For instance, we might be told that phenomenal information concerns the intrinsic character of experience. A friend of phenomenal information might indeed believe that it reveals certain special, nonphysical intrinsic properties of experience. He might even believe that it reveals the existence of some special nonphysical thing or process, *all* of whose intrinsic properties are nonphysical. But he is by no means alone in saying that experience has an intrinsic character. Plenty of us materialists say so too. We say that a certain color-experience is whatever state occupies a certain functional role. So if the occupant of that role (universally, or in the case of humans, or in the case of certain humans) is a certain pattern of neural firing, then that pattern of firing *is* the experience (in the case in question). Therefore the intrinsic character of the experience is the intrinsic character of the firing pattern. For instance, a frequency of firing is part of the intrinsic character of the experience. If we materialists are right about what experience is, then black-and-white Mary knows all about the intrinsic character of color-experience; whereas most people who know what color-experience is like remain totally ignorant about its intrinsic character.[6]

To say that phenomenal information concerns 'qualia' would be tendentious in much the same way. For how was this notion introduced? Often thus. We are told to imagine someone who, when he sees red things, has just the sort of experiences that we have when we see green things, and vice versa; and we are told to call this a case of 'inverted qualia'. And then we are told to imagine someone queerer still, who sees red and responds to it appropriately, and indeed has entirely the same functional organization of inner states as we do and yet has no experiences at all; and we are told to call this a case of 'absent qualia'. Now a friend of phenomenal information might well think that these deficiencies have something to do with the nonphysical subject matter of phenomenal information. But others can understand them otherwise. Some materialists will reject the cases outright, but others, and I for one, will make sense of them as best we can. Maybe the point is that the states that occupy the roles of experiences, and therefore *are* the experiences, in normal people are inverted or absent in victims of inverted or absent qualia. (This presupposes, what might be false, that most people are enough alike.) Experience of red—the state that occupies that role in normal people—occurs also in the victim of 'inverted qualia', but in him it occupies the role of experience of green; whereas the state that occupies in him the role of experience of red is the state that occupies in normal people the role of experience of green. Experience of red and of green—that is, the occupants of those roles for normal people—do not occur at all in the victim of 'absent qualia'; the occupants of those roles for him are states that don't occur at all in the normal. Thus we make good sense of inverted and absent qualia; but in such a way that 'qualia' is just the word for role-occupying states taken *per se* rather than *qua* occupants of roles. Qualia, so understood, could not be the subject matter of phenomenal information. Mary knows all about them. We who have them mostly don't.[7]

It is best to rest content with an unhelpful name and a *via negativa*. Stipulate that 'the phenomenal aspect of the world' is to name whatever is the subject matter of phenomenal information, if there is any such thing; the phenomenal aspect, if such there be, is that which we can become informed about by having new experiences but never by taking lessons. Having said this, it will be safe to say that information about the phenomenal aspect of the world can only be phenomenal information. But all we really know, after thus closing the circle, is that phenomenal information is supposed to reveal the presence of some sort of nonphysical things or processes within experience, or else it is supposed to reveal that certain physical things or processes within experience have some sort of nonphysical properties.

The Knowledge Argument

If we invoke the hypothesis of phenomenal information to explain why no amount of physical information suffices to teach us what a new experience is like, then we have a powerful argument to refute any materialist theory of the mind. Frank Jackson (see note 1) calls it the "knowledge argument." Arguments against one materialist theory or another are never very conclusive. It is always possible to adjust the details. But the knowledge argument, if it worked, would directly refute the bare minimum that is common to *all* materialist theories.

It goes as follows. First in a simplified form; afterward we'll do it properly. Minimal materialism is a supervenience thesis: no difference without physical difference. That is: any two possibilities that are just alike physically are just alike *simpliciter*. If two possibilities are just alike physically, then no physical information can eliminate one but not both of them. If two possibilities are just alike *simpliciter* (if that is possible) then no information whatsoever can eliminate one but not both of them. So if there is a kind of information—namely, phenomenal information—that can eliminate possibilities that any amount of physical information leaves open, then there must be possibilities that are just alike physically, but not just alike *simpliciter*. That is just what minimal materialism denies.

(Analogy. If two possible locations in our region agree in their x-coordinate, then no amount of x-information can eliminate one but not both. If, *per impossibile*, two possible locations agreed in all their coordinates, then no information whatsoever could eliminate one but not both. So if there is a kind of information—namely, y-information—that can eliminate locations that any amount of x-information leaves open, then there must be locations in the region that agree in their x-coordinate but not in all their coordinates.)

Now to remove the simplification. What we saw so far was the knowledge argument against materialism taken as a necessary truth, applying unrestrictedly to all possible worlds. But we materialists usually think that materialism is a contingent truth. We grant that there are spooky possible worlds where materialism is false, but we insist that our actual world isn't one of them. If so, then there might after all be two possibilities that are alike physically but not alike *simpliciter*; but one or both of the two would have to be possibilities where materialism was false. Spooky worlds could differ with respect to their spooks without differing physically. Our minimal materialism must be a *restricted* supervenience thesis: within a certain class of worlds, which includes our actual world, there is no difference without physical difference. Within that class, any two possibilities just alike physically are just alike *simpliciter*. But what delineates the relevant class? (It is trivial that our world belongs to *some* class wherein there is no difference without physical difference. That will be so however spooky our world may be. The unit class of our world is one such class, for instance. And so is any class that contains our world, and contains no two physical duplicates.) I think the relevant class should consist of the worlds that have nothing wholly alien to this world. The inhabitants of such a nonalien world could be made from the inhabitants of ours, so to speak, by a process of division and recombination. That will make no wholly different kinds of things, and no wholly different fundamental properties of things.[8] Our restricted materialist supervenience thesis should go as follows: throughout the nonalien worlds, there is no difference without physical difference.

If the hypothesis of phenomenal information be granted, then the knowledge argument refutes this restricted supervenience nearly as decisively as it refutes the unrestricted version. Consider a possibility that is eliminated by phenomenal information, but not by any amount of physical information. There are two cases. Maybe this possibility has nothing that is alien to our world. In that case the argument goes as before: actuality and the eliminated possibility are just alike physically, they are not just alike *simpliciter*; furthermore, both of them fall within the restriction to nonalien worlds, so we have a counterexample even to restricted supervenience. Or maybe instead the eliminated possibility does have something X which is alien to this world—an alien kind of thing, or maybe an alien fundamental property of nonalien things. Then the phenomenal information gained by having a new experience has revealed something negative: at least in part, it is the information that X is *not* present. How can that be? If there is such a thing as phenomenal information, presumably what it reveals is positive: the presence of something hitherto unknown. Not, of course, something alien from actuality itself; but something alien from actuality as it is inadequately represented by the inexperienced and by the materialists. If Mary learns something when she finds out what it's like to see the colors, presumably she learns that there's *more* to the world than she knew before—not *less*. It's easy to think that phenomenal information might eliminate possibilities that are impoverished by comparison with actuality, but that would make a counterexample to the restricted supervenience thesis. To eliminate possibilities without making a counterexample, phenomenal information would have to eliminate possibilities less impoverished than actuality. And how can phenomenal information do that? Compare ordinary perceptual information. Maybe Jean-Paul can just *see* that Pierre is absent from the café, at least if it's a small café. But how can he just see that Pierre is absent from Paris, let alone from the whole of actuality?

(Is there a third case? What if the eliminated possibility is in one respect richer than actuality, in another respect poorer? Suppose the eliminated possibility has X, which is alien from actuality, but also it lacks Y. Then phenomenal information might eliminate it by revealing the actual presence of Y, without having to reveal the actual absence of X—but then I say there ought to be a third possibility, one with neither X nor Y, poorer and in no respect richer than actuality, and again without any physical difference from actuality. For why should taking away X automatically re-store Y? Why can't they vary independently?[9] But this third possibility differs *simpliciter* from actuality without differing physically. Further, it has nothing alien from actuality. So we regain a counterexample to the restricted supervenience thesis.)

The knowledge argument works. There is no way to grant the hypothesis of phenomenal information and still uphold materialism. Therefore I deny the hypothesis. I cannot refute it outright. But later I shall argue, first, that it is more peculiar, and therefore less tempting, that it may at first seem; and, second, that we are not forced to accept it, since an alternative hy-pothesis does justice to the way experience best teaches us what it's like.

Three More Ways to Miss the Point

The hypothesis of phenomenal information characterizes information in terms of eliminated possibilities. But there are other conceptions of 'infor-mation'. Therefore the hypothesis has look-alikes: hypotheses which say that experience produces 'information' which could not be gained other-wise, but do not characterize this 'information' in terms of eliminated possibilities. There look-alikes do not work as premises for the knowledge argument. They do not say that phenomenal information eliminates possi-bilities that differ, but do not differ physically, from uneliminated possibil-ities. The look-alike hypotheses of phenomenal 'information' are consistent with materialism, and may very well be true. But they don't make the knowledge argument go away. Whatever harmless look-alikes may or may not be true, and whatever conception may or may not deserve the name 'information', the only way to save materialism is fix our attention squarely on the genuine hypothesis of phenomenal information, and deny it. To avert our eyes, and attend to something else, is no substitute for that denial.

Might a look-alike help at least to this extent: by giving us something true that well might have been confused with the genuine hypothesis, thereby explaining how we might have believed the hypothesis although it was false? I think not. Each of the look-alikes turns out to imply not only that experience can give us 'information' that no amount of lessons can give, but also that lessons in Russian can give us 'information' that no amount of lessons in English can give (and vice versa). I doubt that any friend of phenomenal information ever thought that the special role of experience in teaching what it's like was on a par with the special role of Russian! I will have to say before I'm done that phenomenal information is an illusion, but I think I must look elsewhere for a credible hypothesis about what sort of illusion it might be.

The Fourth Way. If a hidden camera takes photographs of a room, the film ends up bearing traces of what went on in the room. The traces are distinctive: that is, the details of the traces depend on the details of what went on, and if what went on had been different in any of many ways, the traces would have been correspondingly different. So we can say that the traces bear information, and that he who has the film has the information. That might be said because the traces, plus the way they depend on what went on, suffice to eliminate possibilities; but instead we might say 'information' and just mean 'distinctive traces'. If so, it's certainly true that new experience imparts 'information' unlike any that can be gained from lessons. Experience and lessons leave different kinds of traces. That is so whether or not the experience eliminates possibilities that the lessons leave open. It is equally true, of course, that lessons in Russian leave traces unlike any that are left by lessons in English, regardless of whether the lessons cover the same ground and eliminate the same possibilities.

The Fifth Way. When we speak of transmission of 'information', we often mean transmission of text. Repositories of 'information', such as libraries, are storehouses of text. Whether the text is empty verbiage or highly informative is beside the point. Maybe we too contain information by being storehouses of text. Maybe there is a language of thought, and maybe the way we believe things is to store sentences of this language in some special way, or in some special part of our brains. In that case, we could say that storing away a new sentence was storing away a new piece of 'information', whether or not that new piece eliminated any possibilities not already eliminated by the sentences stored previously. Maybe, also, the language of thought is not fixed once and for all, but can gain new words. Maybe, for instance, it borrows words from public language. And maybe, when one has a new experience, that causes one's language of thought to gain a new word which denotes that experience—a word which could not have been added to the language by any other means. If all this is so, then when Mary sees colors, her language of thought gains new words, allowing her to store away new sentences and thereby gain 'information'. All this about the language of thought, the storing of sentences, and the gaining of words is speculation. But it is plausible speculation, even if no longer the only game in town. If it is all true, then we have another look-alike hypothesis of phenomenal 'information'. When Mary gains new words and stores new sentences, that is 'information' that she never had before, regardless of whether it eliminates any possibilities that she had not eliminated already.

But again, the special role of experience turns out to be on a par with the special role of Russian. If the language of thought picks up new words by borrowing from public language, then lessons in Russian add new words, and result in the storing of new sentences, and thereby impart "information" that never could have been had from lessons in English. (You might say that the new Russian words are mere synonyms of old words, or at least old phrases, that were there already; and synonyms don't count. But no reason has been given why the new inner words created by experience may not also be synonyms of old phrases, perhaps of long descriptions in the language of neurophysiology.)

The Sixth Way. A philosopher who is skeptical about possibility, as so many are, may wish to replace possibilities themselves with linguistic *ersatz* possibilities: maximal consistent sets of sentences. And he may be content to take 'consistent' in a narrowly logical sense, so that a set with 'Fred is married' and 'Fred is a bachelor' may count as consistent, and only an overt contradiction like 'Fred is married' and 'Fred is not married' will be ruled out.[10] The *ersatz* possibilities might also be taken as sets of sentences of the language of thought, if the philosopher believes in it. Then if someone's language of thought gains new words, whether as a result of new experience or as a result of being taught in Russian, the *ersatz* possibilities become richer and more numerous. The sets of sentences that were maximal before are no longer maximal after new words are added. So when Mary sees colors and her language of thought gains new words, there are new *ersatz* possibilities; and she can straightway eliminate some of them. Suppose she knows beforehand that she is about to see green, and that the experience of seeing green is associated with neural firing pattern F. So when she sees green and gains the new word G for her experience, then straightway there are new, enriched *ersatz* possibilities with sentences saying that she has G without F, and straightway she knows enough to eliminate these *ersatz* possibilities. (Even if she does not know beforehand what she is about to see, straightway she can eliminate at least those of her new-found *ersatz* possibilities with sentences denying that she then has G.) Just as we can characterize information in terms of elimination of possibilities, so we can characterize *ersatz* 'information' in terms of elimination of *ersatz* 'possibilities'. So here we have the closest look-alike hypothesis of all, provided that language-of-thoughtism is true. But we still do not have the genuine hypothesis of phenomenal information, since the eliminated *ersatz* possibility of G without F may not have been a genuine possibility at all. It may have been like the *ersatz* possibility of married bachelors.

Curiouser and Curiouser

The hypothesis of phenomenal information is more peculiar than it may at first seem. For one thing, because it is opposed to more than just materialism. Some of you may have welcomed the knowledge argument because you thought all along that physical information was inadequate to explain the phenomena of mind. You may have been convinced all along that the mind could do things that no physical system could do: bend spoons, invent new jokes, demonstrate the consistency of arithmetic, reduce the wave packet, or what have you. You may have been convinced that the full causal story of how the deeds of mind are accomplished involves the causal interactions not only of material bodies but also of astral bodies; not only the vibrations of the electromagnetic field but also the good or bad vibes of the psionic field; not only protoplasm but ectoplasm. I doubt it, but never mind. It's irrelevant to our topic. The knowledge argument is targeted against you no less than it is against materialism itself.

Let *parapsychology* be the science of all the nonphysical things, properties, causal processes, laws of nature, and so forth that may be required to explain the things we do. Let us suppose that we learn ever so much parapsychology. It will make no difference. Black-and-white Mary may study all the parapsychology as well as all the psychophysics of color vision, but she still won't know what it's like. Lessons on the aura of Vegemite will do no more for us than lessons on its chemical composition. And so it goes. Our intuitive starting point wasn't just that *physics* lessons couldn't help the inexperienced to know what it's like. It was that *lessons* couldn't help. If there is such a thing as phenomenal information, it isn't just independent of physical information. It's independent of every sort of information that could be served up in lessons for the inexperienced. For it is supposed to eliminate possibilities that any amount of lessons leave open. Therefore phenomenal information is not just parapsychological information, if such there be. It's something very much stranger.

The genuine hypothesis of phenomenal information, as distinguished from its look-alikes, treats information in terms of the elimination of possibilities. When we lack information, several alternative possibilities are open, when we get the information some of the alternatives are excluded. But a second peculiar thing about phenomenal information is that it resists this treatment. (So does logical or mathematical 'information'. However, phenomenal information cannot be logical or mathematical, because lessons in logic and mathematics no more teach us what a new experience is like than lessons in physics or parapsychology do.) When someone doesn't know what it's like to have an experience, where are the alternative open possibilities? I cannot present to myself in thought a range of alternative possibilities about what it might be like to taste Vegemite. That is because I cannot imagine either what it *is* like to taste Vegemite, or any alternative way that it *might* be like but in fact isn't. (I could perfectly well imagine that Vegmite tastes just like peanut butter, or something else familiar to me, but let's suppose I've been told authoritatively that this isn't so.) I can't even pose the question that phenomenal information is supposed to answer: is it this way or that? It seems that the alternative possibilities must be unthinkable beforehand; and afterward too, except for the one that turns out to be actualized. I don't say there's anything altogether impossible about a range of unthinkable alternatives; only something peculiar. But it's peculiar enough to suggest that we may somehow have gone astray.

From Phenomenal to Epiphenomenal

A third peculiar thing about phenomenal information is that it is strangely isolated from all other sorts of information; and this is so regardless of whether the mind works on physical or parapsychological principles. The phenomenal aspect of the world has nothing to do with explaining why people seemingly talk about the phenomenal aspect of the world. For instance, it plays no part in explaining the movements of the pens of philosophers writing treatises about phenomenal information and the way experience has provided them with it.

When Mary gets out of her black-and-white cell, her jaw drops. She says "At last! So this is what it's like to see colors!" Afterward she does things she couldn't do before, such as recognizing a new sample of the first color she ever saw. She may also do other things she didn't do before: unfortunate things, like writing about phenomenal information and the poverty of materialism. One might think she said what she said and did what she did because she came to know what it's like to see colors. Not so, if the hypothesis of phenomenal information is right. For suppose the phenomenal aspect of the world had been otherwise, so that she gained different phenomenal information. Or suppose the phenomenal aspect of the world had been absent altogether, as we materialists think it is. Would that have made the slightest difference to what she did or said then or later? I think not. Making a difference to what she does or says means, at least in part, making a difference to the motions of the particles of which she is composed. (Or better: making a difference to the spatiotemporal shape of the wavefunction of those particles. But let that pass.) For how could she do or say anything different, if none of her particles moved any differently? But if something nonphysical sometimes makes a difference to the motions of physical particles, then physics as we know it is wrong. Not just silent, not just incomplete—wrong. Either the particles are caused to change their motion without benefit of any force, or else there is some extra force that works very differently from the usual four. To believe in the phenomenal aspect of the world, but deny that it is epiphenomenal, is to bet against the truth of physics. Given the success of physics hitherto, and even with due allowance for the foundational ailments of quantum mechanics, such betting is rash! A friend of the phenomenal aspect would be safer to join Jackson in defense of *epiphenomenal* qualia.

But there is more to the case than just an empirical bet in favor of physics. Suppose there is a phenomenal aspect of the world, and suppose it does make some difference to the motions of Mary's jaw or the noises out of her mouth. Then we can describe the phenomenal aspect, if we know enough, in terms of its physical effects. It is that on which physical phenomena depend in such-and-such way. This descriptive handle will enable us to give lessons on it to the inexperienced. But insofar as we can give lessons on it, what we have is just parapsychology. That whereof we cannot learn except by having the experience still eludes us. I do not argue that *everything* about the alleged distinctive subject matter of phenomenal information must be epiphenomenal. Part of it may be parapsychological instead. But I insist that *some* aspect of it must be epiphenomenal.

Suppose that the hypothesis of phenomenal information is true and suppose that V_1 and V_2 are all of the maximally specific phenomenal possibilities concerning what it's like to taste Vegemite; anyone who tastes Vegemite will find out which one obtains, and no one else can. And suppose that P_1 and P_2 are all the maximally specific physical possibilities. (Of course we really need far more than two Ps, and maybe a friend of phenomenal information would want more than two Vs, but absurdly small numbers will do for an example.) Then we have four alternative hypotheses about the causal independence or dependence of the Ps on the Vs. Each one can be expressed as a pair of counterfactual conditionals. Two hypotheses are patterns of dependence.

K_1: if V_1 then P_1, if V_2 then P_2

K_2: if V_1 then P_2, if V_2 then P_1

The other two are patterns of independence.

K_3: if V_1 then P_1, if V_2 then P_1

K_4: if V_1 then P_2, if V_2 then P_2

These dependency hypotheses are, I take it, contingent propositions. They are made true, if they are, by some contingent feature of the world, though it's indeed a vexed question what sort of feature it is.[11] Now we have eight joint possibilities.

$K_1V_1P_1$ $K_3V_1P_1$ $K_3V_2P_1$ $K_2V_2P_1$

$K_2V_1P_2$ $K_4V_1P_2$ $K_4V_2P_2$ $K_1V_2P_2$

Between the four on the top row and the four on the bottom row, there is the physical difference between P_1 and P_2. Between the four on the left and the four on the right, there is the phenomenal difference between V_1 and V_2. And between the four on the edges and the four in the middle there is a parapsychological difference. It is the difference between dependence and independence of the physical on the phenomenal; between efficacy and epiphenomenalism, so far as this one example is concerned. There's nothing ineffable about that. Whether or not you've tasted Vegemite, and whether or not you can conceive of the alleged difference between V_1 and V_2, you can still be told whether the physical difference between P_1 and P_2 does or doesn't depend on some part of the phenomenal aspect of the world.

Lessons can teach the inexperienced which parapsychological possibility obtains, dependence or independence. Let it be dependence: we have either K_1 or K_2. For if we had independence, then already we would have found our epiphenomenal difference: namely, the difference between V_1 and V_2. And lessons can teach the inexperienced which of the two physical possibilities obtains. Without loss of generality let it be P_1. Now two of our original eight joint possibilities remain open: $K_1V_1P_1$ and $K_2V_2P_1$. The difference between those is not at all physical, and not at all parapsychological: it's P_1, and it's dependence, in both cases. The difference is entirely phenomenal. And also it is entirely epiphenomenal. Nothing physical, and nothing parapsychological, depends on the difference between $K_1V_1P_1$ and $K_2V_2P_1$. We have the same sort of pattern of dependence either way; it's just that the phenomenal possibilities have been swapped. Whether it's independence or whether it's dependence, therefore, we have found an epiphenomenal part of the phenomenal aspect of the world. It is the residue left behind when we remove the parapsychological part.

Suppose that someday I taste Vegemite, and hold forth about how I know at last what it's like. The sound of my holding forth is a physical effect, part of the realized physical possibility P_1. This physical effect is exactly the same whether it's part of the joint possibility $K_1V_1P_1$ or part of its alternative $K_2V_2P_1$. It may be caused by V_1 in accordance with K_1, or it may instead be caused by V_2 in accordance with K_2, but it's the same either way. So it does not occur because we have K_1V_1 rather than K_2V_2 or vice versa. The alleged difference between these two possibilities does nothing to explain the alleged physical manifestation of my finding out which one of them is realized. It is in that way that the difference is epiphenomenal. That makes it very queer, and repugnant to good sense.

The Ability Hypothesis

So the hypothesis of phenomenal information turns out to be very peculiar indeed. It would be nice, and not only for materialists. if we could reject it. For materialists, it is essential to reject it. And we can. There is an alternative hypothesis about what it is to learn what an experience is like: the *ability hypothesis*. Laurence Nemirow summarizes it thus:

some modes of understanding consist, not in the grasping of facts, but in the acquisition of abilities. . . . As for understanding an experience, we may construe that as an
ability to place oneself, at will, in a state representative of the experience. I understand the experience of seeing red if I can at will visualize red. Now it is perfectly
clear why there must be a special connection between the ability to place oneself in a
state representative of a given experience and the point of view of experiencer: exercising the ability just *is* what we call 'adopting the point of view of experiencer'. . . .
We can, then, come to terms with the subjectivity of our understanding of experience without positing subjective facts as the objects of our understanding. This
account explains, incidentally, the linguistic incommunicability of our subjective
understanding of experience (a phenomenon which might seem to support the hypothesis of subjective facts). The latter is explained as a special case of the linguistic
incommunicability of abilities to place oneself at will in a given state, such as the
state of having lowered blood pressure, and the state of having wiggling ears.[12]

If you have a new experience, you gain abilities to remember and to
imagine. After you taste Vegemite, and you learn what it's like, you can
afterward remember the experience you had. By remembering how it once
was, you can afterward imagine such an experience. Indeed, even if you
eventually forget the occasion itself, you will very likely retain your ability
to imagine such an experience.

Further, you gain an ability to recognize the same experience if it comes
again. If you taste Vegemite on another day, you will probably know that
you have met the taste once before. And if, while tasting Vegemite, you
know that it is Vegemite you are tasting, then you will be able to put the
name to the experience if you have it again. Or if you are told nothing at
the time, but later you somehow know that it is Vegmite that you are then
remembering or imagining tasting, again you can put the name to the experience, or to the memory, or to the experience of imagining, if it comes
again. Here, the ability you gain is an ability to gain information if given
other information. Nevertheless, the information gained is not phenomenal, and the ability to gain information is not the same thing as information itself.

Earlier, I mentioned 'knowing what an experience is like under a description'. Now I can say that what I meant by this was having the ability
to remember or imagine an experience while also knowing the egocentric
proposition that what one is then imagining is the experience of such-and-
such description. One might well know what an experience is like under
one description, but not under another. One might even know what some

experience is like, but not under any description whatever—unless it be some rather trivial description like 'that queer taste that I'm imagining right now'. That is what would happen if you slipped a dab of Vegemite into my food without telling me what it was: afterward, I would know what it was like to taste Vegemite, but not under that description, and not under any other nontrivial description. It might be suggested that 'knowing what it's like to taste Vegemite' really means what I'd call 'knowing what it's like to taste Vegemite under the description 'tasting Vegemite''; and if so, knowing what it's like would involve both ability and information. I disagree. For surely it would make sense to say: "I know this experience well, I've long known what it's like, but only today have I found out that it's the experience of tasting Vegemite." But this verbal question is unimportant. For the information involved in knowing what it's like under a description, and allegedly involved in knowing what it's like, is anyhow not the queer phenomenal information that needs rejecting.

(Is there a problem here for the friend of phenomenal information? Suppose he says that knowing what it's like to taste Vegemite means knowing that the taste of Vegemite has a certain 'phenomenal character'. This requires putting the name to the taste, so clearly it corresponds to our notion of knowing what it's like to taste Vegemite under the description 'tasting Vegemite'. But we also have our notion of knowing what it's like *simpliciter*, and what can he offer that corresponds to that? Perhaps he should answer by appeal to a trivial description, as follows: knowing what it's like *simpliciter* means knowing what it's like under the trivial description 'taste I'm imagining now', and that means knowing that the taste one is imagining now has a certain phenomenal character.)

As well as gaining the ability to remember and imagine the experience you had, you also gain the ability to imagine related experiences that you never had. After tasting Vegemite, you might for instance become able to imagine tasting Vegemite ice cream. By performing imaginative experiments, you can predict with some confidence what you would do in circumstances that have never arisen—whether you'd ask for a second helping of Vegemite ice cream, for example.

These abilities to remember and imagine and recognize are abilities you cannot gain (unless by super-neurosurgery, or by magic) except by tasting Vegemite and learning what it's like. You can't get them by taking lessons on the physics or the parapsychology of the experience, or even by taking

comprehensive lessons that cover the whole of physics and parapsychology. The ability hypothesis says that knowing what an experience is like
just *is* the possession of these abilities to remember, imagine, and recognize. It isn't the possession of any kind of information, ordinary or peculiar. It isn't knowing that certain possibilities aren't actualized. It isn't
knowing-that. It's knowing-how. Therefore it should be no surprise that
lessons won't teach you what an experience is like. Lessons impart information; ability is something else. Knowledge-that does not automatically
provide know-how.

There are parallel cases. Some know how to wiggle their ears; others
don't. If you can't do it, no amount of information will help. Some know
how to eat with chopsticks, others don't. Information will help up to a
point—for instance, if your trouble is that you hold one chopstick in each
hand—but no amount of information, by itself, will bring you to a very
high level of know-how. Some know how to recognize a C-38 locomotive
by sight, others don't. If you don't, it won't much help if you memorize a
detailed geometrical description of its shape, even though that does all the
eliminating of possibilities that there is to be done. (Conversely, knowing
the shape by sight doesn't enable you to write down the geometrical description.) Information very often contributes to know-how, but often it
doesn't contribute enough. That's why music students have to practice.

Know-how is ability. But of course some aspects of ability are in no sense
knowledge: strength, sufficient funds. Other aspects of ability are, purely
and simply, a matter of information. If you want to know how to open the
combination lock on the bank vault, information is all you need. It remains
that there are aspects of ability that do *not* consist simply of possession of
information, and that we *do* call knowledge. The ability hypothesis holds
that knowing what an experience is like is that sort of knowledge.

If the ability hypothesis is the correct analysis of knowing what an experience is like, then phenomenal information is an illusion. We ought to
explain that illusion. It would be feeble, I think, just to say that we're
fooled by the ambiguity of the word 'know': we confuse ability with information because we confuse knowledge in the sense of knowing-how with
knowledge in the sense of knowing-that. There may be two senses of the
word 'know', but they are well and truly entangled. They mark the two
pure endpoints of a range of mixed cases. The usual thing is that we gain
information and ability together. If so, it should be no surprise if we apply

to pure cases of gaining ability, or to pure cases of gaining information, the same word 'know' that we apply to all the mixed cases.

Along with information and ability, acquaintance is a third element of the mixture. If Lloyd George died too soon, there's a sense in which Father never can know him. Information won't do it, even if Father is a most thorough biographer and the archives are very complete. (And the trouble isn't that there's some very special information about someone that you can only get by being in his presence.) Know-how won't do it either, no matter how good Father may be at imagining Lloyd George, seemingly remembering him, and recognizing him. (Father may be able to recognize Lloyd George even if there's no longer any Lloyd George to recognize—if *per impossibile* he did turn up, Father could tell it was him.) Again, what we have is not just a third separate sense of 'know'. Meeting someone, gaining a lot of information about him that would be hard to gain otherwise, and gaining abilities regarding him usually go together. The pure cases are exceptions.

A friend of phenomenal information will agree, of course, that when we learn what an experience is like, we gain abilities to remember, imagine, and recognize. But he will say that it is because we gain phenomenal information that we gain the abilities. He might even say the same about other cases of gaining know-how: you can recognize the C-38 when you have phenomenal information about what it's like to see that shape, you can eat with chopsticks or wiggle your ears when you gain phenomenal information about the experience of doing so, and so on. What should friends of the ability hypothesis make of this? Is he offering a conjecture, which we must reject, about the causal origin of abilities? I think not. He thinks, as we do, that experiences leave distinctive traces in people, and that these traces enable us to do things. Likewise being taught to recognize a C-38 or to eat with chopsticks, or whatever happens on first wiggling the ears, leave traces that enable us to do things afterward. That much is common ground. He also interprets these enabling traces as representations that bear information about their causes. (If the same traces had been caused in some deviant way they might perhaps have carried misinformation.) We might even be able to accept that too. The time for us to quarrel comes only when he says that these traces represent special phenomenal facts, facts which cannot be represented in any other way, and therefore which cannot be taught in physics lessons or even in parapsychology lessons. That is the part, and the *only* part, which we must reject. But that is no part of his psychological story about how we gain abilities. It is just a gratuitous metaphysical gloss on that story.

We say that learning what an experience is like means gaining certain abilities. If the causal basis for those abilities turns out also to be a special kind of representation of some sort of information, so be it. We need only deny that it represents a special kind of information about a special subject matter. Apart from that it's up for grabs what, if anything, it may represent. The details of stimuli: the chemical composition of Vegemite, reflectances of surfaces, the motions of well-handled chopsticks or of ears? The details of inner states produced by those stimuli: patterns of firings of nerves? We could agree to either, so long as we did not confuse 'having information' represented in this special way with having the same information in the form of knowledge or belief. Or we could disagree. Treating the ability-conferring trace as a representation is optional. What's essential is that when we learn what an experience is like by having it, we gain abilities to remember, imagine, and recognize.

Acknowledgment

Part of this paper derives from a lecture at LaTrobe University in 1981. I thank LaTrobe for support in 1981, Harvard University for support under a Santayana Fellowship in 1988, and Frank Jackson for very helpful discussion.

Notes

1. See Frank Jackson, "Epiphenomenal qualia," *Philosophical Quarterly* 32 (1982), pp. 127–136, and reprinted in this volume; "What Mary didn't know," *Journal of Philosophy* 83 (1986), pp. 291–295.

2. See B. A. Farrell, "Experience," *Mind* 59 (1950), pp. 170–198; and Thomas Nagel, "What is it like to be a bat?" *Philosophical Review* 83 (1974), pp. 435–450, also in Thomas Nagel, *Mortal Questions* (Cambridge: Cambridge University Press, 1979).

3. See Peter Unger, "On experience and the development of the understanding," *American Philosophical Quarterly* 3 (1966), pp. 1–9.

4. For such speculation, see Paul M. Churchland, "Reduction, qualia, and the direct introspection of brain states," *Journal of Philosophy* 82 (1985), pp. 8–28.

5. See my "Attitudes *de dicto* and *de se*," *Philosophical Review* 88 (1979), pp. 513–543, also in my *Philosophical Papers*, vol. 1 (New York: Oxford University Press, 1983); and Roderick Chisholm, *The First Person: An Essay on Reference and Intentionality* (Minneapolis: University of Minnesota Press, 1981).

6. See Gilbert Harman, "The intrinsic quality of experience," *Philosophical Perspectives* 4 (1990).

7. See Ned Block and Jerry A. Fodor, "What psychological states are not," *Philosophical Review* 81 (1972), pp. 159–181, also in Ned Block (ed.), *Readings in Philosophy of Psychology*, vol. I (Cambridge, Mass.: Harvard University Press, 1980); and my "Mad pain and Martian pain," in *Readings in Philosophy of Psychology*, vol. I, and in my *Philosophical Papers*, vol. I.

8. See my "New work for a theory of universals," *Australasian Journal of Philosophy* 61 (1983), pp. 343–377, especially pp. 361–364. For a different view about how to state minimal materialism, see Terence Horgan, "Supervenience and microphysics," *Pacific Philosophical Quarterly* 63 (1982), pp. 29–43.

9. On recombination of possibilities, see my *On the Plurality of Worlds* (Oxford: Blackwell Publishers, 1986), pp. 87–92. The present argument may call for a principle that also allows recombination of properties; I now think that would not necessarily require treating properties as nonspatiotemporal parts of their instances. On recombination of properties, see also D. M. Armstrong, *A Combinatorial Theory of Possibility* (Cambridge: Cambridge University Press, 1989).

10. See *On the Plurality of Worlds*, pp. 142–165, on linguistic *ersatz* possibilities.

11. On dependency hypotheses, see my "Causal decision theory," *Australasian Journal of Philosophy* 59 (1981), pp. 5–30, reprinted in my *Philosophical Papers*, vol. II (New York: Oxford University Press, 1986).

12. Laurence Nemirow, review of Nagel's *Mortal Questions*, *Philosophical Review* 89 (1980), pp. 475–476. For a fuller statement, see Nemirow, "Physicalism and the cognitive role of acquaintance"; and *Functionalism and the Subjective Quality of Experience* (doctoral dissertation, Stanford, 1979). See also Michael Tye, "The subjective qualities of experience," *Mind* 95 (1986), pp. 1–17.

I should record a disagreement with Nemirow on one very small point. We agree that the phrase 'what experience E is like' does not denote some 'subjective quality' of E, something which supposedly would be part of the subject matter of the phenomenal information gained by having E. But whereas I have taken the phrase to denote E itself, Nemirow takes it to be a syncategorematic part of the expression 'know what experience E is like'. See "Physicalism and the cognitive role of acquaintance," section III.

6   Motion Blindness and the Knowledge Argument

Philip Pettit

Introduction

In a now famous thought experiment, Frank Jackson asked us to imagine an omniscient scientist, Mary, who is confined in a black-and-white room and then released into the world of color (Jackson 1982; Jackson 1986; cf. Braddon-Mitchell and Jackson 1996). Assuming that she is omniscient in respect of all physical facts—roughly, all the facts available to physics and all the facts that they in turn fix or determine—physicalism would suggest that there is no new fact Mary can discover after emancipation; physicalism holds that all facts are physical in the relevant sense (for a fuller statement see Pettit 1993; Jackson 1998). Yet we cannot help but feel that coming out of that room would be an occasion of dramatic enlightenment and, in particular, an occasion for learning facts to do with how red or yellow or blue looks or, as it is usually said, with what it is like to see red or yellow or blue.

Mary in the black-and-white room knew all the physical facts about the world, where these may be taken to include three sorts of color facts: objectual facts, as to what surface colors different objects have, assuming—as I shall do throughout—that colors are properties of objects; intentional facts, as to which colors different objects or apparent objects are represented as having in the subject's experience, rightly or wrongly; and nonintentional facts, about what such color experiences are like in their effects on subjects—whether they are comforting, or arousing, or whatever. But, according to the argument, Mary didn't know how any color looks or, equivalently, what color experience is like in itself, not just in its effects on subjects. This particular nonintentional fact about the quality of color experience—this phenomenal fact, as it is often described—she did not know. And so it is said to follow that there are facts—phenomenal color facts—that are not physical in character.

The idea, then, is that for all that Mary's knowledge in the black-and-white room settles, determining which possibilities are realized in the actual world, it leaves open a crucial question. Assume that colors are physical properties in objects—say, spectral reflectances—as it will be natural for physicalists to assume. Mary's knowledge in the black-and-white room, so it is said, does not give her information on whether the actual world is one where red looks phenomenally this way or that way—looks the way red actually looks to us, perhaps, or looks the way green actually looks to us. That issue is resolved for Mary, it appears, only in the light of her color experience: it is only when she actually sees colors that she knows whether one or the other possibility is realized; both possibilities are epistemically in play up to that point. Thus her color experience outside the black-and-white room yields knowledge that is additional to the knowledge of all physical facts that Mary, by hypothesis, had in the room. The phenomenal fact about which it gives her knowledge, therefore, has to be a fact of a nonphysical kind.

One sort of response to this argument holds that Mary could not have known all the physical facts there are to know under the constraints of the black-and-white room: that, not having been exposed to color, she would have lacked the conceptual resources required for knowing all such facts (Harman 1990). The sort of response I favor, however, assumes that she did know all the physical facts in the black-and-white room and maintains instead that what happens when she leaves the room is not that she gains new knowledge but that she changes in some other knowledge-related way: in a broad sense she develops a new mode of knowing. One version of the mode-of-knowing approach, understood in this broad sense, is the know-how response, according to which Mary learns how to discriminate colored things from one another—in experience, in memory, and in imagination—and how to order them in terms of similarity (Lewis 1990). But other, familiar responses to the argument can be seen as versions of the approach too. Mary may be said to learn how to recognize an abstract sort of particular under a new aspect, one we naturally describe as 'the way red looks'; or how to think indexically—that is, in the 'here', 'now', and 'I' way—about a fact previously known nonindexically; or how to form color concepts proper and to use them in expression of familiar facts; and so on (for a review, see Braddon-Mitchell and Jackson 1996).

My version of the mode-of-knowing approach develops from consideration of a case analogous to Mary's—the case of Eva—where the property to which the subject is initially blind is not color but motion. I try to argue that while Eva could have known all the physical facts in a room where motion-blindness is imposed—say, by stroboscopic lighting—she will undergo a change on leaving that room which is so massive that we are first inclined to say that she learns a new fact: the fact of what motion looks like or, equivalently, what it is like to see motion; and yet that it proves completely implausible, on reflection, to maintain that view. What we should maintain, rather, is that Eva comes to believe or know in what I describe as a practical, nonintellectual mode facts that she previously believed or knew only in a purely intellectual way. I think that this analysis of Eva's case is compelling and it should help us to be persuaded that a similar analysis applies in Mary's. There are differences between the cases, of course, deriving from the fact that whereas motion is a primary property that is available to many senses, color is a secondary property discerned by sight alone. But I hold that these are not sufficient to argue for a substantially different treatment of the two.

The essay is in three sections. In the first I analyze the case of Eva, trying to show how she can undergo a massive change on leaving the stroboscopic room and yet, plausibly, learn no new fact, and so learn no new nonphysical fact, about motion: for example, no new objectual fact about which objects are moving at what rate, in what direction; no new intentional fact about how motion vision represents such objects, rightly or wrongly, as moving; and no new nonintentional fact about what motion vision is like in its effects on subjects or in any other way. In the second, I consider and reject an antiphysicalist objection that, to the contrary, Eva will learn on leaving the stroboscopic room about what motion vision is like in itself, not just in its effects: that is, she will learn about phenomenal—visually phenomenal—motion. Then I go on to argue in the third section that although there is an important difference in the spontaneous intuitions we have about the two cases—this difference may explain why the Mary argument has proved so persuasive—it is not sufficient to block our accepting a similar story in the case of Mary.

1 Analyzing the Case of Eva

The Case of Eva

Recent studies have identified akinetopsia or motion blindness of a kind
akin to the phenomenon of color blindness (Zeki 1993, ch. 10). Someone
who suffers this ailment sees motion in a jerky series of static images, as if
in a stroboscopic light (Gazzaniga et al. 1998, p. 146). Thus a sufferer
reports as follows on the difficulty of crossing a road: "When I'm looking at
the car first, it seems far away. But then, when I want to cross the road,
suddenly the car is very near" (Zeki 1993, p. 82). As our awareness of color
blindness makes it easy for us to follow the story about Mary, and to have
intuitions about it, so an awareness of motion blindness can serve us in the
same way with regard to a parallel scenario.

Imagine that an omniscient scientist, Eva, knows all the physical facts
there are to know in just the sense in which Mary does but is confined in a
room—call it a stroboscopic room—where she has never been able to see
phenomenal motion. For Eva, seeing bodies move has only ever meant
seeing them occupy a temporally ordered, gappy succession of distinct
positions. And moving her eyes or rotating her body, so we may presume,
has only ever meant seeing the scene before her jump from one profile to
another; the literature is unclear as to whether this is a feature of those
diagnosed with akinetopsia. Eva will understand motion fully: for her, as
for everybody else, motion is just temporally continuous change of place
(or, if this is thought necessary, temporally continous change of place that
has a suitable metaphysical grounding). Eva will be able to perceive motion
nonvisually, and to have illusory, nonvisual experiences of motion, in virtue of having kinaesthetic sensations of her limbs and body moving and
she will be able to perceive the motion of external objects nonvisually, by
touching and tracking them. But she will be visually blind to motion; she
will have absolutely no visual sense of what motion, as distinct from dis-
continuous change of place, involves. Thus, as Mary does not know what
seeing red is like—what red looks like—Eva does not know what seeing
motion is like or, equivalently, what motion looks like.

So how will things be for Eva when she leaves the stroboscopic room for
the first time? Will the shift that occurs within her, as we intuitively imagine it, involve her learning any new fact? Or can we make good sense of it
just on the assumption that she develops a new way of knowing old facts?

I shall argue that we can make good sense of the transformation in Eva on this latter assumption, so that there is no reason to think that her new visual access provides evidence of a nonphysical fact. The analogy with Mary suggests that a similar lesson will go through there, and I turn to the case of Mary in the last section.

Objectual Facts About Motion

There are three candidate sorts of facts that Eva might be thought to learn on leaving the stroboscopic room. First, facts about the objectual properties of motion: facts to do with whether it is slow or fast, accelerating or decelerating, steady or jumpy, going in this direction or that, and so on. Second, facts about the intentional properties of the visual experience of motion. And third, facts about the nonintentional properties of that experience. Visual experience, here and throughout the essay, is meant to refer to visual representaton, which is registered or conceptualized as a representation—it is overtly a representation—for the subject. The intentional properties of such an experience will determine whether it is as of fast or slow motion, as of accelerating or decelerating motion, and so on. The nonintentional properties will determine whether it is soothing or exciting or threatening and so on.

I think it is clear that Eva will not learn any facts about the objectual properties of motion, since they are clearly physical and she would have known about them already in the stroboscopic room. She knows all the physical facts there, by hypothesis, so she knows that this or that object is moving fast or moving slowly, that it is accelerating or decelerating, and so on for the other objectual properties of its motion. Indeed, she has the capacity to register some of those objectual properties perceptually in the stroboscopic room, though perhaps only on the basis of nonvisual perception.

But though Eva will not learn any new facts about the objectual properties of this or that motion, it may well seem that she does. For there is something new, as we might put it, that such objectual facts are going to be like for her; it's just that there being something that those facts are like for her does not mean that she learns a new fact. Consider how things will be for Eva outside the stroboscopic room, as she surveys a moving object. She will not just know, on the basis of prior information about all physical facts, that it is moving and moving in this or that objectual way. Nor will she be caused on just any old perceptual basis to believe that it is moving, and moving in this or that way. Eva will register the movement visually, and she will be disposed to treat what she sees as evidence of the object moving and of its moving in a certain manner; she will have the visual ability, and the visually based reasoning ability, of a normal human being. And the fact that she has this new visual and reasoning ability means that there is something new that facts about the objectual properties of motion are bound to be like for her.

There is something new that such facts are bound to be like for her because, in registering those facts as such, she will by that very token register them as connected up with other facts in a variety of ways. She will register them as visually salient, of course; that is, she will register the facts in an awareness, explicit or implicit, that the evidence of her eyes—evidence sensitive to distinctively visual obstacles—leads her to do so. And she will register the facts as entailing or supporting other facts, or as being entailed or supported by them. Thus she will not just see the object moving at a certain rate but will see it as moving at such a rate that it is bound to hit a certain obstacle. Or she will register it as moving in such a manner that here or there is the place to reach out and pick it up. Or she will see it as moving in such a way that this or that change of position ought to confirm the appearance. And so on. Seeing motion will involve registering the motion facts in an inferentially rich way, as we might put it; each individual fact will present itself within a network of presumptive implicators and implications.[1]

That Eva registers the familiar motion facts in a manner that displays these connections—those extra facts—means that the familiar facts must present themselves to her in a new way. They are not recorded one by one, in the manner of propositions in an articulated body of prior information, for example; they reveal certain inferential connections more or less immediately. And that means, intuitively, that there is something new that the facts about motion are like for her. It does not mean, however, that there is any new fact she learns. Within the stroboscopic room she already knew all the facts—including all the facts about connections—that she now registers outside. And she was perfectly able to recognize within the room that once outside those facts would present themselves to her in the inferentially rich manner described.

One aspect of the inferential richness with which the familiar facts will present themselves to Eva outside the room is worth mentioning in order to underline the significance of the change involved. With many facts to do with motion, say, with the position of a moving body in her vicinity, she may have registered them previously only in a nonindexical manner; she may have known that the body will occupy such and such a position at such and such a time in objective space, for example, without having any perceptual access to that position. But when she registers the moving body visually before her she will know of the position of the body at the time in question, not just in objective space, but also in egocentric space: she will have knowledge of that very fact in a way that allows her to say 'It's there (at such and such an angle and distance from me)'. This egocentric way of knowing the fact of the body's position facilitates action on the body in a manner that a nonindexical way of knowing it does not; it facilitates relevant practical inferences as to where to reach in order to grasp it—I should reach *there*—and so on. Her knowledge of where she was in objective space would have allowed her in the stroboscopic room to work out that she should reach in a particular way in order to grasp the object. But it would not have facilitated the inference in the same way as the egocentric, visual representation (Perry 1979).

Intentional Facts About Seeing Motion

As the emergence of Eva's new visual and reasoning ability will not give her access to any new facts about the objectual properties of motion, so it will not give her access to any new facts about the intentional or nonintentional properties of the experience of motion. Take facts about the intentional properties, first: facts to the effect that this visual experience is an experience as of slow or fast motion, as of motion that is steady or jumpy, as of upward or downward motion, and so on. These are all facts about the objectual properties that the experience represents the motion, real or apparent, as having.

What is it for a visual experience to have such an intentional or representational capacity? I shall assume that a visual experience represents motion as having certain properties, in the relevant sense, so far as it overtly disposes the subject to make corresponding judgments about those properties. The visual experience of motion will overtly dispose subjects to make judgments about its objectual properties such as its direction or velocity or rate of change insofar as two conditions are fulfilled. First, a condition that is grounded in the conception of experience as an overt representation: subjects have to be aware of what is experienced by them as something they experience—something they register and conceptualize in that way. And second, they have to be aware of what is experienced as disposing them, without compelling them, to judge that the direction or velocity or rate of change of the motion is in such and such a range. This notion of an overt disposition of an experience—that is, an overt-to-the-subject disposition—is important for my purposes, and I will be employing it throughout the essay.

Like the objectual facts about the motion itself, intentional or representational facts about motion vision are bound to be known to Eva in the stroboscopic room, given that she knows all the physical facts there are. The Eva argument, like the analogous argument with Mary, is meant to raise a problem for physicalism, without assuming that other, more basic problems get in the way of the doctrine. And if it is not a physical fact that a visual motion experience represents the motion as having these or those objectual properties—if it is not a physical fact that the experience overtly disposes the subject to ascribe these properties—then physicalism is confounded quite independently of the knowledge argument. Thus it must be presumed within the knowledge argument that Eva knows all the intentional facts about various visual experiences of motion while she is in the stroboscopic room. There is no such fact remaining for her to learn when she emerges from that room.

What happens in this case, of course, as with objectual facts about motion, is that Eva will acquire a new perceptual and reasoning ability, on leaving the room, to read off the intentional properties of the visual experiences that lead her to posit motion. Seeing what she takes to be the motion of a fast-moving object, for example, and being aware that that motion is made visually salient to her—being aware, as human beings are able to be aware, that she makes judgments about it on the basis of what appears before her eyes—she will by that very token register an experience in herself as of fast motion. And so on in the other cases: the intentional properties of the experience will be read off from the objectual properties ascribed, rightly or wrongly, to the motion experienced. Thus there will be something new it is like for her to experience motion. There will be something new, more strictly put, that the intentional facts about her experiences of motion are like for her, as there is something new that the objectual facts about motion itself are like for here. Those facts, known already in the stroboscopic room, will make a new sort of impact as soon as she can visually register motion; they will become available in a new immediate way and, as with the objectual facts, spontaneously display their inferential connections with one another. They will assume a visual life of their own, as we might put it, and cease to be inert items of information recorded in her encyclopedic knowledge of all that there physically is.

Motion vision has certain intentional properties, we assumed, so far as it represents motion as being slow or fast: that is, so far as the experience overtly disposes the subject, in the sense explained, to make corresponding judgments. I shall describe properties that are associated with the effects that an experience overtly has on the subject as overt powers, where the powers are not potential but active. While intentional properties of an experience are overt powers in this sense, being associated with the active effect of the experience in overtly disposing the subject to make certain judgments, they are not the only overt powers an experience may have. Nonintentional properties may be overt powers too, as we shall now see, being associated with the active effect of the experience in overtly disposing the subject toward certain nonjudgmental responses.

Nonintentional Facts About Seeing Motion

Eva will become aware of nonintentional facts about motion vision as soon as she leaves the stroboscopic room, and finds herself soothed by the gentle motion of a falling leaf, enthralled by the elegant motion of a plane coming into land, recoiling or ducking away from the motion of an object in the direction of her face. Are these also facts that she was in a position to register in the stroboscopic room? And if they are, can we adequately account for how they change in Eva's perspective—for how there is something new they come to be like for her—just on the basis of recognizing that Eva gains new visual and related abilities?

The nonintentional facts mentioned in these examples involve effects that the experience overtly has on the subject. What is experienced is conceptualized by the subject as something experienced, and subjects are aware of what is experienced as disposing them appropriately; they are aware of the motion experienced as affectively soothing or exciting, for example, or as prompting them to certain motor responses: say, to recoil or duck. In the word I just introduced, the nonintentional facts mentioned all bear on overt, active powers in the experience. Eva will certainly have known about such overt powers just on the basis of knowing all physical facts. If these sorts of facts were not physical in character—and so, being physical, available to her in the stroboscopic room—there would have been no need to invoke the knowledge argument against physicalism; the doctrine would already have been dismissed.

Plausibly, all nonintentional properties of Eva's visual experience of motion are overt powers in that sense. Were there a nonintentional property of which Eva became aware in her visual experience of motion, where that property was not associated with the effects of an experience in the intimate manner of an overt power, then it would have to be a property that she could imagine manifesting itself in visual experiences with quite different effects, intentional and nonintentional. She would have to be able to imagine it being present here in a visual experience as of fast motion, there in an experience as of slow, here in an experience as of an object moving toward her face and causing her to recoil, there in an experience of an object moving away and allowing her to relax, here in an experience of soothing motion, there in an experience of disturbing, staccato motion, and so on. It would have to be a property that was overtly present in the experience but was dissociable in principle from such overt effects; we would have to be able to conceive of it being present without the effects and of the effects being present in its absence. It would have to be a property that made itself manifest, not in any such effects—that is how an overt power makes itself manifest—but in a character that was related only contingently to such effects. It is very hard indeed to imagine what such a property might be in the case of seen motion.

There is a well-established word in the philosophical lexicon, of course, for a qualitative property of experience whose essence or character is overt, not in virtue of overt effects, but just on the basis of inspection. This is the Latin word *quale* (Lewis 1995). That word is sometimes loaded with other connotations. Functionally, for example, *qualia* may be taken by definition to play a certain role in the subject's capacity to reidentify, recognize, and imagine experiences; epistemically, they may be taken by definition to be capable of a foundational role, being properties about which the subject cannot be mistaken and perhaps cannot overlook or miss; and ontologically, they may be taken by definition to be inconsistent with physicalism. I shall set aside all those connotations, however, and think of qualia just as qualitative properties of experience: properties whose essence is inspectionally or effect-independently overt to the subject of the experience.

As overt, experiential qualities, qualia contrast nicely with the overt, experiential powers that we have been invoking. You see the overt, active powers in an experience by feeling as such the effects of the experience—by being overtly empowered by the experience—so that the powers are conceived in a way that makes them incapable of coming apart from the effects.[2] You see the overt qualities in an experience just by inspecting them—that's the theory at any rate—so that the qualities are conceived as capable of coming apart from any effects the experience may happen to have on the subject.

If qualia in this sense are absent from Eva's visual experience of motion, then there is no problem in thinking that she will have known about all the nonintentional properties of that visual experience while still in the stroboscopic room. And equally, there will be no problem in recognizing that when Eva develops the ability, just on the basis of being able to see motion, to recognize nonintentional facts about visual experience—to feel their overt powers—there is bound to be something new that those facts will be like for her. They will be read off spontaneously from the sorts of feelings and inclinations that prove to be occasioned by visual experience, now of this sort of motion, now of that. A further aspect of the inferential richness of the visual experience of motion is that it will spontaneously deliver information about such nonintentional properties of the experience at the same time that it delivers information about the objectual properties of the motion experienced and about the corresponding, intentional properties of the experience itself.

Old Facts, New Modes of Believing

I say that Eva acquires new perceptual and reasoning abilities on leaving the stroboscopic room, but does not come to learn any new facts. Does that mean that what I am envisaging, then, is that Eva acquires a new causal route to a state she had already reached by virtue of her knowledge of all physical facts: the state of believing in the relevant objectual facts about motion, and the relevant intentional and nonintentional facts about the experience of motion? Not quite. I think that there is a more persuasive gloss to be given to the connection between the new abilities and Eva's beliefs about those facts, one that makes better sense of why we are inclined to think that she really does enjoy a massive transformation and enlightenment—and why we spontaneously say that there is something new that relevant objectual, intentional, and nonintentional facts will be like for her.

When Eva believes in the relevant facts, whether before or after leaving the room, that is by almost all accounts because—or at least partly because—she has the functional profile of such a believer. Thus, to rehearse the standard account of that profile, she is disposed to remain in the belief state so far and only so far as the evidence supports it, and she is disposed to draw the inferences and perform the actions that being in that state makes rational in the presence of her other states. Or at least that is so, when she is operating under intuitively favorable circumstances and within intuitively feasible limits (Pettit 1999). But if this is something that Eva's believing the relevant facts involves, then the profile may be satisfied in virtue of different causal bases, and that is plausibly what happens as between the period when she is confined to the room and the period after release.

While Eva is inside the room she believes a large number of the relevant facts—she has the profile of such a believer—in virtue of having access to scientific formulations of what they involve, being disposed to assent to those formulas and being disposed to let her responses be organized around them. When Eva escapes from the room, however, with many such facts, she comes to display the profile of a believer in a very different way. She comes to be in the state of believing that an object is moving at such and such a rate, for example, not just in virtue of giving assent to the corresponding proposition and allowing it to influence, say, where she concludes that it would be best for her to reach and try to intercept it. She now instantiates that state in virtue of being spontaneously disposed to reach out to that place as she tries to pick up the object—to reach out *there*, as she will think of it—and being spontaneously disposed to make an indefinite range of similar adjustments. If we describe the profile of a believer in the relevant facts as involving dispositions to act and adjust in certain ways, then Eva in the stroboscopic room is disposed to act and adjust appropriately on a very different basis from the basis on which she comes to be so disposed outside. She believes the same set of facts inside the room as she believes outside, but the shift in her perceptual and inferential abilities ensures that her mode of believing many of those facts will be very different.

This comment connects with the more general claim that believing a given fact can come about in different modes: say, as I have described them elsewhere, relatively more intellectual modes, relatively more practical modes, or modes involving both aspects (Pettit 1998). The logician who can formulate and assent to modus ponens—but who may have to take pains to remain faithful to it in practice—believes the principle in a characteristically intellectual way. The regular reasoner who cannot formulate it but who can recognize instances and is naturally disposed to treat the premises in each case as a reason for endorsing the conclusion believes it in a characteristically practical manner. The anthropologist who believes that all berries of a certain plant are edible—but who may lack the ability to identify such berries reliably—believes that proposition in an intellectual mode. The native who has never reflected on that general claim but who is able to identify those berries and is disposed to think of any such berry he or she identifies that it is edible—a disposition that may appear just in their treating it as edible—believes it in a practical mode.

In the same way I say that Eva in the stroboscopic room believes—indeed knows—various objectual facts about motion, and the intentional and nonintentional facts about the visual experience of motion, in one mode of believing, and that Eva outside believes and knows those facts—or at least believes and knows those to which she has been visually exposed—in quite another. Where she previously knew those facts in a purely intellectual way, as we might put it, she now believes them by virtue of having practical dispositions to draw inferences and make adjustments on the basis of continually monitored visual information. What were previously inert items of information that have to be explicitly connected up with any responses they rationalize now give way to modes of belief that materialize in a network of dispositions that source such responses spontaneously. Not only is there a shift in the perceptual and reasoning abilities that Eva enjoys, then; there is, by that very token, a change in the mode in which she believes many of the physical facts that were previously in her possession.

We can put this in another way if we think about belief from the point of view not of the subject in whom it involves a certain sort of disposition, but from the point of view of the possibilities among which it situates the subject. When I believe that something is the case, I situate the actual world and my position within the world in relation to various possibilities, taking it to realize this possibility but not that, and so on (Lewis 1983, essay 10). That there are different modes of believing—different ways of being disposed in the way belief involves—amounts to the fact that there are different modes of locating oneself among the possibilities. With some possibilities self-location will be typically effected by the intellectual means afforded by scientific theory; with others, it will be more usual to locate oneself in the perceptually based manner of regular observation and experience.

Now consider Eva inside and outside the stroboscopic room. And think of those possibilities to do with whether an object in Eva's vicinity is moving quickly or slowly, is going to reach a point early enough to avoid colliding with another moving object, is gathering speed as it moves away from her, and so on. Normally sighted people find their way among such possibilities, ruling these in and those out, by relying on continually updated visual information and on the spontaneous reasoning ability that attends this, and that is the way that Eva will come to locate herself in relation to those possibilities when she leaves her room. But within the room things are very different, for here the means of self-location that Eva relies on in relation to those possibilities will often have the very intellectual cast associated with theoretical, scientific knowledge; only occasionally will her kinesthetic and tactile experiences give her any more practical take on the relevant motion possibilities. Thus we have to say that while she may not achieve any more specific level of self-location after leaving the room, she will come to be able to locate herself among the possibilities in a very different manner. She may have nothing to learn in the matter of which possibilities are realized in the actual world and which not, but she does have to learn how to situate herself in a wholly novel way among those possibilities.[3]

2 Defending the Analysis

I argued in the last section that though Eva in the stroboscopic room knows all the physical facts there are to know, she does undergo a great shift in the way she can know things on leaving the room. She comes to be able to believe in a new, practical way facts that she previously believed only in quite a different, purely intellectual manner; there is something new that objectual facts about motion, and intentional and nonintentional facts about seeing motion, come to be like for her. Yet I maintained that nothing in this transformation should lead us to think that Eva learns any new fact. And nothing about Eva, therefore, should suggest that physicalism is false: that there are facts of a nonphysical kind that she did not know in the stroboscopic room and that she learned on leaving that room.

One crucial step in my analysis was the argument that as the intentional properties of a visual experience of motion are all overt powers—as, say, the property of being as of slow motion is an overt power of evoking the judgment that the motion is slow—so too all the plausible nonintentional properties are overt powers. They consist in the experience's being such as to dispose the subject overtly toward this or that response, whether it be a response of being soothed or excited, ducking away from a moving object, or reaching out in its direction. All the intentional and nonintentional properties of the experience, so I argued, should be thought of as overt powers of evoking judgmental or nonjudgmental responses, and powers therefore whose essence is known to the subject only in those very effects. None should be conceived of as an overt quality: a property whose essence is known inspectionally to the subject, not just via the effects that it is found contingently to have.

An Objection to the Analysis

There is an argument that may be invoked against this step in my analysis, however, and used to support an antiphysicalist, counterintuitive reading of Eva's case. I consider that argument in this section and try to show that it is not compelling. It is important to see why the argument should not be allowed to get a hold on us, for the principle driving it represents a powerful source of mistaken, antiphysicalist intuitions; it is liable to influence our general take on the debate between physicalism and nonphysicalism, and not just to warp our reading of Eva's case, or indeed of Mary's.

The argument can be set out as follows.

(1) If Eva's visual experience outside the room has the intentional property of being as of slow motion, or whatever, then it will overtly dispose her to judge that there is motion and that the motion ascribed is slow.

(2) If it overtly disposes her in this way to make this judgment, then there must be an intrinsic property of the visual process that leads her, as a matter of contingent fact, to make it; otherwise, implausibly, the disposition would be bare and unexplained (see Smith and Stoljar 1998).

(3) One possibility is that the property that leads her to make suitable judgments is a covert—say, subpersonal—property; this property would be causally responsible for the capacity to make the judgments but would be unknown to the subject. This possibility appears to be ruled out, however, by the following argument.

(4) Eva will be able to inspect what she experiences more closely to see if the ascription of slow motion is really well supported: to see if it continues to be reliably prompted and presumptively justified. And so she must be able to inspect a property of the motion experienced that can be identified independently of the effect and judged for whether, contingently, it supports the ascription of slow motion.

(5) Thus the property that operates in disposing Eva to ascribe slow motion, by claim (2), is bound to be a property that is inspectionally overt to Eva—or can become inspectionally overt—in its character or essence, and not just in the effects that it is found contingently to have. It is bound to be an essentially overt, qualitative property of the experience: a quale.

(6) But such a property is not one that Eva could have known in its essence within the stroboscopic room. Lacking the ability to see motion, she could not have had the essence of the property revealed to her there. And none of the physical properties she knew in their essence—certainly none of the causal properties that might underpin a disposition—would be capable of having their essence revealed in that way (Lewis 1995).

(7) Thus there is a new fact that Eva learns, contrary to the analysis offered. She learns what the qualitative property that prompts the ascription of slow motion involves: what it is in its essence. She learns how slow motion looks in the sense in which this involves more that its looking slow: in the sense in which it involves its looking a substantive way that happens as an inductive, contingent matter to prompt the ascription of slow motion.

This argument seems to establish, contrary to the analysis of the last section, that the visual experience as of slow motion will have a property that is accessible in its inspected character only to those enjoying the experience—call this the property of being 'slowish'—and will therefore escape Eva in the stroboscopic room. Eva in the stroboscopic room will be able to know that there is such a property—she will have access to the argument given, after all—but as between the possibility that it has this inspectable essence or that one she will not know which possibility is realized; she will not even be able to discriminate such possibilities as candidates that she can properly understand. She will not know what slowishness is like in itself.

Responding to the Argument

How to reply to this line of argument? My intuitive response is to say that there has to be something wrong because, as suggested in the last section, it is really hard to think that motion vision makes salient any qualititative property like that of being slowish or fastish—or there-ish or here-ish, uppish or downish, and so on. Being a property known inspectionally in its character or essence to Eva, not just in any of the effects it is found contingently to have, the sort of property in question should be one that she can imagine remaining constant while the associated effects change, and vice versa. Being a qualitative property—a *quale*—slowishness should be one that might conceivably be present in fast motion and that might be associated for people other than herself with fast motion; and similarly upwardishness should be a property that might conceivably be present in downward motion and in other people's visual experience of downward motion; and so on in other cases. But imagination boggles at the attempt to envisage anything Eva comes to see in slow motion or upward motion that might be dissociable in this way from the effects of seeing slow or upward motion.

This response is strongly reinforced by a body of research in empirical psychology (Kohler 1961; Taylor 1962; Kohler 1964; Kagan 1989; see Hurley 1998, 346–349 for a useful discussion). The subjects in a familiar series of experiments were fitted with glasses that turned the visual world upside down or inverted it on the left-right axis: in one sort of experiment what appeared up was really down, what appeared down was really up; in the other what appeared on the right was really on the left, what appeared on the left was really on the right. This would have affected, not just what was statically up and down, or statically on the right and left, but also what moved up and moved down, or what moved right and moved left; it would have affected perception of every such objectual property of motion. Now if there are qualia of the experiences as of upward movement and as of downward movement, to take that case, then in this sort of experiment what we ought to predict is the following: that while people are likely to learn in time to make correct judgments—and related, motor adjustments—on the basis of the inverted qualia, they should continue to find that upward motion looks the way downward used to look, and vice versa. After all, if the argument is sound, then the people in the experiment have inverted certain qualia and merely learned to change their wonted, judgmental and related responses to those qualia.

But this is not what people in the experiment reported. They did indeed learn to make correct judgments and adjustments after a week or so of wearing the glasses, but as their dispositions changed in this respect so at the same time did the way things looked to them. They gave no report of continuing, unchanged qualia—unchanged qualia playing different roles in producing judgment—but said rather that after the period of correction everything was as it had been for them before they began wearing the glasses: what was up now looked up, once again, and what was down looked down. And equally in the other case, subjects reported that what was to the right now looked to the right, what was to the left now looked to the left. In neither case was there anything that remained constant in the way in which we might have expected qualia to remain constant.

If this is what happened in an attempt to switch the alleged qualia of experiences as of upward and downward motion, and indeed as of rightward and leftward motion, it seems reasonable to suppose that the same sort of thing would happen in any attempted switch of the other qualia that must attend visual motion, according to the antiphysicalist argument. There must be a false premise in that argument, then, or perhaps a mistake of reasoning. But where is the error to be found?

I suggest that the problem is in the fourth claim in the argument, according to which the property that grounds the disposition to ascribe slow motion must have an inspectable, independent character if the experience is to be sensitive to inspection. That claim supposes that if Eva attends closely to the motion seen in the attempt to determine whether she should really ascribe slow motion, then in scutinizing the evidence of her eyes she must be paying attention to a property under an aspect that is independent of the experience's overtly disposing her to ascribe slow motion. The experience may come overtly to dispose her—more or less strongly—

to ascribe slow motion, as she concentrates her gaze. But the idea is that this can only be because her concentration is giving her access to a distinct, qualitative property that causes such strengthening or weakening. It is this idea that lends plausibility to the fourth premise and drives the argument.

But why should we accept that idea? Why shouldn't things go rather as follows? As Eva concentrates her gaze, various things happen in the subpersonal realms of her visual processing, as a result of which the experience that was previously as of slow motion gives way to an experience with a different overt power and a different intentional cast. Perhaps it is now more sharply as of slow motion, as we say, or perhaps it ceases to be as of slow motion. But in either case the only properties that are ever available to her in the experience are the property in the motion ascribed of being more or less slow and—by the same token—the property in the experience of being more or less as of slow motion.

If you and I and Eva are designed by mother nature to operate like this, then in determining whether to trust our eyes as to the speed of observed motion, we will certainly go back to the experience itself and find properties in it—being as of slow motion, looking slow—that we can quote as reasons for the corresponding judgment. Thus there will be something available in experience that supports the ascription of slow motion. But that something—the experience's being as of slow motion—will be an overt power through and through. The experience will dispose me or you overtly to ascribe slow motion but it will have no other aspect than that. It will not be an overt quality of the kind invoked in the antiphysicalist argument.

Situating This Line of Response

This line of response suggests, in the spirit of Wilfrid Sellars's (1997) attack on the myth of the given, that consistently with becoming better available on the basis of increased attention, a property may be nothing other than an overt power: something that empowers the perceiving subject, without giving him or her access to the property in itself that grounds the power. There is a property given to me, the subject of a visual experience as of slow motion. But what is given is not anything in the nature of a quale, with an inspectable character that is related in only a contingent and inductive way to my becoming disposed to make a certain judgment. What is given is nothing more or less than the character of that experience that is exhausted in its disposing me in that way; what is given is just an overt power of the experience.

That overt power will have a categorical grounding under any plausible metaphysics, but this can be unmysterious and physical and need not be available to the subject (Lewis 1995). For me the property will reveal itself in the fact that the experience overtly disposes me to ascribe slow motion. But the ground of that disposition will be discernible only within the realms of neuropsychological analysis. Things will conform to the pattern acknowledged as a possibility in the third premise of the argument given.

The position adopted—and, more generally, the rejection of the myth of the given—is supported by a certain class of discoveries in neuroscience. What these show is that perceptual data may elicit in a subject a disposition to behave in a certain way, quite independently of the subject's being aware of the character of those data that explains that disposition; and that with the disposition in place the subject is then positioned to see the data under a corresponding gestalt: that is, as having a suitable character, a suitable overt power. The nature of what is registered, in its subpersonally available profile, prompts a certain response, and, given the tendency to make that response, the subject then sees what is registered as having a corresponding character: in effect, as being the sort of thing that is fitted to that response.

Consider the findings of a recent study in which subjects are asked to gamble with four decks of cards, where two of the decks are stacked against them (Bechara et al. 1997). While the subjects do eventually come to register those two decks as stacked, and so to resist them, it turns out that the resistance response—or at least the disposition toward that response—is present long before any perception of the decks as stacked, or even as suspect, emerges. This is evident from imaging of what is going on in their brains when they are dealing with those decks, as distinct from the fair ones, and from associated skin conductance responses. Unconscious resistance materializes in these subjects on the basis of a subpersonal registering of the fact that things are going wrong with the suspect decks. And the eventual registering of the decks as suspect—'there's something I don't like about them'—takes the form of registering them simply as decks that occasion that resistance.

The myth of the given may be sourced in the idea that the explicitly registered charactered of what is presented—what is inertly given—

prompts the subject's response and so must have a character for the subject that is dissociable from that response.[4] However, the truth may rather be, as this sort of finding suggests, that often things are the other way around. It may be that what perception first of all provides is an unconsciously effective response-guidance system, and that as responses congeal, the percepts get articulated as having a character fit to support them.[5] So far as that is the case, the properties revealed in preception will be overt powers, not qualia; they will be known to the subject in the effects they elicit, not on an inspectional, effect-independent basis.

3   The Case of Mary

From Eva to Mary: A Parallel Analysis

By the analysis offered, Eva gains a practical, visual way of knowing about motion, and hence about the vision of motion, on leaving the room. What she gains is not new factual knowledge but a new mode of registering and believing facts already known. Why shouldn't things be the same for color? And why shouldn't we then think that Mary's enlightenment as she leaves the black-and-white room involves nothing more than Eva's: that Mary comes at that moment to know in a spontaneous, practical way facts that she previously knew in a different mode? Why, more particularly, shouldn't we say that the sense in which Mary learns what it is like to see colors is just the sense in which Eva learns what it is like to see motion? There is something new that the objectual facts about the colors of things—facts to do with hue and saturation and brightness—will be like for Mary. And there is something new that the intentional and nonintentional facts about color experience will be like for Mary. But there will be nothing new that Mary discovers when those facts assume that profile for her.

On this story, Mary will be able on leaving the room to scrutinize the colors of things with a view to making more reliable judgments about their objectual properties; with a view to becoming surer about the properties her vision represents things as having—about the intentional properties of her experience; and perhaps with a view to savoring various nonintentional effects that she enjoys in the experience. But in doing this she will not be eye-balling anything in the way of a quale: a property with a character or essence that is inspectionally revealed to her for the first time. Rather, she will be putting herself under the control of the overt powers of seen color; she will be putting herself in a position to let the powers of color work on her.

There is no good reason, I believe, why we shouldn't go along with the lesson of Eva's case and endorse these claims about Mary. For the Mary argument to have any point, it has to be assumed that color is a physically analyzable property that is detected by human beings in a physically analyzable way; otherwise physicalism would be undermined before the argument ever got going. But that being so, it seems that the points made in discussion of Eva's case will carry over smoothly to Mary's. Mary in the black-and-white room is bound to know the facts about the objectual properties of color, including the color of this or that object, since she knows all the physical facts. She is bound to know all the corresponding intentional facts to do with which color experiences are experiences as of which colors. And she is bound to know all the facts to do with how far experiences as of this or that color have certain nonintentional properties. Yet such antecedent knowledge is consistent with Mary's enjoying a radical transformation on leaving the black-and-white room; in particular, a transformation that may incline us to think that she learns a new fact. For on leaving that room, by the lesson of our analysis in Eva's case, there will be something new that the objectual, intentional, and nonintentional facts about color are like for her. She will be in a position, given color vision, to believe in a new and practical mode facts that she previously registered only in an intellectual or theoretical manner. She will be able to locate herself among those possibilities on a new basis—to rule this possibility out, that possibility in—but she will continue to locate herself at the same place.

The analogies between the two cases are sufficient in themselves to make it plausible that Mary's case should be analyzed on such parallel lines. But one particular attraction to that strategy is that it suggests a nice account of what it is for something experienced to look red or blue, or to look bright or saturated, or indeed to look warm and comforting or cold and disturbing. We are invited to think about those properties of experienced color as overt powers of what is experienced: as powers that are exhausted for subjects in the experience's overtly disposing them toward relevant responses, judgmental or nonjudgmental. Those powers may wax or wane with attention and focus but the important thing is that they are not qualia. They are not properties whose essence is available in the visual experience on the basis of inert inspection, as something that just happens to prompt the judgmental and nonjudgmental responses. They are not properties such that we can imagine them varying independently of such effects: remaining present while the effects change, or changing while the effects remain the same.

Experienced color has overt powers, under this story, but no overt character that is independent of the powers it exercises, relating only inductively and contingently to the effects involved. And that being so, we can see why Mary in the black-and-white room will be able to know about those properties and yet not be able to form beliefs about them in the manner of ordinary people. She will know the overt powers of colors, through knowing that color properties—surface reflectance properties, as we are taking them to be—have effects of the required sort. But she will not know them in the manner of ordinary people. While knowing that the properties have such and such effects, none of those effects will materialize in her. She will not undergo those effects, in the manner of ordinary people, as effects overtly prompted by what is seen in the experience of color.

Objection: There Is a Difference

But while there are many analogies between Eva's case and Mary's, and many advantages in defending a parallel analysis, there is one salient difference of intuition between the cases. Most of us will agree that there really seems to be nothing distinct from the overt powers of seen motion that is identified in seeing objects move; there is no quale that might in principle vary independently of overt effects, being only inductively and contingently associated with such effects. But it is not so clear that most of us will be equally moved by the parallel claim in Mary's case.

On the contrary, so it may be said. When I see or seem to see a color, I don't just know that the color experience has the intentional property of being as of a certain color, nor that it has the nonintentional properties of soothing or boring or exciting me, though I certainly do know those things. Beyond knowing that it has such overt powers—beyond experiencing those powers—I also know that the experience has a certain quale, unexhausted by any particular effect. I know not just that what is experienced looks red or yellow, for example—that is, overtly disposes me to make corresponding judgments—but that it looks reddish or yellowish, where 'reddish' is understood in the same manner as 'slowish' and registers the presence of an overt quality that is only inductively and contingently associated with disposing subjects in certain ways. If I know this just in virtue of having color experience, then what I know—that red things look this or that substantive, reddish way—is something that Mary will come to know only after emerging from the black-and-white room.

This intuition about what Mary has to learn is associated with the intuitive plausibility, long recorded in the philosophical literature, of an inversion in the space of color experience. The idea is that there is nothing incoherent in imagining that the qualia of different color experiences might be exchanged, or that the qualia of your experience and mine of one and the same color might be different. I can imagine my experience as of red being the overt, substantive way that my experience as of green currently is, and vice versa. And, for parallel reasons, I can imagine my experience as of red being the overt, substantive way that your experience as of green currently is. What looks red to me now is reddish, so it is suggested, whereas what looks red to me later, or to you now, may look greenish. And this may be so without our performance being in any way impaired. The idea is not that this inversion is a real-world possibility, being consistent with the actual laws governing color and the perception of color—that claim has been laid to rest, though it had life for a time (Hardin 1997)—but that it is at least a logical or metaphysical possibility.

We saw in the first section that it is very hard to envisage what the quale of slowishness in seen motion—or any such property—could be, given that it would have to be capable in principle of varying while the effects of the motion seen remained the same, and vice versa. What now appears, however, is that things are very different in the case of color. We do seem to find color qualia intuitive posits, so that we will be naturally disposed to think that Mary, unlike Eva, learns something new on escaping confinement.

Explaining the Difference

How to explain this difference of intuition? How to explain why we find it almost impossible to imagine what a quale of slowishness in seen motion might be, while having no difficulty in envisaging a quale like the reddishness of a color seen? Why does it require an abstract, specious argument to give life to the idea of qualia in the case of motion but not in the case of color? Happily, I think that there is quite a plausible answer available and that it allows us to maintain the view that Eva's and Mary's cases should be treated on a par.

The motion of an object concerns me as an ordinary visual observer, not just in its intentional or judgmental effects, and not just in nonintentional effects of an affective kind: its being soothing or exciting and so on. It concerns me above all, and for reasons that reach deep into our nature, in the motor adjustments it requires. If I have an experience as of an object accelerating in the direction of my face, for example, then what I experience had better prompt me to duck and, *qua* experience, overtly prompt me to duck. If I have an experience as of an object beginning to move in the direction of my child then, assuming the object can be stopped, what I experience had better prompt me—and prompt me overtly—to reach out here or there in order to intercept it. And so on. Motion is a primary property that is associated not just with effects on a single sense like that of sight, but also with an indefinite range of other effects. Thus, in learning to see motion, what I see had better be something that overtly prompts me in corresponding ways. Otherwise it will not constitute an experience as of the primary property of motion: an experience as of a property that has the wide range of effects typical of primary properties.

The color of an object concerns me in a very different way, since color is a secondary property that we conceptualize as something that is revealed only to a single sense, sight. There are no responses to color that I clearly must have, in the way in which I must have various responses to motion. And so the color that I see in an object, unlike the motion that I see there, is not something that is so obviously required to dispose me overtly in this or that manner. I will not count as seeing motion unless what I see prompts me overtly to respond with certain bodily adjustments. I will count as seeing color, for all that is obvious to us as ordinary subjects, just so far as what I see prompts me overtly to make suitable judgments. Motion is a primary, multisensory property that concerns me in various ways, so that seen motion must overtly dispose me to respond in that variety of ways. Color is a secondary, unisensory property that concerns me only in its effects on the eyes, so that seen color need only overtly dispose me—so at least it seems—to respond with suitable visual judgments.

Consider the case of motion. The fact that the visual experience of motion is experience that has to overtly prompt a variety of nonvisual effects—in particular, the fact that this is something salient to all of us—

makes it hard to think of anything given in the experience, any quale, that might change while the experience continues to prompt those effects, or vice versa. The quale of a particular visual experience of motion, if there is any, will have to be capable of varying independently of the effects the experience overtly has on the subject. And yet it will also have to mediate—and overtly mediate—those effects; it is supposedly the overt character of the experience in virtue of which it disposes the subject to respond in this or that manner. But it is hard to see how it could simultaneously satisfy these two demands: these constraints of independence, on the one side, and mediation on the other. As the range of effects to be mediated overtly by the experience increases, it is going to seem less and less plausible that the mediating property could be independent enough to vary while those effects remain in place, or vice versa.

For this reason the space in which we can imagine a purely qualititative change occurring in the visual experience of motion is restricted to a vanishing point, as we consider the range of effects, in particular effects of a nonvisual kind, that the experience will overtly have to elicit. The overt powers of the visual experience are so rich and salient that they leave us little room for envisaging the possibility that apart from those powers, the experience might also have a dissociable, overt quality.

Think of the case where people wear glasses that turn the visual world upside down and make upward movement look downward, and downward movement look upward. Imagine those people becoming accustomed to this shift. Imagine them learning to put their heads down, for example—this will be kinesthetically registered as down—when they see an object coming up at them, as it will seem. And imagine this learning becoming second nature, until the way things are visually presented automatically produces required nonvisual responses. It is very hard indeed to think of what it is that might remain the same in the subjective quality of the motion seen, as all of those responses are adjusted. How could the motion continue to look as if it comes from down there, for example—where 'there' will be identified in egocentric space—while the way it looks automatically leads them to put their heads down?

This line of thought explains very well, I think, why it requires an abstract and specious argument to give any life to the idea of qualia in the visual experience of motion. Were there a quale to a visual experience of motion it would have to mediate so many overt effects, that it would be hard to see how it might have an independent, overt character: a character capable of independent variation.

But now think of color. Things are very different here, since color is a unisensory, secondary property. The objectual properties of color that correspond to properties of motion like speed, acceleration, and direction involve hue, saturation, brightness, and so on. And those are all properties that involve vision, and vision only. That an experience is as of a deeply saturated, brightly illuminated red object, for example, signifies nothing about it—so far as we can tell—that directly impacts on any nonvisual sense. And in this respect it differs greatly from an experience that is as of an accelerating object that is moving in the direction of my face.

The fact that objectual color properties are purely visual means that the demands on experiences as of objects having those properties are not so obviously rich as the demands on visual experiences as of objects having various motion properties. And that in turn makes it intuitively more imaginable that there might be color qualia: properties of seen color that satisfy the dual constraints of mediating certain overt effects and of being able, at least in principle, to vary independently of those effects. It makes it intuitively imaginable that consistently with taking on the greenish quale, for example, the experience as of something red might continue to function perfectly well in overtly disposing us to discriminate red objects from objects of other colors, to see them as similar to objects of the same color, and to judge that they are red; all that would be needed is that a compensating change occur in experiences as of something green.

This being so, it is understandable why we might give credence to color qualia and expect that Mary will learn something when she leaves the black-and-white room. Color qualia are intelligible posits, where it is doubtful if motion qualia—the qualia of seen motion—are. Or at least they are intelligible against the background of our received folk psychology, which identifies much that seen motion has to dispose us to do and little that seen color has to effect.

But the fact that color qualia are folk-psychologically intelligible posits does not imply, of course, that they are posits we are well advised to make, and it does not imply that Mary will actually learn something on leaving the room. There are three points to make in support of sticking with the lesson from the analogy with Eva (for more detail see Pettit 2003). These are: first, that color qualia may be folk-psychologically intelligible without being intelligible, period; second, that however intelligible, they are not economical posits; and third, that there are some experiments in which they might well have been confirmed but weren't.

First Point: Color *Qualia* May Not Be Intelligible Posits   What is it for something to look red? In particular, what is it for something to look red, putting aside the possibility that there is a reddish quale present? Our spontaneous folk-psychological intuition—by contrast with intuitions in the motion case—is to think that something rather bare and simple is involved; if the possibility of a *quale* is put aside, it seems that to look red is just to look discriminable in ordinary conditions from orange and yellow and green and so on. It is this intuition that leaves us with the feeling that there has to be more than this occurring when an object looks red: there has to be a distinctive quale on offer also. The intuition is highly suspect, however, and may only survive in the absence of reflection on what color vision has to achieve for us, and in the absence of information about how it does that.

Consider someone who has the sort of discriminatory capacity mentioned. He or she is able to discriminate any two objects on the basis of their having different colors, at least in ordinary conditions: say, where the light is good, the background steady, and the subject's viewpoint unchanging. This ability falls well short of the portfolio of abilities associated with color vision, as a little reflection makes clear, particularly in light of recent scientific investigations. That portfolio must also include these capacities:

• to discriminate two objects of shades of the same color;
• to discriminate two objects of different colors under varying illumination, against changing backgrounds, and from a changing viewpoint;
• to recognize one of the objects as having the same color as a third object which lies at a little distance from it, or even in a different visual context;
• to track an object on the basis of its color—to reidentify it through time as the same-colored object—across different levels of illumination, different backgrounds, and from a changing viewpoint.

Once we take account of the need for these capacities in color vision, we see that to look red, in quale-free terms, involves much more than looking discriminable from other colors in ordinary conditions. Something will look red to a person so far as it looks fit, not just to be discriminated from things of other colors in ordinary circumstances, but to satisfy a much wider range of situation-response connections. It must look fit to stand out in contrast to objects of other shades and colors, under different intensities of incident light; against different backgrounds of landscape and objects; and from different spatial and subjective viewpoints. It must look fit to stand out as similar to other red objects, or to objects of the same shade of red, under parallel variations in lighting, background, and viewpoint. And consistently with looking fit to sustain such contrasts and comparisons, it must also look fit to transform in systematic and distinctive ways, while remaining determinably the same color and determinably reidentifiable, through various changes of lighting, background, and viewpoint.

With this enriched sense of what is involved in something's looking red, it is worth asking whether the quale intuition remains as firm as it seemed to be originally. Can we really imagine something's continuing to have the rich, discriminable, classifiable, reidentifable color profile of an object that looks a certain shade of red, while the supposed, substantively reddish way it looks changes? Can we really be sure that it is reasonable to think that there is a substantive way it looks that is dissociable from the discriminatory, classificatory, and reidentificatory capacities that its looking that way gives us? Isn't it just possible that there is no change conceivable in how the object looks that would not disturb one or another of those capacities? I surmise that this is possible, even plausible, and that a doubt must arise, therefore, as to whether qualia are intelligible posits. It may be that they are intelligible only against a background of an unreflective, uninformed folk psychology of color perception (Pettit 2003).

Second Point: Color *Qualia* Are Not Economical Posits   Even if we think that color *qualia* are intelligible posits, however, it does not follow that they are posits worthy of credence. And a consideration that suggests they are not is that there is a more economical qualia-free story available to us. We have seen that it is perfectly possible to explain Eva's transformation on leaving her confinement—and so to explain Mary's in parallel— without positing qualia or the learning of a new fact. So why should we posit qualia in the color case and why should we give an antiphysicalist reading to Mary's transformation?

I see no reason why we should do so. Being forced to explain what happens with Eva without invoking qualia—this, because we could not plausibly invoke qualia there—we learned that we could do without qualia. We learned that it makes sense to think of the motion of a body looking slow or fast, upward or downward, without thinking that there is any substantive way it looks: any slowish or upwardish, fastish or downwardish, way it looked. We learned that seen motion can have overt powers, in other words, without having any overt qualities. It would make good sense to invoke the same economical sort of story in the case of Mary, arguing that the ways colors look are not substantive ways that might vary independently of the judgmental and related effects they overtly prompt: that they too are overt powers, not overt qualities.

In particular it would make good sense to do this, given that the status of color as a secondary property explains why there is a quale-intuition in this case, but none in the case of seen motion. That difference in status shows why it is natural in Mary's case, though not in Eva's, to endorse the conclusion that on escaping confinement she learns what certain qualia are. And in explaining away the quale-intuition, it shows why it is not compelling to invoke such learning in explanation of what happens to Mary when she effects her escape.

Third Point: Color *Qualia* Have Failed Empirical Confirmation The line taken on motion vision was supported by empirical reseach on how various experiments that should have switched unchanged qualia from one role to another, if there were qualia available to shift, failed to have any such effect. It is worth noting, in conclusion, that the parallel line on color perception is supported in a similar fashion. An experiment in which we might have expected color *qualia* to remain unchanged, while judgmental adaptations shifted, suggests that there was nothing at all that remained constant and so no qualia that remained constant (Kohler 1964; Taylor 1962; for a good discussion see Hurley 1998, pp. 287–288).

The experimenter in this case fitted the subjects with spectacles in which the left side of each lens was tinted blue, the right side yellow—in another variation the top part was red, the bottom green—so that when the wearers looked left things had a blue tinge, when they looked right things had a yellow tinge. But as the subjects learned to adapt in the color judgments they made, and in the associated discriminations and comparisons—this took some weeks—so the way things looked adapted too; all signs of an inappropriate yellow or blue tinge disappeared. Indeed when the subjects removed the lenses, according to the reports, distortions reappeared for an initial period: things had a blue tinge when subjects looked in the direction that the goggles had been yellow, things had a yellow tinge when subject looked in the direction that the goggles had been blue.

These results suggest that as a movement's looking slow or fast just involves the visual experience of the motion having the overt power of disposing the subject to make suitable judgments and adjustments, so something similar holds in how color looks. Let something's looking red or blue consist in its looking fit to satisfy the range of situation-response connections mentioned above; let it consist in its exercising that richly profiled, overt power. When a subject wore glasses of the kind described, then that overt power was disrupted and the subject lost information that was previously available. The information was still there in what reaches the retina, but its encoding was distorted; "the light delivered by the spectacles to the eyes still carried the same information about the environment, but in an altered form. This information had not been destroyed, but only biased" (Gibson 1964, p. 8). What happens, then, when the look of red is restored? On this quale-free story, there is an obvious answer. What happens is that the brain adapts so as to retrieve the customary information from the distorted encoding and, as that adaptation occurs, the things again look exactly as they did without glasses.

If we think that there are color qualia, however, then it is hard to know what to say. Allow that there are qualia of that kind and we should expect that, short of an unexplained shift in quale occurring at the appropriate time, the subjects who began to see normally through a blue or a yellow lens would report that the quale of how things looked in the relevant part of the visual field had changed from what it was without the glasses but that they had learned to make corrected judgments and adjustments in its presence. They reported no such thing, however, giving us serious, additional ground to doubt the reality of color qualia and so to doubt whether there is any reason to treat Mary's case as different from Eva's.

Conclusion

It may be useful, in conclusion, to sum up the main points argued in the paper.

1. When Eva leaves the stroboscopic room and sees motion for the first time, then she gains a new mode of access to three sorts of facts: facts about the objectual properties—direction, velocity, and so on—of the motion she sees or seems to see; intentional facts about which properties her visual experiences represent such motion, rightly or wrongly, as having; and nonintentional facts about those experiences, to do with how far they are affectively exciting or soothing, or elicit motor responses like ducking or reaching.

2. Eva, knowing all physical facts, would have known all those facts previously. But when she leaves the room there is something new that those facts are like for her, in the sense that she will now see the connections between them in new, spontaneous ways. She will come to believe or know those facts in a practical, engaged way, as distinct from the purely intellectual way she knew them previously. She will situate her world and herself in a new way among the possibilities but the place where she self-locates in this epistemic sense will be just the same place as before.

3. The shift that occurs in Eva is sufficiently significant for it to be understandable why we should be inclined to say, without thinking, that she must learn a new fact. Holding that there is something that such new facts are like for her is close to saying that she becomes acquainted with something new. But we need not, and should not, indulge this inclination. There is no further fact that it is plausible to think she learns when she escapes confinement.

4. Antiphysicalists may resort to a certain argument at this point. Under the story told, when a movement seen or apparently seen looks slow or fast or whatever, then it overtly disposes the subject to judge that it is slow or fast, and when it prompts a response of an affective or motor kind then it overtly disposes the subject toward that response. But the overt power thereby registered in the movement seen or apparently seen—if you like, in the experience of motion—is not a property that has any inspectable character for the subject that is independent of this disposing effect. The antiphysicalist argument I envisage would maintain that apart from such overt powers we also have to acknowledge overt qualities or qualia, and we have to say that Eva learns what the qualia of such motion are on leaving her room.

5. On this usage, qualia are properties whose essence or effect-independent character is something that the subject grasps inspectionally in having an experience like the visual experience of motion. The anti-physicalist argument is that the overt powers of an experience must be grounded in independent properties, and that the fact that subjects can inspect what they experience as they explore how far to let those powers prevail—how far to draw the judgments prompted or make the responses elicited—shows that those independent properties must have a character or essence that is inspectionally overt to the subjects; that is, they must be qualia. The argument implies, then, that Eva will learn new facts on leaving her room: she will learn that when a motion looks slow it has a slowish quale—it looks a slowish way—and so on for other properties seen in motion.

6. This argument is counterintuitive. Qualia have to satisfy two constraints: on the one hand, mediate to the subject in an overt way the judgments and other responses elicited; and second, be independent of those effects and so capable, in principle, of varying while the effects remain the same—and vice versa (Block 1990). But it is highly implausible that anything could fit that bill in the case of seen motion. For being a primary property, any experience that counts as an experience of motion must overtly prompt the subject in a variety of nonvisual ways: the movement of an object toward one's face must prompt one to duck, and so on. And it is all but impossible to see how any property could have all those effects and yet, in principle, be capable of independent variation in an overt dimension. It is almost impossible to imagine, for example, how a fast motion could have a slowish quale, or an upward motion a downish quale. This observation is supported by empirical results to the effect that if people's visual experiences of motion are disturbed by lenses of various kinds—so that upward motion, for example, is presented as downward used to be—then as people learn to adjust and make the correct judgments, they report that motion begins to look appropriate once again; there is no continuing, downwardish quale in motion that they now judge to be upward, and so on.

7. But the argument is not only counterintuitive in Eva's case. It is also uncompelling, since we can plausibly hold, in line with a Sellarsian tradition, that when Eva attends to the seen motion of a body in order to be

clearer about its velocity or rate, she may merely be exposing herself to the overt power of the experience to dispose her judgmentally in this or that way. There is no need to postulate that there is an independent property she is inspecting—slowishness, as it might be—which is only found to be associated contingently with slow motion, and so on. This line fits quite well with recent neuroscientific observations. These show that things we experience may have effects on us without our being aware of what it is about them that elicit those effects and that, with the effects in place, we may see the things we experience as possessed of corresponding properties: the property in each case of overtly disposing us toward the relevant effect.

8. There is every reason why we should take a similar line in Mary's case to that which is defended here for Eva's. The story is economical and plausible. It requires us to acknowledge that when something looks red, there is no substantive way it looks to us—there is no quale on offer—and that it just looks the way that goes with our judging that it is red, making the required discriminations and comparisons. It requires us to think of the looks of color, as we think of the looks of seen motion, as overt powers rather than overt qualities. But this is something that is quite coherent, as argued in the case of motion.

9. All that said, it must be acknowledged that while the antiphysicalistic argument is as uncompelling in the case of color as in the case of seen motion, it is not as counterintuitive in the color case. This is because color is a secondary property that affects vision alone, so that seen color does not have to activate the rich array of effects that seen motion is required to do. It is all but impossible in the case of visually registered motion to see how anything could fill the dual constraint on a quale of mediating such effects but being capable in principle of independent variation: to see how downward motion could continue to have the quale of upward and so on. But no such argument is available with color. And so we can envisage that there is a reddish way that red things look—we can envisage a reddish quale that is registered in seeing red—so that green things might look that way instead of red, and vice versa.

10. We can, but we shouldn't. For it remains possible, as already observed, to hold instead by the economical story motivated by consideration of Eva's case. And two other arguments also offer grounds for rejecting color qualia. The first is that for something to look red is for it to look

fit to sustain a very wide range of situation-response connections, as investigations of color vision have made clear, and that the intuition that there are color qualia is put under pressure by a recognition of this fact. And the second is that as the story told in the case of seen motion was supported by some empirical results, so a parallel story is supported in the same way in the case of color. The earlier results were that people who compensate for lenses that disturb the visual perception of motion do not continue to find the old *qualia* still in place. The results relevant to color show that people who compensate for lenses that disturb the sight of color slightly do not continue to find old qualia in place either. Where their judgment of color goes—and their associated adjustments—so the way color looks to them appears to go also. And that is just what we should expect on the story developed here.[6]

Notes

1. I discovered in presenting the paper at the Tucson Consciousness Conference 2002 that the views I favor on this topic, and on other matters related to perception—see the discussion of color vision in the last section—are close to the very engaging 'sensorimotor' view defended by O'Regan and Noë (forthcoming). I have adjusted some phrasing in response to their influence. The views are close, more generally, to a range of recent work that emphasizes the role of perception as a skill and the importance of perceptual-practical connections (see Thompson 1995; Hurley 1998; Clark 1999; Myin 2001; Myin and O'Regan 2002). The paper is a companion piece to Pettit 2003.

2. It may be useful to think of the power as a higher-order, disposing property that consists in the experience's having lower-order properties that produce those effects. Why is it said to be a disposing rather than a dispositional property? Because the power is understood in the sense of active, not just potential, power: it exists only so far as the effects are actually materializing. Why is it said to be a higher-order rather than a lower-order property? Because it is overt, being recognized as such by the subject who is exposed to it; the lower-order properties responsible for the effects could not be overt in that way.

3. Perry (1979) argued that a very important shift occurs whenever an agent comes to be able to think indexically, say, in 'I', 'here', or 'now' terms, about themselves or their position; nonindexical thought cannot motivate my acting, or my acting here or now. Such a shift may occur for Eva, as emphasized in the earlier discussion of her being able to think of an object as moving 'there', in egocentric space. I do not think that this sort of transformation reduces the space of epistemic possibilities and represents knowledge of a new fact. But even if that were denied, it should be clear that

the kind of knowledge gained in this indexical shift is not the sort that would vindi-
cate the rejection of physicalism; it does not point us toward a realm of general,
physically nonsupervenient facts.

4. Taylor (1962, p. 3) writes: "a great many human actions are preceded by perception, and it is commonly believed that such actions are, by virtue of the preceding
perception, essentially different from others, the so-called 'unconsciously motivated'
actions. It is assumed that the former are 'guided' by perception while the latter are
not. Indeed the truth of this proposition appears self-evident. Nevertheless I propose
to doubt it."

5. It may seem strange that perception could prompt responses without first eliciting
a conscious recognition that things are such and such, where their being such and
such provides a reason for the response. But quite a lot of work suggests that this is
so. It can even happen in the extreme cases that subjects are perceptually prompted
to respond in a manner that fails to make sense on the basis of their conscious
reports. Subjects who prove incapable of distinguishing between letter-boxes with
different orientations (north–south, east–west, etc.) can nevertheless adjust their
hands appropriately in seeking to insert a letter (Kelly forthcoming). And subjects
who are subjected to a visual illusion that makes one disk seem bigger than another
of equal size—this is what they report—still adjust their grip as if they were free of
that illusion when asked to reach out and grasp one or other of the disks (Milner and
Goodale 1995).

6. I was introduced to akinetopsia, and to much else, through my association with
the McDonnell Project in Philosophy and the Neurosciences, directed by Kathleen
Akins from Simon Fraser University. I am very grateful for helpful observations
received in exchanges with David Braddon-Mitchell, Frank Jackson, Sean Kelly, Victoria McGeer, Eric Myin, Alva Noë, and Michael Ridge; for detailed comments given
by Laura Schroeter and Daniel Stoljar; and for discussions of presentations made at
the University of Queensland, the University of Michigan, and the Tucson Consciousness Conference, 2002.

References

Bechara, A., H. Damasio, D. Tranel, and A. R. Damasio (1997). "Deciding advanta-
geously before knowing the advantageous strategy." *Science* 275: 1293–1295.

Block, N. (1990). "Inverted Earth." *Philosophical Perspectives* 4: 52–79.

Braddon-Mitchell, D., and F. Jackson (1996). *Philosophy of Mind and Cognition.*
Oxford: Blackwell.

Clark, A. (1999). "A Case Where Access Implies Qualia." *Analysis* 60: 30–38.

Gazzaniga, M. S., et al. (1998). *Cognitive Neuroscience.* New York: Norton.

Gibson, J. J. (1964). "Introduction to Ivo Kohler 'The Formation and Transformation of the Perceptual World.'" *Psychological Issues* 3(4): 5–13.

Hardin, C. L. (1997). Reinverting the Spectrum. In *Readings on Color*, volume 1: *The Philosophy of Color*. Eds. A. Byrne and D. R. Hilbert. Cambridge, Mass.: The MIT Press: 289–301.

Harman, G. (1990). "The Intrinsic Quality of Experience." *Philosophical Perspectives* 4: 31–52.

Hurley, S. (1998). *Consciousness in Action*. Cambridge, Mass.: Harvard University Press.

Jackson, F. (1982). "Epiphenomenal Qualia." *Philosophical Quarterly* 32: 127–136. Reprinted in this volume.

Jackson, F. (1986). "What Mary Didn't Know." *Journal of Philosophy* 83: 291–295. Reprinted in this volume.

Jackson, F. (1998). *From Metaphysics to Ethics: A Defence of Conceptual Analysis*. Oxford: Oxford University Press.

Kagan, S. (1989). *The Limits of Morality*. Oxford: Oxford University Press.

Kelly, S. D. (forthcoming). "The Logic of Motor Intentional Activity." *Ratio*.

Kohler, I. (1961). "Experiments with Goggles." *Scientific American* 206 (May): 62–72.

Kohler, I. (1964). "The Formation and Transformation of the Perceptual World." *Psychological Issues* 3(4, monograph 12): 1–173.

Lewis, D. (1983). *Philosophical Papers*, Vol 1. Oxford, Oxford University Press.

Lewis, D. (1990). What Experience Teaches. In *Mind and Cognition: A Reader*. Ed. W. G. Lycan. Cambridge, Mass.: Blackwell: 499–519. Reprinted in this volume.

Lewis, D. (1995). "Should a Materialist Believe in Qualia?" *Australasian Journal of Philosophy* 73: 140–144.

Milner, A. D., and M. Goodale (1995). *The Visual Brain in Action*. Oxford: Oxford University Press.

Myin, E. (2001). "Color and the Duplication Assumption." *Synthese* 129: 61–77.

Myin, E., and J. K. O'Regan (2002). "Perceptual Consciousness, Access to Modality and Skill Theories." *Journal of Consciousness Studies* 9: 27–45.

O'Regan, J. K., and A. Noë (forthcoming). "A Sensorimotor Account of Vision and Visual Consciousness." *Behavioral and Brain Sciences* 24.

Perry, J. (1979). "The Problem of the Essential Indexical." *Noûs* 13: 3–21.

Pettit, P. (1993). "A Definition of Physicalism." *Analysis* 53: 213–223.

Pettit, P. (1998). "Practical Belief and Philosophical Theory." *Australasian Journal of Philosophy* 76: 15–33.

Pettit, P. (1999). "A Theory of Normal and Ideal Conditions." *Philosophical Studies* 96: 21–44.

Pettit, P. (2003). "Looks as Powers." *Philosophical Issues* (supp. to *Noûs*) 13: 221–252.

Sellars, W. (1997). *Empiricism and the Philosophy of Mind.* Cambridge, Mass.: Harvard University Press.

Smith, M., and D. Stoljar (1998). "Global Response-dependence and Noumenal Realism." *Monist* 81: 85–111.

Taylor, J. G. (1962). *The Behavioral Basis of Perception.* New Haven, Conn.: Yale University Press.

Thompson, E. (1995). *Colour Vision: A Study in Cognitive Science and the Philosophy of Perception.* London: Routledge.

Zeki, S. (1993). *A Vision of the Brain.* Oxford: Blackwell Scientific.

7 Knowing What It Is Like: The Ability Hypothesis and the Knowledge Argument

Michael Tye

Mary, as the familiar story goes (Jackson 1982), is imprisoned in a black-and-white room. Never having been permitted to leave it, she acquires information about the world outside from the black-and-white books her captors have made available to her, from the black-and-white television sets attached to external cameras, and from the black-and-white monitor screens hooked up to banks of computers. As time passes, Mary acquires more and more information about the physical aspects of color and color vision. She comes to know all the familiar color names and the objects to which they apply, the physical character of the surfaces of those objects, the way the light is reflected, the changes in the retina and the optic nerve as different colors are perceived, the physical changes in the visual cortex. Eventually, she becomes the world's leading authority on color and color vision. Indeed she comes to know *all* the physical facts pertinent to everday colors and color vision.

Still, as the years go by, she becomes more and more dissatisfied. She wonders to herself: What do people in the outside world *experience* when they see the various colors? *What is it like* for them to see red or green? No matter how often she reads her books or how long she spends examining the printouts from her computers, she still can't answer these questions fully.[1] One day her captors release her. She is free at last to see things with their real colors (and free too to scrub off the awful black-and-white paint that covers her body). She steps outside her room into a garden full of flowers. "So, that is what it is like to experience red," she exclaims, as she sees a red rose. "And that," she adds, looking down at the grass, "is what it is like to experience green."

Mary here seems to make some important discoveries. She seems to find out things she did not know before. How can that be, if, as seems possible at least in principle, she has all the physical information there is to have about color and color vision—that is, if she knows all the pertinent physical facts?

One popular explanation among philosophers (so-called "qualia freaks") is that that there is a realm of subjective, phenomenal qualities associated with color, qualities the intrinsic nature of which Mary comes to discover upon her release, as she herself undergoes the various new color experiences. Before she left her room, she only knew the objective, physical basis of those subjective qualities, their causes and effects, and various relations of similarity and difference. She had no knowledge of the subjective qualities in themselves.

This explanation is not available to the physicalist. If what it is like for someone to experience red is one and the same as some physical quality, then Mary already knows *that* while in her room. Likewise, for experiences of the other colors. For Mary knows all the pertinent physical facts. What, then, can the physicalist say?

Some physicalists respond that knowing what it is like is know-how and nothing more. Mary acquires certain abilities—for example, the ability to recognize red things by sight alone, the ability to imagine a green expanse. She does *not* come to know any new information, any new facts about color, any new qualities. This is the view of David Lewis. In the postcript to "Mad Pain and Martian Pain," he comments:

... knowing what it is like isn't the possession of information at all. It isn't the elimination of any hitherto open possibilities. Rather, knowing what it is like is the possession of abilities: abilities to recognize, abilities to imagine, abilities to predict one's behavior by imaginative experiments. (1983, p. 131)

In a similar vein, in his essay "What Experience Teaches," Lewis says:

The ability hypothesis says that knowing what an experience is like just *is* the possession of these abilities to remember, imagine, and recognize.... It isn't knowing-that. It's knowing-how. (1990, p. 516)

Lawrence Nemirow holds the same (or almost the same) view:

Knowing what an experience is like is the same as knowing how to imagine having the experience. (1990, p. 495)

Is the ability hypothesis true? Moreover, if it is true, is it really the case that captive Mary poses no problem for physicalism? In what follows, I argue that the answer to both of these questions is "No." I also propose an alternative hybrid account of knowing what it is like that ties it conceptually both to knowing-that and to knowing-how. Given this account, I maintain, the physicalist still has a satisfactory response to the case of Mary and the knowledge argument.[2]

1.1   The Hypothesis Clarified

Lewis identifies knowing what an experience is like with certain abilities. What exactly are these abilities supposed to be? To begin with, there is the ability to remember the experience in question. Suppose you smell a skunk for the first time, and you thereby learn what it is like to smell a skunk. Afterward, you can remember the experience. Moreover, by remembering it, you can imaginatively recreate it. This will be the case, even if, as Lewis notes, you eventually forget the occasion on which you had the experience. By having the experience of smelling a skunk, you gain new abilities to remember and imagine.

Included within the ability to imagine is more than just the ability to imagine the experience you underwent earlier. After seeing something red, for example, and seeing something yellow, you are able to imagine something red with yellow spots, even if you have never seen anything red with yellow spots. By imagining certain situations you could not imagine before, you also gain the ability to predict with a fair degree of confidence what you would do were the situations to arise. For example, having seen the color purple, you can now imagine how you would likely react if you were offered a purple shirt to wear.

Another important ability you gain is the ability to recognize the experience when it comes again. Lewis says:

If you taste Vegemite on another day [your second encounter with it], you will probably know that you have met the taste once before. And if, while tasting Vegemite, you know that it is Vegemite that you are tasting, then you will be able to put the name to the experience if you have it again. (1990, p. 515)

These abilities—to remember, imagine, and recognize—constitute knowing what it is like, in Lewis view. There is no claim that you *could* not possibly have these abilities without having the relevant experiences. After all, you might acquire them by some possible future neurophysiology or by magic. The point is that, given how the world actually works, lessons alone won't do the trick, no matter how complicated they become. Experience, as Lewis puts it, is the best teacher about what a new experience is like.

1.2   The Three Ls (Levin, Lycan, and Loar): Some Unpersuasive Objections to the Ability Hypothesis

Janet Levin suggests that the ability hypothesis has a number of undesirable consequences. She comments:

First of all, it would be perverse to claim that bare experience can provide us only with practical abilities.... By being shown an unfamilar color, I acquire information about its similarities and compatibilities with other colors, and its effects on other of our mental states: surely I seem to be acquiring certain facts about that color and the visual experience of it. (1990, p. 479)

This seems to me to miss the point. It is certainly true that *I* can gain information about a color I have never seen before by experiencing it. The real question, however, is whether Mary could or whether I could in a comparable situation. In actual fact, I myself do not know all the relevant physical facts; so, of course, *I* can learn things about similarities and differences and causes and effects by undergoing new color experiences. Mary's situation is different, however. Arguably, she already knows all such relations for the case of color even though she does not know what it is like to experience the various colors. As Lewis observes,

Maybe Mary knows enough to triangulate each color experience exactly in a network of resemblances, or in many networks of resemblance in different respects, while never knowing what any node of any network is like. (1990, p. 502)

The ability hypothesis has it that Mary's failure to know what any node in any network is like consists in her lacking certain crucial abilities. Nothing in Levin's first objection undercuts this claim.

Levin has a second objection:

... it is not implausible to suppose that experience is the *only* source of at least some of these facts.... [H]ow *does* one convey the taste of pineapple to someone who has not yet tried it, and does that first taste not dramatically increase, if not fully constitute, the knowledge of what the taste of pineapple is?

Again, this seems uncompelling. The first taste of pineapple provides one with knowledge of what the taste of pineapple is like, as everyone agrees. In Lewis's view (1990, p. 519), the expression "what experience *E* is like" denotes experience *E*. So, Lewis can happily grant that knowledge of what the taste of pineapple is like is knowledge of the taste of pineapple, of what that taste is.[3] The real issue concerns the *kind* of knowledge acquired here.

Lewis says that it is knowledge-how. Having tasted pineapple, one has the ability to remember what the taste of pineapple is, to imagine the taste, and so on. Levin evidently takes the opposing view. But she has not given us a clear reason in her second objection for taking her side.

Levin's final objection follows:

... there seem to be important cognitive differences between ourselves and those incapable of sharing our experiences. It would seem extremely natural to explain this by appeal to differences in our knowledge of the facts about experience: indeed what other explanation could there be? (1990, p. 479)

The obvious reply by the advocate of the ability hypothesis is that the difference can be explained by differences in cognitive abilities. If you have never experienced a certain experience E, you lack the ability to remember E, to recognize E when it comes again, to imagine E.

All of the above objections by Levin to the ability hypothesis are endorsed by Lycan (1996). He has some further objections of his own, none of which seems to me very persuasive. I shall briefly discuss four.

Lycan tells us that instances of "S knows wh- ..." are closely related to "S knows that ..." For example, "I know where Tom is" is true by virtue of my knowing that Tom is in such-and-such place. Likewise, "You know who Bill Clinton is" is true by virtue of your knowing that Bill Clinton is so-and-so (e.g., the president of the United States). This model leads Lycan to propose that "S knows what it is like to see blue" means (roughly): "S knows that it is like Q to see blue," where 'Q' names the pertinent phenomenal quality. So, according to Lycan, the "knowing what it is like" locution does not pick out an ability at all.

Presumably Lycan introduces the name 'Q' into the proposed analysis rather than an indexical for a phenomenal quality, since one can know what it is like to experience blue at times at which one is not experiencing it and hence at times at which one does not know that experiencing blue is like *this*. But the presence of a qualia name within a propositional attitude context creates a difficulty. If I can know that Hesperus is a planet without knowing that Phosphorus is a planet, even though 'Hesperus' and 'Phosphorus' are coreferential, I can surely likewise know that seeing blue is like Q without knowing that seeing blue is like R, or vice versa, even though 'Q' and 'R' denote the same phenomenal quality. So, which name is the appropriate one for the analysis? Presumably whichever name S antecedently knows or introduces for the relevant phenomenal quality. Still, what if S

neither introduces a name nor knows one already? This surely does not
preclude S from knowing what it is like to see blue. Moreover, even if S has
a suitable name, she can satisfy Lycan's analysans without satisfying the
analysandum.

Consider again Mary. Arguably, as Lewis suggests, Mary knows enough to
triangulate each color experience within a network of resemblances. Hence,
she knows of the experience of indigo, for example, that it is like seeing
blue. If she names the former experience 'Q', Mary knows that seeing blue
is like Q. However, Mary does not know what it is like to see blue (or indigo) until she leaves her cell. This objection, I might add, also refutes the
suggestion that 'S knows what it is like to see blue' means 'There is a phenomenal quality (or state) such that S knows that seeing blue is like it'.

So Lycan has not shown that 'knowing what it's like' sentences are analyzable as 'knowing-that' sentences. Nor is it obvious how to revise Lycan's
proposal satisfactorily.

A rather different objection Lycan raises is that comparisons can be made
between what it is like to experience one thing (e.g., hydrogen sulphide)
and what it is like to experience another (e.g., rotten eggs). What it's like,
then, is a matter of fact. "The facts in question per se are not about imagining but about actually smelling," Lycan asserts, "[a]nd what is factual is
propositional" (1996, p. 99).

It seems to me that Lewis would deny none of this. He explicitly allows
that color experiences can be compared, and also that what it is like to taste
Vegemite can be compared to what it is like to taste Marmite (Lewis 1990,
pp. 501–502). He explicitly asserts that what experience E is like is the same
as E. So, what it's like, according to Lewis, is a matter of fact. The issue, to
repeat what I said earlier, concerns *knowledge* of what it's like. Lycan's argument for the conclusion that the relevant knowledge is propositional is a
non sequitur.[4]

Lycan has another objection from success or failure. If knowing what it is
like to experience red is largely being able to imagine experiencing red, the
imagining here must be accurate. I do not know what it is like to experience red, if, when I take myself to be imagining it, I am really visualizing
blue. From this, Lycan concludes:

... there is such a thing as getting 'what it's like' right, representing truly rather than
falsely, from which it seems to follow that 'knowing what it's like' is knowing a
truth. (1990, p. 99)

This is a blatant non sequitur. From the fact that the abilities with which knowing what it is like is identified are abilities to be in certain propositional states, it certainly does *not* follow that knowing what it is like is knowing a truth. What follows is that knowing what it's like consists in abilities, the exercise of which demands (at the time of exercise) the representation of certain truths. So what?

Lycan also objects that the ability hypothesis leaves us without a satisfactory explanation of why we have the abilities it describes. Consider our ability to visualize red. How is this best explained? According to Lycan, the answer is that we have factual knowledge of what it is like to experience red. No such explanation is available to Lewis.

This again seems to me inconclusive. Lewis can respond that we have the ability to visualize red because we have experienced red, and we can generate a mental image of red from a suitable memory representation of the experience. Of course, the ability to generate images from memory representations itself needs some sort of explanation. However, this explanation (which lies within the domain of cognitive science) is not obviously one that need appeal to factual knowledge of what it is like to see red. For it is not at all obvious that the relevant memory representations will be propositional at all. One alternative possibility is that they are stored representations with a picture-like format.[5]

The third objector to the ability hypothesis, Brian Loar (1990), cites two objections. His initial complaint (echoed again by Lycan 1996) is as follows:

One can have knowledge not only of the form 'pains feel like such and such' but also of the form '*if* pains feel like such and such then Q'. Perhaps you could get away with saying that the former expresses (not a genuine judgement but) the mere possession of recognitional know-how. There seems however no comparable way of accounting for the embedded occurrence of 'feels like such and such' in the latter; it seems to introduce a predicate with a distinct content. (1990, p. 96)

It is not easy to evaluate this objection since Lewis and Nemirow focus on the locution 'knows what it is like', not the locution 'feels like such and such'. Their claim is simply that the former expresses an ability. Still, let us take a concrete example: Suppose I have never felt any pains before, and I remark about my current experience (P): "If pains feel like *this*, then I do not want to feel pain ever again." As noted earlier, Lewis claims that 'what experience E is like' denotes E. So, in Lewis's view, (P) may be recast as simply 'If this is pain, then I do not want to experience it again'.[6]

What is supposed to be the problem here? No one who endorses the ability hypothesis should deny that the final quoted sentence expresses a genuine judgment. Lewis, for example, is a realist about pain. Pain, in his view, is both a brain state and a functional state (1983a). Abilities enter only with respect to *knowing what pain is like*. One's knowledge of the state of pain, when one knows what it is like, consists in the possession of certain cognitive abilities, all of which pertain to that state (e.g., the ability to recognize *it* when it comes again, the ability to imagine *it*, and so forth).

So far so good, then, for the ability hypothesis. But Loar has one further objection:

> For many conceptions of phenomenal qualities, there simply is no candidate for an independently mastered term, instances of which one then proceeds to learn how to recognize: my conception of a peculiar way my left knee feels when I run (a conception that occurs predicatively in various judgments) is not my knowing how to apply an independently mastered predicate. (1990, p. 86)

The obvious riposte is: Whoever said that the conceptions pertinent to the relevant abilities must be ones that correlate neatly with linguistic terms? If I know the way my left knee feels when I run, then, according to the ability theorist, I must have certain abilities. These abilities (to recognize, to imagine) require conceptions. But the conceptions need not be ones that their subjects can articulate publicly in language. Of course, if Loar here has in mind terms in the language of thought, then this response is inappropriate. But Loar's initial claim now needs defense. For why should the ability theorist accept that there are no suitable terms in the language of thought, terms that are deployed when the pertinent abilities are exercised?

Still, there is, I believe, a real difficulty lurking here in the background for the ability hypothesis. It is to the development of this difficulty that I turn in the next section.

1.3 The Problem as I See It

Human sensory experience is enormously rich. Take color experience. There is a plenitude of detail here that goes far beyond our concepts. Humans can experience an enormous number of subtly different colors, something on the order of ten million, according to some estimates. But we have names for only a few of these colors, and we also have no stored representations in memory for most colors. There simply isn't enough room.

My experience of red_{19}, for example, is phenomenally different from my experience of red_{21}, even though I have no stored memory representations of these specific hues and hence no such concepts as the concepts red_{19} and red_{21}. This is why I cannot go into a paint store and reliably identify a color on a chart as *exactly* matching the precise hue of my dining room walls. I possess the concept *red*, of course, and I exercise it when I recognize something as red, but I lack the concepts for determinate hues. My ordinary color judgments are, of necessity, far less discriminating than my experiences of color. Human memory simply isn't up to the task of capturing the wealth of detail found in the experiences. Beliefs or judgments abstract from the details and impose more general categories. Sensory experience is the basis for many beliefs or judgments, but it is far, far richer.

This point is not restricted to color, of course. The same is true for our sensory experiences of sounds, to mention another obvious example. They, too, admit of many more fine-grained distinctions than our stored representations of sounds in memory. Experiences of shapes are likewise nonconceptual. Presented with an inkblot, for example, Mary will likely have an experience of a shape for which she has no corresponding concept.[7]

When Mary first sees the rose and exclaims, "So, that is what it is like to see red," she certainly acquires certain abilities, as Lewis and Nemirow suppose. She is now able to recognize red things by sight; she can identify the experience of red when it comes again; afterward, she can remember the experience of red; she can imagine what it is for something to be red. So far no obvious difficulty. But she knows more than just what it is like to experience red. As she stares at the rose, it is also true of her at that time that she knows what it is like to experience the particular determinate hue of red—call it 'red_{17}'—she is seeing. Of course, she does not know that hue *as* red_{17}. Her conception of it is indexical; she thinks of it only as *that* shade of red. But she certainly knows what it is like to experience that particular hue *at the time at which she is experiencing it.*

What is the new ability that Mary acquires here? She is not now able to recognize things that are red_{17} as red_{17} by sight. Ex hypothesi, Mary is one of us, a human being. She lacks the concept red_{17}. Nor is she able to recognize things other than the rose as having that very determinate color (whatever it is). She has no mental template that is sufficiently fine-grained to permit her to identify the experience of red_{17} when it comes again. Presented with two items (one red_{17} and the other red_{18}) in a series of tests, she cannot say with any accuracy which experience her earlier experience of the rose matches. Sometimes she picks one; at other times she picks the other. Nor is she able afterward to imagine things as having hue, red_{17}, or as having that very shade of red the rose had; and for precisely the same reason.

Mary lacks the abilities Lewis lists. But, as she stares at the rose, she certainly knows what it is like to experience the particular shade of red she is experiencing. If you doubt this, suppose we inform Mary that she is seeing red_{17}. She replies, "So, this is what it is like to see red_{17}. I had always wondered. Seventeen, you see, is my favorite number; and red the color of my mother's favorite dress." We then say to her, "No, you don't know what it is like to see red_{17}. For you won't remember it accurately when you take your eyes from the rose; you won't be able to recognize it when it comes again; you won't be able to imagine the experience of seeing red_{17}." Should Mary then admit that she doesn't really know what it is like to see red_{17} even while she is staring at the rose? She won't know it later certainly. But it seems intuitively bizarre to deny that she knows it *at the time*.

Perhaps it is correct to say that Mary never really *learns* what it is like to see red_{17}, for learning arguably requires not just knowledge but the retention of that knowledge. You haven't learned that the distance of the earth from the sun is 93 million miles if you only know it at the moment your teacher tells you. You need to retain that knowledge to have genuinely learned what the distance is. But the knowledge argument against physicalism is just that: an argument from knowledge. It makes no essential use of the concept of learning. The main claim is that Mary comes to *know* things she didn't know before even though she knows all the physical facts.

I conclude that the ability hypothesis, as elaborated by Lewis, does not afford us a satisfactory *general* account of knowing what it is like. The knowledge argument still presents physicalism with a very serious difficulty.

1.4 A Possible Revision to the Ability Hypothesis

When Mary leaves her room, she gains certain abilities. Among them is the ability to recognize certain experiences when they come again. Another more basic ability is the ability to *cognize* the experience for as long as it is present. The latter ability, it might be said, is one Mary possesses even with respect to the experience of red$_{17}$. For when Mary first sees that particular shade of red, she does have the ability then and there to cognize her experience as an experience with *that* phenomenal character. Perhaps knowing what it is like should be identified not with the cluster of abilities Lewis cites—for they may all be lacking while knowing what it is like is present—but rather with the more basic ability to apply an indexical concept to the phenomenal character of her experience via introspection.

This, it seems to me, still won't save the ability hypothesis. Mary, when she is shown the rose for the first time, may be distracted. Perhaps she is still thinking hard about a theoretical problem that occupied her in her black-and-white room. The fact that she is distracted does not entail that she doesn't undergo any color experience any more than the fact that I am sometimes distracted by philosophical thoughts when I drive entails that I no longer see the road and the cars ahead. I am able at such times to attend to my visual sensations even though I do not do so. But the visual sensations are there all right. How else do I keep the car on the road? And the same points apply *mutatis mutandis* to Mary. She has her eyes open. The rose is immediately before her. She is not cognitively blocked from her visual experiences by a psychological impairment. She *can* introspect those experiences even if, in fact, she does not do so.

Now if Mary sees the rose, as I see the road ahead in the driving example, then she must have a visual experience caused by it. If, say, she has massive damage to the visual cortex, then it won't matter what activity the rose elicits in the cells of her retina: she won't have any visual experiences and she won't *see* anything.[8] But if Mary has visual *experiences*, then she must have consciousness at the phenomenal level. There must be something it is like for her as she sees the rose. Her state must have a certain phenomenal character. What it is like for her is something she can become aware of by introspection. Had she paid attention to her visual state, she would have been conscious of it in the higher-order sense. She would have formed a thought about it. She would have been aware that she was undergoing that visual experience. But, in fact, Mary is distracted. And being distracted, she does not actually apply *any* concept at all to her experience. In these circumstances, she clearly does not know what it is like to have the experience in question. For she has no conception, no cognitive awareness of her phenomenal state. But she certainly has the *ability* to mentally point to the phenomenal character of her experience with an indexical concept via introspection. So, here the proposed ability is present, but knowing what it is like is absent. In the earlier examples, the reverse had been true. Cut the pie any way you like, then, the ability hypothesis is false.

Of course, I am not claiming that knowing what it is like is never the possession of abilities. In particular, I am not claiming that in those cases where the subject has the appropriate concept knowing what it is like is not the possession of abilities. Nothing that I have said undercuts the claim that knowing what it is like to experience red, for example, is a cluster of abilities of the sort Lewis proposes. But the 'is' here cannot be the 'is' of identity. Knowing what it is like to experience red and knowing what it is like to experience red$_{17}$ have something in common: they are both cases of knowing what it is like. This common feature is lost if knowing what it is like to experience red is literally one and the same as the possession of certain abilities.

It is also worth stressing that even if some specimens of knowing what it is like could be identified with various abilities, this would not help the physicalist with the knowledge argument. For if there are *any* examples of knowing what it is like that do not conform to some version of the ability hypothesis, then physicalism is threatened. And that there are such examples is what I have been primarily at pains to show.

I now want to make the case for something stronger: that physicalism is threatened by the knowledge argument, even if knowing what is is like *is* an ability or cluster of abilities. If this is correct, then the ability hypothesis has less significance than is usually supposed. Consider again Mary as she remarks, "So, this is what it is like to experience red." Intuitively, in making this remark, Mary is expressing a discovery that she has made. But what has she discovered? Well, she now knows what it is like to experience red. So, on the ability hypothesis, she has acquired some know-how. But that know-how she retains even after she stops having any experience of red; and intuitively, there is a cognitive difference between Mary at the time at which she makes her remark and Mary later on, after the experience ceases (at least at those times at which she is not exercising any of the pertinent abilities). If we agree with Lewis that what experience E is like is the same as E, then the difference seems well captured by saying that while she is attending to her experience, Mary has knowledge-that she didn't have before, knowledge (in part) that this is the experience of red.[9] Moreover, even if we distinguish what experience E is like from E, we can still say that Mary has knowledge-that she didn't have before, namely, knowledge that this is the phenomenal character of the experience of red. So, either way, Mary does make a genuine propositional discovery. And that, according to advocates of the knowledge argument, spells trouble for physicalism.

1.5 More on Knowing What It Is Like and the Knowledge Argument

In the case described in the section above in which Mary is distracted, Mary has knowledge of how to do something. She knows how to mentally point to the phenomenal character of her experience in introspection. But, being distracted, she doesn't exercise her know-how. Were she to do so, she would turn her knowledge-how into knowledge-that. Intuitively, she would come to know that *that* is the phenomenal character of her experience. And in so doing, she would come to know what it is like to have an experience of that sort. So, introspective knowing-that is sufficient for knowing what it is like. Such knowing-that is not necessary, however. One need not be paying attention to one's current experiences to know what it is like to experience red. Intuitively, in such a case, it is necessary and sufficient to have abilities of the sort Lewis describes. It seems, then, that knowing what it is like is best captured by a disjunction of introspective knowing-that and knowing-how along the following lines:

S knows what it is like to undergo experience E = df Either S is now undergoing E, and S has knowledge-that with respect to the phenomenal character of E obtained via current introspection, or S has the Lewis abilities with respect to E.

This proposal is similar to one I made some years ago (Tye 1986), and it still seems to me to do more justice to our ordinary understanding of the expression 'know what it is like' than does any other I have seen. But prima facie it leaves the physicalist with a problem. For how can it now be denied that Mary gains some new propositional knowledge when she leaves her room as she introspects her new experiences—for example, knowledge that this is the experience of red, while viewing a ripe tomato; or knowledge, on the same occasion, that she is having an experience of this phenomenal type? The worry, of course, is that physicalism cannot allow such discoveries.

Let us focus first on Mary's discovery that this is the experience of red. It will not suffice for the physicalist to try to explain this discovery by saying simply that, confined to her cell, Mary can form no indexical conception of the experience of red or any particular shade of red. For if the experience of red is physical state, then it is not at all obvious that captive Mary cannot perceptually demonstrate it, as it is tokened in others outside her room— given the appropriate finely focused, high-tech, viewing apparatus.

A more promising strategy is to argue that Mary, while she is confined, lacks the phenomenal concept *red*.[10] This is not to say that she attaches no meaning to the term 'red'. On the contrary, given the information at her disposal, she can use the term correctly in a wide range of cases. Still, the concept Mary exercises here is nonphenomenal. She does not know what it is like to experience red; and intuitively knowing what it is like to have that experience is necessary for possession of the phenomenal concept *red*.[11] It follows that there is a thought that Mary cannot think to herself while in her room, namely the thought *that this is the experience of red*, where the concept *red*, as it is exercised in this thought, is the one she acquires upon her release after seeing red things. But if she cannot think this thought as she languishes in her cell, she cannot know its content then. Since she does know that content upon her release, she discovers something. Experience is her teacher even though, according to the physicalist, there is nothing nonphysical in the world that makes her new thought true.

Perhaps it will be replied that if Mary acquires various phenomenal concepts pertaining to color experience upon her release, then she cannot really know all there is to know about the nature of color vision from within her room; for where a difference between the old and the new concepts obtains, a difference in the world between the properties these concepts stand for or express must also obtain. Some of these properties she knew in her cell; others she became cognizant of only upon her release. That I simply deny, however. Properties individuate no more finely than causal powers, but conceptual differences exist even between concepts that are analytically equivalent. So, conceptual differences need not be mirrored in worldly differences. Sense is one thing, reference another.[12]

Consider now Mary's thought *that she is having an experience with this phenomenal character*, as she introspects her first experience of red. Here it is certainly the case that she cannot think this thought truly, while she is held in her room. For the concept *this*, exercised in her thought, refers to the phenomenal character associated with her experiencing red and Mary, in her room, never experiences red. So, once again, when she thinks a thought of this sort on the appropriate occasion, she is making a genuine discovery.

The position sketched above assumes that demonstrative thoughts and thought-contents are partly individuated by the item picked out by the demonstrative and partly by the various general concepts and associated modes of presentation exercised in the thoughts. That real-world items play a role in individuating indexical thoughts and thought contents is an externalist claim that is very widely accepted, and one which needs no further argument here. That concepts and modes of presentation are also involved in the individuation of thought-contents should also be un-controversial, given one sense of the term *content*—the sense in which thought-content is whatever information that-clauses provide that suffices for the purposes of even the most demanding rationalizing explanation. In this sense, what I think, when I think that Cicero was an orator, is not what I think when I think that Tully was an orator. This is precisely why it is possible to discover that Cicero is Tully. The thought that Cicero was an orator differs from the thought that Tully was an orator not at the level of truth-conditions—the same singular proposition is partly constitutive of the content of both—but at the level of concepts and modes of presenta-tion. The one thought exercises the concept *Cicero*; the other the concept *Tully*. The concepts have the same reference; but because they present the referent in different ways, the two thoughts can play different roles in rationalizing explanation.

So, there is no difficulty in holding that Mary comes to know some new things upon her release, while already knowing all the pertinent real-world physical facts, even though the new experiences she undergoes and their introspectible qualities are wholly physical.[13] In an ordinary, everyday sense, Mary's knowledge increases. And that is all the physicalist needs to answer the knowledge argument.

Some philosophers (including Lewis) individuate thought contents more coarsely than I have above, as, for example, sets of possible worlds. On this view, the thought that $7 + 5 = 12$ has the very same content as the thought that all bachelors are unmarried. However, it seems intuitively undeniable that the event type, thinking that $7 + 5 = 12$, plays a different role in rationalizing explanation than the event type, thinking that all bachelors are unmarried. So, on this approach, thought-types cannot be individuated for the purposes of rationalizing explanations by their contents alone. Two different thought types can have the same content. Likewise for belief types.

It follows that even on this two-factor theory of thought-types (according to which thought-types are individuated by their contents plus some other factor), the physicalist can insist that there is a perfectly good sense in which Mary discovers that so-and-so is the case after she is released. For she comes to instantiate cognitive thought-types (knowing-that types) she did not instantiate before, even though, given her exhaustive knowledge of the physical facts, the contents of her thought-types before and after remain unchanged. And if Mary or anyone else knows that p at time t without knowing that p before t, then surely it is correct to say, in ordinary parlance, that the person has made a discovery at t.

My overall conclusion is that there is much that is right in the ability hypothesis, but that it cannot be the whole truth about the nature of knowing what it is like. Moreover, even if it were the whole truth, there would still be propositional cases of knowing, not themselves properly classifiable as knowing what it is like, that advocates of the knowledge argument might well take to refute physicalism. This should not overly concern the physicalist, however. Even with the demise of the ability hypothesis, these cases can be comfortably handled in the manner I have indicated. Either way, then, the knowledge argument can be answered.

Notes

1. For a real life case of a visual scientist (Knut Norby) who is an achromotope, see Sacks 1996, chapter 1.

2. Of course, the case of Mary is a threat not only to physicalism with respect to phenomenal qualities but also to functionalism: Mary has all the pertinent functional information, too. To simplify exposition, I focus on physicalism. But what I say applies *mutatis mutandis* to functionalism.

3. Nemirow (1990) takes a different view. His claim is that 'what E is like' is a syncategorematic part of the expression 'know what experience E is like'. This creates difficulties for him of a sort that Lewis can avoid.

4. A response of the same sort can be given to Lycan's argument from attempting-to-describe (1996, p. 98).

5. See, for example, Kosslyn 1980. These representations (in Kosslyn's view) are also importantly dissimilar from pictures.

6. For Lewis, pain and the feeling of pain are one and the same (Lewis 1983, p. 130).

7. For more on this topic, see chapters 3 and 4 of Tye 2000.

8. I ignore here blindsight. My remark is made with respect to normal, everyday seeing.

9. By parallel reasoning, we may infer that Mary has other new knowledge-that associated with her experience of red, notably knowledge that she is having an experience of this particular shade of red and knowledge that she is having an experience of this phenomenal type. The latter knowledge, incidentally, should be granted even by those who deny that what experience E is like is the same as E.

10. Those who take the view that inversion scenarios show that no phenomenal character need be shared by all actual and possible tokens of the experience of red will want to deny that Mary discovers *that this is the experience of red* and, correspondingly, that there is any such concept as the *phenomenal* concept *red*. This position is compatible with holding that Mary nonetheless makes some discoveries as she introspects her first experience of red: for example, *that this is R*, where the concept *R* is a phenomenal concept of the phenomenal character associated with the experience of red in Mary, and *that I am having an experience with this phenomenal character*. The concept *R* is one Mary lacks in her room. For a discussion of the latter discovery, see below, pp. 17–18. The former discovery may be handled in a way parallel to that given in the text for the discovery that this is the experience of red.

11. Phenomenal concepts are discussed in detail in chapter 2 of Tye 2000.

12. For more here, see chapter 2 of Tye 2000.

13. The term 'fact' is itself ambiguous. Sometimes it is used to pick out real-world states of affairs alone; sometimes it is used for such states of affairs under certain conceptualizations. When I speak of the physical facts here, I refer either to physical states of affairs alone or to those states of affairs under purely physical conceptualizations. (For more on 'fact', see Tye 1995.)

References

Jackson, F. 1982. "Epiphenomenal Qualia." *Philosophical Quarterly* 32: 127–136. Reprinted in this volume.

Lewis, D. 1983. "Mad Pain and Martian Pain." In his *Philosophical Papers*, vol. 1. Oxford: Oxford University Press.

———. 1990. "What Experiences Teaches." In *Mind and Cognition: A Reader*, ed. W. Lycan. Oxford: Blackwell. Reprinted in this volume.

okl.

Levin, J. 1990. "Could Love Be Like a Heat-Wave? Physicalism and the Subjective Character of Experience." In *Mind and Cognition: A Reader*, ed. W. Lycan. Oxford: Blackwell.

Loar, B. 1990. "Phenomenal States." In *Philosophical Perspectives* 4, ed. J. Tomberlin. Northridge, Calif.: Ridgeview.

Lycan, W. 1996. *Consciousness and Experience*. Cambridge, Mass.: The MIT Press.

Nemirow, L. 1990. "Physicalism and the Cognitive Role of Acquaintance." In *Mind and Cognition: A Reader*, ed. W. Lycan. Oxford: Blackwell.

Tye, M. 1986. "The Subjective Qualities of Experience." *Mind* 95: 1–17.

———. 1995. *Ten Problems of Consciousness*. Cambridge, Mass.: The MIT Press.

———. 2000. *Consciousness, Color, and Content*. Cambridge, Mass.: The MIT Press.

Part IV The Acquaintance Hypothesis

8 Knowing Qualia: A Reply to Jackson (with Postscript: 1997)

Paul M. Churchland

In a recent paper concerning the direct introspection of brain states (1985a) I leveled three criticisms against Frank Jackson's "knowledge argument" (Jackson 1982). At stake was his bold claim that no materialist account of mind can possibly account for all mental phenomena. Jackson has replied to those criticisms in "What Mary Didn't Know" (1986). It is to those replies, and to the issues that prompted them, that the present note is directed.

Jackson concedes the criticism I leveled at my own statement of his argument—specifically, that it involves an equivocation on 'knows about'—but he insists that my reconstruction does not represent the argument he wishes to defend. I accept his instruction, and turn my attention to the summary of the argument he provides at the bottom of p. 293 [p. 54, this volume]. Mary, you will recall, has been raised in innocence of any color experience, but has an exhaustive command of neuroscience.

1. Mary (before her release) knows everything physical there is to know about other people.
2. Mary (before her release) does not know everything there is to know about other people (because she *learns* something about them on her release).

3. There are truths about other people (and herself) which escape the physicalist story.

Regimenting further, for clarity's sake, yields the following:

1. $(x)[(Hx \& Px) \supset Kmx]$
2. $(\exists x)[Hx \& \sim Kmx]$ (namely, 'what it is like to see red')

3. $(\exists x)[Hx \& \sim Px]$

Here m = Mary; Kyx = y knows about x; Hx = x is about persons; Px = x is about something physical in character; and x ranges over 'knowables', generously construed so as not to beg any questions about whether they are propositional or otherwise in nature.

Thus expressed, the argument is formally valid: the salient move is a modus tollens that applies the second conjunct of premise (2), '$\sim Kmx$', to the waiting consequent of premise (1), 'Kmx'. The question now is whether the premises are jointly true, and whether the crucial notion 'Kmx' is univocal in both of its appearances. Here I am surprised that Jackson sees any progress at all with the above formulation, since I continue to see the same equivocation found in my earlier casting of his argument.

Specifically, premise (1) is plausibly true, within Jackson's story about Mary's color-free upbringing, only on the interpretation of 'knows about' that casts the object of knowledge as something propositional, as something adequately expressible in an English sentence. Mary, to put it briefly, gets 100 percent on every written and oral exam; she can pronounce on the truth of any given sentence about the physical characteristics of persons, especially the states of their brains. Her 'knowledge by description' of physical facts about persons is without lacunae.

Premise (2), however, is plausibly true only on the interpretation of 'knows about' that casts the object of knowledge as something nonpropositional, as something inarticulable, as something that is non-truth-valuable. What Mary is missing is some form of 'knowledge by acquaintance', acquaintance with a sensory character, prototype, or universal, perhaps.

Given this prima facie difference in the sense of 'knows about' or the kind of knowledge appearing in each premise, we are still looking at a prima facie case of an argument invalid by reason of equivocation on a critical term. Replace either of the 'K's above with a distinct letter, as acknowledgment of the ambiguity demands, and the inference to (3) evaporates. The burden of articulating some specific and unitary sense of 'knows about', and of arguing that both premises are true under that interpretation of the epistemic operator, is an undischarged burden that still belongs to Jackson.

It is also a *heavy* burden, since the resources of modern cognitive neurobiology already provide us with a plausible account of what the difference in the two kinds of knowledge amounts to, and of how it is possible to have the one kind without the other. Let me illustrate with a case distinct from that at issue, so as not to beg any questions.

Any competent golfer has a detailed representation—perhaps in his cerebellum, perhaps in his motor cortex—of a golf swing. It is a *motor* representation and it constitutes his 'knowing how' to *execute* a proper swing. The same golfer will also have a discursive representation of a golf swing— perhaps in his language cortex, or in the neighboring temporal and parietal regions—which allows him to describe a golf swing or perhaps draw it on paper. The motor and the discursive representations are quite distinct. Localized brain trauma, or surgery, could remove either one while sparing the other. Short of that, an inarticulate golf champion might have a superb representation of the former kind, but a feeble representation of the latter kind. And a physicist or sports physiologist might have a detailed and penetrating representation of the mechanics of a good swing, and yet be unable to duff the ball more than ten feet, by reason of lacking an adequate *motor* representation, of the desired behavioral sequence, in the brain areas that control his limbs. Indeed, if our physicist is chronically disabled in his motor capacities, he may have no motor representation of a golf swing whatsoever. In one medium of representation, his representational achievements on the topic may be complete, while in another medium of representation, he has nothing.

A contrast between 'knowing how' and 'knowing that' is one already acknowledged in common sense, and thus it is not surprising that some of the earliest replies to Jackson's argument (Nemirow 1980; Lewis 1983) tried to portray its equivocation in these familiar terms, and tried to explicate Mary's missing knowledge solely in terms of her missing some one or more *abilities* (to recognize red, to imagine red, etc.). While the approach is well motivated, this binary distinction in types of knowledge barely begins to suggest the range and variety of different sites and types of internal representation to be found in a normal brain. There is no reason why we must be bound by the crude divisions of our prescientific idioms when we attempt to give a precise and positive explication of the equivocation displayed in Jackson's argument. And there are substantial grounds for telling a somewhat different story concerning the sort of nondiscursive knowledge at issue. Putting caution and qualification momentarily aside, let me tell such a story.

In creatures with trichromatic vision (i.e., with three types of retinal cone), color information is coded as a pattern of spiking frequencies across the axonal fibers of the parvocellular subsystem of the optic nerve. That massive cable of axons leads to a second population of cells in a central body called the lateral geniculate nucleus (LGN), whose axonal projections lead in turn to the several areas of the visual cortex at the rear of the brain's cerebral hemispheres, to V1, V2, and ultimately to V4, which area appears especially devoted to the processing and representation of color information (Zeki 1980; Van Essen and Maunsell 1983; Hubel and Livingstone 1987). Human cognition divides a smooth continuum of color inputs into a finite number of prototypical categories. The laminar structure at V4 is perhaps the earliest place in the processing hierarchy to which we might ascribe that familiar taxonomy. A creature competent to make reliable color discriminations has there developed a representation of the range of familiar colors, a representation that appears to consist in a specific configuration of weighted synaptic connections meeting the millions of neurons that make up area V4.

That configuration of synaptic weights partitions the "activation-space" of the neurons in area V4: it partitions that abstract space into a structured set of subspaces, one for each prototypical color. Inputs from the eye will each occasion a specific pattern of activity across these cortical neurons, a pattern or vector that falls within one of those subspaces. In such a pigeonholing, it now appears, does visual recognition of a color consist (see P. M. Churchland 1989a, chapters 9 and 10, for the general theory of information processing here appealed to). This recognition depends upon the creature possessing a prior representation—a learned configuration of synapses meeting the relevant population of cells—that antecedently partitions the creature's visual taxonomy so it can respond selectively and appropriately to the flux of visual stimulation arriving from the retina and LGN.

This distributed representation is not remotely propositional or discursive, but it is entirely real. All trichromatic animals have one, even those without any linguistic capacity. It apparently makes possible the many abilities we expect from color-competent creatures: discrimination, recognition, imagination, and so on. Such a representation is presumably what a person with Mary's upbringing would lack, or possess only in stunted or incomplete form. Her representational space within the relevant area of neurons would contain only the subspace for black, white, and the intervening shades of gray, for the visual examples that have shaped her synaptic configuration were limited to these. There is thus more than just a clutch of abilities missing in Mary: there is a complex representation, a processing framework that deserves to be called cognitive, which she either lacks entirely or has in severely reduced form. There is indeed something she 'does not know'. Jackson's premise (2), we may assume, is thus true on these wholly materialist assumptions.

These same assumptions are entirely consistent with the further assumption that elsewhere in Mary's brain—in the language areas, for example—she has stored a detailed and even exhaustive set of discursive, propositional, truth-valuable representations of what goes on in people's brains during the experience of color, a set she has brought into being by the exhaustive reading of authoritative texts in a completed cognitive neuroscience. She may even be able to explain her own representational deficit, as sketched above, in complete neurophysical detail. Jackson's premise (1), we may thus assume, is also true on these wholly materialist assumptions.

The view sketched above is a live candidate for the correct story of sensory coding and sensory recognition. But whether or not it is true, it is at least a logical possibility. Accordingly, what we have sketched here is a consistent but entirely *physical* model (i.e., a model in which Jackson's conclusion is false) in which both of Jackson's premises are true under the appropriate interpretation. They can hardly entail a conclusion, then, that is inconsistent with physicalism. Their compossibility, on purely physicalist assumptions, resides in the different character and the numerically different medium of representation at issue in each of the two premises. Jackson's argument, to refile the charge, equivocates on 'knows about'.

An argument form with one invalid instance can be expected to have others. This was the point of a subsidiary objection in my 1985 paper: if valid, Jackson's argument, or one formally parallel, would also serve to refute the possibility of *substance dualism*. I did not there express my point with notable clarity, however, and I accept responsibility for Jackson's quite missing my intention. Let me try again.

The basic point is that the canonical presentation of the knowledge argument, as outlined above, would be just as valid if the predicate term 'P' were everywhere replaced by 'E'. And the resulting premises would be just as plausibly true if

i. 'E' stood for 'is about something ectoplasmic in character' (where 'ecto-plasm' is an arbitrary name for the dualist's nonphysical substance), and

ii. the story is altered so that Mary becomes an exhaustive expert on a completed *ectoplasmic* science of human nature.

The plausibility would be comparable, I submit, because a long discursive lecture on the objective, statable, law-governed properties of ectoplasm, whatever they might be, would be exactly as useful, or use*less*, in helping Mary to *know-by-acquaintance* 'what it is like to see red', as would a long discursive lecture on the objective, statable, law-governed properties of the physical matter of the brain. Even if substance dualism were true, therefore, and ectoplasm were its heroic principal, an exactly parallel "knowledge argument" would "show" that there are some aspects of consciousness that must forever escape the *ectoplasmic* story. Given Jackson's antiphysicalist intentions, it is at least an irony that the same form of argument should incidentally serve to blow substance dualism out of the water.

Though I am hardly a substance dualist (and neither is Jackson), I do regard substance dualism as a theoretical possibility, one that might conceivably succeed in explicating the psychological ontology of common sense in terms of the underlying properties and law-governed behavior of the nonmaterial substance it postulates. And I must protest that the parallel knowledge argument against substance dualism would be wildly unfair, for the very same reason that its analog against physicalism is unfair. It would equivocate on 'knows about'. It would be no more effective against dualism than it is against materialism.

The parallel under examination contains a further lesson. If it works at all, Jackson's argument works against physicalism not because of some defect that is unique to physicalism; it works because no amount of discursive knowledge, on *any* topic, will *constitute* the nondiscursive form of knowledge that Mary lacks. Jackson's argument is one instance of an indiscriminately anti*reductionist* form of argument. If it works at all, an analogue will work against any proposed reductive, discursive, objective account of the nature of our subjective experience, no matter what the reducing theory might happen to be. I see this as a further symptom of the logical pathology described earlier. Since the argument "works" for reasons that have nothing essential to do with physicalism, it should "work" against the explanatory aspirations of other ontologies as well. And so it does. The price of embracing Jackson's argument is thus dramatically higher than first appears. For it makes *any* scientific account of our sensory experience entirely impossible, no matter what the ontology employed.

We can appreciate the equivocation more deeply if we explore a version of Jackson's argument that does *not* equivocate on 'knows about'. The equivocation can quickly be closed, if we are determined to do so, and the results are revealing. Given that the problem is a variety in the possible forms of knowing, let us simply rewrite the argument with suitable quantification over the relevant forms of knowing. The first premise must assert that, for any knowable x, and for any form f of knowledge, if x is about humans and x is physical in character, then Mary knows(f) about x. The second premise is modified in the same modest fashion, and the conclusion is identical. Canonically,

1'. $(x)(f)[(Hx \text{ \& } Px) \supset K(f)mx]$
2'. $(\exists x)(\exists f)[Hx \text{ \& } \sim K(f)mx]$

3'. $(\exists x)[Hx \text{ \& } \sim Px]$

This argument is also formally valid, and its premises explicitly encompass whatever variety there may be in forms of knowing. What can we say about its soundness?

Assume that Mary has had the upbringing described in Jackson's story, and thus lacks any knowledge-by-acquaintance with 'what it is like to see red'. Premise (2') will then be true, as and for the reasons that Jackson's story requires. What will be the truth-value of premise (1') on these assumptions?

Premise (1') is now a very strong claim indeed, much stronger than the old premise (1), and a materialist will be sure to insist that it is false. The reason offered will be that, because of her deprived upbringing, Mary quite clearly *lacks one form* of knowledge of a certain physical aspect of people. Specifically, she lacks a proper configuration of synaptic connections meeting the neurons in the appropriate area of her visual cortex. She thus lacks an apropriately partitioned activation vector space across those neurons, and therefore has no representation, at that site, of the full range of sensory coding vectors that might someday come from the retina and the LGN. In other words, there is something physical about persons (their color sensations = their coding vectors in their visual pathways), and there is

some form of knowledge (an antecendently partitioned prelinguistic taxonomy), such that Mary lacks that form of knowledge of that aspect of
persons. Accordingly, premise (1') is false and the conclusion (3') is not
sustained.

From a materialist's point of view, it is obvious that (1') will be false on
the assumptions of Jackson's story. For that story denies her the upbringing
that normally provokes and shapes the development of the relevant representation across the appropriate population of cortical neurons. And so, of
course, there is a form of knowledge, of a physical aspect of persons, that
Mary does not have. As just illustrated, the materialist can even specify that
form of knowledge, and its objects, in neural terms. But this means that
premise (1'), as properly quantified at last, is false. Mary does *not* have
knowledge of everything physical about persons, in every way that is possible for her. (That is why premise [2'] is true.)

There is of course no guarantee that the materialist's account of sensations and sensory recognition is correct (although the experimental and
theoretical evidence for a view of this general kind continues to accumu-
late). But neither is Jackson in a position to insist that it must be mistaken.
That would beg the very question at issue: whether sensory qualia form a
metaphysically distinct class of phenomena beyond the scope of physical
science.

To summarize. If we write a deliberately nonequivocal form of Jackson's
argument, one that quantifies appropriately over all of the relevant forms
of knowledge, then the first premise must almost certainly be false under
the conditions of his own story. So, at any rate, is the materialist in a strong
position to argue. Jackson's expressed hope for "highly plausible premises"
is not realized in (1'). The original premise (1) was, of course, much more
plausible. But it failed to sustain a valid argument, and it was plausible only
because it failed to address all the relevant forms of knowledge.

My final objection to Jackson was aimed more at breaking the grip of the
ideology behind his argument than at the argument itself. That ideology
includes a domain of properties—the qualia of subjective experience—that
are held to be metaphysically distinct from the objective physical properties addressed by orthodox science. It is not a surprise then, on this view,
that one might know all physical facts, and yet be ignorant of some domain of these nonphysical qualia. The contrast between what is known

and what is not known simply reflects an antecendent metaphysical division in the furniture of the world.

But there is another way to look at the situation, one that finds no such division. Our capacity for recognizing a range of (currently) inarticulable features in our subjective experience is easily explained on materialist principles—the relevant sketch appears earlier in this essay.... Our discursive inarticulation on those features is no surprise either, and signifies nothing about their metaphysical status. Indeed, that veil of inarticulation may itself be swept aside by suitable learning. What we are now able spontaneously to report about our internal states and cognitive activities need not define the limit on what we might be able to report, spontaneously and accurately, if we were taught a more appropriate conceptual scheme in which to express our discriminations. In closing, let me again urge on Jackson this exciting possibility.

The intricacies of brain function may be subjectively opaque to us now, but they need not remain that way forever. Neuroscience may appear to be defective in providing a purely "third-person account" of mind, but only familiarity of idiom and spontaneity of conceptual response are required to make it a "first-person account" as well. What makes an account a "first-person account" is not the *content* of that account, but the fact that one has earned to *use* it as the vehicle of spontaneous conceptualization in introspection and self-description.

We all of us, as children, learned to use the framework of current folk psychology in this role. But it is entirely possible for a person or culture to learn and use some other framework in that role—the framework of cognitive neuroscience, perhaps. Given a deep and practiced familiarity with the developing idioms of cognitive neurobiology, we might learn to discriminate by introspection the coding vectors in our internal axonal pathways, the activation patterns across salient neural populations, and myriad other things besides.

Should that ever happen, it would then be obvious, to everyone who had made the conceptual shift, that a completed cognitive neuroscience would constitute not a pinched and exclusionary picture of human consciousness, one blind to the subjective dimension of self, as Jackson's argument suggests. Rather, it would be the vehicle of a grand reconstruction and expansion of our subjective consciousness, since it would provide us with a conceptual framework which, unlike folk psychology, is at last equal to the kinematical and dynamical intricacies of the world within. (See also P. M. Churchland 1979, section. 16; 1981.)

Real precedents for such a reformation can be drawn from our own history. We did not lose contact with a metaphysically distinct dimension of reality when we finally stopped seeing an immutable, sparkle-strewn quintessential crystal sphere each time we looked to the heavens, and began to see instead an infinite space of gas and dust and giant stars structured by gravitational attractions and violent nuclear processes. On the contrary, we now see far more than we used to, even with the unaided eye. The diverse 'colors' of the stars allow us to see directly their absolute temperatures. Stellar temperature is a function of stellar mass, so we are just as reliably seeing stellar masses. The intrinsic luminosity or brightness of a star is tightly tied to these same features, and thus is also visually available, no matter how bright or faint the star may appear from Earth. Its 'visual magnitude' or 'apparent' brightness is visually obvious also, of course, and the contrast between the apparent and the intrinsic brightnesses gives you the star's rough distance from Earth. In this way is the character and three-dimensional distribution of complex stellar objects in a volume of interstellar space hundreds of light-years on a side made visually available to your unaided eyes from your own back yard, given only the right conceptual framework for grasping it, and observational practice in using that framework. From within the new framework, one finds a systematic significance in experiential details that hitherto went largely or entirely unnoticed (cf. Feyerabend 1963b; P. M. Churchland 1979).

The case of inner space is potentially the same. We will not lose contact with a metaphysically distinct dimension of self when we stop introspecting inarticulable qualia, and start introspecting "instead" sensory coding vectors and sundry activation patterns within the vector spaces of our accessible cortical areas. As with the revolution in astronomy, the prospect is one we should welcome as metaphysically liberating, rather than deride as metaphysically irrelevant or metaphysically impossible.

Postscript: 1997

The following remarks concern the attempt to repair or avoid the charge of equivocation by quantifying over the possible diversity in any relevant forms of knowing, as briefly discussed two sections ago. Some time after publishing the original version of this paper, I discovered there was yet more to be learned from this exercise. Let me begin by giving the proof for the original version of the multiply quantified argument. (As before, $Hx = x$ is a fact about humans; $Px = x$ is a physical fact; $K(f)mx$ = Mary knows$_f$ x.)

ATTEMPT No. 1

1. $(x)(f)[(Hx \,\&\, Px) \supset K(f)mx]$	**False!**
2. $(\exists x)(\exists f)[Hx \,\&\, \sim K(f)mx]$	____/ .. $(\exists x)[Hx \,\&\, \sim Px]$
3. $(\exists f)[Hr \,\&\, \sim K(f)mr]$	2, E.I. (flag constant r)
4. $Hr \,\&\, \sim K(i)mr$	3, E.I. (flag constant i)
5. $(f)[(Hr \,\&\, Pr) \supset K(f)mr]$	1, U.I.
6. $(Hr \,\&\, Pr) \supset K(i)mr$	5, U.I.
7. $\sim K(i)mr \,\&\, Hr$	4, Comm.
8. $\sim K(i)mr$	7, Detach
9. $\sim(Hr \,\&\, Pr)$	6, 8, M. Tollens
10. $\sim Hr \lor \sim Pr$	9, DeMorgan
11. Hr	4, Detach
12. $\sim\sim Hr$	11, Dbl. Neg.
13. $\sim Pr$	10, 12, Dis. Syl.
14. $Hr \,\&\, \sim Pr$	11, 13, Conj.
15. $(\exists x)[Hx \,\&\, \sim Px]$	14. E.G.

As remarked in the original paper, this argument is valid, but premise (1) is clearly false. The universal quantifier, (f), claims far too much about Mary's knowledge (because there *is* a form of knowledge about red sensations that Mary most famously *lacks*: introspective knowledge or knowledge-by-acquaintance).

But there are other possibilities here. Perhaps Jackson can get by with a slightly weaker first premise. To this end, let us replace the universal quantifier, (f), with an existential quantifier, $(\exists f)$. Premise (1) is now circumspect enough to be perfectly true on the assumptions of Jackson's story; for the specific case of *propositional* knowledge, Mary knows all there is to know.

Moreover, it might seem that this (true) premise is adequate to sustain a closely parallel argument.

ATTEMPT No. 2

1. $(x)(\exists f)[(Hx \And Px) \supset K(f)mx]$
2. $(\exists x)(\exists f)[Hx \And \sim K(f)mx]$ ___/ $\therefore (\exists x)[Hx \And \sim Px]$
3. $(\exists f)[Hr \And \sim K(f)mr]$ 2, E.I. (flag constant r)
4. $Hr \And \sim K(i)mr$ 3, E.I. (flag constant i)
5. $(\exists f)[(Hr \And Pr) \supset K(f)mr]$ 1, U.I.
6. $(Hr \And Pr) \supset K(i)mr$ 5, E.I.   **Invalid!**
7. $\sim K(i)mr \And Hr$ 4, Comm.
8. $\sim K(i)mr$ 7, Detach
9. $\sim(Hr \And Pr)$ 6, 8, M. Tollens
10. $\sim Hr \lor \sim Pr$ 9, DeMorgan
11. Hr 4, Detach
12. $\sim\sim Hr$ 11, Dbl. Neg.
13. $\sim Pr$ 10, 12, Dis. Syl.
14. $Hr \And \sim Pr$ 11, 13, Conj.
15. $(\exists x)[Hx \And \sim Px]$ 14, E.G.

Unfortunately, this argument is invalid by reason of violating (in line [6]) the standard restriction on Existential Instantiation to an already instantiated individual constant: in this case, the constant *i*. This failure is not random. It is revealing. The inference from (5) to (6) invalidly assumes that the form of knowledge, *i*, of which line (6) presumes to speak, is the *same thing* as the introspective form of knowledge of which line (4) quite correctly speaks. If these are indeed the premises from which Jackson wishes to proceed, then even the blind machinery of the predicate calculus finds him guilty of the classic charge against him—the illegitimate conflation of two possibly distinct (indeed, presumptively distinct) forms of knowledge.

There remains the possibility that, while the specific deduction of attempt no. 2 is invalid, there is some other deductive route that *will* take us validly from its two premises to its conclusion. But this hope is vain also, since the two premises are formally and jointly consistent with the negation of the conclusion. As I showed above, there exists a model—indeed, a purely physical model—in which both premises are true and yet the conclusion is false.

Still, perhaps the logical gap here can be closed and the argument's validity recaptured by leaning, this time, on a stronger version not of the first, but rather of the *second* premise. Specifically, let us replace the existential quantifier, (Ef), with a universal quantifier, (f). This will yield the following argument:

ATTEMPT No. 3

1. $(x)(\exists f)[(Hx \ \& \ Px) \supset K(f)mx]$
2. $(\exists x)(f)[Hx \ \& \sim K(f)mx]$ **False, or Question-Begging**
3. $(f)[Hr \ \& \sim K(f)mr]$ 2, E.I. (flag constant r)
4. $Hr \ \& \sim K(i)mr$ 3, U.I.
5. $(\exists f)[(Hr \ \& \ Pr) \supset K(f)mr]$ 1, U.I.
6. $(Hr \ \& \ Pr) \supset K(i)mr$ 5, E.I. (flag constant i)
7. $\sim K(i)mr \ \& \ Hr$ 4, Comm.
8. $\sim K(i)mr$ 7, Detach
9. $\sim (Hr \ \& \ Pr)$ 6, 8, M. Tollens
10. $\sim Hr \ V \sim Pr$ 9, DeMorgan
11. Hr 4, Detach
12. $\sim \sim Hr$ 11, Dbl. Neg.
13. $\sim Pr$ 10, 12, Dis. Syl.
14. $Hr \ \& \sim Pr$ 11, 13, Conj.
15. $(\exists x)[Hx \ \& \sim Px]$ 14, E.G.

As expected, this new argument is formally valid. The problematic restriction on instantiating to the constant i in line (6) has now disappeared, because i was never flagged in any earlier line. In this argument, its first appearance came by U.I. rather than by E.I.

Alas, premise (2) is now a very strong claim indeed, and deeply problematic as a result. The materialist can plausibly maintain that it is false, and it begs the question in any case. As stated here, it claims that there is a fact or facts about humans (e.g., the character of their red sensations) that is unknown to Mary, not just via her introspection, but via *any* form of knowledge whatsoever. The materialist, however, is bound to claim that Mary does indeed know about sensations and their qualities (the alleged lacuna) via a discursive or propositional form of knowledge, namely, her exhaustive and completed neuroscience. The materialist's position, after all, is that sensations and their qualities are (either type- or token-) *identical* with brain states and their properties, something of which it has been stipulated that Mary has extensive, indeed, exhaustive, knowledge. *If* this identity claim is correct, then knowledge of the latter is *bound to be* knowledge of the former, despite the doubly opaque epistemic context arising from two distinct *forms* of knowledge (knowledge-by-acquaintance vs. knowledge-by-description) and two distinct descriptive vocabularies: folk psychology on the one hand, and cognitive neuroscience on the other. Accordingly, premise (2) would then be false: Mary would know a great deal—indeed, *everything*—about the qualitative characters of people's sensations, but only as those characters get represented within a single (discursive) form of knowledge, and only under a set of (scientific) descriptions mostly unfamiliar to the rest of us.

Materialists have also argued that, with nothing more than extensive practice on our part, the originally "unfamiliar" neuroscientific descriptions can come to displace entirely the more primitive vocabulary of our current folk psychology, even as the conceptual vehicle for our spontaneous self-conscious introspections. In that event, the descriptive opacity here lamented would disappear entirely. (Good riddance, too, if all it represented was our own ignorance.)

To be sure, the materialist cannot simply insist that Mary's neuroscientific knowledge truly constitutes a knowledge of sensations and their qualities: that would beg the question against the property dualist. Whether such identities do or do not hold is for our unfolding science to show in the fullness of time. But equally sure, neither can Jackson simply insist that neuroscience must *fail* to encompass qualia, which is precisely what the inflated version of premise (2) is attempting to blow past us. That would be to *assume at the outset* that materialism is false, rather than to *show* that it must be false.

We have now explored three of the four combinations possible. There are two premises in Jackson's argument, and two forms of quantification over *f* for each. The last and least of the possible combinations deploys the strong version of both premises.

ATTEMPT No. 4

1. $(x)(f)[(Hx \& Px) \supset K(f)mx]$ **False!**
2. $(\exists x)(f)[Hx \& \sim K(f)mx]$ **False, or Question-Begging**

$\vdots$

15. $(\exists x)[Hx \& \sim Px]$

As in attempts no. 1 and no. 3, the ensuing argument will be valid, but here the premises make up the least compelling package of all, for the reasons already discussed singly.

In summary, then, the only argument whose premises are broadly and uniformly acceptable is attempt no. 2, but that argument is formally invalid by reason of conflating possibly distinct (presumptively distinct) forms of knowledge. And the only valid argument whose premises have even an outside chance of being true is attempt no. 3, but its second premise blithely begs the very question at issue.

As I remarked earlier in a similar context, Jackson has surely profited from the ambiguities here. The difference between attempts no. 2 and no. 3 is subtle—an $(\exists f)$ vs. an (f) buried within premise (2). Further, attempt no. 2 clearly has true premises, and attempt no. 3 is clearly valid. What is important, however, is that neither attempt meets both conditions, and so nothing whatever has been accomplished.

Curiously, Jackson's "color-blind Mary" argument is still regularly cited as a decisive critique of reductive materialism (e.g., Chalmers 1996; Searle 1992). It is curious because this somewhat vague and elusive argument shows up as either invalid, unsound, or question-begging on every rigorous interpretation in the neighborhood. If Jackson has some further version of the argument he would like to propose—preferably in canonical form, for clarity's sake—we should all be eager to address it. As it stands, we seem to have exhausted the available possibilities. None of them teaches us anything about the status of materialism: only about the dangers of equivocation, conflation, and begging the question at issue.

References

Chalmers, D. 1996. *The Conscious Mind*. Oxford: Oxford University Press.

Churchland, P. A. 1979. *Scientific Realism and the Plasticity of Mind*. Cambridge: Cambridge University Press.

———. 1981. "Eliminative Materialism and the Propositional Attitudes." *Journal of Philosophy* 78: 67–90.

———. 1985. "Reduction, Qualia, and the Direct Introspection of Brain States." *Journal of Philosophy* 82: 8–28.

———. 1989. *A Neurocomputational Perspective: The Nature of Mind and the Structure of Science*. Cambridge, Mass.: The MIT Press.

Feyerabend, P. K. 1963. "How to Be a Good Empiricist: A Plea for Tolerance in Matters Epistemological." In *Philosophy of Science: The Delaware Seminar*, vol. 2, ed. B. Baumrin, 3–19. New York: Interscience Publications.

Hubel, D. H., and M. S. Livingstone. 1987. Segregation of Form, Color, and Stereopsis in Primate Area 18." *Journal of Neuroscience* 7: 3378–3415.

Jackson, R. 1982. "Epiphenomenal Qualia." *Philosophical Quarterly* 32: 127–136. Reprinted in this volume.

———. 1986. "What Mary Didn't Know." *Journal of Philosophy* 83: 291–295. Reprinted in this volume.

Lewis, D. 1983. "Postscript to 'Mad Pain and Martian Pain.'" In his *Philosophical Papers*, vol. 1. Oxford: Oxford University Press.

Nemirow, L. 1980. "Review of Thomas Nagel's *Mortal Questions*." *Philosophical Review* 89: 473–477.

Searle, J. R. 1992. *The Rediscovery of the Mind*. Cambridge, Mass.: The MIT Press.

Van Essen, D. C., and J. Maunsell. 1983. "Hierarchical Organization and Functional Streams in the Visual Cortex." *Trends in Neuroscience* 6: 370–375.

Zeki, S. 1980. "The Representation of Colors in the Cerebral Cortex." *Nature* 284: 412–418.

9 Acquaintance with Qualia

John Bigelow and Robert Pargetter

1 Physicalism and the Knowledge Argument

There is a crucial argument which seems to work against any physicalist account of phenomenal properties. The argument is particularly powerful, because it does seem to apply to any physicalist account of phenomenal properties whatever. It does not trade on any of the details of any particular physicalist account. The argument may be called the knowledge argument. In this paper, we show that the knowledge argument does not provide a conclusive case against physicalism. We do not prove, nor do we presuppose, that physicalism is true, only that it can withstand the knowledge argument.

The knowledge argument can be introduced through a variety of different illustrations. Here are three.

(i) Consider a complete physical theory of the light spectrum, including the effects different wavelengths of light have on the neural systems of humans. There are also the phenomenal properties we experience when we see the spectrum. The physical facts would remain exactly the same even if the phenomenal properties were systematically transposed. When you see the spectrum, you *know* which phenomenal property is present during your current neural states, and so you know something which could not be known from the physical theory alone.[1]

(ii) Suppose our neurophysiological theory told us that there are two kinds of mental states humans have in fact never experienced, though they are capable of experiencing them, and suppose our theory went on to give us the complete physical specification of those states. Suppose we then brought those states about in ourselves and experienced the corresponding phenomenal properties. The physical story would have been exactly the same even if the phenomenal properties associated with the two states had been interchanged. Hence knowledge of "which way around" the phenomenal properties are is knowledge unobtainable in physcial theory alone.[2]

(iii) Mary lived in a black-and-white world, and learned all her physical theory on black-and-white television. There is nothing within physical theory she could not learn that way. In fact she becomes an expert on the physics of color, including the way in which colors are perceived in humans. But the day that Mary leaves her black-and-white world, and experiences the qualia of a colored world, she learns something. Yet she learns no new part of physical theory.[3]

2   Responding to the Knowledge Argument

There are a number of responses to the knowledge argument, which, in one way or another, resist the intuitive case for saying that there is knowledge which reaches beyond the scope of scientific, physical theory. We think all these responses are unsatisfactory. We think that the knowledge argument does establish that the complete story of physical science fails to exhaust all the knowledge relating to the mental, and that there is no satisfactory reduction of the *knowledge* of phenomenal properties to *knowledge* of physical theory. Yet we maintain this does not force us to abandon the physicalist's program: it does not refute physicalism. Before explaining how this can be, however, we will look briefly at one misguided yet particularly instructive physicalist response.

The most straightforward physicalist response to the knowledge argument would be to protest that we *do* have all knowledge when we have all knowledge expressible within physical theory, and thus that we in fact *do* have knowledge of the phenomenal properties. The phenomenal properties of the spectrum could not be reversed without altering physical theory, the qualia of the two new mental states could not have been interchanged, and Mary would not be surprised.[4] We cannot decisively refute such a response, but we will restrict our attention to only those responses which are compatible with the crucial premiss of the knowledge argument. We do not take ourselves to have proved beyond dispute that even when we have all knowledge expressible within physical theory, when we have an experience for ourselves then we learn something new. But we do restrict our attention to responses which do grant this much.

Consider for instance the third example, the scientist Mary who emerges from a black and white world to experience colors for the first time. Mary does come to know what colors are like. Furthermore, it must not be underestimated just how much Mary learns. She now knows what colors are like. She may now know how to discriminate colors. She is probably now able to visualize colors at will—if asked to imagine a man in a blue jacket, she knows what to do. She also learns things about herself. She now knows, of herself, that she is having a specific color experience of, say orange. Later, she can remember having that experience. Obviously she could not know these things without having the experience. Yet this knowledge of herself is not the only sort of knowledge she has gained. As a result of having color experiences for herself, Mary has probably also learned something about the mental states of others.[5] She now may know that others too will be having color experiences like those she is now having—she may know what their experiences are like (supposing of course that there is some reply to blanket skepticism about other minds). Yet she knew all the physical facts about other people all along, and nothing new has happened to *them*. She knows something new about other people, as well as about herself.

We thus reject responses which deny that there is any knowledge one can have about qualia, beyond that found in physical theory. We accept that there is knowledge of phenomenal properties which is not reducible to knowledge of physical theory. Yet we will argue that this is compatible with the physicalist program of accounting for the mental in purely physical terms. This is problematic, however, since on the face of it we seem to be caught in a contradiction, saying that ideal physical theory is complete, and yet also incomplete, at the same time. The resolution of this apparent contradiction is to be found by freeing ourselves from a seductive yet oversimplified theory of knowledge.

3 A Taxonomy for Belief and Knowledge

Let us begin with a sketch of a taxonomy of beliefs. Different instances, or tokens, of belief, different instances of believing, may be classified in a variety of ways.

In the first place, instances of believing may be classified on the basis of their truth-conditions. Given a person's belief at a time, we may often find that there are claims of the following form which can be made:

If ... then that person's belief would be true.

If ... then that person's belief would be false.

If ... then that person's belief might be true and might be false, depending on whether ...

It is a task for another occasion to justify claims of these sorts; here we take them as given.

All such truths about the person's belief may be summed up in a function which maps possible worlds to truth values. Such a function may map any given possible world to the value 'true', or to 'false', or to some intermediate degree of truth or falsity; or else the function may be a partial function, which is undefined for the possible world in question.

As a simplification, we will consider only the set of worlds in which a belief is true. This enables us to introduce a classification of beliefs in terms of the possible worlds in which they are true. There is a respect in which two different instances of believing will be of the same type, when they are true in the same set of possible worlds.

This taxonomy can then be refined to yield a more finegrained classification. At least sometimes, and arguably always, when an instance of believing is related to a set of possible worlds in which it is true, then there will be more which can be said about what those worlds are like, what they contain, in what ways they are different from the possible worlds which are excluded from the truth-set. Sometimes (arguably always) we will be able to identify some *things*, some individuals, properties, and relations, such that all and only the worlds in which the belief is true, are worlds which contain those things interrelated in a determinate way. A nexus of things (individuals, properties, and relations), interrelated in a determinate way, may be called a *structure*. There is a respect in which two different instances of believing are of the same type, when they are both true in the same set of possible worlds *because* those worlds contain a specific structure. This yields a classification which is more fine-grained than one which hinges only on the truth-sets for beliefs. Two instances of believing may be of the same type with respect to the set of possible worlds in which they are true, yet may differ with respect to the manners in which they are related to the various structures within those possible worlds.

Consider an illustration which owes much to a puzzle concocted by David Lewis. Imagine a trial in which there is a judge called Hoffman, and a defendant called Hoffman who is being tried as a result of disruptive behaviour during political protests on the streets of Chicago. During the trial, which goes on for weeks, the defendant engages in incessant disruptive behavior. Two people, Willard and Hilary, are hearing news of the trial. Willard is politically conservative, and has a strong inclination to sympathize with Hoffman, the Judge. One piece of news, however, causes Willard to think to himself, 'Oh dear, Hoffman is just as bad as Hoffman!', meaning that the judge is just as bad as the defendant.

Meanwhile, Hilary reacts differently to the news. He is an anarchist and has a strong inclination to sympathize with Hoffman the defendant. The piece of news, however, causes Hilary to think to himself, 'Oh dear, Hoffman is just as bad as Hoffman!', meaning that the defendant is just as bad as the judge.

Willard's belief and Hilary's belief are different, and yet also the same. They are true in the very same set of possible worlds. (For simplicity, let us take their thoughts to be that one Hoffman is as bad but no worse than the other, so that the relation 'just as bad as' is a symmetrical relation: necessarily A is just as bad as B if and only if B is just as bad as A.)

Furthermore, in any possible world in which both Willard's and Hilary's beliefs are true, we can also say that the reason why this is a world in which both are true, is that the world contains both Hoffmans, and each Hoffman is just as bad as the other. Thus, Willard's and Hilary's beliefs are relevantly related not only to the same set of possible worlds, but also to the same constituents within those possible worlds.[6]

Nevertheless, the beliefs are different. Willard's belief is relevantly related to a different structure than Hilary's. The two relevant structures involve the same ingredients, but relate those ingredients in a different *order*. We may represent the difference by saying that Willard's belief is relevantly related to the structure:

$\langle$just as bad as, x, $y\rangle$

(where x is Hoffman the judge and y is Hoffman the defendant); while in contrast, Hilary's belief is relevantly related to the structure:

$\langle$just as bad as, y, $x\rangle$.

The beliefs of Willard and Hilary differ only in structure, and not in either truth-conditions, or in the things that the belief is about.[7]

Other examples can be used to make the same point. Clear illustrations can be drawn from arithmetical beliefs; and these illustrations have been extensively exploited by Cresswell in his extended examination of the structures of beliefs. Consider for instance the differences between the thought that three fours are twelve, and the thought that four threes are twelve. Another memorable illustration is one we learned from Smullyan's *What Is the Name of This Book?* Outside an expensive restaurant there are said to have been two notices: 'Good food is not cheap', and 'Cheap food is not good'. It takes some concentration to see that these are logically equivalent. Also consider an old teaser: a man looks at a photograph of someone and says (truthfully): 'Brothers and sisters have I none, but this man's father is my father's son'. This thought has the same truth conditions as the thought that he has a father, he has no brothers or sisters, and the person in the photograph is his son. There are two different thoughts possible here, and these thoughts are strikingly different to such a degree that people have been known to debate heatedly about whether or not the man is looking at a photograph of his son. Yet the thoughts do not differ in truth conditions. The striking difference between the two thoughts derives solely from differences in the ordering of the elements which they involve.

The notion of a 'relevant relation', holding between a belief and a structure, stands in need of further attention. Philosophers are painfully aware that everything is related to everything else in ever so many ways, and so a belief will stand in all sorts of relations to ever so many structures which have nothing to do with the issues at hand. Willard's belief is relevantly related to a different structure from Hilary's, but also stands in many irrelevant relationships to both the structures under discussion, and also to all the other structures you might mention. What makes a relationship to a structure a 'relevant' one? Such a relation is a 'relevant' one, when the belief is true in worlds which contain that structure *because* they contain that structure. This structure mediates between the belief and the set of worlds in which it is true. Other structures do not.

In order for a structure to mediate between a belief and a set of worlds, the believer must stand in some suitable relationship to the constituents of that structure. When will a believer's relationships to individuals, properties and relations count as 'suitable relations'? They are 'suitable' provided they relate the believer to a structure in such a way as to make the belief true in the set of possible worlds which contain that structure. It is a topic for another occasion, to discover what sorts of relationships will be 'suitable' in this sense. Here, we take it as given that sometimes the relationships between a believer and other things (individuals, and properties, and relations) are relationships in virtue of which the person's belief is true in certain possible worlds and not in others. These relationships, whatever they turn out to be like in detail, will be called *acquaintance relations*. When a person stands in such acquaintance relations to constituents of a structure, this makes it possible for them to stand in a relevant relation to the structure, and this in turn enables them to stand in a relevant relation to the set of possible worlds which contain that structure.

A person's relation to a structure, then, is underpinned by acquaintance relations to the constituents of that structure. This opens a further taxonomic possibility. Two people could stand in different relations to the same structure. Although these relations may be different, each of these relations may have whatever it takes to qualify as an acquaintance relation, and to entail that the belief is true in all and only the worlds which contain the structure. If two people may stand in different acquaintance relations to the same structure, then this opens the possibility that their beliefs may be the same and yet different, in a further respect. They may be the same with respect to the set of worlds in which they are true, and also with respect to the structure in those worlds in virtue of which they are true, yet they may nevertheless be different in a further important respect. The beliefs may be different with respect to the specific acquaintance relations which link the two believers, in different ways, to one and the same structure.

To illustrate, consider again the Hoffmans. Imagine that the judge is driving home and is absent-mindedly listening to the radio. He hears a report on a court debacle between a judge and a disruptive defendant, and thinks to himself, '*He* is just as bad as he is', meaning that the judge is just as bad as the defendant. Hoffman could conceivably even hear that the judge and defendant are both called 'Hoffman', and he could then think to himself, 'Hoffman is just as bad as Hoffman'. At this point his thought is just like Willard's in all relevant respects—in the set of worlds in which it is true, in the structure within those worlds in virtue of which it is true, and in the mode of acquaintance in which he stands to that structure, hearing it as he does through a news broadcast just as Willard did.

Yet then Hoffman wakes from his reverie and thinks to himself, 'Oh no, it's me! *I* am just as bad as Hoffman!' At this time, he forms a belief which is significantly different from the one he formed initially, and so from Willard's belief too. Yet his new belief is not different with respect to the set of worlds in which it is true. Nor is it different from Willard's in the way that Hilary's is different from Willard's. His belief is not different because it is related to different individuals, properties or relations, or because it relates to them in a different order. His new belief differs from his initial belief, rather, because it involves a different mode of acquaintance with the very same structure. The earlier belief involved an indirect, causal acquaintance with himself; the later belief involves a more intimate, direct acquaintance with himself. Arguably, the acquaintance relation involved in the "first-person" thought is simply the *identity* relation. This could be contested, but whatever account we give of the "first-person" acquaintance relation, it is clearly *not* the same as the one which involves hearing of a person on news broadcasts.

Beliefs, therefore, may differ significantly from one another even if they are true in the same possible worlds, and in virtue of the very same structure of individuals, properties and relations in those possible worlds.

Since this holds for beliefs, the same will hold also, *mutatis mutandis*, for knowledge. One instance of knowing may differ from another, even though the sets of worlds, in which what is known would be true, are the same, and even though the structures in those worlds, with which the knower is acquainted, are the same. These instances of knowing may differ only with respect to the mode of acquaintance in which the knower stands to the structures with which she or he is acquainted.

4   Knowledge of Our Mental States

The epistemic taxonomy which we have developed can now be applied to the knowledge of qualia. The judge, who thinks 'It's me!', comes to be in a knowledge-state which is new and different from any of his previous states. So too, a person who comes to have certain experiences may come to be in knowledgestates which are new and different from any of her previous states. Such a person may, like the judge, feel as though she has had a dramatic revelation. And yet this revelation need not involve any change in the sets of possible worlds compatible with her beliefs, or in the contents of those worlds with which she is acquainted. The new knowledge state may differ only in a new mode of acquaintance with things in the world, things with which she was already acquainted, although under a different mode of acquaintance.

Usually when a person has a new experience, their knowledge states change at three levels at once. In addition to changes at the levels of worlds and of structures, there may also be changes at a third level, the level of acquaintance relations. It is because this third level has been too often neglected, that Jackson's imaginary colour scientist, Mary, is so instructive. Her case is one in which there clearly is a change in what she knows, but arguably there is no change at the level of worlds or structures—and hence we cannot in this case neglect the third level of change, the level of modes of acquaintance.

It is important that we resist the misleading associations which emanate from the word 'acquaintance'. In the present context, an acquaintance relation is one which enables a person to hold a belief which is true in all and only the possible worlds containing a specific structure. A specific structure, in turn, will be one containing specific individuals, properties and relations. Thus, a person will be acquainted with a visual experience, when that person is capable of having beliefs which are true if and only if *that very experience* is involved in certain determinate structures. A person may become acquainted with an experience, in the required sense, when they have that experience themselves. But there is no reason why that should be the only conceivable way they could be acquainted with that experience. There is no reason why a person could not be acquainted with the experience, in virtue of causal interactions between that person and the experience, even though the experience occurs only in other people. After all, a person *can* be acquainted, in the relevant sense, with the physical processes in other people's bodies. If physicalism is true, some of these physical things with which they are acquainted *will be* the very experiential qualities under debate. So a person can be acquainted with experiences they have not had—provided we construe 'acquaintance' in the sense relevant to the present debate.

For a physicalist, then, it must be possible for a person, like Jackson's color scientist Mary, to be acquainted with all the physical structures in the world, and to know exactly which possible world she is in. When she sees colors, she enters a new knowledge state, significantly different from any that she was in before. Yet this new state does not differ in virtue of its being true in different possible worlds, nor in virtue of the fact that its truth in these worlds is explained by the presence of different structures in those possible worlds. Not if physicalism is true. Her new state can differ only in a third respect—in the nature of the acquaintance relations which link her to the structures in question, and thereby to the relevant set of possible worlds. Before Mary had color experiences, she was acquainted with all the relevant structures which there are in the world. After having color experiences, she is acquainted in a new way with some of those structures. Her new knowledge state differs from the old ones, not at the level of truth-conditions, nor at the level of structures, but only at the third significant level, that of her modes of acquaintance with those structures.

Consider again the three sample presentations we have given of the knowledge argument against physicalism. These fail, because they overlook the third level at which beliefs or knowledge states may differ, namely, the level of modes of acquaintance.

The first illustration appealed to the idea of a spectrum reversal within our visual experience. In knowing all there is to know about the physical structures involved, we *do* thereby know which experiences have which properties. We just come to know, *in a new way*, what we already knew, but under other, less direct modes of acquaintance.

The second illustration involved the theoretical study of two brain states which are possible for humans, but which no one has experienced yet. When someone does experience these states, this does not entail the discovery of any new individuals, or properties, or relations, which were unknowable before. Everything knowable was known before, but is now known in a new way, under a new mode of acquaintance.

The third illustration of the knowledge argument was that of Jackson's nearly omniscient colour scientist, Mary, who never experiences colors for herself until she has completed her comprehensive study of the topic, both theoretically and experimentally. In her black-and-white laboratory, Mary is both theoretically and practically acquainted with colours, and with color experiences in others, and with all the properties of color experiences in others. She can identify all these things using demonstratives; and she can hold beliefs which are true only in worlds containing just those very colors, those very color experiences, and those very properties and relations among colors and color experiences. In one sense, there is nothing she does not know about the world she is in, even though she has never seen colors for herself. Nevertheless, there is a new way of knowing the things she knows, and she cannot instantiate this new way of knowing until she gains a new mode of acquaintance, a mode which requires her to have color experiences for herself.

In attaining a new mode of acquaintance, Mary thereby opens the doors to a wide range of new thoughts which she can formulate. This expands the number of distinctions she can make among her representations of the world. Even though the set of worlds compatible with her beliefs does not alter, there will be an alteration in the range of representations she can construct, corresponding to those worlds. Worlds which she could represent in one way, she can now represent in a new way as well.

This expansion of representational powers may confer on Mary the potential to generate combinations and permutations of representations, yielding more representations than there are possible worlds to represent. Suppose for instance that Mary is acquainted with two experiential properties, firstly under a "third-person" mode of acquaintance, as two neurological properties. Then she becomes acquainted with those properties under a more direct mode of acquaintance, when she experiences them for herself. She may then say to herself:

So *this* is what *this* experiential property is like, and *that* is what *that* one is like. I now know that *this* one is *not that* one, and *that* one is *not this* one. I now know "which way around" the experiential properties in fact happen to be. They are *this* way around, rather than the other way around.

These thoughts of Mary's arise by recombining several distinct representations of a smaller number of things. The state with which she is indirectly acquainted, experimentally, can be represented as identical with either of two states with which she is acquainted experientially. One of these represented identities is correct, the other is not. The erroneous representation does not correspond to any genuine possibility. The state with which she is "experimentally" acquainted *is identical* with one of her experiential states and not the other (according to physicalism). Given this, there will be *no* possible world in which it is identical with the other experiential state. So there is in fact no real possibility corresponding to Mary's representation of '*this* one being *that* one, and *vice versa*'. What she represents is a logical impossibility. Yet there is also a sense in which this representation is itself a "possibility"—something she can imagine, even though it could not really be true. It is, in a loose sense, a doxastic or even an epistemic possibility, even though it is not a logical possibility.

This split between doxastic and logical possibilities is one which is very difficult for physicalists to evade. Most physicalists believe that dualism is, or was, an epistemic possibility. So in some sense it is an epistemic possibility for them that an experience of theirs (which they say is *in fact* physical) *could be* nonphysical. Yet it is extremely implausible to suggest that a physical process *could have been* a nonphysical process, in the sense that there is a possible world in which that *same process* exists but has the property of being nonphysical. So there is an epistemic possibility that 'this state' might be something nonphysical. Yet there is no possible world in which 'this state' *is* nonphysical. Hence the physicalist is committed to an epistemic possibility which is paired with no possible world in which it is true. The epistemic predicament of Mary is, we argue, of this very sort—when she experiences colors for herself, she can then represent 'possibilities' which are not in fact logically possible. This, however, is not a result of any queer sort of privacy attaching in a peculiar way to qualia. It is a result of very general phenomena concerning knowledge of the outer world, just as much as the inner world.

Compare Mary's new knowledge with that sought by Lewis's insomniac,[8] who wonders what time it is. We will call him Kim. Kim knows that, for each time t between dusk and dawn, he is awake at t. There is no new proposition Kim seeks to learn—the nature of the actual world is all too clear to him. What he cannot do, at t, is to self-ascribe the property of 'being at t'. He has, at t, an acquaintance relation to his time-slice at t, and this generates a representation of himself of the form, '*this* time-slice'. Until he finds out the time, there are many representations which he is unable to discriminate among, of the form '*this* time-slice is located at t_n'. When he finds out the time, he comes to know which of these representations corresponds to actuality. This is new knowledge of a sort, even though it gives no new knowledge of which world he is in: the set of worlds compatible with what he knows is unchanged. Nor is he now aware of a new structure within the worlds compatible with what he knows: he always knew, of each moment, that he would be awake at that moment. And yet there is nevertheless something he does not know, namely, which of a number of representations is the true one.

Note that the representations which turn out to be false, in Kim's case, are *not* ones which represent genuine possibilities. If 'this' time-slice is actually located at time t_n, then there is no possible would in which this very time-slice is located at some other time t_m. It would not be the time-slice it is, if it were located at a different time. Of course, Kim may say 'I could have been wondering what time it is, at another time instead of now'. But that is quite different from the thought that now might have *been*, say, 4 A.M. instead of 3 A.M. There is no possible world in which that is so. Nevertheless, there is a sense in which it is an epistemic possibility for Kim, that 'now' *might* be any of a number of different times. Not all epistemic possibilities are logically possible. Something may be 'epistemically possible' even though there is no possible world in which it is true.

Similarly with Mary. She, like Kim, obtains no new knowledge of which world she is in. But due to new acquaintance relations, she can represent the world in new ways, and she can locate the actual world within this richer array of representations. She knows that '*this* state' has '*this* property', and she can exclude the *representable* possibility that '*this* state' has '*that* property'. Mary, like Kim, has a new knowledge state, which enables her to discriminate among new representable possibilities, even though her knowledge of which world she is in, and which structures are in that world, has not changed. All that has changed is the addition of a new mode of acquaintance with structures she was already acquainted with under a less 'immediate' mode. Not all new knowledge uncovers new objects, or properties, or real (nonepistemic) possibilities. Some new knowledge arises simply from old acquaintances being renewed in new ways.

5   Knowledge and Abilities

David Lewis[9] has borrowed an idea from Laurence Nemirow[10] which he employs to defend physicalism against the knowledge argument. Basically, the idea is that when we 'know what it's like' to have a certain experience, this is practical knowledge, *know-how*, not theoretical knowledge. Hence the fact that total physical theory leaves out this 'knowledge' does not show any genuine incompleteness in physical theory. Any knowledge required to underpin these abilities is already accommodated in physical theory, no new *propositional information* is required.

Consider again the scientist, Mary, who experiences colors for the first time. Nemirow and Lewis point out that after experiencing color, Mary will be able to exercise new abilities, ones that she could not possibly exercise before experiencing colors for herself. She will be able to *remember, recognize*, and *visualize at will*. She will be able to remember what orange looked like when she saw it for the first time. She will now be able to instantly recognize the colour of something—by sight—whereas before, she could only determine the color or something with the aid of instruments. When she hears someone describe say a pumpkin, she will now be able to visualize it, color and all, which is something she could not do before she had experienced colors. And undoubtedly there are further abilities she will have acquired as a result of experiencing color vision for herself. Clearly, however, the acquisition of such abilities is no threat to physicalism if no new, "theoretical" information is required.

It is important to focus on the normal way in which people acquire such abilities. By far the most common way is by becoming *acquainted* with the experiences in question. Acquaintance by itself is not enough: memory, willpower and other faculties also must be brought to bear. But in most cases, acquaintance is one essential ingredient in the acquisition of the relevant abilities. Furthermore, once a person becomes acquainted with a kind of experience, it will in *most* cases follow almost automatically that they acquire such abilities. Hence the plausibility of the hypothesis of Lewis and Nemirow, that the abilities simply constitute 'knowing what it's like'.

It is interesting to note that the abilities to which Lewis and Nemirow appeal are all ones which have a tight connection with knowledge by introspective acquaintance. There are many other abilities which are not plausible candidates for an analysis of knowing what an experience is like. After experiencing colors, Mary can classify frequencies of light *without* using instruments. She may also have improved depth vision. These abilities will also be explained, in part, by the new information she gains by acquaintance with color experiences. But they are not the sorts of abilities which could be proposed as part of the analysis of knowing what it's like— their connection with the introspective acquaintance relation is too tenuous. Memory, recognition, and visualization are much more tightly linked to introspective acquaintance: hence the plausibility of using them in an analysis of knowing what it is like.

Insofar as abilities and introspective acquaintance can be kept separate, knowing what it is like follows acquaintance rather than abilities. There are cases where knowing what it is like is not so tightly linked with abilities like remembering, recognizing, or visualizing at will. For instance, a child looking at an orange may know at that moment what it's like to experience that color, but may not have any of the associated abilities. The child's memory for colors may be embryonic, and consequently she may not be sure of "recognizing" the color when she sees it again; and her powers of visualization may be totally nonexistent. Conversely, a person who has never experienced colors might conceivably acquire a state of what is called "blind sight," which permits certain people to discriminate colored objects using their eyes, without any conscious visual experience whatever.[11] Such a person could acquire *all* the practical abilities of someone with visual experience, *except* those essentially involving experience by first-person acquaintance. Such a person would not know what the experiences are like—not because of lack of ability, but because of lack of knowledge by first-person acquaintance. Knowing what an experience is like is knowledge essentially resting on acquaintance by introspection.

Nevertheless, there clearly is an intimate relationship between knowing what an experience is like, and the possession of various abilities. Even though this relationship is not an essential one, it does play an important role in our theory. Knowledge of what an experience is like is not epiphenomenal. It does make a difference to a person's life. One of the things it does is to generate a host of new practical abilities. It is a mistake to identify the relevant knowledge with the abilities; but it is not a mistake to see the abilities as consequences of that knowledge.

6 Conclusion

The physicalist's program has a response to the knowledge argument. There is a kind of knowledge of the phenomenal properties of your own mental state that is not available to other persons unless they stand in an introspective acquaintance relation to one of their own mental states, and that state shares the phenomenal properties of your mental state. Thus there is no problem for physicalism in people having a kind of knowledge of their mental states which would not be available to them without having experienced those states for themselves. Physicalists can allow the existence of knowledge of that kind. Yet to concede this much is to transform significantly our image of physicalism. It is to abandon the idea that there could ever be an impersonal textbook which not only recorded all the physical facts about the world, but which also expressed all the kinds of knowledge which it is possible for a person to have concerning those physical facts. There are kinds of knowledge which could not be had without distinctive modes of acquaintance. Some kinds of knowledge are not mere items in an impersonal theory. Some kinds of knowledge are not mere items in an impersonal theory. Some kinds of knowledge require distinctive forms of engagement between the knower and the known. That is why, although qualia are physical, people cannot know all there is to know about them unless they experience them for themselves.

Notes

1. The idea of spectrum reversals is widely discussed. See for instance D. M. Armstrong, *A Materialist Theory of the Mind* (London: Routledge and Kegan Paul, 1968), pp. 256–260. Philosophers have used the possibility of spectrum reversal to make a wide variety of philosophical points, some of them quite independent of the point we are using it to make. Our use is specifically epistemological though not skeptical and not metaphysical.

2. Brian Ellis, "Physicalism and the Contents of Sense Experience" in *Philosophical Aspects of the Mind-Body Problem*, ed. Chung-ying Cheng (Honolulu: University Press of Hawaii, 1975), pp. 64–77.

3. Frank Jackson "Epiphenomental Qualia," *Philosophical Quarterly* 32 (1982): 127–136.

4. See, for instance, Paul Churchland, "Reduction, Qualia, and the Direct Introspection of Brain States," *Journal of Philosophy* 82 (1985): 8–82.

5. Frank Jackson, "What Mary Didn't Know," *Journal of Philosophy* 83 (1986): 291–295. David Lewis has also influenced us in discussions of what Mary learns.

6. For another illustration, though one which raises many more tangled issues, consider Wittgenstein's *Philosophical Investigations*, p. 18n:

What is it to *mean* the words 'That is blue' at one time as a statement about the object one is pointing to—at another as an explanation of the word 'blue'?

Here Wittgenstein treats 'blue' as a nominalist would, and overlooks the possibility that we might mean the words 'That is blue' as a statement about the color blue, rather than as a statement about either the object or the word 'blue'. Nevertheless, his point does clearly illustrate a phenomenon very similar to that of the differing thoughts about the two Hoffmans.

7. Extended developments of this idea can be found in M. J. Cresswell, *Structured Meanings* (Cambridge, MA: MIT Press, 1985), or J. Barwise and J. Perry, *Situations and Attitudes* (Cambridge, MA: MIT Press, 1983). Bertrand Russell, *The Problems of Philosophy* (London: Oxford University Press, 1912) contains an early precursor of such theories, in chapter 12.

8. David Lewis, "Attitudes *De Dicto* and *De Se*," *Philosophical Review* 88 (1979): 513–543; the insomniac is introduced to us on p. 527.

9. David Lewis, "Knowing What It's Like," Public lecture, La Trobe University, 1981, unpublished. See his "Postscript to 'Mad Pain and Martian Pain'," *Philosophical Papers*, vol. 1 (New York: Oxford, 1983). We are indebted to David Lewis for further expansion of this view in private communications.

10. Lawrence Nemirow, "Physicalism and the Cognitive Role of Acquaintance" and David Lewis, "What Experience Teaches," both in William Lycan, ed., *Mind and Cognition: A Reader* (Oxford: Blackwell, 1989). See another objection to this approach in Frank Jackson, "What Mary Didn't Know," *Journal of Philosophy* 83 (1986): 291–295.

11. See Lawrence Weiskrantz, *Blindsight: A Case Study and Implications* (Oxford: Oxford University Press, 1986.) Methodologically, this book is remarkably "behavioristic"; it is exceedingly cautious in its discussion of the "bold jump" we are tempted to make, in inferring from a person's verbal reports (that they can see nothing) to the conclusion that they have no visual experiences. In fact, there is room for caution here. Comparisons can be made to the philosophically problematic "split brain," commissurotomy patients, who seem to have visual experiences in the right hemisphere of the brain, which are not communicated to the regions in the left hemisphere which controls speech. It is not obvious that verbal reports of a lack of specific experiences, in such cases, proves that there are no such experiences. Similar doubts may be raised about the interpretation of the data on blindsight.

10   Phenomenal Knowledge

Earl Conee

I   Introduction

Frank Jackson has presented a simple and powerful argument against physicalism (5, 6). The physicalism that Jackson contests is the thesis that all correct information is physical information. Jackson's argument against this version of physicalism goes roughly as follows. Complete knowledge of physical information would not provide someone who never had the experience of seeing a certain color with knowledge of what it is like to see the color. Form this Jackson infers that knowledge of what an experience is like is knowledge of nonphysical information. He concludes that not all correct information is physical information.

This is the knowledge argument against physicalism. The argument has received extensive critical attention.[1] The main line of critical response proceeds by acknowledging that Jackson has identified knowledge which is not knowledge of physical information, while denying that it is knowledge of nonphysical information. It is claimed not to be knowledge of information at all. Its existence thus poses no threat to the physicalist thesis asserting that all correct information is physical information.

This sort of response has a structure which is suitable for refuting the knowledge argument. In order to accomplish a convincing refutation of this form, the response must include some persuasive explanation of what does constitute knowing what it is like to see a color. Several critics contend that knowing what an experience is like is a kind of knowing how, a kind of knowledge consisting in having abilities rather than information.[2] It will be argued here that this is an untenable view of the knowledge at issue. It will be argued that the knowledge consists in acquaintance with the experience. Acquaintance with an experience does not require having either information or abilities. Acquaintance constitutes a third category of knowledge, irreducible to factual knowledge or knowing how. Knowledge by acquaintance of an experience requires only a maximally direct cognitive relation to the experience. The principal work of the present paper is to offer an exposition and defense of this position. The epistemic considerations on which the knowledge argument is based have considerable plausibility. An appeal to knowledge by acquaintance is particularly useful in accounting for them in a way that casts no doubt on physicalism.

II The Knowledge Argument Reviewed

Let us review in more detail Jackson's presentation of the knowledge argument against physicalism. Jackson uses two examples, the example of Mary and the example of Fred. Mary is a neurophysiologist in the distant future. She has managed to become extremely well informed while living in a peculiar state of deprivation. She has always been confined to an entirely black and white environment. She has never experienced any other hue. Yet Mary has learned all of the facts that can be learned in her drab world of black and white. In particular, she has learned all such facts about color vision. All accurate physical information about color vision has been conveyed to Mary in black and white via textbooks, television monitors, or the like.

Using this example Jackson argues against physicalism as follows (6, p. 291). In spite of Mary's exhaustive physical knowledge, she does not know all that there is to know. When Mary is released and sees ripe red tomatoes, she will learn what it is like to see something red. Jackson claims that this will be for Mary to learn a fact about others' color experiences, a fact that she did not previously know. Since by hypothesis she already knew all of the physical information about color vision, Jackson infers that this is nonphysical information. He concludes that not all information is physical.

The other example that Jackson uses in presenting the knowledge argument is that of Fred. Fred has extremely keen color vision throughout the visible spectrum. In addition, Fred is able quite reliably to discriminate objects into two color classes where the rest of us see things of only a single shade of red. Fred experiences a phenomenal difference. The objects in the two classes do not look to him to be of the same color. The members of at least one class do not produce in him the experience that all of these red things produce in the rest of us, the experience of a certain shade of phenomenal redness.

Jackson uses this example as follows. He claims that no physical information would 'tell us what [Fred's] color experience is like' (5, p. 473), something that Fred himself knows. Furthermore:

[T]he special quality of [Fred's] experience is certainly a fact about it, and one which Physicalism leaves out because no amount of physical information [tells] us what it is. (5, p. 473)

Physical information fails to include facts like this fact about Fred's experience. So again it is implied that not all correct information is physical information.

III Objections from Ability Analysts

Philosophers critical of Jackson's knowledge argument have largely accepted his 'knows-what-it-is-like' description of the sort of knowledge that is new to Mary and special to Fred, and they have largely agreed that knowledge of what an experience is like is not knowledge of physical information. They contend that nonetheless it is not knowledge that threatens physicalism. One leading approach is to analyze the knowledge as a kind of know-how. For instance, Laurence Nemirow proposes an analysis of knowing what a certain visual experience is like that is framed in terms of an ability to visualize. Nemirow writes:

The expression 'x knows how to visualize red' either should replace, or can be used to paraphrase, 'x knows what the experience of seeing red is like'. (8, p. 494)

Similarly, David Lewis proposes that knowing what it is like e.g. to taste Vegemite is identical to possessing certain sorts of abilities. Lewis contends that one who comes to taste Vegemite ordinarily gains the ability to remember that experience, and the abilities to imagine it and to recognize it. New experiences ordinarily yield such abilities. Lewis writes:

The Ability Hypothesis says that knowing what an experience is like just is the possession of these abilities to remember, imagine, and recognize. (7, p. 516)

Thus, the ability analysts' response to Jackson's argument is to contend that in learning what it is like to see something red Mary gains abilities rather than factual knowledge. This permits the inference that her learning does not imply the existence of information that is new to her. Physical information can be exhaustive.

IV Problems for Ability Analyses

Analyses of knowing what an experience is like in terms of abilities are objection able. First, knowing how to visualize any given colour is not sufficient for knowing what it is like to see the color. Suppose that Martha is a superlative color interpolator. She is highly skilled at visualizing an intermediary shade that she has not experienced between pairs of shades that she has experienced. Martha happens not to have any familiarity with the shade known as cherry red. She has seen, and vividly recalls, the look of burgundy red and the look of fire engine red. Suppose that Martha is now informed that there is a common shade of red, cherry red, which is a hue midway between burgundy red and fire engine red. At this moment, before Martha has imaginatively interpolated between those two shades, it is clear that Martha does not yet know what it is like to see something cherry red. She does not know this, although she is fully prepared to find out by exercising her imagination.[3] Yet Martha already knows how to visualize cherry red, since she knows how to perform the imaginative interpolation between burgundy and fire engine red. Thus, knowing how to visualize something cherry red at will is not sufficient for knowing what it is like to see the color.

Someone in Martha's situation poses no problem for David Lewis's proposal that knowing what an experience is like is identical to being able to remember, imagine, and recognize the experience. Lewis's proposal correctly implies that Martha does not yet know what it is like to see something cherry red. Martha is unable to remember an experience of seeing cherry red because she has never had this experience.

Lewis's ability hypothesis is subject to a different objection. It requires too much of a person in order to know what an experience is like. Nemirow's ability analysis also makes this mistake. To see this, let us suppose that Mary is in the epistemic condition that Jackson ascribes to her during her confinement. She is as well informed about color vision as can be accomplished by lessons in black and white. But suppose too that Mary has no visual imagination. She is unable to visualize anything. Now the story continues as before. Mary is released from her black-and-white confinement and sees something red for the first time. At that point, while she is intently gazing at the color of red ripe tomatoes, it is clearly true that she knows what it is like to see something red. She has made an exciting discovery. 'Aha!', she might well exclaim. Yet she is unable to imagine anything. A *fortiori*, she is not able to imagine, remember, and recognize the experience, as Lewis's ability hypothesis requires in order of her to know what it is like to see red. In light of her incapacity to imagine, it is also true that she does not know how to visualize red at will. Hence, knowing what an experience is like does not imply having any such abilities.

This version of the case of Mary enables us to see that knowing what an experience is like requires nothing more than noticing the experience as it is undergone. That is all Mary did, and yet it was enough to justify her issuing an 'Aha!' exclaiming a revelation. Memory and imagination are unnecessary. In fact, no ability to do anything other than to notice an experience is required.

This point does not require that we deny all role for abilities in the phenomenon that we call 'knowing what an experience is like'. *Continuing to know* what an experience is like may require mnemonic or imaginative abilities. But the knowledge argument against physicalism has no need of any such continued knowledge. If Mary, who is fully physically informed, learns some new fact when first she see a spectral color, then it follows that not all information is physical, however tenuously or fleetingly Mary may know the new fact.

V   An Initial Acquaintance Hypothesis

When we consider someone in Mary's epistemic condition prior to seeing any spectral color, it is entirely plausible that the person is in some way ignorant concerning color experiences. She may know all about them, but this knowledge is pallid and abstract. She does not know these vivid experiences first hand. Jackson maintains that this is factual ignorance, a lack of information. We have seen that it is a mistake to construe this ignorance as a lack of ability. There is a third alternative. It is suggested by a close look at one way in which Jackson himself describes the ignorance. Concerning Fred, who has differing color experiences in cases where we see just one shade of red, Jackson writes:

[T]here [is] something about his colour experience, a property of it, of which we [are] ignorant. (5, p. 473)

Jackson goes on to claim that this special quality of Fred's color experience is a fact about it. But the ignorance that Jackson actually attributes to us in this citation is ignorance of a *property* of Fred's color experience. To be ignorant of a property is not to fail to know a fact. Factual knowledge is knowledge of truths, not properties. Nor is ignorance of a property identical to a lack of ability. A person is ignorant of a property when the property is unfamiliar to the person. In order to be ignorant of a property, it suffices to lack acquaintance with the property. To come to know a property is to become acquainted with the property, just as to come to know a city is to become acquainted with the city, and to come to know a problem is to become acquainted with the problem. It is uncontroversial that some knowledge attributions ascribe a relation of acquaintance, as when we say things like 'Sam knows Bill', or 'Bob knows the agony of defeat'. These considerations suggest a hypothesis about the examples in question to the effect that the difference between ignorance of what an experience is like and knowledge of what an experience is like is a matter of acquaintance.

A simple acquaintance hypothesis about what Mary learns is that learning what an experience is like is identical to becoming acquainted with the experience. When first Mary sees red ripe tomatoes, she learns what it is like to see something red. It is also true of this episode that it is the first time that she undergoes an experience with the phenomenal quality that ordinarily results from seeing something red, phenomenal redness.

Suppose that this quality is a physical property of experiences.[4] If phenomenal redness is a physical property, then from the assumption that Mary already knew all of the physical facts it follows that she already knew that experiences have this property. But during her confinement phenomenal redness was not a property of any of her visual experiences. It seems also to be true that she never knew the property itself, in spite of her knowing all about it. This suggests the more specific acquaintance hypothesis that becoming acquainted with a phenomenal quality consists in experiencing the quality. This further hypothesis puts us in a position to account for Mary's learning what it is like to see something red. The learning is a matter of Mary's becoming acquainted with the visual experience that ordinarily results from seeing something red, and this acquaintance consists in Mary's experiencing phenomenal redness. She experiences the quality, and that teaches her what seeing red things is like. She does not learn any new fact. Rather, she comes to know the quality itself. Likewise, Fred knows the special quality of his experience, and not any special fact.

According to this account, Mary already knew all of the physical facts without knowing what it is like to see something red. Mary came to have the latter knowledge simply by having the right sort of experience, and not by acquiring any new information. So the knowledge argument fails to establish the existence of any nonphysical information, if this acquaintance account is correct.

VI   Three Objections Calling for Clarifications

An explanation will soon be offered for why knowledge by acquaintance in such cases consists in experience. But first let us consider whether there is good reason to think that learning what it is like to see something red requires something more than experiencing phenomenal redness.

i. Herbert Feigl appears to have argued that merely experiencing does not constitute knowledge of any sort. Feigl writes: '[M]erely having or living through ("erleben") is not knowledge in any sense' (4, p. 68). Feigl himself accepts the existence of a sort of knowledge by acquaintance. But he takes it to be a species of factual knowledge.

Feigl's cited claim is surely right if it means that in general a person's merely having some property or living through some condition is not sufficient for the person to know the property or the condition. If we need to persuade ourselves of this with an example, we can suppose that a certain fellow Barney is a man of modest means, but not in such dire straits as to be pitiable in any respect. Barney wins a very large cash lottery prize. As unkind fate would have it, an accident renders Barney comatose before he finds out about his winnings. Barney might well come to be pitied as his loss of income goes beyond his lottery winnings while he remains unconscious. Thus, Barney lives through the condition of being affluent and has the property of being pitied without knowing either affluence or pity.

The crucial cases for the knowledge argument are relevantly dissimilar to this one. The crucial cases involve only knowledge of experiences. It is plausible that having experiences is sufficient for knowing those experiences. It is most plausible to hold that this is almost sufficient. The 'almost' is called for because qualities that are quickly and inattentively experienced may not be thereby known. Momentary peripheral awareness of some new shade of colour is not sufficient really to know that shade. The one thing more that is required in order to know an experienced quality is to notice the quality as it is being experienced.

This slightly amended account still implies no need for factual knowledge in order to have knowledge by acquaintance. Ordinarily we do also acquire factual knowledge when we notice a novel sort of experience. We usually acquire factual knowledge about accompaniments of the experience, and sometimes of its causes and effects. Novel experiences also ordinarily bring about new abilities to imagine and recognize. But these are contingent epistemic associates of learning what an experience is like. In the latest version of the case of Mary, the version in which she is wholly lacking in imagination, some of these ordinary epistemic companions are not present. None of them need be present in order to know what an experience is like. Mere attentive awareness will do. The acquaintance hypothesis accommodtates this possibility by holding that all that it takes for a person to come to know what an experience is like is to notice the experience while undergoing it. This hypothesis, which is restricted to knowing experiences, is not refuted by Feigl's correct point that in general having a property or living through a condition does not imply knowing it in any sense. Knowledge of experiences is exceptional in this way.

ii. By experiencing red things, Mary learns what red things look like. Any knowledge by acquaintance aside, this may continue to appear to be a fact that Mary has learned about red things.[5] But this appearance dissipates when we concentrate on the content of this learning. Learning what red things look like is identical to learning how red things look, and this is identical to learning the look of red things. When we have reached this last formulation of the content of the learning, any appearance of factual content is gone. Clearly this does not say that what is learned is some fact to the effect that something or other is so.[6] It says, concerning a certain look, that what is learned is *it*. A look is not a fact. This learning seems to be unproblematically classified as a relation of a person to a phenomenal quality, just as the acquaintance approach would have it.

There are closely related facts, such as the fact concerning phenomenal redness that red things look *that* way. But we have no reason to doubt that

Mary knew all such facts before knowing how red things look. Mary already had the capacity to form thoughts using this demonstrative sort of reference to phenomenal qualities. She was able to demonstrate them with comprehension, at least via others' experiences of them, e.g. as 'that look' while indicating another person's attentive experience of phenomenal redness.

iii. Laurence Nemirow objects to a certain type of analytic proposal that construes knowledge of what an experience is like in terms of acquaintance (8, p. 491). The proposal to which Nemirow objects both asserts that knowing what an experience is like amounts to acquaintance with the experience and denies that this is genuine knowledge. Nemirow observes that this denial of genuine knowledge fails to account for our extensive use of epistemic terms other than 'know' in connection with what an experience is like, epistemic terms such as 'learn', 'remember', and 'forget'.

We can see that this objection does not threaten the present proposal be nothing that the acquaintance hypothesis advocated here does not offer the sort of eliminative reduction to which Nemirow properly objects. The hypothesis has it that Fred does know something in knowing what his special color experience is like, and Mary does learn something in coming to know what it is like to see something red. These are to be cases of having knowledge by acquaintance in the former case, and gaining it in the latter case. They are not implied to be cases of acquaintance rather than knowledge. Thus, Nemirow's objection to any acquaintance proposal that eliminates knowledge does not apply to the present suggestion.

The acquaintance hypothesis under consideration is the view that coming to know what an experience is like requires only noticing the experience as it is undergone. It should be added that continuing to know what an experience is like is not quite so simple. This knowledge can be sustained either by continuing to notice the experience as it is undergone, or by retaining a memory of the experience. It is plausible that having a memory of the experience requires being able to recreate it in imagination. So the abilities to which Nemirow and Lewis appeal in their analyses, abilities to imagine, to remember, and the like, are plausibly regarded as part of the nature of the general phenomenon that we call knowing what an experience is like. But again, what is needed to refute the knowledge argument is an account according to which this knowledge can be gained in the absence of any new abilities. We have seen that no such ability is implied by Mary's initial learning of what it is like to see something red, and this initial learning implies all of the knowledge of what an experience is like that the knowledge argument needs. It is this initial learning that the acquaintance hypothesis accounts for purely in terms of acquaintance.[7]

VII   An Objection Calling for Justification

The response to the knowledge argument that is being advocated here is intended to be compatible with the truth of physicalism. The account is intended to be neutral on the question of whether or not the event of a person's experiencing a phenomenal quality is an entirely physical event. In order to accomplish this neutrality, the account must allow for the possibility that every property is a physical property and all factual information is physical information. It must allow for the physicalist view that during Mary's confinement in a black-and-white environment she already knew every fact about colour vision, including every fact about experiencing phenomenal qualities. If this view is correct, then during her confinement Mary would already know all about chromatic phenomenal qualities. This knowledge would make every visual phenomenal quality a topic of many facts known to Mary. It might be contended that, in virtue of having all of this factual knowledge about the qualities, Mary would be thoroughly acquainted with them. Yet during her confinement Mary does not know what it is like to see something red. So it appears that this knowledge cannot be acquired simply by becoming acquainted with phenomenal redness after all.

This objection depends on the assumption that when someone has a familiarity with phenomenal qualities that is acquired by knowing all of the facts about the qualities, the person is acquainted with those qualities. The acquaintance hypothesis that we are considering denies this. The view has it that someone becomes acquainted with a phenomenal quality only by noticing the quality in experience. Knowing every fact about phenomenal qualities does not imply experiencing them, and thus on the present account it does not imply being acquainted with them.

This appears to be a special requirement for acquaintance with phenomenal qualities, and thus it appears to stand in need of some special justification. If someone is thoroughly familiar with say, Cambridge, then the person 'knows Cambridge' in the sense of being acquainted with the city. So why is Mary's thorough familiarity with the facts about visual phenomenal qualities not likewise sufficient for her to know those qualities by acquaintance?

An answer to this question can be derived from something which is plausibly held to be common to all attributions of knowledge: factual knowledge, knowledge consisting in the possession of an ability, and knowledge by acquaintance. Having knowledge of any sort implies achieving some optimal cognitive accomplishment with reference to the object of knowledge. For instance, in order to know a proposition for a fact, it is not enough for a person simply to believe the proposition with good reason. Factual knowledge requires that the person believe the proposition on the best sort of basis that a person can have for believing propositions of the relevant kind. Similarly, in order to know how to drive a car, it is not enough simply to be able to direct the car's motion in some fashion under some conditions. Knowing how to do something requires being adept at doing it throughout some full normal range of occasions on which it is done. Likewise for the case in point. In order for someone to know something by acquaintance, it is not enough for the person simply to have one or another sort of familiarity with the thing. In fact, however it is with the two other forms of knowledge, it seems particularly clear that knowing something by acquaintance requires a person to be familiar with the known entity in the most direct way that it is possible for a person to be aware of that thing.

Thus, in order for someone to know Cambridge, it is sufficient for the person to be thoroughly familiar with Cambridge by sensory observations. There is no substantially more intimate sort of awareness of a city that a person can have. But in order for someone to know a phenomenal quality, it is not sufficient for the person to know facts about the quality, not even all such facts. The reason for this appears to be that whereas a person's awareness of such a quality in knowing a fact about the quality can be mediated by a conceptual representation of the quality, we seem to be capable of a more direct sort of awareness of any such quality. When the quality is a property of someone's experience, the person need not use any such representation to be aware of the property. Perhaps awareness is experiential pure and unmediated; perhaps awareness of an experienced quality is mediated by some particularly transparent sensory form of representation. What matters for the present account is that experiencing a quality is the most direct way to apprehend the quality. That much seems beyond reasonable doubt.

Even that much need not be true, however. A weaker supposition is usable, though an acquaintance-based objection to the knowledge argument that uses it must be otherwise adjusted accordingly. Let us suppose that all forms of cognition of phenomenal qualities are equally direct, perhaps because they all employ representations. Still, it is quite plausible to think otherwise. Attentively experiencing phenomenal qualities certainly appears to be the most direct sort of awareness of them that we can have. This appearance can be used to explain why we reasonably think that Mary must experience such qualities in order to know them. First we should note that it is an implication of the present supposition, together with the acquaintance hypothesis, that Mary is already acquainted with the qualities simply by knowing facts involving them. This follows because on the present hypothesis her factual knowledge about the qualities renders her as directly aware of them as we can be. So the acquaintance approach would count as false the assumption of the knowledge argument to the effect that Mary learns something by experiencing phenomenal redness for the first time. Since on the current supposition Mary is already acquainted with the experience, she already knows what the experience is like. The plausibility of our initial judgment to the effect that Mary does learn something can be attributed to the plausibility of the thought that experience is required in order to come to know the quality. The knowledge argument would fail by incorrectly assuming that Mary learns what it is like to see something red only when she experiences the quality. It is difficult to believe that this assumption is incorrect, just as difficult as it is to deny that experiencing a quality is a more direct way to be aware of the quality than is thinking abstractly about it. On the present approach, the difficulty in accomplishing this denial would explain the difficulty in believing that Mary did not learn something by experience.

Such an account is available to be used if the best theory of the nature of cognition ultimately supports the assumption that all awareness employs equally indirect representations. But at least currently this assumption seems quite wrong. It is more plausible to maintain that the most direct sort of awareness of a phenomenal quality that is possible for a person consists in noticing the quality while experiencing it. Knowledge by acquaintance requires an appropriate optimal cognitive achievement. In the case of acquaintance with phenomenal qualities, the relevant sort of optimal cognition is a maximally direct sort of awareness. Thus, knowledge by acquaintance of a phenomenal quality requires attentively experiencing the quality.[8]

VIII A Final Objection and Reply

The present view includes an acknowledgement that when Mary becomes acquainted with phenomenal redness for the first time, she apparently thereby becomes able to think about that property in a new way. Suppose that she does. Suppose that either she then has some new and specially intimate sensory form of representation of the property, or she then apprehends the property directly, unmediated by any representation. This might occasion the following objection. It might be contended that after acquiring this new representational resource Mary can have certain accurate thoughts that she could not have had before. These accurate thoughts consist in attributions of properties to phenomenal redness, such as the property of being true of some experiences. These thoughts are new, the objection continues, because the topic of the thought, phenomenal redness, is presented to Mary via the new way which Mary now has to think of that quality. New accurate thoughts imply new correct information about phenomenal redness. Thus it might be held that Mary's gainning a new way of thinking about phenomenal redness implies Jackson's anti-physicalist conclusion that there is correct information beyond what is included in Mary's exhaustive physical knowledge.

To have a new way to introduce the topic of a thought is to have a new means of referring to that topic. We have a new means of referring to a topic if we have a new symbol for that topic. Plainly the same thought can be newly symbolized. So the conceded representational difference by itself does not show that Mary has a new thought.

We also have a new way of referring to a topic when we have found a new characteristic which is true solely of that topic. So if the new way of referring to phenomenal redness that Mary acquires is a new singular property of phenomenal redness, then Mary does acquire a means for forming new thoughts about it. But nothing in Jackson's example gives us any reason to think that Mary's new means of singling out phenomenal redness is afforded her by some new singular property. The cognitive novelty which is required by the facts of the example is that Mary learns what it is like to see something red upon visually experiencing red things for the first time. If the approach advocated here is correct, then this learning is wholly accounted for by Mary's new experience. The learning consists in becoming acquainted with the visual phenomenal quality which is normally produced by viewing red things, and this is done by experiencing the quality. In this account, no property is otherwise new to Mary. The objection does not challenge this account of Mary's cognitive change. It does not provide reason to think that there is also some singular property that Mary learns to use in order to bring the topic of phenomenal redness into new thoughts.

Perhaps Jackson himself supplies the grounds for justifying the sort of claim about new thoughts that we are considering. At one point he describes Mary's ignorance by saying that there is something about other people that she 'was quite unaware of'. He continues:

... [Others'] experiences ... had a feature conspicuous to them but until now hidden from her ... (6, pp. 292–293)

These comments by Jackson are plausible. Our question is whether they show that there was more than a representational change in Mary's thinking. Do they show that Mary underwent a cognitive change by which she gained access to some new thought?

The lack of awareness that Jackson ascribes to Mary and the fact that a certain feature was conspicuous to others and hidden from Mary are both accounted for by a difference in acquaintance. Others were acquainted with phenomenal redness and Mary was not. But Mary did know all facts about color vision that can be learned in black and white. This gives us reason to affirm, and no reason to deny, that this visual quality was conceived of by Mary by use of various scientific representations. We have no reason to deny that it was present in her thoughts in this way. Such thinking is not what we call being aware of the quality itself. In such thinking a phenomenal quality is not 'conspicuous' to the thinker. For someone to be aware of a phenomenal quality, for it to be conspicuously present, is for the person to know the quality by current acquaintance. Only experiencing it accomplishes that. We have no reason to think that Mary also dicovers some new property which was previously unavailable to her to use in her thinking. Jackson's example gives us no reason to think that Mary's new way of representing phenomenal redness yields any new thought.

IX   Minimality

The present response to the knowledge argument is epistemologically substantial, but it is very lean. The claim is that there is a kind of knowledge of
a phenomenal quality, knowledge by acquaintance, which can consist in
attentively experiencing the quality rather than possessing information or
abilities. This is not an exotic epistemic state. It is neither ineffable nor
unmistakeable. It is the familiar sort of knowledge to which refer when we
discuss knowing people and places as well as experiences.

The acquaintance approach is metaphysically noncommittal. The relation of experiencing need not be some simple relation to a phenomenal
quality. for all that the approach implies, attentively experiencing a quality
might be a brain state with a complex neurophysiological nature, and
equally it might be a simple unanalyzable relation of a soul to a nonphysical quality. Physicalism is neither implied nor excluded. The present
reply to the knowledge argument contends that the differences in experience that are by hypothesis included in Jackson's examples constitute the
differences in knowledge that are actually present in the examples. The
examples thus do not support the existence of any nonphysical information. This says nothing metaphysical about experiences.

X   The Basic Intuition Sustained

The knowledge argument begins with a powerful intuition. It seems quite
manifest that knowing all of the physical facts about color vision does
not imply having all knowledge of chromatic phenomenal qualities. It
does not imply knowing these qualities in the most vivid way. In Jackson's
words, "the qualia are left out of the physicalist story" (5, p. 472). An
acquaintance-based response to the knowledge argument enables us to find
truth in this intuition, a truth that does not conflict with physicalism.

Thinking abstractly about a phenomenal quality by use of some conceptual representation for the quality is phenomenologically different from
thinking about the quality while attentively experiencing it. For instance,
we who know how red things look can, while neither seeing nor imagining
red, have the thought that some experiences are phenomenally red. This
thought does not then seem as it does when we have the same thought
while attending to phenomenal redness in experience. During the latter

thinking, the thought appears to be much more … colourful. The phenomenal quality itself seems to do the work in the thinking that is done in the former case by some representation of the quality. Yet whether or not there is this representational difference, by hypothesis and manifestly it is the same thought.

This sort of difference in the phenomenology of the thinking is easily mistaken for a difference in the identity of the thought. In considering Jackson's example of Mary we see that in her thinking phenomenological difference would accompany the cognitive change that occurs when first she sees something red. This is the very point at which she learns what it is like to see something red. It is tempting to infer that Mary must have a new thought as she sees something red for the first time, and to conclude that the learning is acquisition of the knowledge that the new thought is true.

This temptation to attribute a new thought to Mary should be resisted. Reflection on our own thinking has shown us that a similar phenomenological difference does not imply having a different thought. The acquaintance approach is especially helpful here. It explains how such a phenomenological difference can contribute to acquiring new knowledge without having any new thought. The acquaintance approach seizes on the phenomenological novelty of Mary's experience in order to account for Mary's learning. The content of the learning is just the novel quality experienced, not any fact. The learning consists in becoming acquainted with a phenomenal quality. Since this is all it takes to come to know what an experience is like, no new thought is needed.

The physical facts may include every fact about qualia. Still, the physical story does "leave out the qualia," in the sense that knowledge of the physical facts does not imply knowledge of the qualia. Gaining knowledge of phenomenal qualities, though, is no more than a matter of making their acquaintance by attentive experience. It requires only entering into a new cognitive relation to the qualities, not learning any new information. It gives us no reason to doubt that everything is physical.

Appendix: Similar Views

Other philosophers have offered responses to the knowledge argument which are similar in some ways to the present approach. In (10) Michael Tye offers an analysis of knowing what it is like to have an experience with a certain phenomenal quality. Though Tye's analysis is not formulated in terms of acquaintance, it resembles the acquaintance account developed in the present work. A main difference is that Tye holds (10, p. 9) that knowledge of what an experience is like is "grounded upon" factual knowledge, while the present account explains this knowledge in a way that does not imply factual knowledge. The present account thus avoids any objection that questions the adequacy of a physicalist account of the factual grounding.

In (2) Paul Churchland very briefly sketches an acquaintance analysis and suggests that it may be the sort of knowledge that Mary acquires (2, pp. 23–24). Churchland's sketch has it that acquaintance knowledge may involve a special "prelinguistic or sublinguistic medium of representation for sensory variables," or it may involve sensory discriminative abilities (2, p. 23). The latter alternative is subject to the objection that no such ability is needed for Mary to learn what it is like to see something red. The former alternative seems similar in spirit to the acquaintance hypothesis elaborated and defended in the present work.

In (1) John Bigelow and Robert Pargetter explain in terms of acquaintance what Mary learns. They hold that Mary was already acquainted with all correct information about phenomenal redness via some mode of acquaintance or other (1, p. 144). When she experiences this quality she acquires new knowledge in virtue of being in a new mode of acquaintance and thereby having a new way of knowing what she knew before (1, p. 141). This account locates distinctions among items of knowledge where there is no distinction in what is known. Mary is to gain new knowledge, even though everything that she knows is something that she already knew. That is doubtful. This sort of is difficulty is avoided in the present account, according to which what Mary comes to know—phenomenal redness—is something which she did not know before, although she may have known all facts about it. Bigelow and Pargetter's work is otherwise quite congenial to the present approach. The two papers are largely mutually reinforcing. I regret that I did not have the benefit of studying their paper until its existence was made known to me by an anonymous referee of this manuscript for [the *Australasian Journal of Philosophy*].

In (9) Paul Teller proposes that what is new to Mary is an experience rather than any factual knowledge. Teller concurs, however, with Lewis and Nemirow's ability analyses of knowing what an experience is like. This seems to preclude an adequate response to the version of Jackson's argument discussed above that employs a case in which Mary lacks the relevant abilities.

Acknowledgments

I am grateful for discussions of the knowledge argument with Dorit Bar-On, Mark Crimmins, Richard Feldman, David Lewis, and members of the Philosophy Department at Wayne State University. I am also grateful for comments on previous drafts from Joseph Tolliver and anonymous referees for the *Australasian Journal of Philosophy*.

Notes

1. The following critical writings are particularly pertinent to the work of the present paper: Bigelow and Pargetter (1), Churchland (2), Lewis (7), Nemirow (8), and Tye (10).

2. This is the approach of David (7), Nemirow (8), and Teller (9).

3. Whether or not she really is ready to find out what it is like to see cherry red is questionable in a way that does not affect the present point. See n. 8 below.

4. This is not a pellucid supposition. It is not trivial to give an appropriate sense to 'physical property', nor to the expression 'physical information' in terms of which Jackson formulates physicalism. Presumably the rough idea is that all such properties and information are somehow included in the proper subject matter of the physical sciences, whether or not actual science ever happens to address them. Giving a clear account of the relevant notion of 'proper subject matter' would be no mean feat. Fortunately, for the purposes of the present work any reasonable conception of the physical will do. The main contention here is that Fred's knowledge of the special quality of his experience and Mary's knowledge of what it is like to see something red are initially matters of acquaintance with the relevant phenomenal qualities. Having this knowledge does not imply possessing of any sort of information. This response to the knowledge argument leaves entirely open the ontological status of all properties and accurate information. Because of this, the present work does not depend on having a satisfactory answer to the question of what it takes for properties or information to fall into the category of physical things.

5. An anonymous referee for the *Australasian Journal of Philosophy* suggests that this appearance remains.

6. It is notable that, at least in (5) and (6), Jackson never attempts to formulate the content of Mary's learning with a 'that'-clause. I attempt to do so in (3, p. 300). For

considerations which now seem to me to eliminate any good reason to think that a 'that'-clause formulates new information, see the reply to the present objection, and sections VIII and X below.

7. In the appendix, this acquaintance-based response to the knowledge argument is briefly compared to similar proposals in the literature.

8. Hence the quality can come to be known by being imagined rather than being perceived, if the imagining produces an experience that actually has the quality. If imagination cannot do this, then it cannot initiate acquaintance with a phenomenal quality.

References

1. J. Bigelow and R. Pargetter, "Acquaintance With Qualia," *Theoria* 61 (1990) pp. 129–147.

2. P. M. Churchland, "Reduction, Qualia, and the Direct Introspection of Brain States," *Journal of Philosophy* 83 (1985) pp. 8–28.

3. E. Conee, "Physicalism and Phenomenal Qualities," *Philosophical Quarterly* 35 (1985) pp. 296–303.

4. H. Feigl, *The "Mental" and the "Physical"* (Minneapolis: University of Minnesota Press, 1958).

5. F. Jackson, "Epiphenomenal Qualia," *Philosophical Quarterly* 32 (1982) pp. 127–136. Reprinted in this volume.

6. F. Jackson, "What Mary Didn't Know," *Journal of Philosophy* 83 (1986) pp. 291–295. Reprinted in this volume.

7. D. Lewis, "What Experience Teaches" in W. G. Lycan (ed.), *Mind and Cognition* (Oxford: Blackwell, 1990) pp. 499–519. Reprinted in this volume.

8. L. Nemirow, "Physicalism and the Cognitive Role of Acquaintance" in W. G. Lycan (ed.), *Mind and Cognition* (Oxford: Blackwell, 1990) pp. 490–499.

9. P. Teller, "Subjectivity and Knowing What It's Like" in A. Beckermann, H. Flohr, and J. Kim (eds.), *Emergence or Reduction? Essays on the Prospects of Nonreductive Physicalism* (New York: Gruyter, 1992), pp. 180–200.

10. M. Tye, "The Subjective Qualities of Experience," *Mind* 95 (1986) pp. 1–17.

Part V Old Facts, New Modes

11 Phenomenal States (Revised Version)

Brian Loar

On a natural view of ourselves, we introspectively discriminate our own experiences and thereby form conceptions of their qualities, both salient and subtle. These discriminations are of various degrees of generality, from small differences in tactual and color experience to broad differences of sensory modality, for example, those among smell, hearing, and pain. What we apparently discern are ways experiences differ and resemble each other with respect to *what it is like to have them*. Following common usage, I will call these experiential resemblances *phenomenal qualities*, and the conceptions we have of them, *phenomenal concepts*. Phenomenal concepts are formed "from one's own case." They are *type-demonstratives* that derive their reference from a first-person perspective: 'that type of sensation', 'that feature of visual experience'. And so third-person ascriptions of phenomenal qualities are projective ascriptions of what one has grasped in one's own case: 'she has an experience of that type'.

'Phenomenal quality' can have a different sense, namely, how the *object* of a perceptual experience appears. In this sense, a phenomenal quality is ascribed to an object and not directly to an experience. Some have argued that all we discern phenomenologically are phenomenal qualities in this sense; they deny that experiences themselves have introspectible qualities that are not ascribed primarily to their objects (Harman 1990; Block 1990). I will not pursue the issue here, but will assume a certain view of it. For the present objective is to engage antiphysicalist arguments and entrenched intuitions to the effect that conscious mental qualities cannot be identical with ordinary physical properties, or at least that it is problematic to suppose that they are so. Antiphysicalists typically suppose that such mental properties are not relational—that is, that they present themselves as not intrinsically involving relations to things outside the mind. They may allow that, say, visual experiences are in some sense intrinsically representational. That is hard to deny because, as regards ordinary visual experiences, we cannot apparently conceive them phenomenally in a way that abstracts from their *purporting* to represent things in a certain way. The antiphysicalist intuition is compatible with visual experiences' having (some sort of) internally determined intentional structure, so that it is an introspectable and nonrelational feature of a visual experience that it represents things visually as being thus and so. Antiphysicalists suppose that we have conceptions of how visual experiences differ and resemble each other with respect to what it is like to have those experiences. These conceptions then are of qualities of experiences, whatever allowances one may also make for the apparent qualities of the intrinsic objects of those experiences. I will assume that the antiphysicalists' phenomenological and internalist intuitions are correct. The idea is to engage them over the central point, that is, whether those aspects of the mental that we both count as phenomenologically compelling raise substantive difficulties for the thesis that phenomenal qualities (thus understood) are physical properties of the brain that lie within the scope of current science.

We have to distinguish between *concepts* and *properties*, and this chapter turns on that distinction. Antiphysicalist arguments and intuitions take off from a sound intuition about concepts. Phenomenal concepts are conceptually irreducible in this sense: they neither a priori imply, nor are implied by, physical-functional concepts. Although that is denied by analytical functionalists (Levin 1983, 1986), many other physicalists, including me, find it intuitively appealing. The antiphysicalist takes this conceptual intuition a good deal further, to the conclusion that phenomenal qualities are themselves irreducible, are not physical-functional properties, at least not of the ordinary sort. The upshot is a range of antireductionist views: that consciousness and phenomenal qualities are unreal because irreducible;[1] that they are irreducibly non–physical-functional facts;[2] that they are forever mysterious, or pose an intellectual problem different from other empirical problems, or require new conceptions of the physical.[3]

It is my view that we can have it both ways. We may take the phenomenological intuition at face value, accepting introspective concepts and their conceptual irreducibility, and at the same time take phenomenal qualities to be identical with physical-functional properties of the sort envisaged by contemporary brain science. As I see it, there is no persuasive philosophically articulated argument to the contrary.

This is not to deny the power of raw metaphysical intuition. Thoughtful people compare phenomenal qualities and kinds of physical-functional property, say the activation of neural assemblies. It appears to them to be an evident and unmediated truth, independent of further premises, that phenomenal qualities cannot be identical with properties of those types or perhaps of any physical-functional type. This intuition is so compelling that it is tempting to regard antiphysicalist arguments as rationalizations of an intuition whose independent force masks their tendentiousness. It is the point of this chapter to consider the arguments. But I will also present a positive account of the relation between phenomenal concepts and physical properties that may provide some relief, or at least some distance, from the illusory metaphysical intuition.

In recent years the central problem with physicalism has been thought by many to be "the explanatory gap." This is the idea that we cannot *explain*, in terms of physical-functional properties, what makes a certain experience 'feel like this', in the way we can explain what makes a certain substance a liquid, say. It is concluded that physicalism is defective in some respect, that there cannot be a (proper) reduction of the mental to the physical. Before we consider this explanatory gap, we must first examine, in some detail, a more basic antiphysicalist line of reasoning that goes back to Leibniz and beyond, a leading version of which is now called the knowledge argument. Answering this argument will generate a framework in which to address antiphysicalist concerns in general.

1   The Knowledge Argument and Its Semantic Premise

The knowledge argument is straightforward on the face of it. Consider any phenomenal quality and any physical property however complex. We can know that a person has the physical property without knowing that she experiences the phenomenal quality. And no amount of a priori reasoning or construction can bridge this conceptual gap. That is the intuitive premise. The conclusion is drawn that the phenomenal quality cannot be identical with the physical property. The argument is equivalent to this: since physical and phenomenal conceptions can be connected only a posteriori, physical properties must be distinct from phenomenal properties.

The best known and liveliest version of the knowledge argument is Frank Jackson's, which features the physiologically omniscient Mary, who has never seen color and so does not know what it is like for us to see red, despite her knowing all the physical-functional facts about us.[4] She later sees colors, and thus learns what it has been like all along for us to see red. She learns a new fact about us. Jackson concludes that this fact is not among the physical facts, since Mary already knew them. It is not difficult to see that this argument depends on a more or less technical premise.

In my view, the physicalist should accept Jackson's intuitive description of Mary: she fails to know that we have certain color experiences even though she knows all relevant physical facts about us. And when she acquires color experience, she does learn something new about us—if you like, learns a new fact or truth. But this is to be granted, of course, only on an *opaque* reading of 'Mary learns that we have such and such color experiences', and on corresponding readings of 'learns a new fact or truth about us'. For as regards the transparent versions of those ascriptions of what Mary did not know and then learned, they would beg the question, amounting to this: 'as for the property of having such and such color experiences, Mary did not know, but then learned, *of* that property that we have it'. Physicalists reject this, for according to us those experiential properties are physical properties, and Mary already knew of all our physical properties that we have them—under their physical descriptions. What she lacked and then acquired, rather, was knowledge of certain such properties couched in experiential terms.

Drawing metaphysical conclusions from opaque contexts is risky. And in fact inferences of Jackson's form, without additional premises, are open to straightforward counterexamples of a familiar sort. Let me describe two cases.

(1) Max learns that the bottle before him contains CH_3CH_2OH. But he does not know that the bottle contains alcohol. This holds on an opaque reading: he would not assert that there's stuff called alcohol in the bottle, or that the bottle contains the intoxicating component of beer and wine. Let sheltered Max even lack the ordinary concept 'alcohol'. After he acquires that ordinary concept, he learns something new—that the bottle contained alcohol. If the knowledge argument has a generally valid form, we could then infer from Max's epistemic situation that alcohol is not identical with CH_3CH_2OH. Evidently this does not follow.

(2) Margot learns about the element Au and reads that people decorate themselves with alloys of Au. But she has never seen gold and cannot visually identify it: she lacks an adequate visual conception. She later is shown some gold and forms a visual conception of it, "that stuff," and she acquires a new piece of information—individuated opaquely—to the effect that those previously read about embellishments are made of that stuff. Again, if the knowledge argument were unrestrictedly valid, it would follow that that stuff is not identical with Au. This case differs from the case of Max by involving not a descriptive mode of presentation but (as we might say) a perceptual mode of presentation.

It is not difficult to find a difference between both these cases and the case of Mary. Max lacks knowledge of the bottle's contents under a contingent description of it—'ingredient of wine and beer that makes you intoxicated'. What Margot lacks is a certain visual conception of Au, which is to say gold. This typically would not be a descriptive conception; it would not self-consciously take the form 'the stuff that occasions this type of visual experience'. Still on the face of it such a concept implicates a visual-experience type. For it picks out the kind it picks out by virtue of that kind's occasioning experiences of that type. And that is a crucial *contingency* in how the concept that Margot lacks is related to its reference. I hope I will be understood, then, if I say that the visual take on Au that Margot lacks would have conceived Au 'under a contingent mode of presentation'.

This brings us back to Mary, whose acquired conception of what it is like to see red does not conceive it under a contingent mode of presentation. She is not conceiving of a property that presents itself *contingently* thus: it is like such and such to experience P. Being experienced like that is essential to the property Mary conceives. She conceives it directly. When Mary later acquires new information about us (construed opaquely), the novelty of this information cannot be explained—as in the case of Margot—as her acquiring a new contingent mode of presentation of something she has otherwise known of all along. She has a *direct* grasp of the property involved in the new information; she conceives of it somehow, but not under a contingent mode of presentation. Proponents of the knowledge argument will say that is why it is valid on an opaque reading: there is no contingency in Mary's conception of the new phenomenal information that explains it as a novel take on old facts. She learns new facts simpliciter and not new conceptions of old facts.

Notice how close this comes to Saul Kripke's well-known antiphysicalist argument (1980). Kripke assumes that a phenomenal concept such as 'pain' cannot be a priori linked with a physical concept such as that of the stimulation of C-fibers. The case of Mary is a vivid way of making the same point. Kripke points out that property identities can be true even if not a priori, for example, 'heat = such and such molecular property'. It seems fair to represent the next step in his argument as follows. 'Heat' has a contingent higher-order mode of presentation that connotes the property 'feeling like this'. That is what accounts for the a posteriori status of the identity. But, as Kripke points out, this cannot be how 'pain' works: the phenomenal concept 'pain' does not pick out its referent via a contingent mode of presentation; it conceives pain directly and essentially. Kripke concludes that pain is not identical with a physical property.

The two arguments then turn on the same implicit assumption. The only way to account for the a posteriori status of a true property identity is this: one of the terms expresses a contingent mode of presentation. This ought to be given a place of prominence.

(Semantic premise) A statement of property identity that links conceptually independent concepts is true only if at least one concept picks out the property it refers to by connoting a contingent property of that property.

The knowledge argument and Kripke's argument then depend on two assumptions: the conceptual independence of phenomenal concepts and physical-functional concepts, which I accept, and the semantic premise, which I deny.

The antiphysicalist intuition that links concept-individuation and property-individuation (more closely than is in my view correct) is perhaps this. Phenomenal concepts and theoretical expressions of physical properties both conceive their references essentially. But if two concepts conceive a given property essentially, neither mediated by contingent modes of presentation, one ought to be able to see a priori—at least after optimal reflection—that they pick out the same property. Such concepts' connections cannot be a posteriori; that they pick out the same property would have to be transparent.

But as against this, if a phenomenal concept can pick out a physical property directly or essentially, not via a contingent mode of presentation, and yet be *conceptually independent* of all physical-functional concepts, so that Mary's history is coherent, then Jackson's and Kripke's arguments are ineffectual. We could have two conceptually independent conceptions of a property, neither of which connote contingent modes of presentation, such that substituting one for the other in an opaquely interpreted epistemic context does not preserve truth. Even granting that our conception of phenomenal qualities is direct, physicalism would not entail that knowing the physical-functional facts implies knowing, on an opaque construal, the phenomenal facts; and so the failure of this implication would be quite compatible with physicalism. The next few sections give an account of phenomenal concepts and properties that would justify this claim.

2 Recognitional Concepts

Phenomenal concepts belong to a wide class of concepts that I will call recognitional concepts. They have the form 'x is one of *that* kind'; they are type-demonstratives. These type-demonstratives are grounded in dispositions to classify, by way of perceptual discriminations, certain objects, events, situations. Suppose you go into the California desert and spot a succulent never seen before. You become adept at recognizing instances, and gain a recognitional command of their kind, without a name for it; you are disposed to identify positive and negative instances and thereby pick out a kind. These dispositions are typically linked with capacities to form images, whose conceptual role seems to be to focus thoughts about an identifiable kind in the absence of currently perceived instances. An image is presumably 'of' a given kind by virtue of both past recognitions and current dispositions.

Recognitional concepts are generally formed against a further conceptual background. In identifying a thing as of a recognized kind, we almost always presuppose a more general type to which the kind belongs: four-legged animal, plant, physical thing, perceptible event. A recognitional concept will then have the form 'physical thing of that (perceived) kind' or 'internal state of that kind', and so forth.[5]

Here are some basic features of recognitional concepts that it will help to have in mind in connection with the account of phenomenal concepts that follows.

1. You can understand 'porcelain' from a technical description and only later learn visually, tactually, and aurally to recognize instances. By contrast, in the phenomenon I mean the concept is recognitional at its core; the original concept is recognitional.

2. A recognitional concept need involve no reference to a past instance, or have the form 'is of the same type as that (remembered) one'. You can forget particular instances and still judge 'another one of those'.

3. Recognitional abilities depend on no consciously accessible analysis into component features; they can be irreducibly gestalt.

4. Recognitional concepts are perspectival. Suppose you see certain creatures up close and form a recognitional concept—'those creatures$_1$'; and suppose you see others at a distance, not being able to tell that they are of the same kind (even when they are), and form another recognitional concept—'those creatures$_2$'. These concepts will be a priori independent. Now the respect in which they differ is *perspectival*, in some intuitive sense. A recognitional concept is in part individuated by its constitutive perspective. Here is the important point: a recognitional concept can be ascribed outside its constitutive perspective; 'that thing (seen at distance) is one of those creatures$_1$ (seen up close)' makes perfectly good sense. This plays a key role below in the account of third-person ascriptions of phenomenal concepts.

(This casual invoking of reference-determining dispositions will be a red flag for many who are aware of the vexing foundations of the theory of reference. Problems about referential scrutability, rule-following, naturalizing intentionality—however one wishes to put it—are as frustrating as any in contemporary philosophy. I do not propose to address them here. The idea rather is to appeal to unanalyzed common sense concerning a natural group of concepts and apparent conceptual abilities. The apparent irreducibility of phenomenal qualities itself arises from appeal to intuitions independent of the theory of reference; and it seems reasonable that we should, in resolving that issue, appeal to notions that arise at the same intuitive level. That we *appear* to have recognitional concepts and identifying dispositions that are more or less determinate in their reference is hard to deny. My conception of 'those hedges' [seen around the neighborhood] may unambiguously pick out a variety of eugenia. An example closer to the present topic is this. We can imagine an experiment in which the experimenter tries to determine which internal property is the focus of her subject's identifications: 'again', ... 'there it is again'. There seems no commonsensical implausibility—putting aside foundational worries about the inscrutability of reference—in the idea that there is a best possible answer to the experimenter's question, in the scientific long run.)[6]

3 Phenomenal Concepts as Recognitional Concepts

Here is the view to be defended. Phenomenal concepts are recognitional concepts that pick out certain internal properties; these are physical-functional properties of the brain. They are the concepts we deploy in our phenomenological reflections; and there is no good philosophical reason to deny that, odd though it may sound, the properties these conceptions *phenomenologically reveal* are physical-functional properties—but not of course under physical-functional descriptions. Granted that brain research might discover that (what we take to be) our phenomenal concepts do not in fact discriminate unified physical-functional properties. Failing that, it is quite coherent for a physicalist to take the phenomenology at face value: the property of *its being like this* to have a certain experience is nothing over and above a certain physical-functional property of the brain.

Phenomenal concepts are conceptually independent of physical-functional descriptions, and yet pairs of such concepts may converge on, pick out, the same properties. Rebutting the semantic premise of the knowledge argument requires making sense of the idea that phenomenal concepts conceive physical-functional properties 'directly', that is, not by way of contingent modes of presentation. The objective is to show that the knowledge argument fails for the same reason in the case of Mary as in the case of Max: both arguments require substitution in opaque contexts of terms that are conceptually independent. In the case of Max, the conceptual independence appears to derive from 'alcohol's' connoting a contingent mode of presentation that is metaphysically independent of the property referred to by the chemical concept. In the case of Mary it has a different source.

What then accounts for the conceptual independence of phenomenal and physical-functional concepts? The simple answer is that recognitional concepts and theoretical concepts are in general conceptually independent. It is true that recognitional concepts other than phenomenal concepts

connote contingent modes of presentation that are metaphysically independent of the natural kinds they pick out, and hence independent of the
kind referred to by the theoretical term of the pair. But we need not count
this metaphysical independence as essential to the conceptual independence of coreferring recognitional and theoretical concepts. Concepts of
the two sorts have quite different conceptual roles. It is hardly surprising
that a recognitional conception of a physical property should discriminate
it without analyzing it in scientific terms. Nor should it be surprising that,
if there are recognitional concepts that pick out physical properties *not*
via contingent modes of presentation, they do not discriminate their references by analyzing them (even implicitly) in scientific terms. Basic recognitional abilities do not depend on or get triggered by conscious scientific
analysis. If phenomenal concepts reflect basic recognitions of internal
physical-functional states, they *should* be conceptually independent of
theoretical physical-functional descriptions. That is what you expect quite
apart from issues concerning physicalism.

An antireductionist may reply that the physicalist view depends on an ad
hoc assumption and that it is tendentious to suppose that phenomenal
concepts differ from all other recognitional concepts in not having contingent modes of presentation.

But this is not fair. Even on the antiphysicalist view, phenomenal concepts are recognitional concepts, and we have 'direct' recognitional conceptions of phenomenal qualities, that is, conceptions unmediated by
contingent modes of presentation. Evidently it would be absurd to insist
that the antiphysicalist hold that we conceive of a phenomenal quality of
one kind via a phenomenal mode of presentation of a distinct kind. And
why should the physicalist not agree that phenomenal recognitional concepts are structured in whatever simple way the antiphysicalist requires?
That is after all the intuitive situation, and the physicalist simply claims
that the intuitive facts about phenomenal qualities are compatible with
physicalism. The physicalist makes the additional claim that the phenomenal quality thus directly conceived is a physical-functional property. On
both metaphysical views, phenomenal concepts differ from other recognitional concepts; phenomenal concepts are a peculiar sort of recognitional
concept on any account, and that can hardly count against physicalism.
The two views agree about conceptual structure and disagree about the nature of phenomenal qualities. To insist that physicalism implies, absurdly,

that phenomenal concepts could pick out physical properties only via metaphysically distinct phenomenal modes of presentation is unmotivated. There is, though, still more to be said about whether phenomenal concepts should be regarded as having modes of presentation of some sort, and we continue the account in section 5.

Suppose this account of how phenomenal concepts refer is true. Here is a semantic consequence. The physicalist thesis implies that the judgments 'the state *a* feels like that' and 'the state *a* has physical-functional property *P*' can have the same truth condition even though their joint truth or falsity can be known only a posteriori. I mean, same condition of truth in a possible world. For truth conditions are determined in part by the possible world satisfaction conditions of predicates; and if a phenomenal predicate directly refers to a physical property, that property constitutes its satisfaction condition.

On this account, a phenomenal concept rigidly designates the property it picks out. But then it rigidly designates the same property that some theoretical physical concept rigidly designates. This could seem problematic, for if a concept rigidly designates a property not via a contingent mode of presentation, must that concept not capture the *essence* of the designated property? And if two concepts capture the essence of the same property, must we not be able to know this a priori? These are equivocating uses of 'capture the essence of'. On one use, it expresses a referential notion that comes to no more than 'directly rigidly designate'. On the other, it means something like 'be conceptually interderivable with some theoretical predicate that reveals the internal structure of' the designated property. But the first does not imply the second. What is correct in the observation about rigid designation has no tendency to imply that the two concepts must be a priori interderivable.

4   The Concept 'Phenomenal Concept'

Not all self-directed recognitional concepts are phenomenal concepts, as may be seen in these two cases.

(1) Cramps have a characteristic feel, but they are not feelings. Cramps are certain muscle contractions, while feelings of cramp are, if physical, brain states. (Witness phantom-limb sufferers.) One has a recognitional concept that picks out certain muscle contractions in the having of them.

This is not a phenomenal concept, for it does not purport to pick out a phenomenal quality. But of course, in exercising this concept, one often conceives its reference by way of a phenomenal mode of presentation, a cramp feeling or a cramp-feeling image.

(2) A more fanciful self-directed nonphenomenal concept can be conceived. To begin with, consider blindsight. Some cortically damaged people are phenomenally blind in restricted retinal regions; and yet when a vertical or horizontal line (say) is presented to those regions, they can, when prompted, guess what is there with a somewhat high degree of correctness. We can extend the example by imagining a blindsight that is exercised spontaneously and accurately. At this point we shift the focus to internal properties and conceive of a self-directed recognitional ability, which is like the previous ability in being phenomenally blank and spontaneous but which discriminates an internal property of one's own. If this recognitional ability were suitably governed by the concept 'that state', the resulting concept would be a self-directed recognitional concept that is phenomenally blank.

The two examples show that 'phenomenal concept' cannot mean 'self-directed recognitional concept'. This is compatible with my proposal. For it implies neither (a) that we can reductively explicate the concept 'phenomenal quality' as 'property picked out by a self-directed discriminative ability', or (b) that we can reductively explicate the concept 'phenomenal concept' as 'self-directed recognitional concept'. Phenomenal concepts are certain self-directed recognitional concepts. Our higher-order concept 'phenomenal concept' cannot be reductively explicated, any more than can our concept 'phenomenal quality'. The higher-order concept 'phenomenal concept' is as irreducibly demonstrative as phenomenal concepts themselves.

5 Phenomenal Modes of Presentation

Self-directed recognitional concepts of the blindsight type might appear to raise a problem for the claim that phenomenal concepts pick out physical-functional properties directly. Here is a way to put the point.

The difference between a self-directed blindsight recognitional concept and a phenomenal concept appears to be that the latter involves a phenomenal mode of presentation while the former conceives its referent in some other, odd, way. So, if the phenomenal concept is taken to discriminate some physical property, it then does so via a phenomenal mode of presentation. But that conflicts with your assertion that phenomenal concepts refer directly, with no contingent mode of presentation. A similar point arises concerning recognitional concepts of cramps and of cramp feelings. Both concepts must presumably have modes of presentation. It is far-fetched to suppose that one of them has and the other lacks a mode of presentation; the phenomenal concept does not pick out a physical state *nakedly*. The 'cramp' concept connotes a mode of presentation of the form 'the physical state that causes such and such phenomenal state'. If we attempt to capture the phenomenal concept analogously, its mode of presentation would have the form 'the state that has such and such phenomenal aspect'. But then, contrary to what the physicalist must say, phenomenal concepts point to physical states only by way of phenomenal modes of presentation.

What might an antiphysicalist say about these various self-directed recognitional concepts? Let me make a good-faith attempt to present a reasonable version.

(1) A cramp concept picks out a muscular property indirectly, by way of a causal chain that is mediated by the phenomenal quality associated with the concept. In addition to this mode of presentation type—the phenomenal quality, we can also note the role of, as we might say, "token modes of presentation." One and the same cramp concept (type) can on different occasions be focussed differently: by an actual cramp feeling, by a cramp-feeling image, or by an imageless inclination to identify cramp feelings when they occur (with a cramp-feeling image on the tip of one's imagination).

(2) We turn from cramp concepts to cramp-feeling-concepts. These do not refer (i.e., to cramp feelings) by way of contingent modes of presentation. But they can mimic the working of cramp concepts as regards "token modes of presentation." If one can focus attention on the bodily property of cramp by way of a token cramp feeling, surely one can focus attention on the phenomenal quality cramp feeling by way of a token cramp feeling. The same goes for cramp-feeling images and those gossamer identifying inclinations. Should antiphysicalists say that cramp-feeling concepts have 'noncontingent' modes of presentation? We might say that a phenomenal concept has as its mode of presentation the very phenomenal quality that it picks out. We might also say that phenomenal concepts have "token modes of presentation" that are noncontingently tied to the phenomenal

qualities to which those concepts point: particular cramp feelings and images can focus one's conception of the phenomenal quality of cramp feeling.

(3) As for self-directed blindsight concepts, the antiphysicalist then ought to say, they differ from phenomenal concepts in the obvious way, whether one puts it by saying that they lack the noncontingent phenomenal modes of presentation (types) that phenomenal qualities have, or that they lack their phenomenal "token modes of presentation."

The main point is by now more than obvious. Whatever the antiphysicalist has said about these cases the physicalist may say as well. The idea that one picks out the phenomenal quality of cramp feeling by way of a particular feeling of cramp (or image, etc.) is hardly incompatible with holding that that phenomenal quality is a physical property. The contrast between phenomenal concepts and self-directed blindsight concepts and cramp concepts finds physicalist and antiphysicalist equally able to say something sensible.

A phenomenal concept exercised in the absence of the phenomenal quality it stands for often involves not merely a recognitional disposition but also an image. And so, as a psychological state in its own right, a phenomenal concept—given its intimate connection with imaging—bears a phenomenological affinity to a phenomenal state that neither state bears to the entertaining of a physical-theoretical concept. When we then bring phenomenal and physical-theoretical concepts together in our philosophical ruminations, those cognitive states are phenomenologically so different that the illusion may be created that their references must be different. It is as though antiphysicalist intuitions rest on a resemblance theory of mental representation, as though we conclude from the lack of resemblance in our phenomenal and physical-functional conceptions a lack of sameness in the properties to which they refer.

6 Third-person Ascriptions

Ascriptions of phenomenal qualities to others ostensibly refer to properties that others may have independently of our ascribing them:[7] we have realist conceptions of the phenomenal states of others. But at the same time they are projections from one's own case; they have the form '*x* has a state of this sort', where the demonstrative gets its reference from an actual or possible state of one's own.

Can phenomenal concepts as we predicate them of others be identified with the recognitional concepts we have characterized? A question naturally arises how essentially self-directed recognitional concepts can be applied in cases where it makes no sense to say that one can directly apply these concepts. This is a question that exercised Wittgensteinians.

As we have already pointed out, recognitional concepts are perspectival, in the sense that their reference is determined from a certain constitutive perspective (depending on the concept). The above concept 'those creatures$_1$' (seen up close) picks out a creature-kind that one discriminates on close sightings. But nothing prevents ascribing the recognitional concept 'one of those creatures$_1$' to something observed from a different perspective, seen in the distance or heard in the dark. We have to distinguish the perspective from which reference is determined and the far broader range of contexts in which the referentially fixed concept can be ascribed. The former perspective hardly restricts the latter contexts. This holds also for phenomenal concepts. We acquire them from a first-person perspective, by discriminating a property in the having of it. Assuming that we successfully pick out a more or less determinate physical property, the extraperspectival ascription 'she is in a state of *this* kind' makes complete sense. And so it is not easy to see that Wittgensteinians succeeded in raising a philosophical problem that survives the observation that we can discriminate physical properties and so fix the reference of phenomenal concepts from a first-person perspective, and then go on to ascribe those concepts third-personally.

There is though a more up-to-date worry about the interpersonal ascribability of first-person concepts, however physical we suppose their references to be. Evidently there will be vagueness, and indeterminacy, concerning whether another person—whose neural assemblies will presumably always differ from mine in various respects—has a certain physical property that I discriminate phenomenally. And this on the face of it poses a problem, which may be framed as follows:

The question whether another person's phenomenal states resemble yours can hardly consist in their neural assemblies' resembling yours. Any physical similarity you choose will be arbitrarily related to a given phenomenal similarity. Suppose there is a small physical difference between a neural state of yours and another person's state. What makes it the case that this small neural difference constitutes a small phenomenal difference or a large one or no phenomenal difference at all? It appears that there cannot be a fact of the matter.

But this objection appears to me to overlook a crucial element of the physicalist view we have presented—that phenomenal concepts are (type-) demonstrative concepts that pick out physical properties and relations. A first step in answering it is to consider the connection between interpersonal and intrapersonal phenomenal similarity. It appears that one's phenomenological conception of how others' phenomenal states resemble one's own has to be drawn from one's idea of how one's own phenomenal states resemble each other. A person's quality space of interpersonal similarity must derive from her quality space of intrapersonal similarity. How else is one to get a conceptual grip on interpersonal phenomenal similarity? This seems inevitable on any account—physicalist or antiphysicalist—on which phenomenal concepts are formed from one's own case.

But conceptions of phenomenal similarity relations are as much type-demonstrative concepts as those of phenomenal qualities. All one can apparently mean by 'that spectrum of phenomenal similarity' is '*that ordering* among my phenomenal states'. Physicalism implies that if such a type-demonstrative refers, it picks out a physical ordering. And there is no obvious philosophical difficulty (if we put aside skepticism in the theory of reference) in the idea that discriminations of resemblances and differences among one's own phenomenal properties pick out reasonably well defined physical relations.

Now I have to confess some uneasiness about extending this to interpersonal similarity without qualification; but the implications of the foregoing remarks are clear enough. If they are correct, whatever physical ordering relations are picked out by one's personal notions of phenomenal similarity must also constitute (what one thinks of as) interpersonal phenomenal similarity. It is easy to see that there still is room here for further trouble. But the difficulty the objection raises seems considerably diminished if one insists on the demonstrative nature of all phenomenal concepts, however relational and of whatever order. For the objection then becomes, "Suppose there is a small physical difference between a neural state of yours and another person's state. What makes it the case that this small neural difference constitutes a small difference of *that* type, or a large one, or no difference of *that* type at all?" If 'that type' picks out a physical relation, then the question answers itself, and there seems no gloomy philosophical threat of phenomenal incommensurability.

Naturally there is the risk that physical investigation will not deliver the right physical properties and relations. Even if the risk is increased by bringing in interpersonal similarities, the nature of the risk is the same as in one's own case: the phenomenal might turn out to be not adequately embodied.

It goes without saying that one can coherently conceive that another person has P, conceived in physical-functional terms, and doubt that she has any given phenomenal quality; that has been central to this chapter. But one cannot coherently wonder whether another person in a P state has a state with *this* phenomenal quality if one acknowledges that one's concept 'this quality' refers to the property the concept discriminates in oneself (what else?) and that moreover it discriminates P.

Why then is there an apparent problem of other minds? It is as if one wishes to do to others as one does to oneself—namely, apply phenomenal concepts directly, apply phenomenal recognitional capacities to others from a first-person perspective. The impossibility of this can present itself as an epistemological barrier, as something that makes it impossible to know certain facts. Doubtless more can be said in explanation of the naturalness of the conflation of the innocuous conceptual fact with a severe epistemological disability. It is not easy to shake the grip of that conflation or therefore easy to dispel the problem of other minds. The cognitive remedy, the fortification against the illusion, is the idea of recognitional concepts that can be ascribed beyond their constitutive perspective, coupled with the reflection that there is no reason to doubt that it is physical-functional properties that those recognitional concepts discriminate.

7 Knowing How versus Knowing That

Consider a different physicalist reply, to an antiphysicalist argument posed in this form: "knowledge of physical-functional facts does not yield knowledge of the phenomenal facts; therefore phenomenal facts are not physical-functional." Lawrence Nemirow and David Lewis have replied in effect that the premise is true only if you equivocate on 'knowledge'.[8] The first occurrence means theoretical knowledge, the second the ability to discriminate introspectively or to imagine certain properties. But theoretical knowledge of physical-functional properties that are identical with phenomenal qualities does not yield the other sort of knowledge of the same properties, that is, the ability to discriminate them in introspection or to imagine them. There are two epistemic relations to one class of properties.

Now this suggests something significantly different from my account. On the Nemirow–Lewis proposal, the only knowledge "that such and such" is knowledge couched in physical-functional terms, while what corresponds to (what we have been calling) phenomenal concepts is knowing how to identify or to imagine certain states. What I have proposed is evidently different. Knowing that a state feels a certain way is having distinctive information about it, couched in phenomenal conceptions. There is of course a central role for recognitional abilities, but that is in the constitution of phenomenal concepts. Antiphysicalists are right to count phenomenal knowledge as the possession of distinctive information, for it involves genuinely predicative components of judgment, whose association with physical-functional concepts is straightforwardly a posteriori.

Physicalists are forced into the Nemirow–Lewis reply if they individuate pieces of knowledge or cognitive information in terms of possible-world truth-conditions, that is, hold that 'knowing that p' and 'knowing that q' ascribe distinct pieces of knowledge just in case 'that-p' and 'that-q' denote distinct sets of possible worlds. Then knowing that x's phenomenal qualities are such and such will be distinct from knowing that x's physical properties are so and so only if the former qualities are distinct from the latter properties. So then a physicalist who counts the basic antiphysicalist premise as true on some interpretation must deny either that knowledge, cognitive information, is individuated in terms of possible-world truth-conditions or deny that knowing the phenomenal facts (in the sense that makes the basic antiphysicalist premise true) is knowing that such and such or having distinctive information about it. Nemirow and Lewis deny the latter. Of course I deny the former; there are ample independent reasons to deny it, and it seems otherwise unmotivated to deny the latter.

There are straightforward reasons to prefer the phenomenal concept view.

1. A person can have thoughts not only of the form 'coconuts have *this* taste' but also of the form 'if coconuts did not have *this* taste, then Q'. You

may get away with saying that the former expresses (not a genuine judgment but) the mere possession of recognitional know-how. But there is no comparable way to account for the embedded occurrence of 'coconuts have this taste'; it occurs as a predicate with a distinctive content.

2. We entertain thoughts about the phenomenal states of other people— "she has a state of that type"; this clearly calls for a predicative concept. It does of course involve a recognitional ability, but one that contributes to the formation of a distinctive concept.

3. For many conceptions of phenomenal qualities, there is no candidate for an independently mastered term that one then learns how to apply: thinking of a peculiar way my left knee feels when I run (a conception that occurs predicatively in various judgments) is not knowing how to apply an independently understood term. I suppose a functionalist might say that, in such cases, one implicitly individuates the state in terms of some functional description that is fashioned on the spot, but this appears psychologically implausible.

Notes

1. Cf. Rey 1996 and Dennett 1991.

2. Jackson 1982, 1986.

3. Nagel 1974, 1986; McGinn 1993.

4. Jackson 1982, 1986.

5. How such background concepts themselves arise is not my topic; but we might think of them variously as deriving from more general recognitional capacities, or as functions of complex inferential roles, or as socially deferential; or they may be components of innate structures. Background concepts are not always presupposed. Someone may be extremely good at telling stars from other objects (e.g., lightning bugs, airplanes, comets, planets) without having any real idea of what they are.

6. For more on recognitional concepts and on the determinacy of reference, see Loar 1990, 1991, 1995.

7. The earlier version of this chapter made heavy weather of third-person ascription of phenomenal concepts. General considerations about the perspectival nature of recognitional concepts permit a far neater account, which I here present.

8. Nemirow 1980; Lewis 1983.

References

Block, N. (1978). "Troubles with Functionalism," in C. Wade Savage, ed., *Perception and Cognition: Issues in the Foundations of Psychology*. Vol. 9, *Minnesota Studies in the Philosophy of Science*. Minneapolis: University of Minnesota Press.

————. (1990). "Inverted Earth." *Philosophical Perspectives* 4, 53–79.

Dennett, Daniel (1991). *Consciousness Explained*. Boston: Little Brown.

Harman, Gilbert (1990). "The Intrinsic Quality of Experience," *Philosophical Perspectives* 4, 31–52.

Jackson, Frank (1982). "Epiphenomenal Qualia," *Philosophical Quarterly* 1982, 127–136. Reprinted in this volume.

————. (1986). "What Mary Didn't Know," *Journal of Philosophy* 83: 291–295. Reprinted in this volume.

————. (1994). "Armchair Metaphysics," in M. Michael ed., *Philosophy in Mind*. Norwell, MA: Kluwer.

Kripke, Saul (1980). *Naming and Necessity*. Cambridge, MA: Harvard University Press.

Levin, Janet (1983). "Functionalism and the Argument from Conceivability," *Canadian Journal of Philosophy*, Supplementary Volume 11.

————. (1986). "Could Love Be Like a Heatwave?" *Philosophical Studies*, 49: 245–261.

Levine, Joseph (1983). "Materialism and Qualia: the Explanatory Gap," *Pacific Philosophical Quarterly*, 64: 354–361.

————. (1993). "On Leaving Out What It Is Like," in M. Davies and G. Humphreys, eds., *Consciousness*. Oxford: Blackwell.

Lewis, David (1983a). "Mad Pain and Martian Pain," in *Philosophical Papers*, vol. 1. Oxford: Oxford University Press.

————. (1983b). "Postscript" to the foregoing.

Loar, Brian (1990). "Personal References," in E. Villanueva, ed., *Information, Semantics and Epistemology*. Oxford: Blackwell.

————. (1991). "Can We Explain Intentionality?" in G. Rey and B. Loewer, eds., *Meaning in Mind*. Oxford: Blackwell.

————. (1995). "Reference from a First-Person Perspective," in *Philosophical Issues*.

McGinn, Colin (1930). "Consciousness and Cosmology: Hyperdualism Ventilated," in M. Davies and G. Humphreys, eds., *Consciousness*. Oxford: Blackwell.

Nagel, Thomas (1974). "What Is It Like To Be a Bat?" *Philosophical Review*, 1974: 435–450.

———. (1986). *The View From Nowhere*. Oxford: Oxford University Press.

Nemirow, Lawrence (1980). Review of Nagel's *Mortal Questions*, *Philosophical Review*, July 1980.

Rey, Georges (1996). "Towards a Projectivist Account of Conscious Experience," in T. Metzinger, ed., *Conscious Experience*. Paderhorn: Ferdinand-Schoningh-Verlag.

Warner, Richard (1986). "A Challenge to Physicalism," *Australasian Journal of Philosophy*, 64: 249–265.

———. (1993). "Incorrigibility," in H. Robinson, ed., *Objections to Physicalism*. Oxford: Oxford University Press.

12   What Mary Couldn't Know: Belief About Phenomenal States

Martine Nida-Rümelin

I   Introduction

Everyone familiar with the current mind–body debate has probably heard about Frank Jackson's neurophysiologist Mary.[1] So I tell her story very briefly. Mary knows everything there is to know about the neuro-physiological basis of human color vision but she never saw colors herself (she always lived in a black-and-white environment). When Mary is finally released into the beauty of the colored world, she acquires new knowledge about the world and—more specifically—about the character of the visual experiences of others. This appears clear at first sight. In the ongoing philosophical debate, however, there is no agreement about whether Mary really gains new knowledge and about whether this would, if it were so, represent a problem for physicalism. Those who defend the so-called argument from knowledge (or knowledge argument) think that it does.[2]

Most participants in the debate agree that there is a strong inuition in favor of the thesis that Mary makes a genuine epistemic progress after her release. But there is disagreement about whether this intuition survives critical investigation and also about how the apparent or genuine epistemic progress can be adequately described. Most work about the argument from knowledge has focused on the question whether it leads—as was originally intended—to the ontological result that there are nonphysical facts. The epistemologically interesting questions raised by the Mary-example, how-ever, have not yet been considered in much detail. It seems clear to me that an intuitively adequate theoretical description of what Mary learns after her release has not been proposed so far—neither by those who attack nor by those who defend the knowledge argument. Such a description requires,

I think, the use of an epistemological distinction (between phenomenal and nonphenomenal belief) that will be proposed in the present paper. Using this distinction it will be possible to say in a precise manner what Jackson's Mary learns, when she finally is allowed to see colors and why she could not have learned all this before. Most philosophers use Nagel's term of 'knowing what it's like' in this context.[3] But this metaphorical locution is misleading and does not capture the intuition underlying the knowledge argument.

I have been considering Mary's specific epistemic situation so far. But, of course, the controversy addressed in this paper is not—or only at a superficial level—about how we should describe the counterfactual situation of a fictitious person. One of the deeper questions behind this is, whether there really is—as Mary's example seems to suggest—a specific kind of factual knowledge about the experiences of others that is only accessible to an epistemic subject who is acquainted by personal experience with the type of mental state at issue. The answer to this question is 'yes' for phenomenal knowledge as introduced below. Once we accept that there is such knowledge (knowledge that presupposes acquaintance with certain specific phenomenal states), then it appears that any description of a conscious being capable of phenomenal experience that uses only terms that the physicalist accepts as unproblematic will be—in a sense—epistemically incomplete, since it is characteristic for such a description that it can be understood and believed to be true by any rational epistemic subject independently of the specific kinds of phenomenal qualities it is able to experience given its physiological 'apparatus'. (See Nagel 1986: 13ff.)

My main concern in this paper is to convince the reader that the epistemological distinction I propose between phenomenal and nonphenomenal belief concerning the experiences of others makes sense and that it is useful for certain philosophical purposes. I hope to show this by using the distinction in the following. (I will introduce the distinction only for the special case of belief and other propositional attitudes concerning colors and color experiences, but the distinction naturally carries over to belief about other phenomenal states.[4]) You might convince yourself of the usefulness of this distinction, e.g. for explicating certain philosophical intuitions, even if you do not—in the end—agree with the view here presented about the knowledge argument.

II   An Unusual Epistemic Situation

To introduce the distinction between phenomenal and nonphenomenal belief, I will change Mary's example. Like Mary, Marianna has always lived in a black-and-white environment. Also, there are no colors, we may suppose, in her dreams and visual fantasies and imaginations. Maybe Marianna has—like Mary—detailed knowledge about physiology, but this is of no importance for the following.[5] Marianna has agreed to participate in a psychological experiment which requires that she does not leave the house where she has always been living. But the interior decoration is now radically changed. She sees artificial objects (walls, tables, etc.) of all colors, but is not taught the names of these colors. She already knows of a number of natural objects (like leaves, sunflowers, etc.) that they are called 'green', 'yellow', etc. But she is not allowed to see any of these objects (she is not allowed to see ripe tomatoes, photographs of landscapes or realistic paintings, she is somehow prevented from seeing the natural colours of her own body, she does not see the sky, etc.). In the course of the psychological experiment Marianna undergoes the following test: She is visually presented with four slides showing clear cases of blue, red, green and yellow, and she is asked which of the four slides shows a clear case of the color she believes to be experienced by normal people when they look at the sky. Marianna is especially impressed by the beauty of the red slide. Having been told about the beauty of the sky on a sunny summer day she says after some reflection, pointing to the red slide: 'I believe it's this one'. Two more details are relevant for the following discussion: Marianna believes herself to be normally sighted and this belief is correct.[6]

Already, before she has been presented with colors for the first time, Marianna has acquired the belief that the sky appears blue to people with normal color perception. It appears correct to ascribe this belief to her since a number of those conditions are clearly fulfilled which normally—according to the usual practice of belief ascription—lead us to the claim that a person believes that p: Marianna would say (when asked the appropriate question) 'the sky appears blue to normally sighted people'; she intends to thereby express the belief that is normally expressed using these words and she belongs to a language community where people normally use the above sentence to claim that the sky appears blue to normally sighted people.[7] So, if we wish to describe the beliefs Marianna holds before her acquaintance with colors, then we have reason to claim:

(1) Marianna believes that the sky appears blue to normally sighted people.

But, when she was finally presented with colours, Marianna did not give up this original belief. Her answer in the above described experiment is not accompanied by a revision of her original opinion about how the sky appears to normally sighted people. Therefore, (1) is still correct when claimed about Marianna with respect to the later moment considered. In a sense, Marianna still believes that the sky appears blue to normally sighted people. She still trusts those who told her that this is so. Furthermore, Marianna would therefore contradict the verbally (and without ostension) expressed opinion that the sky appears red to normally sighted people. So we also have reason to claim (with respect to her later epistemic situation):

(2) Marianna does not believe that the sky appears red to normally sighted people.

On the other side, there are strong intuitions against (1) and (2). Marianna believes herself to be normally sighted and she is normally sighted. The red slide appears red to her and she is right in assuming that she has the same type of color experience when looking at the slide as other people with normal color vision.[8] In a sense she believes, therefore, that the slide appears to others like it appears to her, namely red. And she believes that the sky appears to normally sighted people with respect to color like this slide, red therefore, and not blue. Viewed in this way it appears correct to ascribe to Marianna the following beliefs:

(3) Marianna believes that the sky appears red to normally sighted people.

(4) Marianna does not believe that the sky appears blue to normally sighted people.

So, on the one side, there is a tendency to claim that Marianna believes that the sky looks blue and not red to normally sighted people, where this intuition is based on the fact that Marianna belongs to a certain language community. On the other side, it appears obvious that Marianna believes of the wrong visual quality (namely with respect to red) that it is the color experienced by normally sighted people, when looking at the sky on a sunny day. She clearly has, in a sense, mistaken beliefs about the character of the color experiences of others. When imagining the sky in the way it appears to others, she would imagine a red sky. In a certain sense she does not know which color is the color of the sky.

To account for these conflicting intuitions with respect to Marianna's epistemic situation, we should distinguish two readings of belief descriptions containing color terms in their that-clause. One quickly realizes that the distinction makes sense not just for cases where the that-clause contains a 'color appearance term' like 'appears red to ...' but for any occurrence of a color term (as in 'Marianna believes that the sky is red' or in 'Marianna believes that Peter saw a red flower in his dream last night').[9] A first attempt to resolve the conflict between (1) and (4) and (2) und (3) could consist in distinguishing phenomenal and nonphenomenal belief in the following way:

(1′) Marianna believes nonphenomenally that the sky appears blue to normally sighted people.

(2′) Marianna does not believe nonphenomenally that the sky appears red to normally sighted people.

(3′) Marianna believes phenomenally that the sky appears red to normally sighted people.

(4′) Marianna does not believe phenomenally that the sky appears blue to normally sighted people.

But consideration of examples with several occurrences of color terms in the belief context shows that we need to distinguish for every occurrence of a color term in the that-clause whether it is used to ascribe phenomenal or nonphenomenal belief (compare belief description (5) below). I therefore propose to attach the subscripts 'p' (for 'phenomenal') and 'np' (for 'nonphenomenal') to color terms within belief contexts to express the intended distinction. Using this subscripting convention we may describe Marianna's epistemic situation by the following claims:

(1′) Marianna believes that the sky appears $blue_{np}$ to normally sighted people.

(2′) Marianna does not believe that the sky appears red_{np} to normally sighted people.

(3′)   Marianna believes that the sky appears red$_p$ to normally sighted people.

(4′)   Marianna does not believe that the sky appears blue$_p$ to normally sighted people.

(5)   Marianna believes that blue$_{np}$ objects appear red$_p$ to normally sighted people.

Color terms should only be thus subscripted within belief contexts and—more generally—within the description of propositional attitudes and they are used to distinguish different possible readings of the description as a whole. Accepting this subscripting convention within the description of propositional attitudes does not force us to introduce subscripts for color terms also outside such contexts. In my view, there is no way to introduce a corresponding distinction for color terms outside propositional attitudes.[10]

I have been assuming and will argue below that phenomenal belief (and nonphenomenal belief as well) is belief about something that may or may not be the case. Most contemporary philosophers think of such beliefs as having propositions as their content. Therefore, for them the question immediately arises how we should describe the propositions believed in phenomenal and in nonphenomenal belief. Furthermore, who thinks that believing is a relation between a believer and a proposition will ask whether the distinction here introduced is meant as a distinction between two kinds of belief relations (in this case there would be different ways of believing a proposition) or whether the distinction is concerned with the second *relatum* of the belief relation and thus is meant as a distinction between different kinds of propositions. What ontological consequences result from the knowledge argument depends on the view one takes about this question. But a clear understanding of the distinction does not presuppose a decision between the two views about it sketched above.[11]

The distinction is not meant as a diagnosis of a normal kind of ambiguity that is already there in natural language.[12] By a 'normal kind of ambiguity in natural language' I mean cases where a hearer of a sentence containing the ambigious term has first to find out, e.g. by the context or by asking, in which of the two senses the term is presently used, before he can possibly understand the assertion at issue. This is not so in the case of sentences that describe propositional attitudes with respect to color. If someone says in a normal life situation about a person who refuses to buy green salad

tomatoes 'she thinks that green tomatoes are immature', we can understand what he asserts without disambiguating. There is no need to ask 'in
which of the two senses do you mean this belief description?' So, the distinction between phenomal and nonphenomenal belief (and the corresponding distinction for other propositional attitudes) does not correspond
to a normal ambiguity in natural language in the sense explained above.
The reason for this is, simply, the following: in normal life situations the
truth conditions for phenomenal and those for nonphenomenal belief
are always simultaneously fulfilled, or at least we normally implicitly assume that this is so. Unusual epistemic situations that are in relevant
respects analogous to the one of Marianna normally do not occur.[13] But it
is only in these unusual situations that the truth conditions for phenomenal and nonphenomenal belief may 'fall apart', and only when this may
happen is it necessary to add what reading is meant in the relevant belief
descriptions.

III   A Few Remarks About the Status of the Proposed Distinction

This section adresses questions that are likely to occur to readers familiar
with the discussion of propositional attitudes within the analytical tradition when they are first confronted with the present epistemological proposal. The results of this section are only presupposed in the following
discussion in the sense that they answer objections that are likely to be
raised against the proposed distinction between phenomenal and nonphenomenal belief.

One might be tempted to think that the phenomenal–nonphenomenal
distinction here proposed is only a special case of the so-called *de re–de dicto*
distinction. On this view, phenomenal beliefs would be *de re* beliefs that
have a special kind of entity, namely colors, as their objects. But this interpretation is likely to evoke misunderstandings. One might erroneously
conclude that the well-known problems of the *de re–de dicto* distinction
need to be solved before one can reasonably accept the distinction between
phenomenal and nonphenomenal belief. Also, one might be tempted to
conclude that the proposals for a precise account of the *de re–de dicto* distinction proposed in the literature could simply be taken over to account
for the phenomenal–nonphenomenal distinction. I cannot discuss these
possible claims in detail here, but I wish to explain briefly how I think one

should see the interconnection between the phenomenal–nonphenomenal and the *de re–de dicto* distinction.[14]

The intuition behind the *de re–de dicto* distinction can be seen by a comparison of the following two cases. Anna believes that the best dolphin swimmer of Munich is broad-shouldered and her reasons to believe this are certain general convictions: She believes that every good dolphin swimmer is broad-shouldered, she thinks there is one person who is the best at this swimming discipline in the Bavarian capital and she thinks that there are good dolphin swimmers in Munich. Anna has no idea who is the best dolphin swimmer in this city. Maria, by contrast, knows the best dolphin swimmer of Munich (without however knowing that he is the best). Maria saw this person in a swimming competition and she saw that he is broad-shouldered. So Maria too believes (in a certain sense) that this person (the best dolphin swimmer in Munich) is broad-shouldered. Maria's belief is— in a sense—about this individual person (about this 'thing', this 'res', the belief is a paradigm case of so-called '*de re* belief'). Anna, by contrast, does not seem to have any opinion about this particular person. Her belief is a typical example for the idea underlying the notion of a 'mere' *de dicto* belief.

It is common to distinguish between the *de re–de dicto* dichotomy on the level of belief descriptions on the one side and the corresponding dichotomy on the level of the beliefs themselves on the other. The difference between *de re* and *de dicto* belief descriptions can be explained by their hidden logical structure. Thus the following belief description (6) if interpreted on its *de dicto* reading can be paraphrazed by (6′):

(6)   Anna believes that the best dolphin swimmer of Munich is broad-shouldered.

(6′)   Anna believes that there is someone who is the best dolphin swimmer of Munich and who also is broad-shouldered.

By contrast, the assertion (7), if interpreted on its *de re* reading can be paraphrazed by (7′):

(7)   Maria believes that the best dolphin swimmer of Munich is broad-shouldered.

(7′)   There is a person who is the best dolphin swimmer of Munich and who is believed by Maria to be broad-shouldered.

The quantifier ('there is someone who …') appears within the range of the belief predicate in (6′) (the quantifier has 'narrow scopus') whereas in (7′) it appears outside the belief predicate (the quantifier has wide scopus). It is sometimes claimed that there is nothing more behind the so-called *de re–de dicto* distinction than this syntactic ambiguity. Whoever tends to think that way, might suspect that there is nothing more to the phenomenal–nonphenomenal distinction here proposed either. If this were true then the phenomenal reading of (8) could be captured by paraphrasing with 'wide scopus'—see (8′).

(8) Maria believes that the sky appears blue$_p$ to normally sighted people.

(8′) There is a colour such that it is the color blue and it is believed by Marianna to be the color in which normally sighted people see the sky.

But this reformulation of (8) does not exclude a nonphenomenal reading. Marianna has learned the term 'blue' by people who refer to the color blue using this term. Her nonphenomenal belief that the sky appears blue$_{np}$ to normally sigthed people, is, therefore, in a sense a belief about this color, namely about blue. So the phenomenal–nonphenomenal distinction cannot be captured simply by pointing out the syntactic ambiguity at issue and the latter ambiguity cannot replace the distinction between phenomenal and nonphenomenal belief.

De re belief descriptions face the well-known problem that Quine pointed out using his famous Ortcutt-example:

There is a certain man in a brown hat whom Ralph has glimpsed several times under questionable circumstances on which we need not enter here; suffice it to say that Ralph suspects he is a spy. Also there is a gray-haired man, vaguely known to Ralph as rather a pillar of the community, whom Ralph is not aware of having seen except once at the beach. Now Ralph does not know it, but the men are one and the same. (Cited from Quine 1953)

It would be natural to describe Ralph's beliefs as follows:

(9) Ralph believes that the man with the brown hat is a spy.

(10) Ralph does not believe that the man at the beach is a spy.

These beliefs are beliefs about one and the same person whose name is 'Ortcutt' in Quine's story. Interpreted as *de re* belief descriptions (9) and (10) would have to be paraphrased by (9′) and (10′):[15]

(9′) There is a man named Ortcutt who is believed by Ralph to be a spy.

(10′)   There is a man named Ortcutt who is believed by Ralph to be no spy.

We thus have arrived at ascribing conflicting beliefs to Ralph which already appears problematic. Serious problems arise if one further accepts the following belief description (11) for the epistemic situation at issue and then paraphrases (11) with 'wide scopus' as in (11′):

(11)   Ralph does not believe that the man at the beach is a spy.

(11′)   There is a man named Ortcutt who is not believed by Ralph to be a spy.

As is well known, there is a controversy about whether (11′) should be accepted for Ralph's epistemic situation. I cannot enter the debate about Quine's example here. I only recalled Quine's problem because it can help to gain a better understanding of how the phenomenal–nonphenomenal distinction and the *de re–de dicto* dichotomy are related to one another.

Confronted with Quine's problem one might at first think that the problem can be avoided by restricting *de re* belief descriptions to cases where the epistemic subject has a sufficiently direct epistemic access to the object of his or her belief. The reason why the difficulty arises in Quine's example is obviously the fact that Ralph does not recognize a person he already knows in new circumstances. So the relation of a person to the object of his or her belief should be so intimate that such a case is excluded. Restricting *de re* belief descriptions to such cases would therefore solve Quine's problem. But one quickly realizes that there does not seem to be any way to give a general characterization of the 'epistemic intimacy' required which is not *ad hoc* and which still allows *de re* belief descriptions to be at least sometimes adequate. This is so since 'it is in principle always thinkable that we do not recognize even the most familiar object in unusual circumstances and thus mistake one thing for two'.[16] The situation is different in the case of belief about colors. Quine's problem can here be avoided in a natural way by simply restricting *de re* belief descriptions to phenomenal belief about colors. It is impossible for a rational person to have conflicting beliefs about one and the same color. One will immediately see that this is so when trying to find counterexamples.[17] One might describe the situation as follows: We could say that a genuine *de re* belief in an intuitively obvious sense is a belief where the subject is so intimately related to the object of his or her belief that he or she is just incapable to commit the mistake that gives rise to Quine's problem. Phenomenal beliefs about colour are genuine *de re* beliefs in this sense and maybe phenomenal beliefs in general are the only kind of beliefs that are in this sense 'genuinely *de re*'. (This thesis and similar ones about the relation between the two epistemological distinctions at issue obviously can be considered only after having introduced the phenomenal–nonphenomenal distinction independently, without thereby already using the *de re–de dicto* distinction).

The above considerations should have shown among other things: (1) The precise relation between the two epistemological distinctions is a theoretical question that requires detailed examination. (2) It is possible to introduce the phenomenal–nonphenomenal distinction without thereby presupposing the *de re–de dicto* distinction and without thereby being committed to solving first the well-known problems of the latter.[18]

I will not assume in the following (although I think the claim can be defended) that phenomenal belief about colors is *de re* belief about colours. One more reason for not doing so is that this thesis seems to commit its proponent to saying something clarifying about the difficult question of what 'res' these special beliefs are about. But no special philosophical theory about the ontological status of colors is needed for a clear understanding and for a precise account of the epistemological distinction between phenomenal and nonphenomenal belief.

One might furthermore be tempted to think that phenomenal belief about the experiences of others is just a special kind of *de se* belief (of belief about oneself). When Marianna learns that the sky appears blue$_p$ to normally sighted people, she thereby acquires the belief that the sky appears to those people with respect to color like this slide (the blue one) appears to her*.[19] It might therefore appear as if Marianna's progress could be described in the following way: If we select an object that appears blue to Marianna, then we can describe her epistemic progress as consisting in having learned that the sky appears to others with respect to colour like this object appears to her*.

This thesis is interesting in the context of the argument from knowledge if combined with the view that the locution 'O appears to S in the same color as O′ appears to S″' or 'O appears to S with respect to color like O′

appears to S'' can be explicated in purely physicalist terms. Let us call 'physical *de se* knowledge', knowledge that involves self-attribution of physical properties (or of properties that can be explicated in physicalist terminology). Then according to the thesis at issue, phenomenal knowledge about the experiences of others would be physical *de se* knowledge. But, it is common opinion that *de se* belief and *de se* knowledge does not represent a problem for physicalism.[20] It would follow that the notion of phenomenal belief cannot help much in a defence of the knowledge argument.

But the thesis that phenomenal belief (in the sense here introduced) is nothing but physical *de se* belief is untenable. This thesis assumes the equivalence of the following two assertions:

(12)   Marianna believes that the sky appears red$_p$ to Peter.

(13)   Whenever Marianna is visually presented with a red object she forms the *de se* belief that the sky appears to Peter with respect to color like this object presently (*de nunc*) appears to her*.[21]

But the equivalence between (12) and (13) only holds under the assumption that the red object actually appears red to Marianna in the given circumstances. It does not hold if Marianna is pseudonormal or if she is visually presented with the object at issue under unusual lighting conditions that make it appear e.g. brown.[22] So (13) must be changed into (13′) in order to get an assertions that is true just in case (12) holds of Marianna:

(13′)   When Marianna is visually presented with an object that appears red to her under the then prevailing conditions, she forms the *de se* (and *de nunc*) belief that this object presently (*de nunc*) appears to her* (*de se*) with respect to color like the sky appears to Peter.

Now, quite obviously, the equivalence between (12) and (13′) is to be explained in the following way: When Marianna is visually presented with an object that appears red to her under the then prevailing circumstances, she knows that the object presently (*de nunc*) appears red$_p$ to her* (*de se*). That the epistemic subject does have this *de nunc–de se* belief in the circumstances at issue is implicitly assumed in the claim that (12) and (13′) are equivalent. This is not a decisive argument but a hint at what is wrong with the claim under consideration. A genuine refutation of the claim that phenomenal belief is physical *de se* belief can be accomplished using a more complex thought experiment (there is no room, however, to present it here).[23]

Furthermore, phenomenal belief is not just a kind of indexical belief. This idea might appear plausible since we could inform Marianna about what she did not yet know (in the phenomenal sense about the experiences of others, e.g. when they look at the sky) by 'ostensive teaching' (e.g. by pointing to a blue object saying 'this is what we call "blue"'). This might lead to the conclusion that (12) can be paraphrased by (15):

(15)   Every red object O is such that the following holds: If Marianna is visually presented with O, then she will form an indexical belief that she could express saying while demonstratively refering to O (e.g. by pointing): 'The sky appears to Peter with respect to color like *this*'.

However, neither the conclusion of (15) from (12), nor the conclusion of (12) from (15), is valid in general. For example, if Marianna is pseudonormal (green objects appear red to her and red objects appear green to her), (15) can be true and (12) false: If Marianna does not know that she* is pseudonormal then she will express her phenomenal belief that the sky appears red_p to Peter by demonstrative reference to green objects (that appear red to her) and she will have no tendency to express the relevant indexical belief when presented with red objects. The same example refutes the claim that (15) implies (12). The nonequivalence of (12) and (15) can be seen in another way: Suppose there is a measuring instrument that allows blind people to identify the color of objects on the basis of their physical surface properties. Then a blind person who is allowed to use this instrument when confronted with a colored object can fulfill the property ascribed to Marianna in (15) although he or she does not have the belief ascribed to Marianna in (12).[24]

Having this last counterexample in mind a proponent of the indexical interpretation of phenomenal belief might try to defend his position requiring a visual confrontation of the subject with the object at issue in a revised version of (15). But this move does not help for a defence of the claim that phenomenal belief is just a special kind of indexical belief. If phenomenal beliefs were nothing but indexical beliefs then the way in which the corresponding demonstrative reference is achieved should not matter.

IV Marianna's Epistemic Progress

Jackson's example appears in a new light when reconsidered having Marianna's case in mind. When Mary is finally released she acquires new knowledge about the experiences of others (she learns e.g. that the sky appears blue$_p$ to people with normal color perception). But Mary does *not* gain this item of knowledge simply by gaining sight and thereby acquaintance with colors. A disadvantage of Jackson's example is that it fails to distinguish two steps of epistemic progress that can be distinguished clearly in Marianna's case. When Marianna gains sight and thereby acquaintance with blue, green, yellow and red she takes a first step of epistemic progress which consists in her gaining *epistemic access* to questions that she could not have considered before. Only after this first step, namely when she knows red, green, blue and yellow by personal experience, can she consider the question whether the sky appears blue$_p$ or red$_p$ or yellow$_p$ or green$_p$ to normally sighted people. She can weigh these four possibilities against each other, she might assign subjective probabilities to these alternatives. These four possibilities were epistemically inaccessible to her before she left her black-and-white environment. Having gained epistemic access to questions she could not have considered before, is already a kind of *epistemic progress*—although she has not yet gained any new item of the relevant propositional knowledge.

A second step of epistemic progress is required to find out which of the hypotheses she is now able to consider is in fact true. Jackson's Mary seems to take these two steps at once. This is why Jackson's case fails to show explicitly that there is a kind of knowledge inaccessible to blind Mary which *does* involve the elimination of 'hitherto open possibilities'.[25]

Using the notion of phenomenal belief we can describe more in detail what happens when Marianna takes the second step of epistemic progress. Before her release Marianna believes that the sky appears red$_p$ to normally sighted people. She expects the sight of a red$_p$ sky for the moment in which she will leave the house. She entertains—in other words—the *de se* expectation that the sky will appear red$_p$ to her*. When she finally leaves the house on a sunny day she will realize with surprise that her *de se* expectation was mistaken. She will then rationally conclude (since she believes herself to be normally sighted) that—contrary to what she had thought—the sky appears blue$_p$ to normally sighted people. When Marianna finally sees the sky she also detects an error in her former assumptions about the normal use of language. When she still believed that the sky appears red_p to normally sighted people, she thought—so to speak—of the wrong color that it was the color referred to by 'blue'. More precisely her mistake about language should be described this way: She believed that red_p objects are called 'blue' and she believed that 'object O appears blue to person S' is truely asserted of a person S just in case O appears red_p to that person. Note that a precise formulation of her mistake about language already requires the use of the notion of phenomenal belief. Marianna can make this mistake only when she is capable of entertaining phenomenal belief, so only after she has taken the first step of epistemic progress described above. (Her epistemic progress involves the capability to make new errors, which might seem paradox at first sight but is not on a second: who gains epistemic access to new questions also acquires the new ability to believe in the wrong answers.) In the present context it is important to see the following: Marianna's second step of epistemic progress does not *consist* in her revision of a mistake about language (although it goes along with such a revision). It would be a mistake to think that Marianna, when she finally sees the sky, does not learn more than that $blue_p$ objects are called 'blue' and that something is said to appear 'blue' just in case it appears $blue_p$. Given her rich background knowledge this new knowledge about language is necessarily accompanied by the acquisition of a rich body of new phenomenal knowledge. Suppose she had learned that objects appear $blue_{np}$ to a person iff certain physiological conditions are fulfilled. Then her new knowledge about language goes along with the acquisition of the new item of phenomenal belief that things appears $blue_p$ to human beings iff these conditions obtain.

V Phenomenal Knowledge as Knowledge About What Is the Case

Before I answer possible objections against the view that phenomenal knowledge is knowledge in the strict sense about something that is the case, I will briefly sketch a few positive reasons for this claim.

(1) The epistemological notion here introduced allows for the distinction between belief and knowledge. Marianna believes e.g. that the sky appears red_p, but she does not know this, since what she believes is false. There is

no analogous pair of notions (phenomenal belief on the one hand and phenomenal knowledge on the other) in the case of practical capacities, nor is there any such analogous pair of notions in the case of so-called knowledge of what it's like. That there is a corresponding notion of belief is of course typical for knowledge in the full-fledged sense.

(2) In normal cases of belief about something that is the case we can specify the conditions under which the belief of the person is correct using normal assertive sentences. For the case of 'knowing what it's like to have a perception of blue' it is hard to see how one could fulfill this possible requirement. First of all, one would have to explain what could be meant by a corresponding notion of belief about 'what it is like to have a perception of blue', second one would have to find a sentence S such that S is true iff the corresponding belief is true. This task appears almost unsolvable in the case of knowing what it's like. For most cases of phenomenal belief, by contrast, it does not represent any problem.[26] Marianna's phenomenal belief that the sky appears red_p to Peter would be true iff the sentence 'the sky appears red to Peter' were true.

(3) Phenomenal belief and phenomenal knowledge can be ascribed in the normal way, by using that-clauses, which again is typical for belief and knowledge about something that is the case. Also—as in the case of *de re*, *de dicto*, *de se* and *de nunc* beliefs—the distinction naturally carries over to other propositional attitudes: Marianna may hope that the sky appears red_p to normal perceivers, she may wonder whether the sky appears red_p or she may doubt that it appears red_p to normal perceivers, etc.

(4) Also, as in the case of other opinions about what is the case, one can easily construct situations in which Marianna might rationally assign some specific subjective probability to the alternative that the sky appears red_p to normal perceivers. This observation too strengthens the intuition that phenomenal belief is belief about something that might or might not be the case.

(5) It makes sense to ask whether a specific phenomenal belief is rationally justified. Consider the following case. Marianna has seen a painting showing a landscape with a red sky. She has reason to think that the painting is naturalistic. She has reason to think that she* is normally sighted and that she saw the painting under normal lighting conditions. In

this case Marianna may have good reason to think that the sky appears red$_p$ to normally sighted people. The fact that there is room for the notion of rational justification is one more reason to think that phenomenal belief is belief in the full sense of belief about a state of affairs.

The above arguments in favour of the thesis that phenomenal knowledge is factual knowledge would have to be defeated by a proponent of the view that Mary only gains a bundle of practical capacities after her release. But, all the same, I wish to examine this kind of objection more closely (I will call this objection the 'ability objection'). The reason why the ability objection seems to me to deserve a more detailed discussion is the observation that it appears to be surprisingly resistant against counterarguments and conflicting intuitions in discussion with many people (maybe one main cause for this is the celebrity of one of its proponents). The above mentioned properties of phenomenal knowledge that are typical for genuine knowledge are not shared by knowledge of what it's like.[27] This counts against the thesis that knowledge of what it's like is genuine knowledge. So the ability thesis may actually appear plausible as long as one starts from the assumption that Marianna's progress after her release is properly described by saying that she acquires knowledge of what it's like. Let us now see how the analogous objection would have to be formulated once it is accepted that the notion of phenomenal knowledge provides a more adequate account of Mary's real or apparent epistemic progress.

Some of these abilities normally mentioned in this context can quickly be excluded as a possible basis for an analysis of phenomenal knowledge, because Marianna already acquires these abilities after her first step of epistemic progress when she still has not acquired the relevant items of phenomenal knowledge at issue. Marianna is able, for instance, to imagine something blue at will or to remember something blue before she learns that the sky appears blue$_p$ to human beings with normal color perception.

A first answer to this defence against the ability objection could be the following: The relevant sense of 'ability to imagine (or to remember) something blue' is the ability to obey to the verbally given imperative 'imagine something blue' or 'remember an occasion when you saw something blue'. Marianna indeed gains this capacity only after her second step of epistemic progress. At a point of her history when she still believes that the sky appears red$_p$ to normally sighted people she will imagine something red or remember an experience of red when trying to obey to the above imperatives. So the defense above cannot be repeated here. But this does not show that Marianna's progress (after her second step) is not a genuine epistemic one that involves new knowledge of facts. It is quite common that the gaining of factual knowledge goes along with the acquisition of the practical ability to obey to certain imperatives (consider: 'point to the person who is the thief!' or 'choose the right answer!'). In these normal cases the new factual knowledge explains why the person has acquired the capacity at issue. Now, quite obviously, this also applies in the case presently under consideration. Marianna is able to obey to those imperatives after her second step of epistemic progress *because* she now has acquired the phenomenal knowledge needed for this practical ability. Before Marianna corrects her mistake about the normal use of language she believes that a person who wishes to obey to the imperative 'Imagine something blue!' must imagine something red_p and that a person must remember an experience of red_p in order to obey to the second imperative mentioned above. So her incapacity to obey to these imperative is due to a lack of phenomenal knowledge and her capacity to do so after her second step of epistemic progress is due to an acquisition of new phenomenal knowledge.

There is a further interesting capacity sometimes mentioned in this context, namely the capacity to predict the behaviour of others by imaginative experiments. (See Nemirow 1979; 1980.) Now there certainly is an interesting connection between the capacity to make such predictions on the basis of 'correct empathy' on the one hand and phenomenal knowledge on the other, but in this case too it appears obvious to me that the capacity at issue does not constitute the kind of knowledge at issue, but is, rather, in fortunate cases the *result* of phenomenal knowledge. Unfortunately, there is no room for further elaboration of this point in the present paper.[28]

Whoever claims that phenomenal knowledge is nothing but a bundle of practical capacities, should propose a concrete analysis of phenomenal knowledge in terms of such abilities. How could such an analysis look like? A proponent of this view might propose (17) as an analysis of (16):

(16)   Marianna knows that ripe tomatoes appear red_p to normally sighted people.

(17)   Marianna has acquired the practical capacity to select (on the basis of visual perception) those objects that appear to normally sighted people with respect to color like ripe tomatoes.

But this proposal can again be refuted by considering the case of pseudo-normal people. (See note 13.) If Marianna were pseudonormal without knowing that she is, she could fulfill (17) and still believe that ripe tomatoes appear green$_p$ (and do not appear red$_p$) to normally sighted people. Again, this counterexample renders intuitively quite obvious what is wrong with the analysis considered here. Under normal conditions, when Marianna has acquired the item of phenomenal knowledge ascribed to her in (16), then she also has the capacity described in (17) since, when presented with red objects, she knows that these objects appear red$_p$ to her and she believes herself to be normally sighted. The practical capacity described in (17) is only a symptom for her having the phenomenal knowledge at issue but it can be—in unusual circumstances, as is shown by the example of pseudonormal vision—a symptom of a different phenomenal belief as well.

The proponent of the ability objection against the claim that phenomenal knowledge is genuine knowledge, also has to give an analysis of phenomenal belief (not just of phenomenal knowledge). So the question arises how he could interpret for instance (18):

(18) Marianna believes that the sky appears red$_p$ to normally sighted people.

He might consider the following proposal (19):

(19) If Marianna were asked to select those objects (out of several differently colored objects) that have the color that normally sighted people experience when looking at the sky, then she would select the red objects.

But again, (19) could be true of Marianna and (18) false, if Marianna is pseudonormal but does not know that she is.

I wish to leave the development of more sophisticated versions to the proponent of the ability objection. I hope to have convinced the reader that the ability objection loses its intuitive appeal once one accepts that Mary's epistemic progress is adequately described in the way here proposed (as an acquisition of phenomenal knowledge and not as an acquisition of 'knowing what it's like') and that it certainly is not obvious how the claim that phenomenal knowledge too is nothing but a bundle of practical abilities could be argued for in a convincing manner.

VI A New Look at the Argument from Knowledge

Assuming that phenomenal knowledge is a special kind of factual knowledge about phenomenal states (knowledge about something that is the case), the argument from knowledge can be stated quite simply in the following way: There is a kind of knowledge about phenomenal states that is accessible only to an epistemic subject who knows the kind of phenomenal state at issue (the kind of state the relevant item of knowledge is about) by personal experience (by having been in that kind of state). But it is commonly accepted that an understanding of a description given in purely physicalist terms does not presuppose being acquainted with any special kind of phenomenal state by personal experience.[29] Therefore, a description of a conscious being given in purely physicalist terminology is epistemically incomplete in the following sense: A rational epistemic subject who is able to understand any physicalist description of whatever kind, may lack specific items of knowledge about another conscious being that in principle cannot be communicated to the subject at issue by any physicalist description, no matter how detailed and complex this description may be.

Note that for this formulation of the argument it is unnecessary to speculate about the epistemic situation of a person who has 'complete knowledge' in some relevant respect. Instead, it is sufficient to assume that the kind of knowledge at issue (contrary to so-called physical knowledge) presupposes having had certain specific kinds of experiences. When formulated this way several objections raised against the original version of the knowledge argument can be immediately rejected as irrelevant. This is true for those objections that are based on the claim that a physiologist who really knew everything 'physical' there is to know about human color vision could immediately decide which color is the red one when visually confronted with colors for the first time. (Cf. Churchland 1985; Hardin 1992.) The debate about this claim is irrelevant since the argument is already saved if it is accepted that e.g. a person born blind cannot have phenomenal knowledge about the experiences of others although he or she can acquire every kind of 'physical knowledge'. The question when and under what conditions a person born blind would *acquire* phenomenal knowledge when she finally gains sight is then, obviously, of no importance.

I have argued that Mary gains new factual knowledge after her release. But, in general, new factual knowledge does not necessarily involve knowledge of new facts. This can be seen by the example of *de se* knowledge: Maria might know that Maria is in Munich and yet not know that she* is in Munich (she might have forgotten that she* is Maria). When she finds out that she* is in Munich she certainly gains new knowledge. But there is good reason to doubt that she thereby has gained knowledge of a new fact, a fact she did not know before in some other way. After all, what she believes in her belief that Maria is in Munich is true iff Maria is in Munich and the same holds for her *de se* belief: Maria's belief that she* is in Munich is true just in case Maria is in Munich. This observation seems to support the view that in gaining the new item of knowledge that she* is in Munich Maria gets to know an old fact (that she already new before) in a new way, namely in what one might call the '*de se* mode'.

One might consider the view that the analogous claim holds for phenomenal belief. Many philosophers have argued that Mary gains new factual knowledge but thereby gains knowledge of old facts that she already knew before in some other way.[30] The original intention of the knowledge argument was to show that there are nonphysical facts, facts that cannot be expressed in a physicalist language. But the above version of the argument only has an epistemological result that does not yet lead to the intended ontological conclusion. What is needed is a further assumption that can take the following form: The content of phenomenal beliefs are special propositions that cannot be believed in a 'nonphenomenal' way and what is known in phenomenal knowledge are facts that cannot be known otherwise. The following thesis (20) is one possible version of this additional assumption.

(20)   Marianna has knowledge of the fact expressed by 'the sky appears blue to Peter' iff Marianna knows that the sky appears blue$_p$ to Peter.

A possible formulation of the contrary opinion could be based on some version of the view that types of mental states are identical with certain types of physiological states. The proponent of such an identity thesis could base his rejection of (20) on the following claim: for an appropriately chosen brain state S the two sentences 'the sky appears blue to Peter' and 'the sky causes under appropriate circumstances a brain state of kind S in Peter's brain' express one and the same fact. If Marianna knows that the sky produces this kind S of a physiological state in Peter's brain, then she has knowledge of the same fact that is also the content of her item of phenomenal knowledge that the sky appears blue$_p$ to Peter. Therefore, according to the identity theorist, (20) is unacceptable and the argument from knowledge does not lead to the ontological result that was originally intended.[31]

I do not wish to comment this possible objection of the identity theorist here which would require a detailed discussion. Let me just note the following: the claim that new phenomenal knowledge does not involve knowledge of new facts is considerably more problematic than the analogous thesis sketched above for *de se* knowledge. In both cases the claim implicitly assumes a specific view about the conditions under which facts that are verbally expressed in different ways are numerically identical. In the case of the claim at issue for *de se* knowledge, the implicitly accepted sufficient condition for identity of facts is based on the notion of identity of individuals (the facts at issue are considered identical because Maria is identical with the person Maria refers to using the term 'I'). The sufficient condition for 'fact identity' presupposed in the corresponding claim about phenomenal knowledge, by contrast, is based on a notion of identity between properties (between the property of being in a specific brain state and having an impression of blue). Numerical identity is certainly applicable to concrete individual things. It is, however, questionable whether numerical identity between properties is an acceptable notion at all and how—if the answer is positive—identity between properties should be explicated.[32]

So I will content myself with the weaker, only epistemological result of the argument from knowledge here. Actually, it is possible to show that this result is stonger than it might appear at first sight. The result is sufficient for the defense of several central antimaterialist intuitions. For example, using this epistemological result it is possible to argue for the indispensability of phenomenal vocabulary in the empirical sciences of conscious beings. Contrary to a widespread opinion among materialists, certain well-founded epistemic interests that the empirical sciences can and should respond to, cannot be satisfied by these sciences unless they make use of phenomenal terminology. A precise account of this claim and of how it can be argued for can be based on the here proposed version of the argument from knowledge. But there is no room left here to elaborate this point.[33]

Notes

1. For the title compare Jackson 1984b. The example of Mary is presented in Jackson 1984a.

2. The assumption in the example is, more exactly, that Mary knows everything there is to know about human colour perception except for what she cannot possibly know given her colour deprivation.

3. The term was introduced by Thomas Nagel, see his famous paper Nagel 1974.

4. The conditions that must be fulfilled in general in a case where the distinction makes sense are discussed in Nida-Rümelin 1996b, section 3.

5. The example is used here only to introduce an epistemological distinction and, contrary to Jackson's use of his example, it does not serve for a direct attack on physicalism. This is why I do not need the assumption of 'complete physical' knowledge about human color perception.

6. Only under this assumption we are allowed to draw the conclusion that will be drawn in the following, namely that Marianna believes—in a certain sense—that the sky appears red to normally sighted people. If Marianna were red/green blind or pseudonormal (for pseudonormality see note 13), it would be a mistake to conclude this.

7. More precisely, this sentence is normally used to claim that the sky appears blue$_p$ to normally sighted people (see Nida-Rümelin 1996c: section 5). But I have not yet introduced the subscripting convention to distinguish phenomenal and non-phenomenal belief at this point of the present paper.

8. By assuming that normally sighted people have the same type of color experience when looking at the slide I do not mean to claim that they experience exactly the same shade of red. I just assume that for every normally sighted person the slide appears in the same basic hue (red). In every such case, what is seen is a clear case of red.

9. The relation between belief about color properties of concrete objects ('x believes that roses are red') and belief about color appearances ('x believes that roses appear red to normally sighted people') is discussed in Nida-Rümelin 1993, chapter 5.

10. If there were a 'corresponding distinction' (in the sense here intended) between 'red$_p$' (which would be a color term taken on its 'phenomenal' reading) and 'red$_{np}$' (color term on its nonphenomenal reading), then this distinction between

phenomenal and nonphenomenal interpretations of color terms could be used to distinguish the content of phenomenal and nonphenomenal beliefs. The content of the belief that the sky appears blue$_{np}$ would then be given by the content of the sentence 'the sky appears blue$_{np}$' and analogously for phenomenal belief. The reason why I think this picture is completely misguided, is—very roughly—that there is no nonphenomenal concept of red such that whoever believes something of the color red nonphenomenally, believes it about red 'under this nonphenomenal concept'. What people who have nonphenomenal beliefs about a color share is not their conceptual access to the color at issue but rather the way their belief is acquired and the way it is thereby embedded in a certain social context of a specific language community. I do not deny that it might make sense to distinguish different senses of color terms outside belief context. I just deny that such a distinction would correspond, in the simple way sketched above, to the epistemological distinction here proposed.

11. An analogous question arises in the case of *de se* belief. Some have claimed that *de se* belief has a special content (*de se* propositions), others think that *de se* attitudes involve a specific relation to the proposition at issue, still others claim that *de se* belief is not propositional at all. In this case too, one must—in a sense—have gained a clear understanding of what is meant by '*de se*' beliefs before one can start to discuss these issues (see e.g. Perry 1979; Chisholm 1981; Sosa 1983).

12. I owe this insight to a discussion with Andreas Kemmerling.

13. An exception would be the case of pseudonormal people if they really exist which is presented and discussed at length in Nida-Rümelin 1995. I will use this example several times in the following and therefore I here explain the case briefly. According to an empirical hypothesis about the inheritance of red/green blindness, there are people who have their receptors on the retina filled with photopigments in a specific unusual way. For this specific unusual distribution of photopigments, the so-called opponent process theory of colour vision predicts an 'inversion' of red and green, that is to say: what appears greenish to normal people appears reddish to them, and vice versa. Pseudonormal people would call those objects red that appear green to them (and vice versa). They would express the opinion that something appears green$_p$ to a person, using the term 'red'. To describe the epistemic states of pseudonormal people the distinction between phenomenal and nonphenomenal belief is needed (for a discussion of this thesis and its consequences for the philosophy of language see Nida-Rümelin 1996a). The assumption that pseudonormal people exist does not imply the possibility of undetectable qualia inversion, nor the possibility of qualia inversion in a case of functional 'equivalence'. For scientific literature about the empirical hypothesis of pseudonormal vision see Piantanida 1974 and Boynton 1979.

14. For a concise and clear presentation of the *de re–de dicto* debate see Haas-Spohn 1989.

15. In the formulations with 'wide scopus' the terms 'the man with the brown hat' and 'the man at the beach' occur outside the belief context and therefore can be replaced by an expression that designates the same person without thereby changing the truth value.

16. Cited from Haas-Spohn 1989: p. 64 (my translation).

17. This thesis is discussed in more detail in Nida-Rümelin 1993, 61ff. The idea underlying this solution of Quine's problem for belief about colours if of course related to the old idea that colors (and phenomenal qualities in general) are in a sense directly presented to the perceiver in his or her perception (or more general to the subject in his or her experience).

18. Whoever makes a conceptual proposal should of course relate this proposal to concepts that are already commonly accepted. There is no room to do this here (but see Nida-Rümelin 1993: 48–63).

19. I use Castañeda's '*' to indicate *de se* belief. See e.g. Castañeda 1967.

20. It do not subscribe to this view here but it would be bad for my argument if I first had to show that this view is false.

21. *De nunc* belief is belief we normally express using the term 'now'. For a discussion of *de nunc* belief see e.g. Sosa 1983.

22. For pseudonormality see note 13.

23. This refutation is presented in Nida-Rümelin 1993, section 4.3.

24. I owe this example to a comment of Michael Pietroforte. The two articles Spohn 1996 and Nida-Rümelin 1996a discuss in detail the related question whether colour terms are hidden indexicals.

25. David Lewis (1988) has objected to the view that Mary gains propositional knowledge after her release by pointing out that the acquisition of 'knowledge of what it's like' does not seem to be connected with an elimation of hitherto open possibilities. Using the notion of phenomenal belief to describe Mary's epistemic progress allows for an answer to this objection. Every acquistion of an item of phenomenal knowledge involves the exclusion of other hitherto open *epistemic* possibilities.

26. An exception is e.g. the belief that $blue_{np}$ things appear $blue_p$ (for a discussion of this see Nida-Rümelin 1996b, section 6).

27. An analysis of 'knowing what it's like' in terms of phenomenal belief is proposed in Nida-Rümelin 1996b: section 6 and in Nida-Rümelin 1993: 70–76.

28. A precise account of the relation between phenomenal knowledge and successful empathy (correct imagination of what other people experience) is proposed in Nida-Rümelin 1996c.

29. As is common in the discussion 'physicalist' terminology is used here in a very broad sense that includes not just the terms of physics but also of e.g. chemistry and neurobiology. Functionalist and behaviourist terminology is included as well. 'Physicalist terminology' also includes the terminology used in future developments of the mentioned empirical disciplines as long as they do not use mentalist vocabulary in an irreducible manner. 'Physical' knowledge is all knowledge that can be conveyed using physicalist terminology.

30. The thesis that Mary gains new knowledge about facts she already knew before in another way has been sustained by several authors (see e.g. Horgan 1984; Loar 1990; Tye 1986).

31. For a discussion of (20) and other versions of a further assumption that can be used to get to the ontological consequence at issue see Nida-Rümelin 1996b, sections 7 and 9.

32. For a recent discussion of identity theories see Bealer 1994.

33. A detailed presentation of this argument is the topic of Nida-Rümelin 1996b.

References

Bealer, G. (1994). Mental properties. *Journal of Philosophy* **91**: 185–208.

Boynton, R. M. (1979). *Human Color Vision*. New York: Rinehart and Winston.

Castañeda, H.-N. (1967). Indicators and quasi-indicators. *American Philosophical Quarterly* **4**: 85–100.

Chisholm, R. M. (1981). *The First Person*. Brighton: Harvester Press.

Churchland, P. (1985). Reduction, qualia and the direct introspection of brain states. *Journal of Philosophy* **82**: 8–28.

Haas-Spohn, U. (1989). Zur Interpretation von Einstellungszuschreibungen. In G. Falkenberg (ed): *Wissen, Wahrnehmen, Glauben*. Tübingen: Max Niemeyer Verlag.

Hardin, C. L. (1992). Physiology, phenomenology, and Spinoza's true colors. In Beckermann et al. 1992.

Horgan, T. (1984). Jackson on physicalism and qualia. *Philosophical Quarterly* **34**: 147–152.

Jackson, F. (1984a). Epiphenomenal qualia. *Philosophical Quarterly* **34**: 127–136. Reprinted in this volume.

Jackson, F. (1984b). What Mary didn't know. *Journal of Philosophy* **83**: 291–295. Reprinted in this volume.

Lewis, D. (1988). What experience teaches. *Proceedings of the Russellian Society*, University of Sidney. Reprinted in this volume.

Loar, B. (1990). Phenomenal States. *Philosophical Perspectives 4: Action Theory and the Philosophy of Mind*, 81–107. Excerpted in this volume.

Nagel, T. (1974). What is it like to the a bat? *Philosophical Review* **83**: 435–450.

Nagel, T. (1986). *The View from Nowhere*. Oxford: Oxford University Press.

Nemirow, E. L. (1979). Functionalism and the subjective quality of experience. Dissertation at Stanford University Press, unpublished.

Nemirow, E. L. (1980). Review of Thomas Nagel, *Mortal Questions*. *Philosophical Review* **89**: 473–477.

Nida-Rümelin, M. (1993). *Farben und phänomenales Wissen*. St. Augustin: Academia.

Nida-Rümelin, M. (1995). Pseudonormal vision. An actual case of qualia inversion? *Philosophical Studies* **82**: 145–157.

Nida-Rümelin, M. (1996a). The character of color predicates: A phenomenalist view. In M. Anduschus, A. Newen, and W. Künne (eds), *Direct Reference, Indexicality and Propositional Attitudes*. Stanford: CSLI.

Nida-Rümelin, M. (1996b). On belief about experiences: An epistemological distinction applied to the knowledge argument (submitted).

Nida-Rümelin, M. (1996c). Is the naturalization of qualitative experience possible or sensible? In Carrier and Machamer (1996).

Piantanida, T. P. (1974). A replacement model of X-linked recessive colour vision defects. *Annals of Human Genetics*. **37**: 393–404.

Perry, J. (1979). The problem of the essential indexical. *Noûs* **13**: 474–497.

Quine, W. V. (1953). Quantifiers and propositional attitude. *Journal of Philosophy* **53**: 177–187.

Sosa, E. (1983). Consciousness of the self and of the present. In J. E. Tomberlin (ed.), *Agent, Language, and the Structure of the World*. Indianapolis: Hackett.

Spohn, W. (1996). The character of color predicates: A materialist view. In M. Anduschus, A. Newen and W. Künne (eds), *Direct Reference, Indexicality, and Propositional Attitudes*. Stanford: CSLI.

Tye, Michael (1986). The subjective qualities of experience. *Mind* **45**: 1–17.

13 Phenomenal Concepts and the Knowledge Argument

David J. Chalmers

1 Introduction

The classic statement of the knowledge argument against materialism has
been given by Frank Jackson (1982). Mary knows everything that can be
stated in physical terms about the physical processes that are in any way
relevant to color vision. But Mary has never experienced colors other than
black, white, and shades of grey. It seems that Mary has complete physical
knowledge, but she does not have complete phenomenal knowledge: in
particular, she does not know what it is like to see red. Jackson argues that
Mary knows all the physical facts, but does not know all the facts. When
she sees red for the first time, she learns a new fact concerning what it is
like to see red. So there are facts over and above the physical facts, and
materialism is false. In particular, phenomenal facts—facts about the character of conscious experience—are nonphysical facts, and phenomenal
properties are nonphysical properties.

The knowledge argument turns crucially on Mary's new knowledge, and
on her acquisition of new beliefs. To understand the nature of this knowledge, we need to understand the concepts—*phenomenal concepts*—that
are involved in Mary's new beliefs. In this paper, I will give an analysis of
these concepts (in sections 2 and 3), and will then bring it to bear on the
knowledge argument itself (in sections 4 and later). I will argue that the
knowledge argument is basically sound (section 5), and that a correct understanding of phenomenal concepts helps to see why many responses to
the knowledge argument fail (section 6).

In what follows, I will assume *phenomenal realism*: roughly, the view that
Mary acquires new factual knowledge (not a priori deducible form physical
knowledge) when she sees red for the first time. This excludes views on

which Mary merely gains a new ability, or on which she gains no knowledge at all. It is compatible with views on which Mary gains knowledge of an old fact in a new way. The important aspect of this view is that it allows an *epistemic* gap between physical truths and phenomenal truths, in the sense that phenomenal truths are not entailed a priori by physical truths. The view is silent on whether or not there is an ontological gap. As such, the view excludes "type-A" materialist views such as those of Dennett and Lewis, which deny an epistemic gap, but it includes "type-B" materialist views such as those of Loar and Tye, which allow an epistemic gap but denying an ontological gap, as well as including many nonmaterialist views.

(This essay is largely based on material in other papers. The first three sections and the appendix are drawn with minor modifications from Chalmers 2002c [which explores issues about phenomenal concepts and beliefs in much more depth, mostly independently of questions about materialism]. The main ideas of the last three sections are drawn from Chalmers 1996, 1999, and 2002a, although with considerable revision and elaboration.)

2   Phenomenal Concepts

Phenomenal properties are properties characterizing what it is like to be a subject, or what it is like to be in a mental state. Phenomenal beliefs are beliefs that attribute phenomenal properties. I will be especially concerned with first-person phenomenal beliefs, such as *I am now having a red experience*. Phenomenal beliefs attribute phenomenal properties using phenomenal concepts. To understand phenomenal beliefs, we need to understand phenomenal concepts.

(In this paper, I understand beliefs and concepts as psychological entities rather than as semantic entities. Beliefs and concepts have contents, but are not themselves contents.)

Mary looks at a red apple, and visually experiences its color. This experience instantiates a phenomenal property R, which we might call phenomenal redness. It is natural to say that Mary is having a red experience, even though of course experiences are not red in the same sense in which apples are red. Phenomenal redness (a property of experiences, or of subjects of experience) is a different property from external redness (a property of external objects), but both are respectable properties in their own right.

Mary attends to her visual experience, and thinks *I am having an experience of such-and-such quality*, referring to the quality of phenomenal redness. There are various concepts of the quality in question that might yield a true belief.

We can first consider the concept expressed by 'red' in the public-language expression 'red experience', or the concept expressed by the public-language expression 'phenomenal redness'. The reference of these expressions is fixed via a relation to red things in the external world, and ultimately via a relation to certain paradigmatic red objects that are ostended in learning the public-language term 'red'. A language learner learns to call the experiences typically brought about by these objects 'red' (in the phenomenal sense), and to call the objects that typically bring about those experiences 'red' (in the external sense). So the phenomenal concept involved here is *relational*, in that it has its reference fixed by a relation to external objects. The property that is referred to need not be relational, however. The phenomenal concept plausibly designates an intrinsic property rigidly, so that there are counterfactual worlds in which red experiences are never caused by red things.

One can distinguish at least two relational phenomenal concepts, depending on whether reference is fixed by relations across a whole community of subjects, or by relations restricted to the subject in question. The first is what we can call the *community relational concept*, or red_C. This can be glossed roughly as *the phenomenal quality typically caused in normal subjects within my community by paradigmatic red things*. The second is what we can call the *individual relational concept*, or red_I. This can be glossed roughly as *the phenomenal quality typically caused in me by paradigmatic red things*. The two concepts red_C and red_I will corefer for normal subjects, but for abnormal subjects they may yield different results. For example, a red/green-inverted subject's concept red_C will refer to (what others call) phenomenal redness, but his or her concept red_I will refer to (what others call) phenomenal greenness.

Phenomenal properties can also be picked out indexically. When seeing the tomato, Mary can refer indexically to a visual quality associated with it, by saying 'this quality' or 'this sort of experience'. These expressions express a demonstrative concept that we might call E. E functions in an indexical manner, roughly by picking out whatever quality the subject is currently ostending. Like other demonstratives, it has a 'character,' which fixes reference in a context roughly by picking out whatever quality is ostended in that context; and it has a distinct 'content', corresponding to the quality that is actually ostended—in this case, phenomenal redness. The demonstrative concept E rigidly designates its referent, so that it picks out the quality in question even in counterfactual worlds in which no one is ostending the quality.

The three concepts red_C, red_I, and E may all refer to the same quality, phenomenal redness. All of them fix reference to phenomenal redness relationally, characterizing it in terms of its relations to external objects or acts of ostension, and all of them designate this quality rigidly.

There is another crucial phenomenal concept in the vicinity, one that does not pick out phenomenal redness in terms of its relation to external objects or to acts of ostension, but rather picks it out in terms of its intrinsic phenomenal nature. This is what we might call a *pure phenomenal concept*.

To see the need for the pure phenomenal concept, consider the knowledge that Mary is in a position to gain when she learns for the first time what it is like to see red. She may learn that seeing red has such-and-such quality. Mary may learn (or reasonably come to believe) that red things will typically cause experiences of such-and-such quality in her, and in other members of her community. She may learn (or gains the cognitively significant belief) that the experience she is now having has such-and-such quality, and that the quality she is now ostending is such-and-such. Call Mary's "such-and-such" concept here R.

Mary's concept R picks out phenomenal redness, but it is quite distinct from the concepts red_C, red_I, and E. We can see this by using cognitive significance as a test for difference between concepts. Mary is in a position to gain the belief $red_C = R$—that the quality typically caused in her community by red things is such-and-such—and this belief is cognitively significant knowledge. She may gain the cognitively significant belief $red_I = R$ in a similar way. And she may gain the belief $E = R$—roughly, that the belief that *this* quality is such-and-such.

Mary's belief $E = R$ is as cognitively significant as any other belief in which the object of a demonstrative is independently characterized: e.g. my belief *I am David Chalmers*, or my belief *that object is tall*, or my belief *that shape is roundness*. For Mary, $E = R$ is not a priori. No a priori reasoning can rule out the hypothesis that some other quality is the object of her current ostension, just as no a priori reasoning can rule out the hypothesis that I am David Hume, or that the object I am pointing to is short. Indeed, nothing known a priori entails that R is ever instantiated in the actual world.

So the concept R is quite distinct from red_C, red_I, and E. Unlike the other concepts, the pure phenomenal concept picks out the phenomenal quality *as* the phenomenal quality that it is.

(The distinction between pure and relational phenomenal concepts roughly tracks Nida-Rümelin's 1995 distinction between "phenomenal" and "nonphenomenal" readings of belief attributions concerning phenomenal states. "Phenomenal" belief attributions can only be satisfied by beliefs involving pure phenomenal concepts, while "nonphenomenal" belief attributions can be satisfied by beliefs involving either pure or relational phenomenal concepts.)

It may be that there is a broad sense in which R can be regarded as a 'demonstrative' concept. I will not regard it this way: I take it that demonstrative concepts work roughly as analyzed by Kaplan (1977), so that they have an reference-fixing 'character' that leaves their referent open. This is how E behaves: its content might be expressed roughly as 'this quality, whatever it happens to be'. R, on the other hand, is a substantive concept that is tied a priori to a specific sort of quality, so it does not behave the way that Kaplan suggests that a demonstrative should. Still, there is an intimate relationship between pure and demonstrative phenomenal concepts that I will discuss later in the paper; and if someone wants to count pure phenomenal concepts as 'demonstrative' in a broad sense, there is no great harm in doing so, as long as the relevant distinctions are kept clear. What matters for my purposes is not the terminological point, but the more basic point that the distinct concepts E and R exist.

3   The Content of Phenomenal Concepts

The relations among these concepts can be analyzed straightforwardly using the two-dimensional framework for representing the content of concepts. A quick introduction to this framework is given in an appendix; more details can be found in Chalmers 2002b.

According to the two-dimensional framework, when an identity $A = B$ is a posteriori, the concepts A and B have different epistemic (or primary) intensions across epistemically possible scenarios. If A and B are rigid concepts and the identity is true, A and B have the same subjunctive (or secondary) intensions. So we should expect that the concepts red_C, red_I, E, and R have different epistemic intensions, but the same subjunctive intension. And this is what we find. The subjunctive intension of each picks out phenomenal redness in all worlds. The epistemic intension of red_C picks out, in a given centered world, roughly the quality typically caused by certain paradigmatic objects in the community of the subject at the center of the world. The epistemic intension of red_I picks out roughly the quality typically caused by those objects in the subject at the center.

(Note that for the purposes of analyzing the content of phenomenal concepts, epistemic intensions should be taken as functions across epistemically possible scenarios or conceivable worlds, without assuming that these must coincide with metaphysically possible worlds.)

As for the demonstrative concept E: to a first approximation, one might hold that its epistemic intension picks out the quality that is ostended by the subject at the center. This characterization is good enough for most of our purposes, but it is not quite correct. It is possible to ostend two experiences simultaneously and invoke two distinct demonstrative concepts, as when one thinks *that quality differs from that quality*, ostending two phenomenal color qualities associated with symmetrical spatial locations in a symmetrical visual experience (see Austin 1990). Here no descriptive characterization such as the one above will capture the difference between the two concepts. It is better to see E as a sort of indexical, like I or *now* (hence the name E, for a primitive experiential indexical). To characterize the epistemic possibilities relevant to demonstrative phenomenal concepts, we need centered worlds whose centers contain not only a "marked" subject and time, but also one or more marked experiences; in the general case, a sequence of such experiences. Then a concept such as E will map a centered world to the quality of the "marked" experience (if any) in that world. Where two demonstrative concepts E_1 and E_2 are involved, as above, the relevant epistemic possibilities will contain at least two marked experiences, and we can see E_1 as picking out the quality of the first marked experience in a centered world, and E_2 as picking out the quality of the second. Then the belief above will endorse all worlds at which the quality of the first marked experience differs from the quality of the second. This subtlety will not be central for the purposes of this paper.

The epistemic intension of R is quite distinct from all of these. It picks out phenomenal redness in all worlds. When Mary believes *roses cause R experiences*, or *I am currently having an R experience*, she thereby excludes all epistemic possibilities in which roses cause some other quality (such as G, phenomenal greenness), or in which she is experiencing some other quality: only epistemic possibilities involving phenomenal redness remain.

The cognitive significance of identities such as $red_C = R$, $red_I = R$, and $E = R$ is reflected in the differences between the concept's epistemic intensions. The first two identities endorse all epistemic possibilities in which paradigmatic objects stand in the right relation to experiences of R; these are only a subset of the epistemic possibilities available a priori. The third identity endorses all epistemic possibilities in which the marked experience at the center (or the ostended experience, on the rough characterization) is R. Again, there are many epistemic possibilities (a priori) that are not like this: centered worlds in which the marked experience is G, for example. Once again, this epistemic contingency reflects the cognitive significance of the identity.

(The rest of this section is inessential for the discussion of the knowledge argument in the rest of this paper, but is independently relevant to the analysis of phenomenal concepts and phenomenal knowledge in Mary's situation. As with the previous material, the material that follows is developed at greater length in Chalmers 2002c.)

One could even consider the conceivable case of *Inverted Mary*, who is physically, functionally, and environmentally just like Mary, except that her phenomenal color vision is red/green inverted. Like Mary, Inverted Mary learns something new when she sees red things for the first time. But Inverted Mary learns something different from what Mary learns. Where Mary learns that tomatoes cause experiences of (what we call) phenomenal redness, Inverted Mary learns that they cause experiences of (what we call) phenomenal greenness. In the terms given earlier, Mary acquires beliefs $red_C = R$, $red_I = R$, and $E = R$, while Inverted Mary acquires beliefs $red_C = G$, $red_I = G$, and $E = G$ (where G is the obvious analog of R). So Mary and Inverted Mary acquire beliefs with quite different contents.

Even after they see red things for the first time, Mary and Inverted Mary are physical and functional twins. Nevertheless, they have beliefs with different contents. It follows that belief content does not supervene conceptually on physical/functional properties. That is: once we grant that phenomenal properties are conceptually irreducible to physical/functional properties, we must grant that the same goes for at least some intentional properties.

This case might seem analogous to Putnam's familiar case of Twin Earth (Putnam 1975), but something different is going on. On Twin Earth, where the water in our environment is replaced by the superficially identical but chemically distinct XYZ, when Twin Oscar says 'water is wet', he expresses a belief that differs in content from the corresponding belief expressed by Oscar on Earth. Oscar's belief is about XYZ, where Twin Oscar's belief is about H_2O. But one can argue that while these beliefs differ in their subjunctive content, their epistemic content is the same: roughly, the epistemic content of both beliefs endorses all epistemic possibilities in which the watery stuff in the environment of the subject at the center is wet. That is, Oscar's and Twin Oscar's 'water' concepts have different extensions, and different subjunctive intensions, but they have the same epistemic intension.

By contrast, Mary's concept R and Inverted Mary's concept G differ not only in their extension and in their subjunctive intension, but also in their epistemic intension. When Mary thinks *I am having an R experiences*, the epistemic content of her belief endorses only those epistemic possibilities in which the subject at the center has an R experience. When Inverted Mary thinks *I am having a G experience*, the epistemic content of her belief endorses only those epistemic possibilities in which the subject at the center has a G experience. So unlike the Twin Earth cases, this appears to be a case in which the epistemic content of a subject's belief does not supervene conceptually on the subject's physical and functional properties.

Something unusual is going on here. In standard externalism, and in standard cases of so-called "direct reference," a referent plays a role in constituting the subjunctive content (subjunctive intension) of concepts and beliefs, while leaving the epistemic content (epistemic intension) unaffected. In the pure phenomenal case, by contrast, the quality of the experiences plays a role in constituting the *epistemic* content of the concept and of the corresponding belief. One might say very loosely that in this case, the referent of the concept is somehow present inside the concept's sense, in a way much stronger than in the usual cases of "direct reference."

One might say that concepts such as *water* are *subjunctively rigid*, in that their subjunctive intensions pick out the same extension in all possible worlds. Pure phenomenal concepts, by contrast, are not only subjunctively rigid but *epistemically rigid*, in that their epistemic intensions pick out the same extension in all scenarios. Martine Nida-Rümelin suggests in a forthcoming paper that pure phenomenal concepts can be called *super-rigid*: when represented as a two-dimensional matrix, they pick out the same extension in all locations of the matrix. Super-rigidity is clearly a much stronger phenomenon than standard rigidity.

4   Phenomenal Concepts and the Knowledge Argument

This analysis of phenomenal concepts bears on the knowledge argument in a number of ways. For a start, it gives us a better characterization of Mary's new knowledge. The crucial new beliefs that Mary gains do not involve just any phenomenal concept that refers to phenomenal redness, but rather involve a pure phenomenal concept such as R. These beliefs have the form *this experience is R, I am experiencing R, red things typically cause R experiences, other people experience R when they look at tomatoes, R is instantiated*, and so on. The content of R is tied to the phenomenal property R in a very direct way: both the epistemic and subjunctive intensions of the concept pick out instances of R in all possible worlds. And this content appears to be determined directly by the instantiation of R itself in Mary: if Inverted Mary instantiates G instead, she will have a quite different pure phenomenal concept G, and quite different resulting beliefs.

Nevertheless, what I have said so far is already enough to see that certain materialist *responses* to the knowledge argument fail. It is common for materialists to respond to the knowledge argument by invoking specific claims about the nature of phenomenal concepts, or analogies with other concepts. For example, some (e.g. Ismael 1999; Perry 2001) hold that phenomenal concepts are *indexical* concepts, so that the epistemic gap here can be assimilated to the epistemic gap between objective knowledge and indexical knowledge more generally. Others (e.g. Hawthorne 2002; Loar 1997) hold that phenomenal concepts are *demonstrative* or *recognitional* concepts, so that the epistemic gap can be assimilated to that that holds between theoretical knowledge and demonstrative or recognitional knowledge more generally.

From the discussion above, it is clear that Mary's crucial phenomenal concept is not an indexical or a demonstrative concept. Mary does have a concept of this form: it is her demonstrative phenomenal concept E. That concept behaves roughly as the accounts above suggest that phenomenal concepts should. But Mary's important new knowledge involves not E but R, and R is not an indexical or demonstrative concept at all. Rather, it is a pure phenomenal concept, a concept characterizing the phenomenal property in question directly in terms of its phenomenal character.

One can also make a direct case against any analysis of phenomenal knowledge as indexical or demonstrative knowledge, as follows. In the indexical case, any epistemic gaps disappear from an objective perspective. Say that I am physically omniscient, but do not know whether I am in the United States or Australia (let's imagine that there are appropriate qualitative twins in both). Then I have a certain indexical ignorance, and discovering that I am in the United States will constitute new knowledge. But if someone else is watching the world from the third-person point of view and is also physically omniscient, they will have no corresponding ignorance: they will know that A is in Australia and that B is in the United States, and that is all there is for them to know. That is, there is no thought about my location about whose truth-value they are ignorant: they know everything there is to know about my situation. So my ignorance is *essentially* indexical, and evaporates from the objective viewpoint. The same goes for indexical ignorance concerning what time it is, for demonstrative ignorance concerning what *this* is, and so on. In all these cases, the ignorance disappears from the objective viewpoint: an objectively omniscient observer can know everything there is for them to know about my situation, and there will be no doubts for them to settle.

Now consider Mary's ignorance. From her black-and-white room, she is ignorant of all sorts of facts: what it will be like for her to see red for the first time, what it is like for others to see red, and so on. Only the first of these looks even apparently indexical, so let us focus on that. In this case, a physically omniscient observer may have precisely analogous ignorance: even given his complete physical knowledge, he can entertain the question of what it is like for Mary to see red for the first time, and may have no idea what the answer is. So this ignorance does not evaporate from the objective viewpoint. The same goes even more strongly for knowledge of what it is like for others to see red. For any observer, regardless of their viewpoint, there will be an epistemic gap between complete physical knowledge and this sort of phenomenal knowledge. This suggests very strongly that phenomenal knowledge is not a variety of indexical or demonstrative knowledge at all. Rather, it is a sort of non-indexical knowledge of the world, not essentially tied to any viewpoint.

If this is right, then any analysis of phenomenal concepts as indexical or demonstrative concepts fails, and any attempt to explain Mary's epistemic gap in terms of the epistemic gap for indexical or demonstrative concepts fails.

There is more to say here. But to explore these issues, it is useful to first set out the two-dimensional analysis of the knowledge argument.

5   The Two-Dimensional Analysis of the Knowledge Argument

Nothing I have said so far entails that the knowledge argument is sound. So far, what I have said can be embraced in principle by a type-B materialist who holds that phenomenal properties are identical to physical properties, but that phenomenal concepts are distinct from physical concepts. The type-B materialist can take on board everything so far as an epistemic point about the distinctive behavior of phenomenal concepts, and hold that no nonmaterialist ontological consequences follow.

In my view, the knowledge argument is strongest when it is conjoined with the two-dimensional semantic framework, which allows us to think about the connection between epistemic and ontological matters, and between concepts and properties, in a more precise way. Once this is done, we can also bring in the analysis of phenomenal concepts given above, to help see why certain materialist *responses* to the knowledge argument fail.

The basic intuition arising from the knowledge argument is that Mary gains new factual knowledge when she sees red for the first time, knowledge that no amount of physical information and a priori reasoning would have allowed her to possess beforehand. Let P be the complete microphysical truth about the world, and let Q be a truth stating that phenomenal redness is instantiated, deploying a pure phenomenal concept of phenomenal redness. Then the initial moral of the knowledge argument is that Q cannot be deduced from P by a priori reasoning. That is, the material conditional 'P ⊃ Q' is not knowable a priori.

This is an epistemic claim, and as such does not immediately suffice to refute the metaphysical thesis of physicalism. To do this, one needs a bridge from the epistemic claim to a metaphysical claim. As often in philosophy, this can be done by proceeding first from an epistemic claim to a modal claim (about necessity and possibility), and from there to a metaphysical claim. Here, the most straightforward version of such an argument would be the following:

(1) 'P ⊃ Q' is a posteriori.
(2) If 'P ⊃ Q' is a posteriori, 'P ⊃ Q' is contingent.
(3) If 'P ⊃ Q' is contingent, physicalism is false.

(4) Physicalism is false.

Here, premise (1) is a version of the epistemic claim above. Premise (2) is an instance of a traditionally popular thesis relating the epistemic and the modal, holding that when a sentence S is a posteriori, S is contingent. Premise (3) states a modal constraint on the metaphysical thesis of physicalism.

Premise (3) is intended to capture the general idea that if things could have been physically just as they are in our world but mentally different, then physicalism is false in our world. As such, the form of (3) needs minor modification: the truth of physicalism in our world seems compatible with the possibility of physically identical worlds with *additional* nonphysical minds. But this problem can be solved straightforwardly by conjoining to P a "that's-all" claim T, saying that our world is a *minimal* world satisfying P (roughly, a world containing no more than it needs to in order to satisfy P). If we replace P by the conjunction PT, premise (3) states a plausible constraint on physicalism (given that Q is true in our world), and the plausibility of the other premises is unchanged.

A more serious problem is that premise (2) is widely believed to be false. Since Kripke 1980, many have accepted that some statements are both a posteriori and necessary: 'water is H_2O', for example, and 'Hesperus is Phosphorus'. If this is right, then it appears that there is no good reasons to accept premise (2). So the key premise connecting epistemic and modal claims is undercut, throwing doubt on arguments (such as the knowledge argument) that attempt to draw metaphysical conclusions from epistemic premises.

Here, the two-dimensional semantic framework becomes relevant. This framework allows us to draw a slightly different connection between the epistemic and modal domains: a connection that is compatible with the existence of necessary a posteriori statements, but that still allows us to draw metaphysical conclusions from epistemic premises.

Let us say that a sentence S is 1-necessary when its epistemic intension is true at all centered metaphysically possible worlds, and that it is 1-contingent when its epistemic intension is false at some centered metaphysically possible world. Let us also say that a sentence S is 2-necessary when its subjunctive intension is true at all worlds, and that it is 2-contingent when its subjunctive intension is false at some world. Then the following claim is crucial:

2-D thesis: If S is a posteriori, S is 1-contingent.

This thesis is plausibly true of all the a posteriori necessary statements that Kripke considers. For example, the epistemic intension of 'water is H_2O' is false at a Twin Earth centered world. The epistemic intension of 'Hesperus is Phosphorus' is false at a centered world where the evening star near the center is distinct from the morning star near the center. And so on. All these worlds are metaphysically possible. The claims above are quite compatible with Kripke's claim that these sentences are necessary. In effect, Kripke's claim is that the *subjunctive* intension of these sentences are true in all worlds, or that they are 2-necessary. This is quite compatible with their *epistemic* intensions being false in some worlds.

The 2-D thesis above allows us to make inferences from epistemic claims to claims about metaphysical possibility, and from there to metaphysical conclusions. As such the thesis is substantive rather than trivial, and we will look later at attempts to deny it. For now, it is enough to note that the principle appears to fit all of Kripke's cases.

(A related thesis holds that when S is a posteriori, its epistemic intension is false at some epistemically possible scenario. This purely epistemic thesis, by contrast to the last, is more or less trivial on the two-dimensional framework, but does not license inferences from epistemic claims to metaphysical conclusions. In what follows, it will always be metaphysically possible worlds rather than epistemically possible scenarios that are relevant.)

With the 2-D thesis in hand, we can reformulate the version of the knowledge argument above:

(1) 'PT ⊃ Q' is a posteriori.

(2) If 'PT ⊃ Q' is a posteriori, 'PT ⊃ Q' is 1-contingent.

(3) If 'PT ⊃ Q' is 1-contingent, 'PT ⊃ Q' is 2-contingent.

(4) If 'PT ⊃ Q' is 2-contingent, physicalism is false.

(5) Physicalism is false.

Here, (1) is the epistemic thesis arising from the Mary situation, (2) is an instance of the 2-D thesis, and (4) is a version of the modified modal constraint on physicalism, discussed above. Note that it is 2-necessity that is plausibly relevant to physicalism: physicalism requires that it *could not have been* that things were physically just as they are in our world (with nothing more), but mentally distinct. This is a subjunctive rather than an epistemic claim, so that 2-contingency rather than 1-contingency is directly relevant.

The remaining thesis is premise (3), bridging 1-contingency and 2-contingency. It is not true in general that 1-contingent statements are 2-contingent: counterexamples include 'water is H_2O', and 'Hesperus is Phosphorus'. The reason is that expressions such as 'water' and 'Hesperus' have quite different epistemic and subjunctive intensions. However, the principle is true for statements including only *semantically neutral* expressions, whose epistemic intensions are the same as their subjunctive intensions (that is, the epistemic intension's value at any centered world is the same as the subjunctive intension's value at the corresponding uncentered world).

If P, T, and Q were semantically neutral, premise (3) would be true. It is plausible that Q is in fact semantically neutral, as we saw previously that pure phenomenal concepts have the same epistemic and subjunctive intensions, so that Q is semantically neutral. However, it is arguable that P is not semantically neutral. It is plausible that terms for microphysical properties, such as 'charge', refer rigidly to intrinsic properties, but pick out those properties by virtue of the fact that they play a certain causal role in our world (e.g. a certain role in electromagnetic processes). If so, then at any given world, the epistemic intension of 'charge' picks out whatever property plays the relevant causal role in the world, while the subjunctive intension picks out the intrinsic property (charge) that plays the causal role in *our* world. And it is arguable that these intensions differ, since there are arguably worlds where the relevant causal role is played by a property distinct from the property playing the role in our world. If so, premise (3) is false.

However, this opens up only a small loophole in the argument. For premise (3) to be false, there must be a world in which the epistemic intension of 'PT ⊃ Q' is false, but in which its subjunctive intension is true. This must be a world in which the epistemic intension (and subjunctive intension) of Q is false, in which the epistemic intension of PT is true, and in which the subjunctive intension of PT is false. It is not hard to see that this must be a world in which things are structurally just as they are in our world, but with a different array of intrinsic properties playing the causal role that intrinsic microphysical properties play in our world. And this difference in intrinsic properties is responsible for the difference in truth-value of Q between that world and ours. That is, the causal structure of our microphysical world does not necessitate Q, but the intrinsic properties underlying that structure do (perhaps in conjunction with the structure). This is a version of the Russell-inspired view that I have called *panprotopsychism*.

We can therefore say: if 'PT ⊃ Q' is 1-contingent but not 2-contingent, then panprotopsychism is true. Or equivalently: if 'PT ⊃ Q' is 1-contingent, then 'PT ⊃ Q' is 2-contingent or panprotopsychism is true.

This allows us to formulate the final version of the argument:

(1) 'PT ⊃ Q' is a posteriori.
(2) If 'PT ⊃ Q' is a posteriori, 'PT ⊃ Q' is 1-contingent.
(3) If 'PT ⊃ Q' is 1-contingent, 'PT ⊃ Q' is 2-contingent or panprotopsychism is true.
(4) If 'PT ⊃ Q' is 2-contingent, physicalism is false.

(5) Physicalism is false or panprotopsychism is true.

Here, (1) is the epistemic claim arising from the Mary situation, (2) is an instance of the 2-D thesis, (3) is the result of a straightforward piece of reasoning, while (4) is the modal constraint on physicalism. It is not clear whether (5) is as strong as a denial of physicalism, since it is not clear whether or not panprotopsychism is a form of physicalism. But if it is a form of physicalism, it is clearly a strange and unusual form, so the conclusion of the argument remains strong either way.

So here we have a very promising version of the knowledge argument: a valid argument for a strong ontological conclusion about consciousness, based on the epistemic intuition about the Mary case along with three other independently plausible premises.

6 Responses to the Knowledge Argument

We can use the argument above to analyze various responses that have been made to the knowledge argument.

(i) The Ability Reply: According to this type-A response (Lewis 1990; Nemirow 1990), Mary does not gain new factual knowledge, but merely gains an ability. Proponents of this response will deny that there are phenomenal truths that Mary cannot know in her room, and so will deny either premise (1) or the claim that Q is a truth. The same goes for other positions (e.g. Dennett 1991) according to which Mary gains no factual knowledge. The analysis above has no special force against this position, as the discussion here takes Mary's new factual knowledge for granted. Nevertheless, I think there are good reasons to reject the analysis (see e.g. Loar 1997; Nida-Rümelin 1995).

(ii) The No-Concept Reply: Another type-A response holds that the reason Mary lacks knowledge of what it is like to see red is simply that she fails to possess the relevant phenomenal concept. On this account, the conditional 'PT ⊃ Q' is a priori, in that it is knowable a priori by anyone who possesses the concepts involved: it is just that Mary lacks one of the crucial concepts. If so, premise (1) is false, and the argument fails. This reply has not received much attention in the literature to date (although see Harman 1990, Hellie, this vol., and Tye 2000 for suggestions in the vicinity), but in my view it is one of the more powerful replies available to a materialist.

Still, there are natural objections to this reply. While it is plausible that Mary lacks the phenomenal concepts involved in Q, it is less plausible that giving Mary this concept will close all relevant epistemic gaps. For a start, an opponent might appeal to the conceivability of zombies and inverted spectra: these suggest that even if one possess the concepts involved in P, T, and Q, there is no contradiction in the hypothesis 'PT & ∼Q', so that

'PT ⊃ Q' is not a priori. One can also argue that once Mary has the relevant phenomenal concept, she will not automatically know whether or not *other* organisms (bats or Martians, say) are having experiences of the relevant sort, even given a complete physical description of them.

Similarly, one can mount a version of the knowledge argument using weaker phenomenal concepts that Mary possesses inside the black-and-white room. One such concept is that of phenomenal indistinguishability (Lahav 1994). Mary might possess all the physical facts, and possess the concept of phenomenal indistinguishability, while still being unable to know whether two subjects are having phenomenally indistinguishable experiences. If so, an argument analogous to the knowledge argument will go through.

Finally, one can make the case that even once Mary has emerged from the black-and-white room and has the relevant phenomenal concept, she cannot deduce the relevant phenomenal knowledge (e.g. that she is having an experience with such-and-such character) by a priori reasoning from *PT* alone. Rather, she must crucially rely on introspection. Introspection yields a posteriori knowledge, justified by experience rather than by reason alone. If this is correct, then 'PT ⊃ Q' is not a priori.

(iii)   The Indexical Reply: According to this analysis (Bigelow and Pargetter 1990; Ismael 1999; Perry 2001), Mary's new knowledge is likened to indexical knowledge. Proponents of this position will deny premise (1) above. They accept that 'PT ⊃ Q' is a posteriori (and hence are phenomenal realists), but they deny that 'PTI ⊃ Q' is a posteriori: Q is itself indexical knowledge, so if PTI contains full indexical knowledge it will entail Q. Mere indexical knowledge of her identity and the current time will obviously not help Mary to know what it is like to see red, but a proponent might appeal to further aspects of I. In particular, it is not implausible that I needs to build in further indexical information, identifying the referent of indexical phenomenal concepts such as *E*. Even so, this does not help the physicalist, for reasons discussed earlier. As we have seen already, Mary's central new knowledge does not involve any indexical element, so indexical information about the referent of *E* is distinct from Mary's new knowledge.

(One might think that even if Mary's new what-it-is-like knowledge is non-indexical, an indexical claim contained within I might help her derive this knowledge. In particular, a claim of the form *E is such-and-such* might be thought to help, if the right-hand side has the appropriate form: for example, if the indexical claim is $E = R$, it will enable what-it-is-like knowledge. However, if *E is such-and-such* is to be built into PTI, then the right-hand-side must be such that *such-and-such is instantiated* is itself deducible from PT. (The indexical claims in I simply locate indexical referents on the objective map given by PT; see Chalmers and Jackson 2001 for more here.) So given that nonindexical what-it-is-like knowledge of the form *R is instantiated* is not deducible from PT, then $E = R$ cannot be built into PTI. And it is clear that claims of the form $E = X$, where *X is instantiated* is deducible from PT (e.g. because X is a physical-functional concept) does not help Mary to deduce the relevant what-it-is-like knowledge. So if PT does not imply Q, neither does PTI.)

(iv) The Incomplete-Physical-Knowledge Reply: It is occasionally held that the knowledge argument fails as Mary did not have complete physical knowledge inside the black-and-white room. In effect, this reply will question premise (1) of the arguments I have given: rather than showing that 'P ⊃ Q' is not a priori, the Mary case shows only that 'P* ⊃ Q' is not a priori, where P* is encompasses the subset of physical truths that Mary knows inside the room.

There are different versions of this reply, depending on how the proponent understands the notion of 'physical' and the relevant incompleteness. Some proponents (e.g. Horgan 1984) are in effect using 'physical' *broadly*, so that the physical truths encompass high-level truths that are necessitated by microphysical truths. Understood this way, it is nontrivial that knowing all the truths about physics and chemistry (and so on) suffices to know all the physical truths. A physicalist may hold that phenomenal truths themselves are broad physical truths, of which Mary is ignorant. On this view, it begs the question to assert the premise that Mary knows all the physical truths.

To avoid this issue, I think it is best to understand 'physical' *narrowly*, as I do above. On this understanding, the physical is understood as the *microphysical* (or if one likes, the microphysical and the chemical, or some other specified domain). In this sense, it is less arguable that Mary knows all the physical truths: certainly we can stipulate that she knows all the truths in the language of microphysical theory. Of course in this sense, even high-level biological facts and the like will be nonphysical facts, so the existence of nonphysical facts is not enough to defeat physicalism. But the stronger claim that there are facts not *necessitated* by the microphysical facts is enough to defeat physicalism. And this stronger claim is delivered by the argument above.

(The knowledge argument is sometimes formalized as a straightforward inference from the premise that Mary knows all the physical facts but does not know all the phenomenal facts to the conclusion that phenomenal facts are not physical facts. I think this formulation does not provide a compelling argument against physicalism, for the reasons just stated. If 'physical' is understood broadly, the claim that Mary knows all the physical facts is question-begging; if 'physical' is understood narrowly, the conclusion that there are nonphysical facts is compatible with physicalism. For this reason, I think it is much better to formalize the knowledge argument in terms of deducibility and necessitation.)

Another version of this view (e.g. Stoljar 2001) holds that even if 'physical' is restricted to the microphysical, Mary may nevertheless lack physical knowledge. On this view, Mary knows all truths in the language of microphysical theory, but there is more to microphysics than microphysical theory. In particular, microphysical theory gives Mary knowledge of the structural and relational properties of microphysical entities, but not of their intrinsic properties. And these intrinsic properties may be crucial to the necessitation of consciousness. Clearly, this view leads directly to the position that I earlier called "panprotopsychism." As before, one can argue about whether this counts as a version of physicalism, but in any case I think it is a view that the knowledge argument leaves open.

(v) The Old-Fact/New-Way Reply: According to the most popular response to the knowledge argument, Mary gains knowledge of a fact she already knew, under a different mode of presentation (e.g. Horgan 1984; Loar 1997; Tye 2000). In the standard version, this new knowledge is held to be analogous to that of someone who knew Hesperus is a planet and who learns that Phosphorus is a planet, or someone who knew that Superman can fly and who learns that Clark Kent can fly. Each pair of items of knowledge arguably involves a single fact (about a single property instantiated by a single individual), under distinct modes of presentation. Proponents of this response hold that analogously, Mary's new phenomenal knowledge is knowledge of a fact she knew already (about the instantiation of a physical property), under a different mode of presentation. Mary has distinct physical and phenomenal concepts with a common referent, just as with *Hesperus* and *Phosphorus*, or *Superman* and *Clark Kent.*

The two-dimensional argument I have given above is formulated in such a way that it already takes this sort of response into account. In particular, all of the standard cases of new knowledge (involving Hesperus, Superman, and so on) seem to be compatible with premise 2: the claim that a posteriori statements have metaphysically contingent epistemic intensions. The a posteriori identity *Hesperus is Phosphorus* has a necessary subjunctive intensions, but it has a contingent epistemic intensions: the two concepts involved have distinct epistemic intensions across possible worlds, and the epistemic intension of the identity is correspondingly false at some world (e.g., a world where the evening star is distinct from the morning star). The same goes for all the other standard a posteriori identities: none give grounds for questioning premise 2, or any other premise of the argument above. So as it stands, this response does nothing to cast doubt on the knowledge argument as formulated here.

It is also possible to make this sort of point (somewhat less precisely) in ways that do not invoke the two-dimensional framework. For example, one can put the basic point by saying that where two nonindexical concepts a and b involve distinct modes of presentation of a common referent (i.e. when $a = b$ is not a priori), the distinct modes of presentation are associated in some fashion with distinct properties (connected only contingently) of the referent. When one gains new knowledge equating the referents of the two concepts, one gains knowledge of new contingent facts connecting the modes of presentation. In particular, one gains knowledge that a single individual has both associated properties. For example, when one learns that Hesperus is Phosphorus, one learns the new fact that the brightest object visible in the evening is also visible in the morning. When one learns that Superman is Clark Kent, one learns the new fact that the man with the cape works at the Daily Planet. When one learns that water is H_2O, one learns that the liquid in one's pool has a certain molecular structure. And so on. The thesis does not apply to indexical concepts (e.g. an objectively omniscient but indexically ignorant subject who learns *I am X*), but we have seen that indexicality is irrelevant in the case of phenomenal concepts.

This distinct-property thesis is closely related to the 2-D thesis stated above. The 2-D thesis entails that for an a posteriori identity $a = b$, a and b have distinct epistemic intensions across possible worlds. Here, epistemic intensions play much the same role as the associated properties invoked in the distinct-property thesis. The two-dimensional formulation has the advantages that it avoids the imprecise notion of 'association', and that it accommodates indexical cases. (A concept such as I need not be associated with a property distinct from those associated with cognitively distinct coreferential 'objective' concepts, but it does have a distinct epistemic intension.) On the other hand, the distinct-property thesis has the advantage that it requires less semantic theory for its formulation.

In effect the distinct-property thesis allows us to find a new fact associated with any case of new knowledge, so that if Mary gains new knowledge of an old fact, she also gains knowledge of a new fact. One could also run the argument directly, by invoking something like the following thesis:

New fact thesis: In nonindexical cases, whenever one gains new knowledge of an old fact, one simultaneously gains knowledge of some new fact.

This principle (versions of which are put forward by Lockwood 1989, pp. 136–137; Chalmers 1996, pp. 141–142; and Thau 2002, p. 127) is closely related to the 2-D thesis and the distinct-property thesis, but it requires neither two-dimensionalism nor the notion of association between concepts and properties. It can be endorsed even by those with very different views about reference and mental content. An examination of cases, of the sort given above, suggests that it is independently plausible. In all these cases, when one gains knowledge of an old fact under a new mode of presentation, one gains knowledge of a new fact connecting the two modes of presentation.

Applying this principle to Mary: if Mary acquires new knowledge of an old fact, she will also acquire knowledge of a new fact. In effect, the new fact thesis allows us to move from the epistemic claim that Mary gains new factual knowledge (of either an old or a new fact) to the ontological claim that Mary gains knowledge of a new fact. If so, if Mary already knew all the physical facts, then the physical facts do not exhaust all the facts.

Strictly speaking, this conclusion is compatible with physicalism, at least if we understand physical facts as microphysical facts. But to obtain a stronger conclusion, we need only refine the principle slightly.

New fact thesis (modified): In nonindexical cases, whenever one gains new knowledge (not deducible by a priori reasoning from previous knowledge) of an old fact, one simultaneously gains knowledge (or becomes in a position to gain knowledge) of some fact not necessitated by previously known facts.

Once again, this thesis is plausible in all the standard cases. Applying it to Mary: given that Mary gains new knowledge, not derivable from her previous knowledge, it follows that she gains knowledge (or becomes in a position to gain knowledge) of some fact not necessitated by previously known facts. Given that she previously knew all the microphysical facts, it follows that there are facts not necessitated by the microphysical facts, so that physicalism is false.

(vi) Loar's Reply. For an old-fact/new-way analysis to have any hope of succeeding, it must treat Mary's new knowledge as disanalogous to standard cases of coreference, and in particular it must give reason to think that premise (2) fails in this case, as do the related principles discussed above. This is an uphill battle, since it is plausible that these principles hold in all familiar cases. In particular, all familiar a posteriori identities appear to involve distinct epistemic intensions over centered worlds.

A sophisticated attempt in this direction is made by Loar (1997). Loar isolates the "semantic premise" of the knowledge argument:

Semantic premise: A statement of property identity that links conceptually independent concepts is true only if at least one concepts picks out the property it refers to by connoting a contingent property of that property (Loar 1997, p. 600).

Here, two concepts a and b are conceptually independent when an identity judgment $a = b$ is a posteriori. A concept connotes a property when it uses that property to pick out its referent. A concept's connoted property is akin to a property associated with the concept's mode of presentation in the sense discussed above. If we make the translation, Loar's semantic premise is closely akin to the distinct-property thesis discussed above, according to which the concepts involved in an a posteriori identity are associated with contingently coextensive properties. Strictly speaking the distinct-property thesis is weaker than Loar's semantic premise, as distinct properties can be contingently coextensive even when each is a non-contingent property of its bearer (e.g. the properties of containing hydrogen atoms and containing H_2O). There are corresponding exceptions to Loar's semantic premise (as Tye 1997 has pointed out), but (as White forthcoming points out) the weaker premise that the concepts in such an identity connote contingently coextensive properties is enough to make the knowledge argument work.

(Like the distinct-property thesis, Loar's semantic premise is closely related to the 2-D thesis, although like the distinct-property thesis, it has exceptions in the case of indexicals.)

Loar allows that the semantic premise applies to standard a posteriori identities, but denies that it holds in the physical-phenomenal case. He suggests (p. 602) that this can be explained by the fact that phenomenal concepts are recognitional concepts that pick out physical properties without a contingent associated mode of presentation. Here, a recognitional concept is a type-demonstrative ("one of *that* kind"). Loar holds that the fact that phenomenal concepts are recognitional concepts explains the aposteriority of a phenomenal-physical identity: identities involving recognitional and theoretical concepts are always a posteriori.

Most such identities satisfy the semantic premise, but Loar holds that an exception in this case is explained by the fact that phenomenal concepts lack a contingent mode of presentation. Loar's idea of a concept that lacks a contingent mode of presentation corresponds approximately, on the two-dimensional account, to what I called semantically neutral concept above: roughly, a concept with the same epistemic and subjunctive intensions across metaphysically possible worlds (Loar 1999 makes the connection explicitly). Here we can call these *neutral* concepts for short.

Loar's key claims are, in effect: (i) phenomenal concepts are neutral and recognitional; (ii) if phenomenal concepts are recognitional, they will be involved in a posteriori identities with theoretical concepts; (iii) if phenomenal concepts are neutral, these a posteriori identities will not involve contingent modes of presentation. From these claims it follows that the semantic premise is false (as is premise 2), so that the epistemic gap will be compatible with physicalism.

I think there is good reason to reject this account. First, as before, there is good reason to believe that the phenomenal concepts crucial to Mary's argument are not type-demonstratives. Mary's demonstrative phenomenal concepts are type-demonstratives, but her pure phenomenal concepts are quite distinct from these, and it is pure phenomenal concepts that are crucial to the argument. So an account based on an appeal to type-demonstratives cannot succeed here. Loar might respond that he is using 'type-demonstrative' more broadly than I am, so that pure phenomenal concepts still count as type-demonstratives. Or he could drop the appeal to demonstrative concepts, and hold that recognitional concepts need not be demonstrative. But a deeper problem remains.

Let us say that a concept is *opaque* when it can corefer with a conceptually independent neutral theoretical concept. In effect, Loar argues that pure phenomenal concepts are both neutral and opaque: they are themselves neutral, but they can corefer with conceptually independent neutral theoretical concepts. To make discussion easier, I will play along with Loar's view that the relevant theoretical concepts are themselves neutral. (Their nonneutrality complicates matters slightly, but in the end it opens up room only for panprotopsychism.)

If pure phenomenal concepts were both neutral and opaque, the semantic premise (and premise 2) would be false, and the antimaterialist argument would fail. But no reason has been given to believe that any concept can be both neutral and opaque. Every other clear case of an opaque concept (demonstrative concepts, many natural-kind concepts, opaque recognitional concepts) is non-neutral, and their nonneutrality underlies and explains their opacity. By contrast, every other clear case of a neutral concept (certain descriptive concepts, categorical concepts) appears to be nonopaque.

Anticipating a response along these lines (p. 602), Loar says (in effect) that antiphysicalists hold that phenomenal concepts are neutral, and that the physicalist is entitled to the same claim. But the plausibility of the claim that phenomenal concepts are neutral does nothing to resolve the conflict between that claim and the claim that phenomenal concepts are opaque. Insofar as we have reason to believe that phenomenal concepts are neutral, we have reason to believe that they are not opaque, and so we have reason to believe that physicalism is false (or that panprotopsychism is true).

Even if there is a sense in which phenomenal concepts are recognitional, recognitionality alone does nothing to support opacity. The other recognitional concepts that Loar appeals to in order to support the claim of opacity are *nonneutral* recognitional concepts, and it is their nonneutrality that grounds their opacity. (That is, it is because these concepts present their referent under a contingent mode of presentation that they can corefer with conceptually independent neutral concepts.) So if phenomenal concepts are neutral, these analogies give no reason to accept that phenomenal concepts are opaque. We have good reason to believe that all neutral concepts are nonopaque, and no reason has been given to grant an exception.

To sum up: Loar's claims of (i) conceptually independent coreference (opacity) and (ii) lack of contingent mode of presentation (neutrality) stand in strong tension with each other, a tension that Loar's account does nothing to remove. Once we accept the second claim, any support for the first claim is undercut. So there is no reason to believe that the relevant phenomenal concepts have the features that Loar suggests, and there is good reason to deny this claim. I conclude that Loar's attempt to reconcile the distinctive epistemic behavior of phenomenal concepts with physicalism fails.

(Further discussion of Loar's account is given in Chalmers 1999. I have not stressed modal considerations here, but I argue there that Loar's account requires "strong necessities" and a sort of modal dualism that is quite problematic in its own right.)

(vii)   Other Analyses. The materialist might hope that some other account of phenomenal concepts can be given, such that their distinctive epistemic behavior can be reconciled with the claim that they refer to physical properties. I am skeptical that any such account can be given. I think the only remote chance is to attempt to deny premise (2) (and related claims about properties associated with modes of presentation), but as I have argued elsewhere (Chalmers 1999), there is reason to believe that this premise is a deep (nontrivial) conceptual truth. On my view, all other accounts that attempt to deny this premise fall prey to problems that are akin to the problem of Loar's account.

Nevertheless, there is room for fruitful further debate on this topic. And whatever the consequences for the truth of materialism, a deeper understanding of phenomenal concepts is likely to have deep consequences for our understanding of consciousness.

Appendix

What follows is a brief and simplified introduction to the two-dimensional semantic framework as I understand it. See also Chalmers 2002b; forthcoming.

Let us say that it is epistemically possible in the broad sense that S if the hypothesis that S is not ruled out a priori. Then there will be a wide space of epistemic possible hypotheses (in the broad sense; I omit the qualifier in what follows). Some of these will conflict with each other; some of them will be compatible with each other; and some will subsume each other. We have a systematic way of describing epistemic possibilities that differs from our way of describing subjunctive counterfactual possibilities. It is this sort of epistemic description that is captured by the first dimension of the two-dimensional framework.

It is epistemically possible that water is not H_2O, in the broad sense that this is not ruled out a priori. And there are many specific versions of this epistemic possibility: intuitively, specific ways our world could turn out such that if they turn out that way, it will turn out that water is not H_2O. Take the XYZ-world, one containing superficially identical XYZ in place of H_2O. It is epistemically possible that our world is the XYZ-world. When we consider this epistemic possibility—that is, when we consider the hypothesis that *our* world contains XYZ in the oceans, and so on—then this epistemic possibility can be seen as an instance of the epistemic possibility that water is not H_2O. We can rationally say 'if our world turns out to have XYZ in the oceans (etc.), it will turn out that water is not H_2O'. The hypothesis that the XYZ-world is actual rationally entails the belief that water is not H_2O, and is rationally inconsistent with the belief that water is H_2O.

Here, as with subjunctive counterfactual evaluation, we are considering and describing a world, but we are considering and describing it in a different way. In the epistemic case, we consider a world *as actual*: that is, we consider the hypothesis that our world is that world. In the subjunctive case, we consider a world *as counterfactual*: that is, we consider it as a way things might have been, but (probably) are not. These two modes of consideration of a world yield two ways in which a world might be seen to make a sentence or a belief true. When the XYZ-world is considered as actual, it makes 'water is XYZ' true; when it is considered as counterfactual, it does not.

In considering a world as actual, we ask ourselves: what if the actual world is really that way? In the broad sense, it is *epistemically* possible that Hesperus is not Phosphorus. This is mirrored by the fact that there are specific epistemic possibilities (not ruled out a priori) in which the heavenly bodies visible in the morning and evening are distinct; and upon consideration, such epistemic possibilities are revealed as instances of the epistemic possibility that Hesperus is not Phosphorus.

When we consider worlds as counterfactual, we consider and evaluate them in the way that we consider and evaluate subjunctive counterfactual possibilities. That is, we acknowledge that the character of the actual world is fixed, and say to ourselves: what if the world *had been* such-and-such a way? When we consider the counterfactual hypothesis that the morning star might have been distinct from the evening star, we conclude not that Hesperus would not have been Phosphorus, but rather that at least one of the objects is distinct from both Hesperus and Phosphorus (at least if we take for granted the actual-world knowledge that Hesperus is Phosphorus, and if we accept Kripke's intuitions).

Given a statement S and a world W, the *epistemic intension* of S returns the truth-value of S in W considered as actual. (Test: if W actually obtains, is S the case?) The *subjunctive intension* of S returns the truth-value of S in W considered as counterfactual. (Test: if W had obtained, would S have been the case?) We can then say that S is *primarily possible* (or 1-possible) if its epistemic intension is true in some world (i.e. if it is true in some world considered as actual), and that S is *secondarily possible* (or 2-possible) if its subjunctive intension is true in some world (i.e. if it is true in some world considered as counterfactual). Primary and secondary necessity can be defined analogously.

For a world to be considered as actual, it must be a *centered* world—a world marked with a specified individual and time—as an epistemic possibility is not complete until one's "viewpoint" is specified. So a epistemic intension should be seen as a function from centered world to truth-values. For example, the epistemic intension of 'I' picks out the individual at the center of a centered world; and the epistemic intension of 'water' picks out, very roughly, the clear drinkable (etc.) liquid in the vicinity of the center. No such marking of a center is required for considering a world as counterfactual, or for evaluating subjunctive intensions.

Epistemic and subjunctive intensions can be associated with statements in language, as above, and equally with singular terms and property terms. The intension of a statement will be a function from worlds to truth-values; the intension of a term will be a function from worlds to individuals or properties within those worlds. (In some cases, intensions are best associated with linguistic tokens rather than types.)

Epistemic intensions can also be associated in much the same way with the (token) concepts and thoughts of a thinker, all of which can be used to describe and evaluate epistemic possibilities as well as subjunctive counterfactual possibilities. In "The Components of Content" I argue that the epistemic intension of a concept or a thought can be seen as its 'epistemic content' (a sort of internal, cognitive content), and that the subjunctive intension captures much of what is often called 'wide content'.

A crucial property of epistemic content is that it reflects the rational relations between thoughts. In particular, if a belief A entails a belief B by a priori reasoning, then it will be epistemically impossible (in the broad sense) for A to be true without B being true, so the epistemic intension of A entails the epistemic intension of B. Further, if an identity $a = b$ is a posteriori for a subject, then it is epistemically possible for the subject that the identity is false, and there will be an epistemic possibility in which the referents of the two concepts involved differ, so the subject's concepts a and b will have distinct epistemic intensions. So epistemic intensions behave something like Fregean senses, individuating concepts according to cognitive significance at least up to the level of a priori equivalence.

References

Austin, D. F. 1990. *What's the Meaning of 'This'?* Ithaca, NY: Cornell University Press.

Bigelow, J. and Pargetter, R. 1990. Acquaintance with qualia. *Theoria*.

Chalmers, D. J. 1996. *The Conscious Mind: In Search of a Fundamental Theory*. Oxford: Oxford University Press.

Chalmers, D. J. 1999. Materialism and the metaphysics of modality. *Philosophy and Phenomenological Research* 59: 473–496.

Chalmers, D. J. 2002a. Consciousness and its place in nature. In S. Stich and F. Warfield, eds., *The Blackwell Guide to the Philosophy of Mind*. Blackwell. ⟨http://consc.net/papers/nature.html⟩.

Chalmers, D. J. 2002b. The components of content. In D. Chalmers, ed., *The Philosophy of Mind: Classical and Contemporary Readings*. Oxford: Oxford University Press. ⟨http://consc.net/papers/content.html⟩.

Chalmers, D. J. 2002c. The content and epistemology of phenomenal belief. In Q. Smith and A. Jokic, eds., *Consciousness: New Philosophical Essays*. Oxford: Oxford University Press.

Chalmers, D. J. (Forthcoming). The nature of epistemic space. ⟨http://consc.net/papers/espace.html⟩.

Chisholm, R. 1957. *Perceiving: A Philosophical Study.* Ithaca, NY: Cornell University Press.

Dennett, D. C. 1991. *Consciousness Explained.* New York: Little Brown.

Francescotti, R. M. 1994. Qualitative beliefs, wide content, and wide behavior. *Nous* 28: 396–404.

Harman, G. 1990. The intrinsic quality of experience. *Philosophical Perspectives* 4: 31–52.

Hawthorne, J. 2002. Advice to physicalists. *Philosophical Studies* 109: 17–52.

Hellie, B. 2004. Inexpressible truths and the allure of the knowledge argument. In this volume.

Horgan, T. 1984. Jackson on physical information and qualia. *Philosophical Quarterly* 34: 147–183.

Ismael, J. 1999. Science and the phenomenal. *Philosophy of Science* 66: 351–369.

Jackson, F. 1982. Epiphenomenal qualia. *Philosophical Quarterly* 32: 127–136.

Kaplan, D. 1989. Demonstratives. In J. Almog, J. Perry and H. Wettstein, eds., *Themes from Kaplan.* New York: Oxford University Press.

Kripke, S. 1980. *Naming and Necessity.* Cambridge, Mass.: Harvard University Press.

Lahav, R. 1994. A new challenge for the physicalist: Phenomenal indistinguishability. *Philosophia* 24: 77–103.

Lewis, D. 1990. What experience teaches. In W. G. Lycan, ed., *Mind and Cognition.* Oxford: Blackwell.

Loar, B. 1997. Phenomenal states (revised version). In N. Block, O. Flanagan, and G. Güzeldere, eds., *The Nature of Consciousness.* Cambridge, Mass.: MIT Press. Excerpt reprinted in this volume.

Loar, B. 1999. David Chalmers' *The Conscious Mind. Philosophy and Phenomenological Research* 59: 464–471.

Lockwood, M. 1989. *Mind, Brain, and the Quantum.* Oxford: Blackwell.

Nemirow, L. 1990. Physicalism and the cognitive role of acquaintance. In W. G. Lycan, ed., *Mind and Cognition.* Oxford: Blackwell.

Nida-Rümelin, M. 1995. What Mary couldn't know: Belief about phenomenal states. In T. Metzinger, ed., *Conscious Experience.* Ferdinand Schoningh. Reprinted in this volume.

Perry, J. 2001. *Knowledge, Possibility, and Consciousness.* Cambridge, Mass.: The MIT Press.

Putnam, H. 1975. The meaning of 'meaning'. In *Mind, Language, and Reality.* Cambridge: Cambridge University Press.

Stoljar, D. 2001. Two conceptions of the physical. *Philosophy and Phenomenological Research* 62: 253–281. Excerpt reprinted in this volume.

Thau, M. 2002. *Consciousness and Cognition.* Oxford: Oxford University Press.

Tye, M. 1997. Qualia. *Stanford Encyclopedia of Philosophy* (fall 1997 edition). ⟨http://plato.stanford.edu/archives/fall1997/entries/qualia⟩.

Tye, M. 2000. Knowing what it is like: The ability hypothesis and the knowledge argument. In *Consciousness, Color, and Content.* Cambridge, Mass.: The MIT Press.

White, S. Forthcoming. Why the property dualism argument won't go away. *Journal of Philosophy.*

Part VI Did She Know Everything Physical?

14   Jackson on Physical Information and Qualia

Terence Horgan

In a provocative recent paper, Frank Jackson argues against physicalism by appeal to the qualitative or phenomenal features of our mental life.[1] He maintains that physicalism is refuted by the fact that no amount of physical information could ever enable us to know what it is like to undergo a pain, have an itch, taste a lemon, smell a rose, hear a loud noise, or see the sky. He concludes that qualia are epiphenomenal, i.e., "their presence or absence makes no difference to the physical world" (p. 45, this vol.). In the present paper I shall argue that his attack on physicalism is fallacious, being an equivocation on two different senses of the phrase 'physical information'.

I   The Knowledge Argument

Jackson construes physicalism as the thesis that "all (correct) information is physical information" (p. 39, this vol.). He considers it an open philosophical question how exactly to define 'physical information', but he indicates that he employs this expression broadly enough to include whatever information the physical, chemical, and biological sciences provide about the world—including what is often called the *functional role* of various physico-chemical and biological states of humans and other organisms. I myself think that physicalism should instead be formulated as the conjunction of a general supervenience thesis and a general thesis about the physical nature of all substantival individuals,[2] but I shall accept Jackson's characterization for purposes of the present discussion. I also shall follow his practice of speaking of information, and of items of information, as though these are *entities* of some sort, distinct from sentences. I doubt that there are such entities, but avoiding apparent ontological commitment to them is not my present concern.

He does not say which kinds of currently popular mind-body theories count as physicalistic in his sense—i.e., which kinds entail that all information about mentality is physical information. But I take it that he means to include type-type psychophysical identity theories, functionalist theories which embrace type-type identity claims, and functionalist theories which repudiate type-type identity claims.[3] It is less plausible to regard token-token identity theories as physicalistic by themselves, however, since they tell us nothing about identity conditions for mental state-*types*, or mental properties.

He construes qualia, and so shall I, as properties of certain mental states: properties like the hurtfulness of pain, the itchiness of itches, and the qualitative character of one's experience when one is smelling a rose. The question, then, is whether physicalism can accommodate these qualitative, or phenomenal, properties.

He uses the following line of reasoning, which he dubs the *knowledge argument*, in an effort to convince us that qualia are left out of any physicalist story. Suppose that Fred can discriminate two groups of wavelengths in the red spectrum as consistently as we are able to sort out yellow from blue; and suppose he reports that the two kinds of red he can discriminate, which he calls red_1 and red_2, look as different to him as yellow and blue. Then Fred can see at least one more colour than we can; we are to Fred as a totally red-green color-blind person is to us. Jackson writes:

What kind of experience does Fred have when he sees red_1 and red_2? What is the new color or colors like? We would dearly like to know but do not; and it seems that no amount of physical information about Fred's brain and optical system tells us.... There is something about [Fred's color experiences] we don't know. But we know, we may suppose, everything about Fred's body, his behavior and dispositions to behavior and about his internal physiology, and everything about his history and relation to others that can be given in physical accounts of persons. We have all the physical information. Therefore, knowing all this is *not* knowing everything about Fred. It follows that physicalism leaves something out. (This vol., pp. 41–42)

In short, what no amount of physical information can tell us is *what the new color or colors are like*. Physicalism leaves out *qualia*.

This conclusion is reinforced, says Jackson, by supposing that one's own visual physiology is going to be surgically altered to match Fred's. After the operation one will know something about Fred's red_1 and red_2 experiences one did not know before, viz., what they are like. And this new information cannot be physical information, because *ex hypothesi* we had all the relevant physical information beforehand. So physicalism must be false.

He goes on to note that Fred and the new color(s) are inessential to the basic line of reasoning, which instead be formulated this way:

> Mary is a brilliant scientist who is, for whatever reason, forced to investigate the world from a black and white room *via* a black-and-white television monitor. She specialises in the neurophysiology of vision and acquires, let us suppose, all the physical information there is to obtain about what goes on when we see ripe tomatoes, or the sky, and use terms like 'red', 'blue', and so on....
>
> What will happen when Mary is released from her black-and-white room or is given a color television monitor? Will she *learn* anything or not? It seems just obvious that she will learn something about the world and our visual experience of it. But then it is inescapable that her previous knowledge was incomplete. But she had *all* the physical information. *Ergo* there is more to have than that, and physicalism is false. (This vol., pp. 42–43)

In short, what Mary learns are nonphysical items of information: what it is like to see ripe tomatoes, what it is like to see the sky, and so on. She learns about qualia, which thus are nonphysical properties.

II Critique of the Knowledge Argument

Elsewhere I myself have argued, to the contrary, that qualia are physical properties.[4] Yet I am quite prepared to concede that we do not know what Fred's red_1 and red_2 experiences are like, no matter how adequate a physical account we have of Fred's visual processes; and that Mary does not know what seeing ripe tomatoes and seeing the sky are like, prior to her first color-experiences, despite having a fully adequate physical account of human visual processes. What I want to question is Jackson's supposition that a completely adequate physical account of a creature's visual processes gives us complete *physical information* about those processes. In one sense of 'physical information', this supposition is virtually a tautology: for, physical information is just the information that would be provided by a theoretically adequate physical account. But in another sense—the sense really required by the knowledge argument—the supposition is one that physicalists can and should reject.

In order to develop this point, we need to characterize the two relevant senses of 'physical information'. Let S be a sentence that expresses information about processes of a certain specific kind, such as human perceptual processes. We shall say that S expresses *explicitly physical information* just in case S belongs to, or follows from, a theoretically adequate physical account of those processes. And we shall say that S expresses *ontologically physical information* just in case (i) all the entities referred to or quantified over in S are physical entities, and (ii) all the properties and relations expressed by the predicates in S are physical properties and relations. Thus, explicitly physical information is expressed in overtly physicalistic language, whereas ontologically physical information can be expressed by other sorts of language—for instance, mentalistic language.

One might think that information *per se* is independent of the language in which it is expressed, and thus that any sentence which expresses ontologically physical information has the same informational content as some sentence which expresses explicitly physical information. But in fact, the notion of information which Jackson employs in his knowledge argument is heavily intensional. He clearly holds that if one lacks an item of knowledge then one lacks the corresponding item of information: witness his inference from the claim that we don't *know* what Fred's red_1 and red_2 experiences are like to the conclusion that we lack *information* about those experiences, and the parallel inference from the claim that Mary doesn't know what color-experiences are like to the conclusion that she lacks information about them. This close link between knowledge and information means that information inherits the intensionality of knowledge. Thus, since Lois Lane knows that Superman can fly but does not know that Clark Kent can fly, (1) and (2) must express different information even though they each attribute the same property to the same individual:

(1)   Superman can fly.

(2)   Clark Kent can fly.

So it is entirely likely that there are sentences which express ontologically physical information but not explicitly physical information.

Physicalism, construed as the doctrine that all information is physical information, is a claim about ontologically physical information. For, the physicalist obviously does not mean to claim that the only genuine information-conveying language is the language of physical theories.

Rather, he means to claim that whenever a genuine piece of information is conveyed in *any* kind of language (mentalistic language, for instance), the relevant entities, properties, and relations are all physical.

Let us now return to the knowledge argument. We shall focus on the case of Mary, but the following remarks will also apply, *mutatis mutandis*, to the case of Fred. Consider Mary at the moment when she finally has her first color-experience—say, the experience of seeing ripe tomatoes. Jackson maintains, and I agree, that Mary obtains new knowledge at this moment, and thus new information: she finds out what it is like to see ripe tomatoes. How might she formulate this new knowledge? Not with a sentence like

(3)   Seeing ripe tomatoes is like seeing bright sunsets,

because she presumably already has the knowledge expressed by (3) by virtue of having heard the reports of many human subjects in the course of her extensive visual-perception studies. And the same holds for any other similarity judgments that are commonly made about color experiences. Rather, it seems she should express her new knowledge by means of an indexical term, as in (4):

(4)   Seeing ripe tomatoes has *this* property,

where 'this property' is used to designate the color-quale that is instantiated in her present experience.[5] (We shall call this property *phenomenal redness*. It should not be confused, of course, with the redness-property instantiated in the tomatoes themselves.)

Now, (4) as used by Mary certainly doesn't express explicitly physical information; for it expresses new information, and she had all the relevant explicitly physical information beforehand. (The phrase 'this property' is topic-neutral, rather than explicitly physical.) But (4) may very well express *ontologically* physical information. Phenomenal redness, the referent of 'this property', may very well be a physical property. This possibility is not ruled out by the fact that Mary learns something new from her experience.

Sentence (4) expresses new information because Mary has a new perspective on phenomenal redness: viz., the first-person ostensive perspective. Her new information is about the phenomenal color-property *as experienced*. Thus she could not have had this information prior to undergoing the relevant sort of experience herself. But these facts are compatible with physicalism; there is no need to suppose that when she acquires experiential awareness of phenomenal redness, she thereby comes into contact with a property distinct from those already countenanced in her prior physical account of human perception. The perspective is new, and so is the accompanying capacity to designate the relevant property indexically in a first-person ostensive manner. But the property itself need not be new.

Of course if physicalism is correct, then a fully adequate account of human perception and cognition would have to explain the human capacity to discriminate, and then ostensively designate, those physical properties of our own neural activity which are *qualia*. But nothing in the knowledge argument provides any reason to think that such an explanation could not be given.

We may conclude, therefore, that the knowledge argument is fallacious; it rests upon a subtle equivocation between two senses of 'physical information'. Although Mary, prior to her first color experience, does have a complete stock of *explicitly* physical information about human visual processes, it is illegitimate to infer from this that she has a complete stock of *ontologically* physical information. Physicalists can and should claim that the new information she acquires, the information she expresses by using (4), is ontologically physical information. The information is new not because the quale she experiences is a nonphysical property, but because she is now acquainted with this property from the experiential perspective.

Perhaps it will be replied that the phrase 'this property' in (4) cannot designate a physical property, because if it did then (4) would express a piece of information which Mary had already: viz., the information that ripe-tomato perceptions possess the given physical property. But this reply ignores the all-important intensionality of the notion of information. Even though Superman is Clark Kent, nevertheless we must distinguish between the information that Superman can fly and the information that Clark Kent can fly. Similarly, even if phenomenal redness is a physical property, nevertheless we must distinguish between (i) the information that the given property, as physicalistically described, is possessed by ripe-tomato experiences, and (ii) the information which Mary expresses by (4).

Finally, if physicalism is true then qualia presumably have all the effects which common sense attributes to them. The hurtfulness of pain is indeed partly causally responsible for the subject's seeking to avoid pain, for his saying 'It hurts', and so on; and the phenomenal redness of ripe-tomato perceptions is indeed partly causally responsible for the subject's purchasing ripe tomatoes rather than unripe ones, for his calling ripe tomatoes red, and so on. If qualia are physical properties, then there is no need to defy common sense by claiming, with Jackson, that they are epiphenomenal properties, causally impotent with respect to the physical world.[6]

Notes

1. Frank Jackson, "Epiphenomenal Qualia," *Philosophical Quarterly* 32 (1982), 127–136. My subsequent page-references are to this article. Reprinted in this volume.

2. See Terence Horgan, "Token Physicalism, Supervenience, and the Generality of Physics," *Synthese* 49 (1981), 395–413; and "Supervenience and Microphysics," *Pacific Philosophical Quarterly* 63 (1982), 29–43. A number of other philosophers also have argued that physicalism should be understood in terms of supervenience. See Jaegwon Kim, "Supervenience and Nomological Incommensurables," *American Philosophical Quarterly* 15 (1978), 149–156; John Haugeland, "Weak Supervenience," *American Philosophical Quarterly* 19 (1982), 93–103; and David Lewis, "New Work for a Theory of Universals," *Australasian Journal of Philosophy* 61 (1983), 343–377.

3. Functionalists often argue against type-type identity theory on the grounds that creatures who are radically different from humans in their physico-chemical makeup (e.g., Martians) could instantiate the same psychological state-types as humans. Cf. Hilary Putnam, "Psychological Predicates," in *Art, Mind, and Religion*, ed. W. H. Capitan and D. D. Merrill (Detroit, 1967). But D. M. Armstrong and David Lewis are functionalists who embrace type-type identity theory by treating mental state-type names as population-relative nonrigid designators; thus, under the Armstrong–Lewis view, 'pain' designates one physico-chemical state-type relative to humans, and a different one relative to Martians. See D. M. Armstrong, *A Materialist Theory of Mind* (London, 1968); David Lewis, "An Argument for the Identity Theory," *Journal of Philosophy* 63 (1966), 17–25; and especially David Lewis, "Mad Pain and Martian Pain," in *Readings in the Philosophy of Psychology*, vol. I, ed. Ned Block (Cambridge, Mass., 1980).

Jackson, I take it, wants to count as physical not only physico-chemical state-types or properties, but also the more abstract kinds of state-types involved in Putnam's style of functionalism.

4. Terence Horgan, "Functionalism, Qualia, and the Inverted Spectrum," *Philosophy and Phenomenological Research* 44 (1984): 453–469. There I also contend, however, that no form of functionalism can accommodate qualia. I argue, contrary to most functionalists, that qualia-names denote specific physico-chemical properties, rather than abstract functional properties. And I argue, contrary to Armstrong and Lewis (ibid.), that qualia-names are rigid designators, rather than functionally definable nonrigid designators.

5. Does (4) by itself convey the information which Mary expresses by using (4)? I think not. Rather, since (4) employs an indexical term essentially, it seems that in order to obtain the information which Mary expresses by (4), a member of Mary's audience would have to experience phenomenal redness himself, and would have to know that Mary is using 'this property' to designate the same property that he experiences. Knowledge about what qualia are like cannot be obtained by descriptive means alone, but requires the experiencing of those qualia.

6. Indeed, even if qualia are nonphysical they may not be epiphenomenal. As long as they are supervenient upon physical properties, I think it can plausibly be argued that they inherit the causal efficacy of the properties upon which they supervene. Cf. Jaegwon Kim, "Causality, Identity, and Supervenience in the Mind–Body Problem," *Midwest Studies in Philosophy* 4 (1979), 31–49.

15 Two Conceptions of the Physical

Daniel Stoljar

1

One way to view the contemporary debate in philosophy of mind over physicalism is to see it as being organized around an inconsistent tetrad of theses. These are:

(1) If physicalism is true, a priori physicalism is true.

(2) A priori physicalism is false.

(3) If physicalism is false, epiphenomenalism is true.

(4) Epiphenomenalism is false.

It is obvious of course that these theses *are* inconsistent: (1) and (2) entail that physicalism is false, while (3) and (4) entail that it is true. Barring ambiguity, therefore, one thing we know is that one of the theses is false.

On the other hand, each of the theses has powerful considerations, or at least what seem initially to be powerful considerations, in its favor.[1] In support of (1) are considerations of supervenience, articulated most clearly in recent times by Frank Jackson and David Chalmers. A priori physicalism is a thesis with two parts. The first part—the physicalist part—is that the mental supervenes with metaphysical necessity on the physical. The second part—the a priori part—is that mental truths are a priori entailed by physical truths. Many philosophers hold that supervenience stands in need of justification or explanation; Jackson and Chalmers argue that the project of justifying or explaining supervenience *just is* the project of making it plausible that there is an a priori entailment of the mental by the physical. This suggests that the first part of a priori physicalism inevitably involves the second. By considerations of supervenience, therefore, (1) is true: if physicalism is true, a priori physicalism is true.[2]

In support of (2) are considerations of the apparent epistemic distinctness of qualia from anything physical. According to many philosophers,
knowledge of every physical property a person has cannot by itself suffice
to know which qualia, if any, his or her experiences instantiate.[3] The conclusion drawn from this is that a priori physicalism is false; for if physical
truths a priori entail mental truths, one could know qualia merely on the
basis of physical knowledge. By considerations of epistemic distinctness,
therefore, (2) is true: a priori physicalism is false.[4]

In support of (3) are considerations of the causal closure of the physical. Causal closure is the conjunction of two distinct theses. The first is a
thesis about events; it is that for all physical events e, if there is an event e*
such that e* causes e, then e* is a physical event. The second is a thesis
about properties; it is that if any property is causally efficacious in one
physical event's causing another, that property is a physical property. Of
course, neither these theses nor their conjunction implies that there are no
irreducibly mental events or properties. What causal closure does plausibly
imply however is that irreducibly mental events and properties can play
no causal role in the production of physical events, and so, of behavior.
But the thesis that the mental has no causal work to do in the production of behavior *just is* epiphenomenalism. By considerations of causal
closure, therefore, (3) is true: if physicalism is false, epiphenomenalism
is true.[5]

In support of (4) are considerations of evidence, and, in particular, considerations of what constitutes evidence for the existence and instantiation
of qualia. In both ourselves and others, we come to know about qualia via
systems of memory, introspection and perception. According to one natural approach to these systems, however, they provide evidence of aspects of
the world only if those aspects stand in an appropriately direct causal link
to us. But if epiphenomenalism is true, it is hard to see how qualia might
stand in any such link, and thus it is hard to see our reason for saying there
are qualia in the first place. By considerations of evidence, therefore, (4) is
true: epiphenomenalism is false.[6]

Of course, the fact that each of (1–4) has arguments in its favor does not
affect the possibility that, on reflection, one of them might turn out to
be false. Indeed, interpreted in the simplest possible way, most recent
contributions to the debate (and in fact most classical contributions) are
arguments to the effect that, despite initial plausibility, one or more of the

theses is false. Thus, a posteriori physicalists reject (1): according to them, it is not the case that the only way of justifying or explaining the supervenience thesis implied by physicalism is by making plausible the a priori entailment of the mental by the physical. A priori physicalists reject (2): according to them, either physical knowledge can suffice for qualitative knowledge after all, or else the sense in which it cannot poses no threat to a priori physicalism. Interactionist dualists reject (3): according to them, physical closure is false, either because some physical events are caused by irreducibly mental events, or else because the properties which are efficacious in the production of some physical events are irreducibly mental. And epiphenomenalists reject (4): according to them, one thing can be evidence for another even if no direct causal relation obtains between them.

Certainly the rational weight behind each of these options might in the end be such that we ought to endorse it. But it is important to see that rejecting one or more of its constituent theses is only one way of resolving the physicalism debate. Another possibility is to argue for some kind of ambiguity. If we can discern an ambiguity in (1–4) then it would seem possible to believe *all* the theses that make up the debate, rather than rejecting one of them.[7]

My aim in this paper is to suggest that it *is* plausible to discern an ambiguity in (1–4), and to defend a version of physicalism on that basis. There are, I think, two rather different conceptions of the physical, and hence of physicalism, at play in the physicalism debate. What I want to suggest is that if these two conceptions are distinguished, the apparent inconsistency of (1–4) disappears. More particularly, if the two conceptions are distinguished, it becomes clear that there is no *one* notion of the physical according to which it is plausible to believe both (2) and (3): the sense of 'physical' in which a priori physicalism is false is not the sense in which the rejection of physicalism inevitably leads to epiphenomenalism.

This possibility will of course recommend itself to those who find each of (1–4) attractive. But it is also of interest for another reason. Much of the recent discussion in philosophy of mind has had physicalists either denying that one can have propositional knowledge concerning qualia or else appealing to what Chalmers (1996) calls 'strong necessities'—necessities which are a posteriori but are totally unlike the sort of a posteriori necessities discussed by Kripke (1980). Perhaps it will turn out that one cannot have propositional knowledge of qualia, or that there are strong necessities, but it would helpful if we had a way of defending physicalism that did not require taking a stand on such issues.[8]

My approach is as follows. In §2, I set out the two conceptions of the physical I will be interested in. In §§3 and 4, I suggest that distinguishing the two conceptions resolves the contemporary debate. In §5, I defend this suggestion against some objections, with a particular focus on the sort of physicalism one is left with if the suggestion is adopted—as we will see, the position that emerges is similar in important respects to Russell's neutral monism, and to modern versions of that view. Finally, in §6, I close the paper by providing some positive reasons for endorsing the strategy I propose. [Part of §5 and all of §6 are omitted in this volume.]

2

According to the first conception of the physical—which I will call *the theory-based conception*—a physical property is a property which *either* is the sort of property that physical theory tells us about *or* else is a property which metaphysically (or logically) supervenes on the sort of property that physical theory tells us about. According to this conception, for example, if physical theory tells us about the property of having mass, then having mass is a physical property. Similarly, if physical theory tells us about the property of being a rock—or, what is perhaps more likely, if the property of being a rock supervenes on properties which physical theory tells us about—then it too is a physical property. Let us say that any property which is physical by the lights of the theory-based conception is a *t-physical property*.[9]

According to the second conception of the physical—which I will call *the object-based conception*—a physical property is a property which *either* is the sort of property required by a complete account of the intrinsic nature of paradigmatic physical objects and their constituents *or* else is a property which metaphysically (or logically) supervenes on the sort of property required by a complete account of the intrinsic nature of paradigmatic physical objects and their constituents.[10] According to this conception, for example, if rocks, trees, planets and so on are paradigmatic physical objects, then the property of being a rock, tree or planet is a physical property. Similarly, if the property of having mass is required in a complete account of the intrinsic nature of physical objects and their constituents, then having mass is a physical property. Let us say that any property which is physical by the lights of the object-based conception is an *o-physical property*.

Since it is one of the more central and difficult notions that we have, many issues will arise whenever one is discussing *any* notion of the physical. However, the issue I want to focus on here is the sense in which the two conceptions I have described are distinct.[11] Of course, it is obvious that they are distinct in some sense: one concerns theories, the other objects. But what is of interest to me is whether the classes of properties characterized by both are coextensive. I will argue that they are not coextensive for the following reason: some o-physicals are not t-physical.

The point emerges most clearly if we have two theses before us. The first is that physical theory tells us only about the *dispositional* properties of physical objects and so does not tell us about the *categorical* properties, if any, that they have. A thesis of this sort has been held (at least implicitly) by many philosophers, but the following passage from Blackburn provides an effective illustration:

When we think of categorical grounds, we are apt to think of spatial configurations of things—hard, massy, shaped things, resisting penetration and displacement by others of their kind. But the categorical credentials of any item in this list are poor. Resistance is *par excellance* dispositional; extension is only of use, as Leibniz insisted, if there is some other property whose instancing defines the boundaries; hardness goes with resistance, and mass is knowable only by its dynamical effects. Turn up the magnification and we find things like an electrical charge at a point, or rather varying over a region, but the magnitude of a field at a region is known only through its effects on other things in spatial relations to that region. A region with charge is very different from a region without.... It differs precisely in its dispositions or powers. But science finds only dispositions all the way down. (1992, pp. 62–63)

What Blackburn is saying here is that when we consider both the properties of physical objects we normally think of as primary qualities—such as resistance—and the physical properties we normally think of as being associated with modern physics—such as having a certain charge—we find that such properties are dispositional. His final remark suggests that something more general is true and that in scientific theory—Blackburn means, I think, *physical* scientific theory—one only "finds" dispositional properties. It seems reasonable to summarize this by saying that physical theory tells us only about dispositional properties.[12]

The second thesis we need to consider is that the dispositional properties of physical objects *do* require categorical grounds, i.e. for all dispositional properties, there must be a nondispositional property, or nondispositional properties, such that the instantiation of the latter is metaphysically sufficient for the instantiation of the former. For example, if a vase is fragile, there must be a nondispositional property, or nondispositional properties, whose instantiation makes it the case that the vase is fragile; and if a chair is uncomfortable, there must be a nondispositional property, or nondispositional properties, whose instantiation makes it the case that the chair is uncomfortable.[13] It might perhaps be thought that there is some conflict between this thesis and the first. But there is certainly no *logical* inconsistency here. And indeed, many (but not all) philosophers who hold the first thesis also hold the second. A prominent example is D. M. Armstrong, who in *A Materialist Theory of the Mind*, holds that, since physical theory only characterizes the dispositional or relational nature of physical objects, it therefore "does not tell us"—as Armstrong (1968, p. 282) says—about their categorical or nonrelational nature.

With these two theses in place it is easy to argue that the theory-based conception is distinct from the object-based conception. Suppose a physical object x has a dispositional physical property F. From the thesis that dispositional properties require categorical grounds, it follows that x (or its constituents) must also have a further nondispositional property, which we may call G. But now let us ask: is G a physical property of not? If we are operating with the theory-based conception, it would seem that G is *not* physical. For from the thesis that physical theory tells us only about dispositions, it follows that t-physical properties are either dispositional or else supervene on dispositional properties. But neither is true in the case of G; so G itself is not t-physical. On the other hand, if we are operating with the object-based conception, there is no reason at all to deny that G is a physical property. After all, G is—or at least could perfectly well be—the kind of property required in a complete account of the intrinsic nature of paradigmatic physical objects and their constituents. In sum, properties such as G—the properties which are the categorical grounds of the dispositional properties that physical theory tells us about—serve to show that the two conceptions of the physical are distinct. By the lights of the theory-based conception, G and its ilk are not physical; but by the lights of the object-based conception, G and its ilk are.

The chief complication with this argument—apart of course from the issues that we have already set aside (see ns. 12 and 13)—derives from the fact that there are two different senses in which physical theory might fail to tell us about the categorical properties of physical objects. In the first sense, physical theory fails to tell us about a property just in case no expression of the theory *refers* to that property. Now, in this sense, the argument we just considered will not go through. For even if dispositional properties do require categorical grounds, it is still perfectly possible that the expressions of physical theory might refer to those grounds inter alia. But then G and its ilk will count as t-physical as well as o-physical, and there is no reason for supposing that the two conceptions of the physical are distinct.

But there is also is a second sense in which physical theory might fail to tell us about categorical grounds. In this sense, physical theory fails to tell us about categorical grounds just in case there might be two possible worlds w and w^* such that (i) they are exactly alike in terms of their distribution of dispositional properties—in both w and w^*, x has F; but (ii) they are different in terms of their categorical properties—in w, x has G but in w^*, x has a quite distinct categorical property G^*; and (iii) they are from the point of view of the theory epistemically indiscernible—the two worlds are (in Kripke's famous phrase) epistemically and qualitatively identical, though they might nevertheless be semantically different in the sense that in w, an expression of physical theory refers to G while in w^* the counterpart expression refers to G^*. It is this idea that Blackburn and Armstrong are appealing to when they (respectively) say that science finds dispositions all the way down, and that physical theory does not tell us about the categorical nature of physical objects. Similarly, it is this idea that is required by the argument we just considered that some o-physical properties are not t-physical.[14]

The right response to this complication is to acknowledge it and set it aside. Suppose there *are* two senses of what it is for a theory to tell us about a property. Then we will of course have *two* different versions of the theory-based conception of the physical. Moreover, only one of these versions is distinct from the object-based conception. On the other hand, the two different versions of the theory-based conception will *themselves* determine two different classes of properties: according to the version which employs the first sense of 'tells us about', the theory-based conception of the physical will acknowledge both dispositional and categorical properties as physical; according to the version which employs the second sense, the theory-based conception will acknowledge only dispositional properties as physical. And thus our basic point remains the same: there is distinction between two conceptions of the physical and these two conceptions determine two classes of physical properties, the first of which is limited to the dispositional properties of physical objects, the second of which includes both the dispositional and categorical properties of physical objects. More generally, one could run the following discussion in one of two ways: either one could operate with the two versions of the theory-based conception, or else one could operate with the object-based conception and the version of the theory-based conception which employs the second sense of 'tells us about'. I will here adopt the latter course—and thus I will continue to contrast o-physical properties and t-physical properties—but it is important to notice that the former course is also available.

3

So far, I have introduced two conceptions of the physical, and argued that they characterize distinct classes of properties. I turn now to the suggestion that distinguishing the two conceptions provides a way of believing all the constituent theses in the physicalism debate.

The first thing to say is that the issue of the interpretation of the notion of the physical does not seem to affect the reasons for believing either thesis (1) or thesis (4). The arguments that support (1)—viz., the claim that if physicalism is true a priori physicalism is—are arguments of a very general nature about supervenience, and whether or not the defense of supervenience will in the end involve an a priori entailment of the mental by the physical. These arguments are of course highly controversial. But, however things turn out with these arguments, it seems plain that the issues they raise are orthogonal to the issues having to do with the conceptions of the physical.

The same thing applies to the arguments one might adduce in support of (4)—viz., the claim that epiphenomenalism is false. These are arguments to the conclusion that if epiphenomenalism is true, the systems by which we gather evidence of qualia break down. But once again, while these arguments are controversial, I think we can set them aside. However things turn out with these arguments, it seems plain that the issues they raise are irrelevant to the issues with which we are concerned.

However, while the issue of interpretation does not affect the reasons for (1) and (4), it *does* affect the reasons for (2) and (3).

Let us consider first (2), the claim that a priori physicalism is false. Given our distinction between the theory-based and the object-based conceptions, we can distinguish two interpretations of (2). According to the first, (2) asserts that it is not the case that qualia supervene on t-physical properties *and* that t-physical truths a priori entail qualitative truths. We might express this by rendering (2) as:

(2-t)   A priori t-physicalism is false.

According to the second interpretation, (2) asserts that it is not the case that qualia supervene on o-physical properties *and* that o-physical truths a priori entail qualitative truths. We might express this by rendering (2) as:

(2-o)   A priori o-physicalism is false.

It is obvious that (2-t) and (2-o) are, given our assumptions, distinct. After all, if there are properties which are o-physical but not t-physical, it follows that even if t-physicalism is false, o-physicalism might still be true.[15]

Now, earlier I said that what supports (2)—and so counts against a priori physicalism—are considerations of epistemic distinctness. Given that (2) can be disambiguated into (2-t) and (2-o), what we need to ask is whether these considerations support both disambiguations. I think it can be argued, however, that while the considerations of epistemic distinctness do support (2-t), they do not likewise support (2-o). And this means that we can maintain a priori o-physicalism in the face of the considerations of epistemic distinctness even while we cannot maintain a priori t-physicalism.

While there are a number of different kinds of consideration of epistemic distinctness, we will focus here on what is perhaps the clearest and most notorious of them, Frank Jackson's (1982) knowledge argument.[16] As is extremely well known, this argument asks us to imagine Mary, a famous neuroscientist confined to a black-and-white room. Mary is forced to learn about the world via black-and-white television and computers. However, despite these hardships Mary learns (and therefore knows) all that physical theory can teach her. Now, if a priori physicalism were true, it is plausible to suppose that Mary knows everything about the world. And yet—and here is Jackson's point—it seems she does not know everything. For, upon being released into the world of color, it will become obvious that, inside her room, she did not know what it is like for both herself and others to see colors—that is, she did not know about the qualia instantiated by particular experiences of seeing colors. Following Jackson (1986), we may summarize the argument as follows:

(5)   Mary (before her release) knows everything physical there is to know about other people.

(6)   Mary (before her release) does not know everything there is to know about other people (because she learns something about them on being released).

Therefore,

(7)   There are truths about other people (and herself) that escape the physicalist story.

And of course, the truth of (7) entails (2), the thesis that a priori physicalism is false; for, if a priori physicalism were true, there would be no truths about anybody (or anything) that escape the physicalist story. For our purposes, therefore, it is reasonable to bypass (7) and interpret the knowledge argument simply as urging that (5) and (6) entail (2).

Given our distinction between the theory-based and the object-based conceptions of the physical, however, it is clear that the first premise of this argument is subject to interpretation in either of two ways. We might express these as (5-t) and (5-o):

(5-t)   Mary (before her release) knows everything t-physical there is to know about other people.

(5-o)   Mary (before her release) knows everything o-physical there is to know about other people.

Moreover, it is clear that (5-t) and (5-o) differ both in plausibility and in what conclusions they support. (5-t) is certainly very plausible given the story of Mary. After all, if Mary knows all of physical theory, and if physical theory tells us about t-physical properties, she presumably will know everything t-physical there is to know about other people. But the trouble here is that, when combined with (6), (5-t) only yields the falsity of a priori t-physicalism, not a priori o-physicalism, i.e., it only yields (2-t), not (2-o). If some o-physical properties are not t-physical, from the fact that Mary knows everything t-physical about the world, it does not follow that she knows everything o-physical, and it therefore does not follow that when she learns something about the world she has learned something non-physical. The truth of (5-t) and (6), then, leaves us free to endorse a priori o-physicalism, and therefore free to reject (2-o).

But what if we operate with (5-o) rather than (5-t)? It is obvious that the conjunction of (5-o) and (6), unlike the conjunction of (5-t) and (6), *does* entail the falsity of a priori o-physicalism, i.e., does entail (2-o). But the trouble now is that the story of Mary gives us no reason at all to endorse (5-o). The reason for this is that, on the construal that we have adopted, physical theory *will not tell us* about certain of the o-physical properties. After all, if the physical theory does not tell us about the categorical properties of physical objects, and if some o-physical properties are categorical, it would seem that, no matter how much physical theory one knows, one will still not know about certain o-physical properties. But then no matter how much physical theory *Mary* knows, she will still not know about certain of the o-physical properties. Nothing she knows, therefore, rules out the possibility that the truths about herself and others are entirely o-physical. More generally, while (5-o) and (6) certainly provide premises from which one might validly argue to the falsehood of a priori o-physicalism, the argument is a failure nevertheless, because we have no reason to believe its first premise.

In sum, the distinction between the theory-based conception and the object-based conception provides a way in which we might defeat the knowledge argument and at the same time concede the central intuition that motivates it.[17] In consequence, we can both accept and deny thesis (2). On one interpretation, (2) is equivalent to (2-t), and we have seen that the knowledge argument gives us very good reason to grant this. On the other interpretation, (2) is equivalent to (2-o), and we have seen that the knowledge argument gives us no good reason to grant this. To that extent then, we can with good conscience accept (2) if it is interpreted as (2-t), and reject it if it is interpreted as (2-o).

4

The suggestion that one might reject (2) on one interpretation and accept it on another is an important step in resolving the puzzle posed by the inconsistency of (1–4). But this alone does not complete the resolution. For I have conceded that (2) is very plausible on the theory-based conception of the physical; that is, that (2-t) is very plausible. And I have also suggested that the truth of (1) and (4) remains untouched by any issue about how to interpret the physical. But this means that if (3)—viz., the claim that if physicalism is false, epiphenomenalism is true—is plausible on the theory-based conception, we are back where we started. To complete the resolution of the puzzle, therefore, it needs to be argued that (3) is implausible if interpreted from the standpoint of the theory-based conception.

However, (3) *is* implausible if interpreted from the standpoint of the theory-based conception.

Let us first distinguish the two interpretations of (3) just as we did for (2). On the first interpretation, (3) asserts that if qualia do not supervene on t-physical properties, the inevitable result is epiphenomenalism. We might express this by rendering (3) as:

(3-t)   If t-physicalism is false, epiphenomenalism is true.

On the second interpretation, (3) asserts that if qualia do not supervene on o-physical properties, the inevitable result is epiphenomenalism. We might express this by rendering (3) as:

(3-o)   If o-physicalism is false, epiphenomenalism is true.

Once again, it is clear that (3-t) and (3-o) are, given our assumptions, distinct. If there are o-physical properties which are not t-physical, it is clear that we might have grounds for rejecting (3-t) but no grounds at all for rejecting (3-o).

Now, earlier I said that the considerations in favor of (3) are considerations of causal closure. And we also saw that causal closure is the conjunction of two theses, one about events, the other about properties. We might summarize these theses as (8) and (9):

(8)   For all physical events e, if there is an event e* such that e* causes e, then e* is a physical event.

(9)   For all physical events e and e*, if there is a property F such that F is causally efficacious in e's causing e*, then F is a physical property.

Now, (8) can from our point of view be set aside. The reason is that the conceptions of the physical with which we are operating apply in the first instance to *properties*, and do not obviously extend to items of other ontological categories. More particularly, neither conception as it stands says anything about what it is to be a physical event. But this means that the conceptions are silent on the plausibility of (8).

On the other hand, the conceptions are not silent on the plausibility of (9). If we interpret (9) in accordance with the theory-based conception, it asserts that the only properties that are causally efficacious are *t-physical* properties, a thesis we might call (9-t):

(9-t)   For all physical events e and e*, if there is a property F such that F is causally efficacious in e's causing e*, then F is a t-physical property.

If we interpret (9) in accordance with the object-based conception, by contrast, it asserts that the only properties that are causally efficacious are *o-physical* properties, a thesis we might call (9-o):

(9-o)   For all physical events e and e*, if there is a property F such that F is causally efficacious in e's causing e*, then F is an o-physical property.

And once again, it is clear that (9-t) and (9-o) are, given our assumptions, distinct. The first implies that only t-physical properties are causally efficacious, while the second allows that some causally efficacious properties are not t-physical, i.e., those properties which are o-physical but not t-physical.

Now, I think we should concede that *if* (9-t) is true, we have a very good argument for (3-t). Similarly, we should concede that *if* (9-o) is true, we have a very good argument for (3-o). For consider: if (9-t) is true, the only causally efficacious properties in the production of physical events, and therefore of behavioral events, are t-physical; but if t-physicalism is false, qualia are not t-physical. It follows that qualia are not efficacious in the production of behavior. *Mutatis mutandis* for (9-o): if (9-o) is true, the only causally efficacious properties in the production of physical events, and therefore of behavioral events, are o-physical; but if o-physicalism is false, qualia are not o-physical. It again follows that qualia are not efficacious in the production of behavior.

On the other hand, there is an important difference between (9-t) and (9-o), and this is that it is far from obvious that (9-t) is *true*. For let us consider more directly what (9-t) says. (9-t) says that in the realm of physical causation, the only causally efficacious properties are t-physical. In general, however, this seems to be quite mistaken. The reason is that it is very implausible to suppose that the efficacy of dispositional properties has nothing whatsoever to do with the efficacy of their categorical grounds.

To illustrate this point, consider Ned Block's famous example of the bull and the bull-fighter. Block writes:

Consider the bull-fighter's cape. The myth (which we will accept, ignoring the inconvenient color-blindness of bulls) is that its red color provoked the bull, i.e., redness is causally relevant to the bull's anger. The cape also has the second order property of being provocative, of having some property or other that provokes the bull, of having some property or other that is causally relevant to the bull's anger. But does the provocativeness of the cape provoke the bull? Is the provocativeness causally relevant to the bull's anger? It would seem not. The bull is too stupid for that. The provocativeness of the cape might provoke the ASPCA, but not the bull. (1990, p. 155)

The moral that Block wants to draw from this example is the contentious one that provocativeness and similar properties are in a large class of cases not causally efficacious ("causally relevant") while properties such as redness are. For our purposes, it is sufficient to draw the less contentious moral that while dispositional properties are causally efficacious—for of course provocativeness is a dispositional property—they are only efficacious if their categorical grounds are—for of course redness is (or anyway may be taken to be for the purposes of the example) the categorical ground of provocativeness. As Mark Johnston puts it in a related context, if dispositional properties are efficacious, they are so "at one remove and by courtesy" (1992; p. 235). But this means that (9-t) is false. (9-t) tells us that the only properties which are causally efficacious are dispositional, i.e., properties similar to provocativeness. But it seems clear that, if dispositional properties *are* causally efficacious, so too are their categorical grounds. And, if categorical grounds are, as we are assuming, nondispositional, then, contrary to (9-t), dispositional properties are not the only properties that are causally efficacious.

On the other hand, examples such a Block's do nothing whatsoever to undermine (9-o). (9-o), after all, does not restrict itself to dispositional properties, and so is not subject to the criticism that (9-t) is. More generally, if we interpret (9) in accordance with the theory-based conception, we can reasonably regard it as false and therefore as providing no support for (3). On the other hand, if we interpret (9) in accordance with the object-based conception, we can reasonably regard it as true and therefore as providing support for (3). In summary, (9-o) provides support for (3-o), but (9-t) provides no support for (3-t).

How does this bear on the resolution of (1–4)? Well, earlier we saw that thesis (2) has two versions—viz., the version expressed by (2-t) and the version expressed by (2-o)—and that only the *first* of these receives support from considerations of epistemic distinctness; that is, considerations of epistemic distinctness leave us free to reject (2-o). What we have just seen is that thesis (3) also has two versions—viz., the version expressed by (3-t) and the version expressed by (3-o)—and that only the *second* of these receives support from considerations of closure; that is, considerations of closure leave us free to reject (3-t). But this suggests that the predicament which in fact confronts us is not quite the predicament we originally imagined ourselves to be in.

Originally, we imagined ourselves to be confronted with four inconsistent theses (1–4) each of which we had powerful reason to believe:

(1)   If physicalism is true, a priori physicalism is true.

(2)   A priori physicalism is false.

(3)   If physicalism is false, epiphenomenalism is true.

(4)   Epiphenomenalism is false.

If we distinguish between the two conceptions of the physical, however, it is plain that (1–4) fail to articulate *precisely* the theses we have reason to believe. What we in fact have reason to believe is not (1–4) but rather:

(1)   If physicalism is true, a priori physicalism is true.

(2-t)   A priori t-physicalism is false.

(3-o)   If o-physicalism is false, epiphenomenalism is true.

(4)   Epiphenomenalism is false.

But this second tetrad is importantly different from first. The first is inconsistent, the second is not. As a consequence, if you find the considerations of supervenience, epistemic distinctness, closure and evidence compelling, you may believe the second tetrad without fear of contradiction. And our original puzzle is solved.

5

My strategy so far has been to distinguish two conceptions of the physical, and to suggest that, if these conceptions can be kept apart, the appearance of inconsistency of (1–4) is resolved. If we adopt the object-based conception, we can reasonably regard (2) as true and (3) as false. But if we adopt the theory-based conception, we can reasonably regard (3) as true and (2) as false. I turn now to some objections to this strategy.

Broadly speaking, there are two classes of objection to consider. The first class raises questions about the assumptions I required in order to argue that, properly understood, (1–4) do not present a contradiction: the thesis that dispositions require categorical grounds, and the thesis that physical theory tells us only about dispositional properties. The second class raises questions about the outline of the position that one is left with if one pursues our strategy. Obviously, it is no good to resolve the inconsistency of (1–4) only to be forced into an even more unpalatable position. I have already noted that I will set aside the first class of objection, and so here I will concentrate on the second class.

What sort of position is one left with if one accepts (1), (2-t), (3-o), (4) and rejects (2-o) and (3-t)? The answer is that one is left with a view that bears a close resemblance to Russell's in *The Analysis of Matter*, and even closer resemblance to the view discussed by contemporary defenders of a Russell-inspired physicalism such as Maxwell (1978) and Lockwood (1989, 1992).[18]

The broad contours of the position may be brought out by considering the following analogy. Imagine a mosaic constituted by two basic shapes, triangles and pieces of pie, as well as a large number of shapes obtained by a transparent combination of these: squares, half-moons, circles, rhombuses etc. Imagine also that our access to the mosaic is limited to two shape-detecting systems: the first scans the mosaic and detects triangles; the second scans it and detects circles. For one reason or another we spontaneously assume that the triangle-detector tells us everything about the nature of the mosaic—we become trianglists, i.e., those who believe that triangles are the fundamental shape and that all other shapes supervene. The problem of the circle then stares us in the face: the circle-detector tells us the mosaic contains circles, but there is apparently no place for circles in a mosaic totally constituted by triangles. Different people respond to the problem in different ways: some say the circle-detecting system leads us astray, and that properly understood it provides no propositional knowledge of circles; others declare circles a posteriori identical with triangles; still others decide that circles are irreducible, and postulate contingent laws linking them and triangles. Of course all these responses are mistaken, and moreover they make a common mistake. The mistake is that the triangle-detector does not tell us everything about the mosaic: it is selective and only tells us about triangles when in addition there are pieces of pie. Of course the pieces of pie are not themselves circles. But in combination they may constitute circles. When God created the mosaic, all he had to do was to create triangles and pieces of pie, and arrange them in just the way he wanted; in doing so, he created everything else including circles.

As it is with triangles, pieces of pie, and circles so (largely) it is with t-physical, o-physical and qualia, according to the Russell-inspired view. Physical theory tells us about the physical world, and introspection tells us about qualia. For one reason or another we spontaneously assume that physical theory tells us everything about the nature of the world—we become t-physicalists, i.e., those who believe that t-physical properties, properties that physical theory tells us about, are fundamental and all other properties supervene. The problem of qualia then stares us in the face: introspection tells us there are qualia, but there is apparently no place for qualia in a world totally constituted by t-physical properties. Different people respond to the problem in different ways: some say introspection leads us astray, and that properly understood it provides no propositional knowledge of qualia; others declare qualia a posteriori identical with t-physical properties; still others decide that qualia are irreducible, and postulate contingent laws linking them and t-physical properties. Of course all these responses are mistaken, and moreover they make a common mistake. The mistake is that physical theory does not tell us everything about the physical world: it is selective and only tells us about dispositional t-physical properties when in addition there are categorical o-physical properties. Of course, the categorical o-physical properties are not themselves qualia. But in combination—perhaps also in combination with the t-physicals—they may constitute qualia. When God created the world, all he had to do was create the fundamental physical properties—o-physical and t-physical—and arrange them in just the way he wanted; in doing so, he created everything else including qualia.

To put things less picturesquely, the Russell-inspired position as I will understand it here has two parts. The first part—the physicalist part—is that qualia supervene not on the class of properties that physical theory tells us about—the t-physical properties, as I have called them—but on a larger class that includes both the t-physicals and categorical bases of such properties—o-physical properties, as I have called them. The second part—the a priori part—is that mental truths (in particular, qualitative truths) are a priori entailed by physical truths. . . .

Notes

1. It is important to note that I am merely trying to state the considerations in favor of (1) here, not defend them. Likewise, the considerations in favor of (2–4) I consider in a moment.

2. For a statement of this argument, and for an analysis of the notion of a priori entailment, see Jackson 1998, and Chalmers 1996, 1999; for criticism, see Block and Stalnaker 1999, Byrne 1999, Loar 1997, 1999, and Yablo 1999. One should perhaps talk more correctly of mental truths being a priori entailed by physical and *topic neutral* truths, but I will leave this extension largely implicit in what follows.

3. By 'qualia', I mean the properties of experiences in virtue of which there is something it is like (in the phrase made famous by Nagel) to have those experiences.

4. For a recent statement of this argument, see Braddon-Mitchell and Jackson 1996 and Chalmers 1996. Of course, there are other reasons for resisting a priori physicalism—for example, reasons having to do with intentionality—but I will limit my discussion here to qualia.

5. For a recent statement of this argument, see Kim 1999; for criticism, see Yablo 1992. The question of what the relation is between the two parts of causal closure—the thesis about events and the thesis about properties—is a question about the metaphysics of causation, and in particular about the metaphysics of causal relata, which I will set aside here. It is worth noting also that causal closure as I have defined it rules out the possibility of overdetermination—I will set aside this issue also.

6. For a recent statement of this sort of argument, see Shoemaker 1999 and Chalmers 1996; for criticism, see Jackson 1982 and Chalmers 1996, 1998.

7. It is interesting to note that Gilbert Harman's (1986) sharp distinction between what follows from what and what one ought to believe provides yet another possibility here. More particularly, in Harmanesque fashion, one might suppose that, even if (1–4) *are* contradictory, it is nevertheless a rational strategy to resolve to believe all of them so long as one also resolves not to exploit this contradiction in one's reasoning. This suggestion seems to me to present not a resolution of the puzzle posed by (1–4) so much as a way in which one might live with oneself in the absence of such a resolution, but in any event I will set it aside here.

8. For examples of those who deny that one can have propositional knowledge of qualia, see Lewis 1994, and references therein; for strong necessities, see Yablo 1999 and Loar 1999.

9. The theory-based conception bears some relation to the notion of physical discussed in Meehl and Sellars 1956 and in Feigl 1965; more explicit defense is found in Smart 1978, Lewis 1994, Braddon-Mitchell and Jackson 1996, and Chalmers 1996. There is of course the threat that a formulation of physicalism which utilizes the theory-based conception will be trivial: if the notion of a physical theory is sufficiently unconstrained, any property including irreducibly mental properties might be such that physical theory tells us about them. (For this sort of criticism, see Crane and Mellor 1990 and Chomsky 1995.) There are a number of ways in which one might seek to constrain the notion to meet this threat: by speaking of physical theory sufficiently similar to current physical theory; by speaking of physical theory sufficiently similar to commonsense physical theory; or by speaking of physical theory as constrained by the methodology of physics. I will assume here that some such strategy is available, but it will not matter for our purposes to decide which is the best.

10. The best examples of philosophers who operate with the object-conception of the physical are Meehl and Sellars (1956) and Feigl (1965); it is also a position that one encounters regularly in discussion. There is of course the threat that a formulation of physicalism which utilizes the object-based conception will be trivial: if the notion of a paradigm physical object is sufficiently unconstrained, any property including irreducibly mental properties might be such that paradigm physical objects have them. There are a number of ways in which one might seek to constrain the notion to meet this threat: by speaking of physical objects-as-we-currently-conceive-them; by insisting that the notion of a physical object presupposes that such objects cannot turn out to be irreducibly mental; by operating with the notion of a purely physical object, where a purely physical object is something completely nonmental. As with the theory-based conception, I will assume here that some such strategy is available, but it will not matter for our purposes to decide which is best.

11. Two other issues deserve to be mentioned briefly. First, one might object that both conceptions are inadequate because they are circular, i.e., both appeal to the notion of something physical (a theory or an object) to characterize a physical property. The response to this is that circularity is only a problem if the conceptions are interpreted as providing a reductive analysis of the notion of the physical rather than simply an understanding of it. But there is no reason why they should be interpreted in the former way. Second, it might be thought that notion of an o-physical property is open to the following objection discussed by Ned Block: "it is conceivable that there are physical laws that 'come into play' in brains of a certain size and complexity, but that nonetheless these laws are 'translatable' into physical language, and that, so translated, they are clearly physical laws (though irreducible to other physical laws). Arguably, in this situation, physicalism could be true—though not according to [this] account of 'physical property'" (1980, n. 4). However, at least as developed here, the object-based conception does not face this objection because the properties and laws that Block is describing *supervene* on properties required in an

account of paradigmatic physical objects, and so o-physicalism *would* be true in the case he is envisaging.

12. There is of course a large literature in support of the thesis that physical theory tells us only about dispositional properties, a literature which has at least three sources: Russell's (1927) discussion of the nature of physical theory; the approach to the structure of scientific theories and theoretical terms due to Ramsey, Carnap and Lewis (see, e.g., Lewis 1970); and an epistemological thesis that, in perception, we are acquainted only with dispositional properties of physical objects (see, e.g., Armstrong 1961, 1968). I will not in this paper be able to explore this literature or defend the thesis in any detail. My reason is partly space and partly that the contemporary exponents of the antiphysicalist position (or related positions) agree with the thesis, so there is nothing problematic about marking this assumption in the course of defending physicalism; see, e.g., Chalmers 1996, pp. 153–154.

It is worth noting also that it is an oversimplification to say that physical theory tells us only about dispositional properties: physical theory also tells us about what might be called structural properties, i.e. geometrical, spatiotemporal or causal properties. But this complication does not matter for our purposes. The crucial point for our purposes is that there are categorical or nondispositional properties of physical objects which physical theory does not tell us about.

13. There is of course a large literature concerning the thesis that dispositions require categorical grounds, but I will not here explore this literature or defend the thesis in any detail. (For a recent defense, see Smith and Stoljar 1997.) Once again my reason is partly space and partly that contemporary defenders of the antiphysicalists position agree with the thesis; see, e.g., Chalmers 1996, n. 29 on p. 375. To avoid confusion, however, it is worth noting two points: (i) The thesis does not require that if a thing has a dispositional property then there must be a nondispositional property of *that very thing* such that the latter is metaphysically sufficient for the instantiation of the former, i.e., it is perfectly consistent with the thesis that the categorical properties on which the dispositional properties supervene might be properties of constituents of the thing in question rather than the thing itself. (ii) The thesis is a metaphysical thesis, rather than an explanatory one, i.e., it is perfectly consistent with the thesis that to explain the presence of a certain dispositional property one might cite a further dispositional property. All that is being urged is the metaphysical claim that the dispositional supervenes on the nondispositional.

14. For a very similar notion, see the discussion of 'Kantian physicalism' in Jackson 1998.

15. While I will for the most part speak of 'o-physical properties which are not t-physical', I will sometimes speak only of 'o-physical properties'. It will be clear from context whether what is intended is the class of o-physical properties *tout court*— i.e. a class which includes t-physicals—or the class of o-physicals which are not t-physicals.

16. The other main argument against a priori physicalism is the conceivability argument. I think the strategy of this paper also holds good against this argument but I will not discuss this issue here.

17. For a catalog and criticisms of the other main attempts to defeat the knowledge argument, see Braddon-Mitchell and Jackson 1996. They do not consider the kind of proposal that we are considering here.

18. It is important to emphasize that the views at issue here are Russell-*inspired* rather than Russell's. The question of what Russell's actual views are is a difficult scholarly one that I will not address here. Similarly, it is important to emphasize that while there is much similarity between the position discussed in the text and that of Maxwell and Lockwood—for example, Maxwell describes his position as "non-materialist physicalism" (1978; p. 365) which echoes the distinction I have drawn between the theory-based and object-based conception of the physical—neither of these writers develop or defend the position in the way I will do here. For further discussion of Russell-inspired views and related matters, see Chalmers 1996, Foster 1982, 1994 and Unger 1998.

19. It is worth emphasis that the first part of o-physicalism is neutral on the issue of whether qualia supervene on o-physical properties which *exclude* t-physical properties or on o-physical properties which *include* t-physical properties. The general question of the role of t-physical properties in o-physicalism is an interesting question, but it is not a question that I will decide here.

References

Armstrong, D. M. 1961. *Perception and the Physical World*. London: Routledge.

Armstrong, D. M. 1968. *A Materialist Theory of the Mind*. London: Routledge.

Blackburn, S. 1992. "Filling in Space." *Analysis* 52: 60–65.

Block, N. 1980. "Troubles with Functionalism." In Block, N. (ed.), *Readings in the Philosophy of Psychology*, vol. I. Cambridge, Mass.: Harvard University Press.

Block, N. 1990. "Can the Mind Change the World?" In Boolos, G. (ed.), *Meaning and Method: Essays in Honor of Hilary Putnam*. Cambridge: Cambridge University Press.

Block, N., and Robert Stalnaker. 1999. "Conceptual Analysis, Dualism and the Explanatory Gap." *Philosophical Review* 108: 1–46.

Byrne, A. 1999. "Cosmic Hermeneutics." *Philosophical Perspectives* 13: 347–383.

Braddon-Mitchell D., and Jackson F. 1996. *Philosophy of Mind and Cognition*. Oxford: Blackwell.

Chalmers, D. 1996. *The Conscious Mind*. New York: Oxford University Press.

Chalmers, D. 1999. "Materialism and the Metaphysics of Modality." *Philosophy and Phenomenological Research* 59: 473–496.

Chomsky, N. 1995. "Language and Nature." *Mind* 104: 1–61.

Crane, T., and Mellor, D. H. 1990. "There Is No Question of Physicalism." *Mind* 99: 185–206.

Feigl, H. 1967. "The 'Mental' and the 'Physical'." (Minneapolis: University of Minnesota Press. Original Publication: 1958).

Foster, J. 1982. *The Case for Idealism*. London: Routledge.

Foster, J. 1991. *The Immaterial Self: A Defence of the Cartesian Dualist Conception of Mind*. London: Routledge.

Harman, G. 1986. *Change in View*. Cambridge, Mass.: The MIT Press.

Harman, G. 1990. "The Intrinsic Quality of Experience." *Philosophical Perspectives* 4: 31–52.

Jackson, F. 1982. "Epiphenomenal Qualia." *Philosophical Quarterly* 32: 127–136. Reprinted in this volume.

Jackson, F. 1986. "What Mary Didn't Know." *Journal of Philosophy* 83: 291–295.

Jackson, F. 1998. *From Metaphysics to Ethics: A Defense of Conceptual Analysis*. Oxford: Clarendon.

Johnston, M. 1992. "How to Speak of the Colors." *Philosophical Studies* 68: 221–263.

Kim, J. 1993. *Mind and Supervenience*. Cambridge: Cambridge University Press.

Kim, J. 1998. *Mind in a Physical World*. Cambridge: Cambridge University Press.

Kripke, S. 1980. *Naming and Necessity*. Cambridge, Mass.: Harvard University Press.

Kripke, S. 1982. *Wittgenstein on Rules and Private Language: An Elementary Exposition*. Oxford: Blackwell.

Lewis, D. 1970. "How to Define Theoretical Terms." *Journal of Philosophy* 67: 427–446.

Lewis, D. 1994. "Reduction of Mind." In Guttenplan, S. (ed.), *A Companion to the Philosophy of Mind*. Oxford: Blackwell.

Loar, B. 1997. "Phenomenal States." In Block et al. (eds.), *The Nature of Consciousness: Philosophical Debates*. Cambridge, Mass.: MIT Press. Reprinted in this volume.

Loar, B. 1999. "David Chalmers' *The Conscious Mind*." *Philosophy and Phenomenological Research* 59: 465–472.

Lockwood, M. 1989. *Mind, Brain and Quantum*. Oxford: Blackwell.

Lockwood, M. 1992. "The Grain Problem." In Robinson, H. (ed.), *Objections to Physicalism*. Oxford: Oxford University Press.

Maxwell, G. 1978. "Rigid Designators and Mind–Brain Identity." In Savage, C. (ed.), *Perception and Cognition: Minnesota Studies in the Philosophy of Science*, vol. 9. Minneapolis: Minnesota University Press.

McGinn, D. 1989. "Can We Solve the Mind–Body Problem?" *Mind* 98: 349–366.

Moore, G. E. 1922. *Philosophical Studies*. Routledge: London.

Nagel, T. 1970. "Armstrong on the Mind." *Philosophical Review* 79: 394–403.

Nagel, T. 1974. "What Is It Like to Be a Bat." *Philosophical Review* 83: 435–450.

Russell, B. 1927. *The Analysis of Matter*. London: Kegan Paul.

Shoemaker, S. 1994. "Phenomenal Character." *Noûs* 28: 21–38.

Shoemaker, S. 1999. "On David Chalmers' *The Conscious Mind*." *Philosophy and Phenomenological Research* 59: 439–444.

Smart, J. J. C. 1978. "The Content of Physicalism." *Philosophical Quarterly* 28: 239–241.

Smith, M., and Stoljar, D. 1998. "Global Response-Dependence and Noumenal Realism." *Monist* 81: 85–111.

Unger, P. 1998. "The Mystery of the Physical and the Matter of Qualities." *Midwest Studies in Philosophy* 22.

Yablo, S. 1992. "Mental Causation." *Philosophical Review* 101: 245–280.

Yablo, S. 1999. "Concepts and Consciousness." *Philosophy and Phenomenological Research* 59: 455–463.

16   Inexpressible Truths and the Allure of the Knowledge Argument

Benj Hellie

Dualism is a perpetually seductive doctrine; the knowledge argument for dualism (Jackson 1982, reprinted in this vol.) a particularly alluring source of support for the doctrine. Jackson advocated the soundness of the argument for nearly two decades before changing his mind; I and many of my comrades, before we became sophisticated, found the allure of the argument as Jackson presents it hard to avoid; and many other philosophers doubtless have had this experience as well. And, as Stoljar and Nagasawa detail in the introduction to this volume, related ideas have cropped up in the literature throughout the century.

In this essay, I argue that the root of this allure lies in the knowledge argument's involvement with inexpressible concepts. I begin with a discussion of the meaning of a certain version of the knowledge argument: in section 1, I describe this version and argue that it is formally valid; in section 2, I analyze the vexing sentence 'Mary doesn't know what it's like to see a red thing', and argue for the existence of a certain sort of inexpressible concept. In section 3, I assess the knowledge argument for soundness. I argue that no fallacy is involved; rather, the argument is apparently sound. Whether its conclusion should ultimately be accepted hangs on the status of a certain attractive doctrine concerning the ontological impact of inexpressible concepts.

Autobiographical disclosure: I am not a dualist, and I do not intend this essay to establish dualism. Rather, I hope that dualism is not correct: I love desert landscapes, naturalism, and structural explanation as much as the next philosopher. However, I suspect that physicalist philosophers have been overhasty in their treatment of the knowledge argument, being quick to mistakenly accuse it of this or that fallacy. As a result, the real threat posed by the knowledge argument has been missed. My opinion is that this threat won't go away until it is exposed and met head-on; and that it won't be possible to expose this threat unless the argument is treated with the sympathy its allure has earned it.

1 The Knowledge Argument Is Valid

Jackson (1986, p. 293; reprinted in this vol.) explicitly presents the following argument concerning the "black-and-white Mary scenario":[1]

(1$_J$) Mary (before her release) knows everything physical there is to know about other people.

(2$_J$) Mary (before her release) does not know everything there is to know about other people (because she learns something about them on being released).

(C$_J$) Therefore, there are truths about other people (and herself) that escape the physicalist story.

This argument can be weakened and tidied up somewhat to yield the following argument, which will be the focus of this paper:

   At the time immediately before Mary's release,

(1) Mary knows all the physical truths.

(2) Mary does not know what it is like to see a red thing.

(C) There is a truth that is not physical.

The argument (1), (2), therefore (C) is superior to (1$_J$), (2$_J$), therefore (C$_J$) for two reasons: first, (2) is closer to our immediate intuition about the black-and-white Mary scenario than is (2$_J$): while our acceptance of (2) is presumably the source of the plausibility of (2$_J$), some have accepted (2) while denying that the failure to know what something is like is not the failure to know a truth (Lewis 1988; Bigelow and Pargetter 1990) (and although (1) is rather stronger than (1$_J$), the additional strength does not seem in any way to affect the dialectical situation). And second, (C) is slightly clearer than (C$_J$): saying that a truth "escapes the physicalist story" is clearly intended to be a fancy way of calling it nonphysical (compare Jackson 1986, sec. I: "[b]ut she knew all the physical facts about them all along; hence, what she did not know until her release is not a physical fact about their experiences").

I can't find an argument with weaker premises than (1) and (2) that remains true to Jackson's intentions. For this reason, though there are many things that may deserve the title 'the knowledge argument', I will (somewhat stipulatively) reserve the term to denote (1), (2), therefore (C).

If we wish to explain the allure of the knowledge argument, we must establish what we pretheoretically take the knowledge argument to mean. It will be helpful to begin by establishing the most abstract, formal, logical properties of the knowledge argument. The logical form of the knowledge argument can be represented as follows:[2]

(1_{lf}) $(\forall t)(\Phi t \supset Kmt)$

(2_{lf}) $(\exists t)(At \wedge \neg Kmt)$

(C_{lf}) $(\exists t)(\neg \Phi t)$

The nonlogical expressions in this (valid) form are used in the following abbreviations, where small Greek letters are used as syntactic variables and corners represent quasi-quotation: 'Mary' $\Rightarrow$ 'm'; $\ulcorner \tau$ is a physical truth$\urcorner \Rightarrow \ulcorner \Phi\tau \urcorner$; $\ulcorner \mu$ knows $\tau \urcorner \Rightarrow \ulcorner K\mu\tau \urcorner$; and, to put it approximately pending further clarification, $\ulcorner \tau$ "answers" the question 'what is it like to see a red thing?'$\urcorner \Rightarrow \ulcorner A\tau \urcorner$. The next two sections will be primarily concerned with explicating (2_{lf}) and justifying its assignment as logical form to (2).

It's worth pausing a moment to consider the frequently encountered complaint that the knowledge argument is invalid owing to the phenomenon of the "referential opacity" of 'know': where ρ and σ are singular terms, from $\ulcorner \mu$ knows that $\cdots \rho \cdots \urcorner$ and $\ulcorner \mu$ does not know that $\cdots \sigma \cdots \urcorner$, $\ulcorner \rho \neq \sigma \urcorner$ does not follow. If this complaint is directed at the knowledge argument as I am understanding it, it is clearly at odds with my claim that the knowledge argument has the logical form (1_{lf}), (2_{lf}), therefore (C_{lf}).

Fortunately, this complaint can be easily parried. Jackson is clearly aware of the opacity concern and intends to present an argument that is not invalidated by it. In the 1986 essay he insists that "the intensionality of knowledge is not to the point. The argument does not rest on falsely assuming that, if S knows that a is F and $a = b$, then S knows that b is F. It is concerned with the nature of Mary's total body of knowledge before she is released: is it complete, or do some truths escape it?" (sec. I); and he replies to an early expression of the opacity concern as follows: "What is immediately to the point is not the kind, manner, or type of knowledge Mary has, but *what* she knows. What she knows beforehand is ex hypothesi everything physical there is to know, but is it everything there is to know? That is the crucial question" (sec. II).

Charity thus recommends against assigning an invalid logical form to the argument, if possible. And this *is* possible: the standard ordinary language uses of 'truth' and 'know' license the principle that if someone knows that p but does not know that q, then the truth that p is numerically distinct from the truth that q: from $\ulcorner\mu$ knows the truth that $\pi\urcorner$ and $\ulcorner\mu$ does not know the truth that $\rho\urcorner$, $\ulcorner$the truth that $\pi \neq$ the truth that $\rho\urcorner$ *does* follow. In this respect, truths are like (Fregean) propositions. For instance, if someone knows that Hesperus is Hesperus, but doesn't know that Hesperus is Phosphorus, then the truth that Hesperus is Hesperus is numerically distinct from the truth that Hesperus is Phosphorus. 'Know' is not opaque, that is, with respect to terms denoting truths; truths are, in a slogan, the objects of knowledge.[3] There may be some distinction between truths and true propositions; but for my purposes here, this distinction won't matter, so I will ignore it, treating truths and true propositions alike.

2 'What It's Like' and Inexpressibility

I say that the logical form of (2), 'Mary does not know what it's like to see a red thing', can be represented (approximately) by (2_{lf}), '$(\exists t)(t$ "answers" the question 'what is it like to see a red thing?' $\wedge \neg$(Mary knows t))'. Why say this? And what does it mean?

I begin with a methodological discussion of the appropriate way to investigate the logical form of (2). So far as I can tell, the dominant view among philosophers is that uses of the frame 'what $\cdots$ is like' in the context of the philosophy of consciousness are not "normal": i.e., they are not pieces of fully literal ordinary language, but rather involve some use of (for instance) metaphor or idiom or jargon or code. While this opinion is rarely stated explicitly, it is frequently asserted in conversation and is often insinuated in writing—e.g., by putting a completion of the frame in italics or in scare quotes, or by running a completion of the frame together as a single word, or by using such a completion ungrammatically, or by attributing the frame to Nagel, or by calling it a "stock phrase," or by using it in some other self-conscious way to indicate that the frame is somehow not wholly in order. I would guess that most philosophical books or articles on consciousness published in the last decade do this.

Lewis (1995, p. 326) stands out for providing an explicit argument that, in this context, the frame has a "special technical sense." He argues that "[y]ou can say what it's like to taste New Zealand beer by saying what experience you have when you do, namely a sweet taste. But you can't say what it's like to have a sweet taste in the parallel way, namely by saying that when you do, you have a sweet taste!" While this passage is somewhat obscure, I take Lewis to be arguing that, in literal, ordinary use, 'what it's like to do so-and-so' only ever means 'what doing so-and-so resembles'; so, because there is no way to inform someone what experiences of having a sweet taste resemble, and yet there is still something having a sweet taste is like, 'what having a sweet taste is like' must not be used in its only ordinary way when concatenated to 'know'.[4] I reply that Lewis misses the fact that you can also say what it's like to taste New Zealand beer by saying how the experience is, namely pleasant. It is incorrect to assume that literal, ordinary uses of 'what it's like to do so-and-so' solely concern what doing so-and-so resembles: they can also concern how doing so-and-so is, what features or properties it has. I expand on this point below.

The popularity of the nonnormality view is somewhat surprising, because, to my knowledge, no one has ever provided or defended a positive theory of how the frame was assigned its nonnormal meaning. How might such a theory go? Clearly there is not enough in the frame to hang a metaphor on; nor were we ever given explicit instruction in its meaning, as we tend to be when learning idioms.[5] It seems, then, that such a theory must say that the nonnormal meaning is assigned in the manner in which expressions typically acquire technical meaning, that is, in something like the following way. Each of us begins with a grasp of the content the frame is used to express. This content becomes highly salient to one when one engages in the philosophy of consciousness. Once this content has become salient, one can establish an internal convention with oneself to use a certain linguistic expression to express this content. If one's peers have undergone a similar process, a tacit convention may arise whereby all attempt to coordinate their verbal behavior so as to use the same expression to express this content. Obviously any expression would do, so long as everyone uses it: 'the eagle flies at midnight' would do just as well. However, Nagel 1974 happened to show up at just the right historical moment, and as a result, a tacit convention coagulated in the philosophical community around using this frame to express the relevant content.

Whether uses of the frame in discussions in the philosophy of consciousness are, in fact, nonnormal is important, because if they are, it would be very diffcult to assess any claim about the logical form of (2). We would no more be able to appeal, in assessing such claims, to facts about the constituent structure of the sentence or the meanings of its parts than we would in assessing the logical form of the code 'the eagle flies at midnight' or the idiom 'John kicked the bucket'. The best we could hope to do would be to appeal to brute intuition concerning the technical meaning, and such appeals have a slim hope of resulting in any sort of consensus.

But fortunately, it's not very plausible to suppose that the frame in its present use acquires its meaning from an implicit technical convention. Obviously the story of how the convention arose requires a great deal of filling in. But the project of filling in this story does not need to be carried out: even these broad outlines are enough for the story to be empirically refuted in its cradle, because plenty of people who are not plausibly party to the philosophical convention seem to be using the expression in just the way we philosophers are using it. First, the title of Nagel 1974 can be instantly understood by anyone, including those with no exposure to the philosophy of mind. This stands in contrast with the difficulty the uninitiated have understanding the title of Jackson 1982, a contrast which the technical convention view is hard-pressed to explain. Similarly, anyone who has taught undergraduate courses in the philosophy of mind will be aware that, while undergrads have a hard time grasping technical jargon, even such basic pieces of technical jargon as 'substance', 'attribute', and 'supervene', they have no comparable diffculty in understanding (2).

And second, the frame is in wide use in the culture at large, and was so long before the philosophy of mind took on anything like its current shape. Pop songs, from the Beatles' 1966 "She Said, She Said" ("She said 'I know what it's like to be dead'") to Everlast's 1999 "What It's Like" ("God forbid you ever had to walk a mile in his shoes, 'cause then you really might know what it's like to sing the blues"), employ the frame. So do hundreds of thousands of Web pages. Hundreds of Web pages even discuss the question of whether a blind person can know or imagine what it is like to see or the desire of a person who went blind to know what it is like to see again. I do not find it particularly plausible that there is any important difference between the phenomenon these pop songs and Web pages address and the phenomenon (2) concerns.

If (2) can be understood through normal means, then it is possible to investigate its meaning in a systematic manner. We can appeal to our tacit grammatical knowledge in recognizing various sentences as transformations of (2), in recognizing the component expressions of (2) and of these transformations, and in assessing the meanings of these component expressions and how they combine to determine the meaning of the whole.

To begin with, one might wonder, upon looking at (2), "Mary didn't know what *what* is like to see a red thing?" But clearly, 'it' is not intended to refer here: (2) and (2′) 'Mary doesn't know what seeing a red thing is like' are equivalent transformations; all 'it' does in (2) is provide a syntactic subject for 'is' when its semantic subject, the gerund 'seeing a red thing', appears at the end of the sentence in the form of the clause 'to see a red thing'.

Intuitively, 'seeing a red thing' in (2′) concerns experiences of seeing a red thing. Experiences are events. As events in general are particular happenings in the world, such as baseball games or episodes of buttering, so are experiences particular happenings in the world: happenings that are experiencings. Some such events are events of seeing; some events of seeing are events of seeing a red thing. Experiences are events that take place in the mental lives of particular subjects of mentality. An experience is a certain subject's iff the experience takes place in that subject's mental life. In 'seeing a red thing', no subject is specified. Intuitively, it concerns experiences of seeing a red thing in general: normal or typical experiences in normal or typical subjects, within some range. So (2′) is more or less equivalent to 'Mary doesn't know what the typical person's typical experiences of seeing a red thing are like'. This negates (2_T):

(2_T) Mary knows what (the typical person's) (typical) experiences of seeing a red thing are like.

I will briefly explain the frame 'what $\cdots$ is like' and the frame '(someone) knows $\cdots$' as applied to a clause that begins with a question-expression. More detailed argumentation concerning these structures is given in the appendix.

'Like what' can be used to ask questions about the properties of things. When it is, this use has nothing to do with the sorts of comparative questions Lewis focused on in the passage discussed above. This seems fairly obvious: when one asks 'what is San Francisco like?' it is appropriate to respond with a string of predicates, such as 'dense, hilly, and expensive'. The comparative question would be more appropriately answered with a string of NPs (noun phrases), such as 'uranium, Ithaca, and cuts from the tenderloin'. In certain contexts, this might be an apt answer, but in most, it would be bizarre.

Rather, it seems that, in such cases, 'like what' is used to ask which properties a thing has: it serves as a question expression for predicates, in much the same way as 'who' serves as a question expression for noun phrases denoting people. When I ask 'who let the dogs out?' I want you to provide me with names or descriptions of the person or people who let the dogs out; when I ask 'what is San Francisco like?' I want you to provide me with a predicate or some predicates denoting San Francisco's properties.

It is sometimes argued in the philosophical literature that sentences such as, on the one hand, 'John knows that Italian eggplants are white' or 'John knows that one can get an Italian newspaper at Mayer's', and, on the other, 'John knows what color Italian eggplants are' or 'John knows where one can get an Italian newspaper' must express fundamentally different sorts of facts: that sentences of the former sort involving 'that'-clauses report propositional knowledge, whereas sentences of the latter sort involving *wh*-clauses or "embedded questions" report some other, nonpropositional form of knowledge.

Such a claim is not particularly plausible on its face: one can, after all, specify John's knowledge after reporting it with an embedded question: as with 'John knows what color Italian eggplants are—white', or 'John knows where one can get an Italian newspaper—at Mayer's'. It is hard to see what the purpose of giving such a specification would be if it were not to make determinate the content of John's propositional knowledge, which was left undetermined by the initial claim.

Rather, knowledge ascriptions involving embedded questions are intended to ascribe propositional knowledge: knowledge of a proposition that would count, in a context, as an apt answer to the embedded question. So, for instance, the sentence 'John knows where to get an Italian newspaper' communicates that, for some proposition, with a certain contextually salient property—such as concerning newsstands in Ithaca (knowing that one can get an Italian newspaper in Rome might not count)—which answers the question 'where can one get an Italian newspaper?', John knows that proposition. Such a proposition would have the form ||one can get an Italian newspaper at NP||.[6]

So (2_T) reports that Mary knows some proposition that answers the question 'what are experiences of seeing a red thing like?' It is clear that, in the typical context in which one considers the knowledge argument, one is concerned with Mary's knowledge of the properties of experiences of seeing a red thing, and not with Mary's knowledge of what things experiences of seeing a red thing are similar to. Hence such a proposition would have the form ||experiences of seeing a red thing are PRED||.

Suppose then that (2_T) is uttered in a context in which the property of propositions of being F is salient. This utterance would be equivalent to 'there is some truth t such that (i) t is a propositional answer to the question 'which properties do experiences of seeing a red thing have?', (ii) Mary knows t, and (iii) Ft'. This would in turn be equivalent to 'there is some truth t such that (i) t is of the form ||experiences of seeing a red thing are PRED||, (ii) Mary knows t, and (iii) Ft'. (2) negates this claim, and is thus equivalent in such a context to 'no truth t is such that (i) t is of the form ||experiences of seeing a red thing are PRED||, (ii) t is known by Mary, and (iii) Ft'. This is compatible with Mary's knowing all F truths, if there is no F truth of the relevant form. However, in standard discussions of (2), it seems to be presupposed that there is such a truth, and therefore in context (2) seems to be equivalent to 'there is some F truth of the form ||experiences of seeing a red thing are PRED|| that is unknown to Mary'.

This negated claim differs from (2_{1f}) only in that it unpacks the idea of a truth answering a question, and in that the question to be answered, 'what are experiences of seeing a red thing like?', is equivalent to, though distinct from, the question 'what is it like to see a red thing?'[7]

Well that's pretty thin. Strip away the jargon, and what I've argued is that (2) says that there's something about seeing a red thing that Mary didn't know—*you know what I mean*. Nearly all the interesting work of conveying *which* truth about seeing a red thing Mary didn't know needs to be done by context. What then do we mean when we assert (2)?

Although (2) is in itself so insignificant, the fact that we are so drawn to such an insignificant sentence when discussing Mary's situation is itself significant. By refusing to be explicit about the knowledge that Mary lacks, the speaker manages to convey that the knowledge she lacks is of a special sort, which can't be put into words. The speaker exploits the listener's ability to carry out the following line of reasoning:

If you assert of someone that they lack a certain sort of knowledge, but you are inexplicit about what it is, and I know that you know what it is, and I know that you are trying to be as explicit as possible (e.g., you aren't trying to allude to something in a less-than-explicit way because you are playing games, or trying to avoid some bad consequence that would arise from greater explicitness), then I would be reasonable to conclude that you think you can't express this piece of knowledge more explicitly. This might happen because you are having a hard time finding the right words. But usually, in such cases, one hems and haws and makes groping gestures, or apologizes, or talks around the point, or in some other way manifests that one is tongue-tied. So since I don't notice you acting tongue-tied, the only thing to conclude is that you think you aren't alone in your inarticulacy, and that no one can express the piece of knowledge more explicitly: it must be that this piece of knowledge cannot be put into words.

If the listener went through this line of reasoning, this would surely raise to salience, as a feature of the knowledge she lacks, the property of being incapable of being put into words.

This would not stretch the boundaries of common sense: the idea that certain propositions or concepts cannot be put into words, but can only be understood by one who has had a certain experience, is an aspect of our pretheoretic view of the mind.[8] There are a number of places where this pretheoretic idea needs refinement. For instance, there is a sense in which these propositions *can* be put into words: one can say 'this is what it's like to see a red thing!' Such an utterance can even communicate the intended proposition, if the hearer appropriately sympathizes with the speaker. Perhaps the sense in which these propositions are inexpressible is that they cannot be expressed using words that have robust context-invariant semantic content. And there is a sense in which any (noninnate) concept can only be understood by one who has had an experience of a certain sort, an experience which suffices for learning that concept: arguably, in order to grasp the concept 'bachelor', one needs to have an experience of having it defined for one, or perhaps an experience of observing the ostension of a number of paradigms and foils. However, there's no room to provide this refinement here, let alone to address the (interesting and important) question of just what distinguishes grasp of expressible from grasp of inexpressible concepts. I do think that the idea is familiar and serviceable as pretheoretically understood, so I will work with it.

One important class of inexpressible propositions is involved with reflection on our own mental states and sympathetic understanding of those of others.[9] Human adults have the ability to simulate in themselves experiences they are not actually having, such as when one imagines oneself riding a rollercoaster. These experiences do not have the same connections to actual belief and action that genuine experiences have, but they are useful in establishing hypothetical or suppositional lines of thought. This ability to simulate experiences tends to be somewhat limited, in that for the most part one can simulate an experience of a certain type only if one has actually had an experience of a similar type. Human adults also have a general ability to reflect on the character of their own experiences,[10] or of experiences they simulate in themselves, where reflecting in this way brings with it a distinctive way of understanding the character of the experience unavailable to one who has not had or simulated an experience with that character. Once one has this sort of reflective understanding of an experience with a certain character, but not otherwise, one can also sympathetically understand that character as a feature of the experiences of others.[11]

Novel episodes of such understanding seem to be able to underlie the entertaining of thoughts with novel propositional content; for one thing, they seem to have distinctive powers to explain other facts that explanations "in words" lack; and it seems plausible that what explains are propositions (Williamson 2000, sec. 9.5). Clear cases of this novel explanatory power emerge in cases in which one is unable to understand why people with certain experiences feel or behave a certain way: for instance, why many people who are very rich are not happy, why many people who live in areas with above-average rates of street crime do not support more aggressive policing techniques, or why anyone would vote for a certain presidential candidate. One might be presented with certain fairly obvious explanations: it might be explained that a feeling of overcoming challenge or adversity through hard work is rewarding; or that up to a certain point the rate of street crime can increase without demanding much more than slightly increased vigilance, whereas aggressive behavior by arrogant police officers from outside the neighborhood can damage one's sense of pride in community and subject law-abiding residents to the risk of being demeaned by the police; or that the voting behavior is solely determined by the candidate's emotional appeals because of inability to understand the deleterious impact his policies are likely to have. One might hear these explanations, but still feel as though the behavior does not make sense. However, if one were to have or simulate the person's experience—for instance, by taking a month off work to go on a pleasure cruise, or by being treated rudely by a policeman at a traffic stop, or by recalling one's juvenile feelings of patriotism and admiration of power—the behavior might suddenly make sense to one.

This all seems also to be an aspect of our pretheoretic view of mind. Once again, there are nice questions here, which I have no room to address: such as just what grasp of reflective/sympathetic concepts consists in such that thoughts containing them yield explanations that expressible concepts cannot.[12] Still, the presence of this additional explanatory power provides strong support for the view that reflective/sympathetic concepts are genuine concepts, and can enter distinctively into thoughts with propositional content.

I thus propose that what is conveyed by (2) (in the present context) is that, concerning a certain reflective/sympathetic proposition about the nature of experiences of seeing a red thing, Mary didn't know it. Call this proposition 't'. Which proposition is t? Supposing that Mary is a normal subject, and hence much like you, you can entertain t, or at least a proposition much like it,[13] through the following procedure. Cause or simulate in yourself an experience of seeing a red thing, and then focus your attention on the character of the experience.[14] Think to yourself: seeing a red thing is like this.

The link between inexpressible reflective/sympathetic propositions and 'knowing what it's like' has provided much inspiration to writers of pop lyrics, a great many of which complain that someone doesn't know what a certain sort of experience is like. Standardly the singer has been jilted and intends to convey that his or her emotional distress is extraordinarily intense. Such lyrics depend for getting their point across on one's ability to reason as follows:

There's some proposition about the character of the singer's experience of emotional distress I don't know; but since the singer won't tell me exactly what it is, it must be inexpressible; so it must be a reflective/sympathetic proposition; the singer seems to be lamenting my inability to know it; but since the singer won't do anything else to convey it to me, the singer must think I can't grasp it; if I can't grasp it, I haven't had an experience of emotional distress that substantially resembles the singer's experience; the best explanation for this is that the singer's emotional distress is extraordinarily intense.[15]

It is a virtue of my analysis of (2) that it so readily explains the popularity of this lyrical trope.

3   Assessing the Knowledge Argument

The following points are supported by the preceding discussion. I located a certain class of concepts, the reflective/sympathetic concepts. A reflective/sympathetic concept C_X is a predicate, concerning the character X of experiences of a certain type T_X. Reflective/sympathetic concepts are, in some intuitive sense, "inexpressible": this is to say that in general, and subject to the qualifications detailed above, one cannot grasp C_X unless one has had an experience of type T_X. There is a type T_R of experiences of seeing a red thing, which have a character R, and a corresponding reflective/sympathetic concept C_R. Before she is released, Mary has never had an experience of type T_R; consequently she cannot grasp the concept C_R. Standardly, when one says that someone does or does not know what it is like to see a red thing, one means that the person does or does not know the proposition t predicating C_R of experiences of type T_R. Because Mary does not grasp the concept C_R, she cannot entertain any proposition involving C_R, so a fortiori she cannot know a proposition predicating C_R of experiences of type T_R: hence she can't know what it is like to see a red thing.

The knowledge argument can then be recast in a somewhat simpler form as arguing validly from the premises that (1) for every physical truth, Mary knows it, and (2') Mary does not know the truth t, to the conclusion that (C') t is a nonphysical truth.[16] (C') is supposed to suffice for dualism. If a nonphysical truth is a truth that concerns the condition of entities other than physical things, it plausibly does suffice, given the form of t.

How successful is the knowledge argument as an argument for dualism? Any attempt to answer this question is subject, on pain of falling
into either antinaturalism or skepticism, to a requirement of psychological
plausibility: it must capture how we think when we think through the
knowledge argument. Of course a central aspect of our reaction to the
knowledge argument is that it strikes us, pretheoretically, as successful—
or, at least, if it is unsuccessful, it is far from obvious wherein its lack
of success lies: in the introduction to this volume, Stoljar and Nagasawa
list five distinct lines of reply to the knowledge argument, each with its
staunch adherents; obviously, the physicalist opposition is mired in inter-
necine strife—not an easy position from which to make accusations of an
obvious fallacy! So any assessment of the knowledge argument according to
which it doesn't involve some hard-to-unearth error is automatically cast
into doubt.

Stoljar and Nagasawa list five major physicalist accusations against the
knowledge argument. The first denies (2'); the fifth denies (1). Denying (2')
strikes me as pointless for reasons that should become more clear below; I
discuss (1) below. The remaining three allege that the argument is invalid
as an argument for dualism owing to some fallacy of equivocation: we read
the premises in one way and find them plausible; we read the conclusion in
a different way and find it interesting.
  Diagnoses due to equivocation generally face a problem of asymmetry.
If the premises are plausible on disambiguation d_1 but not d_2 and the
conclusion is interesting on disambiguation d_2 but not d_1, why aren't we
equally likely to find the argument for the interesting conclusion implausible, because rather than reading the argument with d_1 premises and d_2
conclusion, we have read it with d_2, d_2; or plausible but uninteresting, because we have read it with d_1, d_1; or implausible and uninteresting, because
we have read it with d_2, d_1?
  Two of the accusations of equivocation concern an alleged equivocation
in 'know'. Even if 'know' is not univocal between uses in which it takes a
clause and uses in which it takes a direct object, it is certainly univocal in
uses in which it takes a clause.[17]
  The remaining accusation of equivocation (which is probably the most
popular physicalist reply to the knowledge argument) appeals to an alleged
distinction between a "Fregean" and a "Russellian" conception of truths,
where this distinction amounts to whether, given some entities "bundled

together in a worldly state of affairs," there can (Fregean) or cannot (Russellian) be more than one truth concerning this bundle. (1) and (2') are plausibly psychological when read along Fregean lines; (C) is interestingly ontological when read along Russellian lines. Allegedly, we succumb, in considering the knowledge argument, to a tendency to equivocate between these conceptions of truths.

But first, it's hard to imagine that this tendency, if it in fact exists, would have been allowed to slip by: the distinction between Fregeanism and Russellianism is incredibly familiar in philosophy. Worse still, as can be seen in the passages I displayed in section 1, Jackson was explicitly aware of opacity concerns in the 1986 essay. It would take a major helping of doublethink to first explicitly cleave to Fregeanism in the statement of the conclusion and then reject it in drawing out the significance of the conclusion.

Second, I doubt that this tendency exists. Although some philosophers advocate that we sometimes or always think of truths as Russellian, I disagree. I never find myself unconsciously slipping into accepting that Lois knows the truth that Clark flies around Metropolis. It is hard to understand what could be the difference between my situation with respect to this truth and the situation of those who regard the knowledge argument as an argument for dualism, such that this difference could ground the alleged distinction in psychological outcomes of these situations.

In recent work, Jackson (1998) has come up with a way of extracting dualism from the knowledge argument that purports to reveal what the argument was after all along. Stoljar and Nagasawa, in section 3.4 of this volume's introduction, boil down this approach as follows: (i) "if physicalism is true, the psychophysical conditional [$\|$if P then $Q\|$, where P "gather[s] together all the [obviously] physical truths of the world into one megatruth" and Q gathers together all the reflective/sympathetic truths of the world into one mega-truth] is a priori" and (ii) there are no a priori connections between obviously physical and reflective/sympathetic propositions.

Whether or not these claims are true, their relation to the knowledge argument as I presented it, and to Jackson's early presentations, is not obvious. Some further explanation of how, pretheoretically, we manage to deduce (i) and (ii) from the principles of the knowledge argument, or regard them as licensed by the black-and-white Mary scenario, is required to make this stick as an explanation of the allure of the knowledge argument.

Moreover, it is not clear that claim (ii) is either true or supported by the black-and-white Mary scenario. It is widely recognized that before her release, no amount of calculation would have enabled Mary to know what it's like to see a red thing. But her problem was not that, like a frustrated mathematician trying to prove Goldbach's conjecture, she was able to entertain t, but couldn't prove it. Unlike the frustrated mathematician—who may spend every waking hour wondering about Goldbach's conjecture— Mary wasn't even in a position to wonder whether t is true. Conjure in yourself an experience of seeing a red thing, focus on its character, and think to yourself 'I wonder whether this is what it's like to see a red thing'. Mary couldn't have done that, before her release. Clearly at least one source of her problem with knowing t was that she couldn't take the constitutive step of even entertaining t. The question whether t is a priori entailed by obviously physical propositions cannot be tested by considering someone who can't even entertain t: a case could count as supporting the negative answer only if it concerned someone who could entertain t, and who found himself incapable of demonstrating it by a priori reasoning from his obviously physical knowledge.

Wait until Mary goes to sleep some night, then perform super-neuro-surgery on her so that she gains the ability to visualize a red thing. This would give her all the concepts required for entertaining t; but would this alone suffice for her coming to know that t is true—as opposed, for instance, to its remaining open for her whether this is what it's like to see a green thing? Aside from the significant departure this example represents from the original black-and-white Mary scenario, I find that my intuitions here are dim—though if anything, it seems she could rule out that she was imagining a green thing on the basis of her knowledge that green things look "cool" and that the thing she imagines would look "hot" (Hardin 1997). The dialectic that emerges from this point is complex: see Hilbert and Kalderon 2000 for some of the details. It seems to me that the question remains open, and extremely vexing, whether there are some obviously physical propositions that a priori entail t.

If the knowledge argument is valid, and (2′) is (as I take it to be) undeniable, then dualism follows if (1) is true. A committed physicalist has an easy out: she can argue from (2′) and the denial of (C′) to the denial of (1). The denial of (1) in the face of the black-and-white Mary scenario can be supported by the familiar Fregean observation that several distinct truths can concern the same "worldly state of affairs": it can be claimed that there is some physical truth Mary already knew, which concerns the same condition as t concerns. t is a physical truth; Mary could not have known all the physical truths before her release.

But one who says this is at risk of saying something highly unintuitive. The knowledge argument is, after all, alluring, and the view that Mary can learn all the physical truths before her release is a particularly alluring subcomponent. None of my undergraduate students in introduction to philosophy of mind have ever objected to this step. Even "post-theoretic" subjects ignore this option: of the five distinct classes of physicalist reply to the knowledge argument detailed by Stoljar and Nagasawa in the introduction, all but the last ignore this reply (and a tiny minority of the articles cited here address this point). Philosophers seem to regard this as a last-ditch escape from dualism, to be adopted only if all other options are exhausted.

There are two reasons why this reply might lack appeal: first, it might not occur to us, because we have some mental block against it; second, we might find it implausible even if it occurs to us. On the first option: we might somehow be distracted from wondering whether t is a physical truth. An intriguing possibility for the source of this distraction (suggested to me by Zoltán Szabó) is that what we are most strongly attending to in assessing the knowledge argument is what Mary *knows*, rather than what is *physical*. The claim that there is such an imbalance in attention is plausible: it's the *knowledge* argument; the article is titled "What Mary Didn't *Know*"; etc. As a result of this imbalance in attention, the questions we will tend to ask about the knowledge argument will tend to concern the scope or nature of Mary's knowledge, rather than the scope or nature of being physical. Stoljar and Nagasawa's survey makes this plausible: four of the five physicalist replies, comprising more than four-fifths of the cited articles, concern the scope or nature of Mary's knowledge.

On the second option: we might simply find it less plausible that t is physical than that (1) is true.[18] Presumably this is because there is some property such that we regard the possession of that property by a proposition as a necessary condition for that proposition's being physical, a property that does not hold of any reflective/sympathetic proposition (note that nothing is special about t: any reflective/sympathetic proposition would do). It is hard to see what property this could be, aside from the property of being expressible: we know little or nothing of the specific content of Mary's lessons, nor do we care to know anything in particular about it. As Lewis (1988, p. 281) notes, "[l]essons on the aura of Vegemite will do no more for us than lessons on its chemical composition.... Our intuitive starting point wasn't just that *physics* lessons couldn't help the inexperienced to know what it's like. It was that *lessons* couldn't help." One thing can be certain about this content, however: because it is conveyed in lessons, it is expressible.[19]

The empiricist thesis that an expressible concept and an inexpressible concept cannot both denote the same entity has a long tradition in the philosophical literature, tracing back, perhaps, at least to Hume (1739/1978, I.I.i).[20] If this is the core idea behind the knowledge argument, the passage through knowledge is largely a detour: a more efficient way to express the core of the argument would be to appeal to this empiricist thesis, together with the thesis that, for any physical entity, there is an expressible concept denoting it.

Assessing the empiricist thesis is the work of another paper, or perhaps a long book; my primary aim in this paper has been to tease out its hidden influence on our reaction to the knowledge argument. However, I will make some (somewhat speculative) evaluative remarks here. A recurrent idea in the philosophical literature is that certain predicate concepts "reveal the natures" of the properties to which they refer (Johnston 1992, pp. 138–139; Lewis 1995, pp. 327–328; Chalmers 2002, p. 256). Contrast such concepts as 'water': one can grasp this concept in complete ignorance of chemistry; and yet, it seems that chemistry reveals the nature of water when it tells us that to be water is to be (or to be constituted by) H_2O. Grasp of a nature-revealing concept, on the other hand, allegedly does not allow for such ignorance about the nature of its referent: such grasp allows only for ignorance about such "extrinsic" matters as its pattern of instantiation.

In this literature, reflective/sympathetic concepts are frequently linked with this idea of Revelation. One who takes a reflective/sympathetic concept to be revelatory in this way might naturally accept that it cannot co-denote with an expressible concept. For suppose that C_x is an expressible concept. Perhaps, possession of a given reflective/sympathetic concept C_r is compatible with ignorance of $\|$to be C_r is to be $C_x\|$, whatever C_x may be.[21] If so, then, given Revelation, that proposition is false.

Why do we feel that there is a link between inexpressibility and Revelation? This opinion can be explained in at least two distinct ways. The first goes by reflection on an allegedly standard pattern of discovery of natures.[22] The concept 'water' allegedly encodes causal structure: water is that substance which plays a certain causal role. And the concept 'H_2O' allegedly encodes causal structure: H_2O is a substance that, as a matter of fact, realizes that causal role. No discovery of nature can be in any way licensed without beginning with a concept that encodes causal structure: without this, the reducing concept cannot get a "toehold." But if a concept is inexpressible, it does not encode causal structure: for causal structure is always expressible.

The second goes by reflection on the functional role of a reflective/sympathetic concept. Perhaps the referent of the concept is somehow "incorporated into" the concept itself: perhaps deploying the concept in a thought involves running a computational process of a certain type, some subprocess of which is of a type that is the referent of the concept; perhaps grasp of the concept requires a primitive relation of "acquaintance" with the referent. Such a concept would be inexpressible, since either way grasp of the concept would essentially involve having an experience of a certain type. And, moreover, such a concept might contribute a feeling of Revelation: since the referent would be, in a sense, part of the concept, the concept would not "stand between" the subject and the referent; rather, the referent would be "present to the mind" of the subject. On this view, incorporation of the referent by a reflective/sympathetic concept lies at the root of both the inexpressibility of the concept and the feeling that it provides Revelation.

Suppose that it is more prima facie plausible that Mary could learn all the physical truths before her release than it is that t is physical, perhaps because we are in fact deeply attracted to the empiricist thesis. Presumably most physicalist philosophers are physicalists because they take it that nothing nonphysical can be involved in the causal order; and because they take it that the characters of experiences are involved in the causal order. If this argument is compelling, we would then be faced with an antinomy:

the characters of experiences must be physical, because they are involved in the causal order; but they cannot be physical, because they can be denoted with inexpressible concepts. This is a serious problem, and I don't see how to make it go away: in part this is because the empiricist thesis has not been adequately investigated. I hope to have shown, however, that this investigation is required. For grant the empiricist thesis, and physicalism falls: it won't do to go out in search of some "fallacy," because there is no fallacy in the neighborhood. One can, of course, stabilize one's epistemic state by turning a blind eye on the antinomy and pleading "antecedent physicalism." But, I hope, most philosophers will find this option uncongenial.

Appendix: Further Formal Properties of (2)

In this appendix, I argue in greater detail for my claims about the formal, logical properties of (2).

The credibility of my claim that 'like what' can be used to ask about the properties of things can be given an additional boost by deriving this behavior from a theory of the deep linguistic properties of 'like what'. I begin with an analysis of the related construction 'like that'.

The familiar "comparative" use of 'like this/that', meaning 'similar to this/that', is composed out of 'like' meaning 'similar to' and the singular pronoun 'this/that'.[23]

But alongside this comparative use, there is also a "propredicative" use of 'like this/that'. A "propredicate" or "predicative proform" is an expression like a pronoun in lacking intrinsic semantic content—in the sense that 'he', 'it', and 'then' have no substantial fixed meaning or denotation, unlike 'dog', 'run', or 'and'—and thereby needing to inherit it from outside (e.g., by demonstration, anaphora, or binding), but which appears in predicate rather than in argument position. 'Like this' seems to have taken over the role as preferred English propredicate from the now somewhat archaic 'thus'. I shall defend three claims about propredicate uses: (I) 'like' does not mean 'similar to'; (II) 'this/that' is not used as a singular pronoun; and (III) 'like this' is semantically incomposite. It follows that the comparative and propredicate uses are totally unrelated.

Consider a demonstrative use of propredicate 'like this': demonstrating red, one utters (d) 'my couch is colored like this'. Here, 'like this' is not used comparatively, but is rather used as a semantically incomposite demonstrative propredicate, referring to red in virtue of one's demonstration.[24] Concerning (I): first, it is intuitively clear that a comparison between the couch and the bearer of the demonstrated instance of redness need not be intended here, and that the utterance may just mean the same as the noncomparative 'my couch is colored red'; so, intuitively, 'like' does not mean 'similar to'. Of course 'my couch is like this' and 'my couch is similar to this object' (said, in the first case, focusing on a property-instance and, in the second case, focusing on its bearer) are necessarily equivalent and obviously so, so it may be easy to convey what is said by uttering either by uttering the other. But necessary equivalence is not, as is familiar, equivalence of meaning. And, according to my intuitive sense of the meaning of the utterances, the former must convey that my couch has the designated property and need not convey that it is similar to any particular object, whereas the latter must convey that my couch is similar to a certain object in a certain respect, but need not convey which property they have in common.[25] Second, 'colored' seems to want to be followed by an adjective, as in 'my couch is colored red'/*'my couch is colored Fred', so that explicit comparatives do not sit happily next to it: *'my couch is colored resembling that'/?'my couch is colored similar to that'; by contrast, (d) does not suffer from this problem.

Concerning (II): first, the process of understanding an utterance of (d) differs from the process of understanding a comparative use. To understand the utterance of (d), one's audience must merely determine which color one is talking about. By contrast, to understand an utterance of (for instance) 'my couch is similar in color to that material body', one's audience must (i) determine which material body in the region of ostension one is talking about, and (ii) determine what its color is. Second, one can wave at a whole range of red objects and sensibly utter (d). By contrast, if one waved at a range of red objects, it would be bizarre to utter %'my couch is similar in color to that'.[26] One's audience might be able to understand the claim, since all the waved-at objects are the same color. But the pronoun could not refer to the color: *'my couch is similar in color to red/redness' is unacceptable. And it could not refer to any individual, since no individual is designated. So it could not refer at all. Only a grammatically plural pronoun could refer given this sort of gesture, as in 'my couch is similar in color to those'.

Concerning (III): one might agree that 'that' is not a pronoun but a pro-predicate used to denote red, yet still dispute my claim that 'like that' is a semantically incomposite propredicate, thinking that 'like' has some other function. But 'like' must disappear along with 'that' when the pro-form is cashed out: *'my couch is like red', unlike 'my couch is, like, red', is unacceptable.

Next, consider a discourse-anaphoric use of propredicate 'like that', in the discourse (a) 'the couches here are red'; 'couches that are colored like that please me'. Here, 'like that' is used not comparatively, but rather as a semantically incomposite anaphoric propredicate, picking up its meaning from the use of 'red' earlier in the discourse. Concerning (I): here, it is also intuitively clear that no comparison need be intended. Concerning (II): the first and second arguments above carry over trivially to this case. An ana-logue to the third argument (from plurals) runs as follows: in (a), the only options for the antecedent to the anaphor are the plural NP 'the couches' and the predicate 'red'. But a plural NP cannot be the antecedent of a grammatically singular discourse-anaphoric pronoun: 'the people here are your friends'; '(they buy/*he buys) me a drink regularly'. So the antecedent of the anaphor in (a) can't be the NP, but must be the predicate; hence the anaphoric proform is not a pronoun but a propredicate.[27] Concerning (III): arguing as above.

Finally, consider a bound use of propredicate 'like that'. The example in this case is somewhat harder to hear in the intended way, so I'll set it up a bit more extensively. Suppose I tell you that I have a rug with squares in Southwestern colors. The following dialogue might ensue: 'Does it have a square that is colored adobe tan?'; 'Yes, my rug has a square that is colored like that'; 'Does it have a square that is colored sage green?'; 'Yes, my rug has a square that is colored like that'; 'Does it have a square that is colored arid-sky blue?'; 'Yes, my rug has a square that is colored like that'; 'Does it have a square that is colored cactus-flower red?'; 'Yes, yes—[(b)] for *every* Southwestern color, my rug has a square that is colored like that'.[28] Here, 'like that' is not used comparatively, but is rather used as a semantically incomposite bound propredicate, ranging over the Southwestern colors in the domain of the NP 'every Southwestern color'. Concerning (I): here we do not need to appeal to intuition to note that no comparison is intended, for interpreting (b) with 'like' as 'similar to' and 'that' as ranging over southwestern colors results in mumbo-jumbo. Squares are parts of my rug, concrete areas of tufting; colors are (if anything) universals. It would be perverse to compare an area of tufting with a universal, which is why %'for every Southwestern color, my rug has a square that is similar to that' is semantically dreadful. Since (b) is not semantically dreadful, clearly no comparison to the entities in the domain of the NP is intended. Concerning (II): the entities in the domain of the NP are properties, and properties are given either with predicates or with such nominalizations as 'redness'. But in the latter case, the matrix clause would not have a sensible predicate: *'my rug has a square that is (colored) (like) redness' is unacceptable; hence, the bound proform must be a propredicate. Concerning (III): arguing as above.

Proforms are closely connected with such "question words" or "wh-forms" as 'who', 'what', and 'where'. Each proform is paired with a wh-form. In English, the members of this pair tend to sound similar (Lycan 1995, p. 245 presents as examples of this phenomenon the pairs 'then'/ 'when', 'there'/'where', and 'thither'/'whither'; compare also 'what'/ 'that'),[29] and, in the most fundamental sense recognized by standard contemporary views in syntax,[30] can occur in the same syntactic positions ('I boiled the potato then'/'when did I boil the potato?'; 'I put the potato there'/'where did I put the potato?'; 'I boiled that'/'what did I boil?'). A proform and the wh-form with which it is paired both lack intrinsic semantic content, but instead range arbitrarily over a certain class of entities, with the members of the pair ranging over the same class: 'where' and 'there' both range over places; 'when' and 'then' both range over times or conditions; 'whither' and 'thither' both range over paths; and 'what' and 'that' both range over arguments. The proform and the wh-form differ only in that the proform has some entity from the range assigned to it by linguistic or extralinguistic context, whereas the wh-form does not have an entity assigned to it but is rather used in asking questions about that range of entities. An appropriate answer to a question consists of a word or string of words denoting entities chosen from this range ('when did you boil the potato?'—'from 3 P.M. to 4 P.M.'; 'where did you put the potatoes?'—'in the lower cabinet, in the basket, and in the boiling water'; 'what did you boil?'—'the potato, the radish, and the cabbage').

We should thus predict as an instance of this generalization that there would be a wh-predicate paired with propredicate 'like that'.[31] The wh-predicate would be pronounced 'like what', would appear syntactically in predicate position, and would be used to ask questions about predicates. This prediction is confirmed: alongside the comparative use, 'like what' is also used as a predicate *wh*-form. Just as one can say 'San Francisco is like that' with propredicate 'like that', one can ask 'What is San Francisco like?' with *wh*-predicate 'like what'.[32] When one does so, an appropriate answer would consist of a predicate or string of predicates such as 'dense, hilly, and expensive'. And, as I noted at the outset, this would be an appropriate answer to this question.

Stanley and Williamson (2001) have recently argued convincingly for the claim that, when an embedded question appears as the complement of 'know', what is reported is propositional knowledge. They argue that this claim is supported by robust results in cognitive syntax and semantics. Here is a brief overview of these results.[33]

Every embedded question corresponds[34] to an "answer-set" of propositions. Which propositions are in this answer-set is related to the syntactic structure of the question in the following way. One can think of the question as corresponding to a string that is like a standard sentence, but which has the question-word standing in for some other word or words (e.g., 'one can get an Italian newspaper at Mayer's'/'one can get an Italian newspaper where'). And then one can think of the question word as a variable: the resulting string is then an open sentence (e.g., 'one can get an Italian newspaper x'). This open sentence does not express a proposition or have a complete sense, since variables do not have senses. But it does have an incomplete sense, and this incomplete sense together with how the world is determines which propositions are in the answer-set: a proposition is in the answer-set iff it is a true completion of this incomplete sense.

So, for instance, the answer-set for the embedded question 'what color Italian eggplants are' has as its only member the proposition that Italian eggplants are white; the answer-set for 'where one can get an Italian newspaper' contains the proposition that one can get an Italian newspaper at Mayer's, the proposition that one can get an Italian newspaper in Rome, the proposition that one can get an Italian newspaper on Arthur Avenue, and so on. (The same goes for the notion of the set of answers to a "root question," which is the sort of sentence uttered in an interrogative speech-act, such as 'what color are Italian eggplants?' and 'where can one get an Italian newspaper?')

Then, the truth-conditions for an utterance, in a context, of a knowledge ascription involving an embedded question with answer-set A are as follows. Such an utterance is true iff the subject of the knowledge ascription knows either some, or all, of those members of A that have a property raised to salience in the context (where whether some or all is required varies from context to context). The contextually variable salience restriction is required. Even if John knows that one can get an Italian news-paper in Rome, 'John knows where to get an Italian newspaper' may be false in a context in which only those members of the answer-set are of interest that concern where to get an Italian newspaper around here. The claim that the members of the answer-set are *propositions* is also required. Even if Lex Luthor knows that Clark Kent works at the *Daily Planet*, 'Lex knows who works at the *Daily Planet*' may be false in a context in which only those members of the answer-set are of interest that concern the day jobs of participants in the Justice League of America. If all this is correct, the view that "knowledge what" is not propositional is in error.

Here's a further argument for the truth-conditions I've assigned to (2). Consider a more ordinary case in which one is asking someone, concerning a certain unfamiliar experience—climbing a mountain, or being in a riot, for instance—'what was it like?' Standardly, an appropriate answer would be something like 'exhilarating'/'terrifying'/'breathtaking'/'enlightening'. (The significance of this phenomenon is highlighted in Lormand in prepara-tion.) On the other hand, it would be somewhat peculiar if one's interloc-utor replied with an NP, such as 'the Tour de France'/'1968'. This is because standardly, when one asks this question, one wishes for a characteriza-tion of the features of the experience, of the sort that would be given by a predicate. However, if what was desired were a comparison, it would only be possible to give an NP answer, and a predicate answer would be very bad. Compare: 'what/which cat is your cat like?' 'Otto'/*'exhilarating'. Given that predicate answers are preferable, let alone permissible, I con-clude that in these ordinary cases, 'like what' is not used with its compara-tive reading. I can of course imagine finding an NP answer appropriate. But I think that I would hear it as elliptical for the comparative predicates 'like the Tour de France'/'like 1968'. What is important here is not that noun phrases cannot be given as answers, but that predicates can be given. In a case in which a comparison is explicitly desired, predicates cannot be given. And I cannot detect any difference between these ordinary cases and Mary's case.

Acknowledgments

Thanks for discussion of these issues to many over the years. I'd especially like to thank Dave Chalmers, Emily Esch, Mike Fara, Gail Fine, Sally McConnell-Ginet, Peter Ludlow, Kieran Setiya, and Jessica Wilson. Harold Hodes, Sydney Shoemaker, Daniel Stoljar, and Zoltán Szabó provided helpful written comments; Sydney's and Zoltán's comments moved me to fundamentally rethink my approach to sizeable portions of the paper, and Daniel's comments on several drafts were impressive both in quantity and in quality. Thanks also to three classes of students in introduction to philosophy of mind for serving as test subjects.

Notes

1. Concerning, of course, superstudent Mary, who, though confined to a room where everything is black, white, or gray, nonetheless acquires a total knowledge of a completed physical (throughout, one may add 'and/or functional', or substitute 'structural' or 'dispositional', making changes as appropriate, without altering the truth of anything I say) science of color and color perception; who is freed, to finally set eyes upon a red thing; who thereupon learns what it is like to see a red thing; and who therefore did not previously know what it is like to see a red thing.

2. By saying that so-and-so 'represents the logical form of' some expression, I mean that so-and-so conveys the meaning of the expression in a way that foregrounds the expression's broadly logical properties and subordinates other aspects of its meaning.

3. Although all I need to make my point is that this is *a* legitimate way of using 'truth', I also accept the stronger claim that there is no legitimate way of using the ordinary language expression 'truth' that violates the principle that truths are the objects of knowledge. Sometimes philosophers use 'truth' (or, more frequently, 'fact') in such a way that truths are truthmakers for true propositions. But it seems to me that if commonsense ontology recognizes entities whose pattern of existence and nonexistence determines which propositions are true and which false, these entities would be something like states or events, such as my couch's redness or the World Series. And it seems to be a linguistic error to use 'truth' to apply to states or events: 'Joan already knew all the truths/facts discussed in the chemistry class'/*'Joan already knew all the states/events discussed in the chemistry class'; 'my couch's redness is a pleasing state'/*'my couch's redness is a pleasing truth/fact'; 'the World Series is a

thrilling event'/*'the World Series is a thrilling truth/fact'. (The asterisks represent syntactic anomalousness.)

If this is correct, the claim often made by advocates of the opacity line that Mary learned an old fact in a new way is incoherent. Since 'x learned that p at t' implies 'x did not know that p immediately before t', the claim that she learned a fact she already knew implies the claim that she didn't and did know some fact immediately before t. I may be misinterpreting advocates of this view, however; they may be intending to give up ordinary language and commonsense ontology for some superior replacements.

4. Thanks to Mike Fara and Kieran Setiya for helping me to figure out Lewis's argument.

5. It will turn out that the phrase gets its significance owing to a considerable amount of reasoning about speaker intentions, but this reasoning proceeds on the basis of a prior understanding of the phrase through normal linguistic processes.

6. Doubled verticals represent "sense–quasi-quotation," so that $\ulcorner\|\varepsilon\|\urcorner$ represents the sense of ε.

7. Lycan (1995) also appeals to the approach to embedded questions outlined here in the analysis of (2). In Lycan's view, "'S knows what it's like to see blue' means roughly 'S knows that it is like Q to see blue', where 'Q' suitably names some inner phenomenal property or condition" (p. 245). This is unclear: what kind of expression names a property? An ordinary proper name, like 'Homer'? Or a definite description denoting a property, like 'the property of redness'? Or a nominalized adjective, like 'redness'? None of these alternatives yields a grammatical sentence when substituted in for 'Q' in Lycan's frame: *'S knows that it is like Homer to see blue'; *'S knows that it is like the property of redness to see blue'; *'S knows that it is like redness to see blue'. The problem is that 'like' is part of the *wh*-form, so that if the answer is given without appeal to a proform (like 'that'), 'like' must go away. So Lycan should say "'S knows what it's like to see blue' means roughly 'S knows that it is Q to see blue', where 'Q' is a suitable predicate denoting an inner phenomenal property." But even still, Lycan's proposal is in one way unmotivated and in another unclear: (i) Lycan does not make it clear what mechanism is at work in ensuring that 'Q' denotes an inner phenomenal property, and (ii) the notion of 'suitability' is left unexplained.

8. Compare Lewis 1988, p. 262: "They say that experience is the best teacher, and the classroom is no substitute for Real Life." Lewis of course does not himself think that such knowledge is propositional or conceptual, though the platitude he mentions amounts to my claim when interpreted in the most natural way. For a somewhat different connection between the knowledge argument and ineffability, see Byrne 2002; also references to other discussions of this connection therein.

Daniel Stoljar points out that Swampman forces this claim to be qualified: compare Lewis 1988, pp. 264–265. To handle such concerns, I could add 'or who is from the standpoint of narrowly individuated apparent memory indistinguishable from one who has had the experience', or make explicit that 'can' is tacitly restricted to normal contexts in this platitude, and that outside of normal contexts, it is unclear what should be said.

9. Stanley and Williamson (2001, pp. 428–430) discuss another class of inexpressible propositions, those one knows when one knows how to do something. Lewis's platitude applies just as well to these. However these are less plausible as relevant in the present context than are reflective/sympathetic propositions.

10. By 'the character of an experience' I'll always intend to pick out the so-called *phenomenal* character of the experience, that feature of experience which is revealed to reflective attention.

11. Harman (1996, p. 259) puts the point nicely: "there is a distinctive kind of understanding that consists in finding an equivalent in one's own case. That is 'knowing what it is like to have that experience'."

12. A substantial obstacle to progress on these questions has been the opinion that reflective/sympathetic concepts are "indexical" concepts. The notion of indexicality was initially presented as a theoretical notion in theories of natural language semantics intended to explain how I assign truth-conditions to your utterances with respect to a context. What relevance such a theory of interpretation is supposed to have to the project of explaining the nature of concepts is, I find, exceedingly unclear; as a result it is unclear how to retrofit this notion of indexicality to the purposes of this project.

13. It might be impossible for you to entertain t exactly. The character of Mary's experience may differ subtly from the character of your experience. Mary's macula may be somewhat more or less yellowed with age than yours, for instance, causing her to regard certain objects you regard as purplish-red as orangey-red, or vice versa. Or red things may be more salient to Mary than to you, since she waited all these years to see one. And your reflective/sympathetic concept 'like this' may be constitutively linked to the character of your experience; so that the proposition she entertains when she thinks 'seeing a red thing is like this' may differ from the proposition you thereby entertain. But, for the most part, we ignore such subtle interpersonal differences in sympathetic understanding. Typically somewhat crude and imprecise understanding meets our purposes in sympathy.

If Mary is not a normal subject, but is rather spectrally inverted, for instance, she does not come to know what it's like to see a red thing: this knowledge concerns what the typical experience of a typical subject is like upon seeing a red thing. If she were aware of her inversion, she could come to know what it is like to see a green thing. In any event, she could come to know what it is like for *her* to see a red thing. Since accounting for this complication would do nothing but encumber the discussion, henceforth I'll ignore it.

14. There's a considerable simplification here: the experience has a great many characters. What I want to focus on is the character that experience has solely in virtue of being an experience of a red thing, the character that experience has in common with all other experiences, in normal subjects, of seeing a red thing. This character will be highly abstract and "determinable"; the character of my present experience of seeing a fire-engine red floppy disk under dim light is a "determinate" of this character. Since accounting for this complication would also do nothing but encumber the discussion, I'll ignore it as well.

15. A less plausible alternative is that the emotional distress is weird: perhaps of the sort one experiences when one's pet bat eats one's pet beetle.

Zoltán Szabó calls my attention to the Patsy Cline lyric, 'You don't know the meaning of the words 'I love you so' until you find your true love—and then you know'. He suggests that 'so' here functions as a pro-adverb, specifying a way of loving using, in context, a reflective/sympathetic concept.

16. This is not fully adequate: here's a better way. Say that a truth is *simple* iff it is either atomic or results from quantifying some or all of the argument places of an atomic truth with quantifiers of positive polarity. The knowledge argument can then be recast in a somewhat simpler form as arguing validly from the premises that (1) for every physical truth, Mary knows it, and ($2'_s$) Mary does not know the (simple) truth t, to the conclusion that (C'_s) t is a nonphysical (simple) truth. The reason for this restriction is that, without it, the truth that e is either an electron or not an electron ends up being counted as physical, as would be the truth that nothing is an electron (if it were a truth). The passage from the physicality of a truth to the physicality of its subject matter would be obscure without this restriction. t is a simple truth, since it results from generically quantifying the argument position of the atomic truth that this experience is like this. Henceforth I'll leave this complication tacit.

17. See, in addition to the discussion above and in the appendix, Lycan 1995 and Stanley and Williamson 2001.

18. Suppose that the proposition p is of the form $\|o$ is $F\|$. I take it that one finds p to be physical just in case (i) when one entertains the sense of o, one finds its referent to be physical, and (ii) the same for F.

19. Some property correlated with expressibility might be at work here: I discuss such a property below. Expressibility is somewhat more obvious than this other property, so I suspect that expressibility is doing the real work here.

20. "We cannot form to ourselves the idea of a pine-apple, without having actually tasted it." See also the citations in Daly 1998.

21. As I remarked above, I am uncertain whether there are a priori connections between obviously physical and reflective/sympathetic concepts.

22. Jackson (1998) and Chalmers (2002) push lines closely resembling this one.

23. Example: (pointing at a dog) 'I want a dog that is like that (dog)' to mean 'I want a dog that is similar to that (dog)'/'I want a dog that resembles that (dog)'.

24. Special thanks to Harold Hodes for incisive comments on the arguments to follow.

25. Following a suggestion due to Harold Hodes, perhaps resemblance must be conveyed, but what is conveyed is not "first-order" resemblance between my couch and the bearer of the demonstrated instance of redness, but rather "second-order" resemblance between my couch's color and the color of that bearer. According to Hodes, this suggestion makes better sense of the fact that utterances of (d), unlike utterances of 'my couch is thus', need not convey that my couch and that bearer exactly resemble in color. But first, I doubt that utterances of 'my couch is thus' require exact resemblance: perhaps the exact-resemblance intuition results from thinking of 'thus' as stressed, which would require exact resemblance. Second, what is demonstrated can be a determinable property, so I also deny that, according to my view, exact resemblance is required. Third, it is unclear what is meant by the suggestion that properties resemble. Bearers of properties resemble one another in virtue of having properties, say, scarlet and crimson, which are close to one another in some metric of determinates, say, the color solid. So, perhaps if scarlet and crimson resemble one another, they too have properties that are close to one another in some metric of determinates. But what properties could these possibly be? Fourth, it would not be so bad for me were Hodes's suggestion correct, since, if Hodes is correct, what is conveyed must concern a property, rather than an individual. It thus does equally well at replying to Lewis's objection and explaining the specification phenomenon.

26. The '%' represents semantic anomalousness.

27. Thanks to Sally McConnell-Ginet for helpful discussion of this argument.

28. Thanks to Sydney Shoemaker for pressing me on this example.

29. Although there are pairs of *wh*-forms and proforms that do not match so closely in their pronunciation and spelling, such as 'he'/'she'/'who' and 'it'/'that'/'this'/ 'what'/*'whis', these are plausibly regarded as "irregular" forms, which persist in the face of general rules owing to their frequency of occurrence.

A defeasible rule can be extracted from this pattern. The phonological realization of the *wh*-form and the proform of a particular semantic type differ only in that the former begins with a 'wh' sound whereas the latter begins with a 'th' sound. This rule seems to be at work with predicate proforms and predicate *wh*-forms. When 'thus' went out of style to be replaced with 'like that' as the dominant predicate proform, the *wh*-form 'like what' became available.

30. Namely, they can be base-generated in the same positions. In English, a *wh*-form is always pronounced at the beginning of the clause, displaced from the positions in which it is base-generated.

31. Unlike 'thus', 'how' has not gone out of fashion. Thus, English is blessed with an abundance of predicate *wh*-forms, and 'I know what it's like' is equivalent to 'I know how it is'.

32. Something slightly odd happens in generating the predicative reading: the semantic unit 'like what', a predicate *wh*-form, is not being treated as a phonological unit, but has rather become scattered over the sentence. However, this does not indicate that 'like' is meaningless, mere phonological junk, as it is in 'this seminar is on, like, presentism'. If 'like' is absent, the result is 'Mary knows what experiences of seeing a red thing are', which has a somewhat different meaning: it seems to be appropriately answered with an NP, rather than with an adjective. Compare: 'Mary knows what lions are'/'Mary knows what lions are like'. 'Dauntless hunters' adequately specifies the former; 'frightening' completes the latter.

I will speculate wildly about how this scattering arises. For whatever reason, English has lost its proper predicate proform 'thus'. A language needs a predicate proform, so for whatever reason, the compound 'like this/that' was pressed into this role. Standardly a *wh*-form sounds like the proform of its semantic type: see n. 29. So the predicate *wh*-form must become 'like what'. Standard rules of question-formation require *wh* to move away from the position it questions. These rules did not bother to check with the rules that formed 'like what' out of 'like this/that', so they do not recognize that 'like what' is a *wh*-form; as a result, only 'what' gets moved and 'like' is left behind.

33. It's also a rather opinionated overview, which is made necessary by my operating with a theory of propositions somewhat at odds with that employed in the literature on questions. Aside from these departures, my discussion follows that in Stanley and Williamson 2001.

34. Contextually set parameters play an important role at every stage here. To keep the presentation reasonably accessible, I'll simply elide this role.

References

Bigelow, John, and Robert Pargetter. 1990. "Acquaintance With Qualia." *Theoria* 56: 129–147.

Byrne, Alex. 2002. "Something About Mary." *Grazer* 63: 123–140.

Byrne, Alex, and David R. Hilbert, editors. 1997. *Readings on Color: The Philosophy of Color*, volume I. Cambridge, Mass.: The MIT Press.

Chalmers, David J. 2002. "Consciousness and Its Place in Nature." In David J. Chalmers, editor, *Philosophy of Mind: Classical and Contemporary Readings*. Oxford: Oxford University Press.

Daly, Chris. 1998. "Modality and Acquaintance with Properties." *Monist* 81: 44–68.

Hardin, Clyde L. 1997. "Reinverting the Spectrum." In Alex Byrne and David R. Hilbert, editors, *Readings on Color: The Philosophy of Color*, volume I. Cambridge, Mass.: The MIT Press.

Harman, Gilbert. 1996. "Explaining Objective Color in Terms of Subjective Reactions." In Enrique Villanueva, editor, *Perception*, volume 7 of *Philosophical Issues* 1–18. Atascadero: Ridgeview. Reprinted in Byrne and Hilbert 1997.

Hilbert, David R., and Mark K. Kalderon. 2000. "Color and the Inverted Spectrum." In Steven Davis, editor, *Color Perception: Philosophical, Psychological, Artistic, and Computational Perspectives*. Oxford: Oxford University Press.

Hume, David. 1739/1978. *Treatise on Human Nature*. Oxford: Oxford University Press.

Jackson, Frank. 1982. "Epiphenomenal Qualia." *Philosophical Quarterly* 32: 127–136. Reprinted in this volume.

Jackson, Frank. 1986. "What Mary Didn't Know." *Journal of Philosophy* 83: 291–295. Reprinted in this volume.

Jackson, Frank. 1998. *From Metaphysics to Ethics*. Oxford: Oxford University Press.

Johnston, Mark. 1992. "How to Speak of the Colors." *Philosophical Studies* 68: 221–263. Reprinted in Byrne and Hilbert 1997.

Lewis, David. 1988. "What Experience Teaches." *Proceedings of the Russellian Society* 29–57. Reprinted in this volume.

Lewis, David. 1995. "Should a Materialist Believe in Qualia?" *Australasian Journal of Philosophy* 73: 140–144. Reprinted in Lewis 1999.

Lewis, David. 1999. *Papers in Metaphysics and Epistemology*. Cambridge: Cambridge University Press.

Lormand, Eric. In preparation. "The Explanatory Stopgap."

Lycan, William G. 1995. "A Limited Defense of Phenomenal Information." In Thomas Metzinger, editor, *Conscious Experience*. Paderborn: Schöningh.

Nagel, Thomas. 1974. "What Is It Like to Be a Bat?" *Philosophical Review* 83: 435–450.

Stanley, Jason C., and Timothy Williamson. 2001. "Knowing How." *Journal of Philosophy* 98: 411–444.

Williamson, Timothy. 2000. *Knowledge and Its Limits*. Oxford: Oxford University Press.

17 So Many Ways of Saying No to Mary

Robert Van Gulick

I Introduction

The knowledge argument (Jackson 1982, reprinted in this vol.) is deceptively simple but radical in aim. We are asked to imagine a hypothetical history of Mary the super color scientist who is held and then released from achromatic isolation. Our intuitions about what Mary would or would not know before and after her release are then alleged to show that physicalism is false, that is, to refute it by purely a priori means rather than empirically with factual evidence.

One is rightly cautious in accepting so radical a conclusion based on merely hypothetical reasoning. Whether or not it is ever possible to achieve so sweeping a result by such austere means, it is surely seldom so, and the standard of proof is justifiably set very high: both for the argument and any assumptions on which it relies. One must always weigh the competing plausibility or implausibility of the argument's alleged radical conclusion against that of its assumptions. If there is a logical conflict of intuitions with established theories, the more empirically well-supported the theories or models, the more likely we are to assign the blame to our intuitions and defer to evidence and theory.

Nonetheless the knowledge argument has a strong intuitive appeal. It is easily understood even by introductory students, and it provides a tangible vehicle for articulating a deep-seated unease about physicalism that may or may not indicate an a priori defect in the position. It has generated philosophical controversy since it was first proposed, and it has continued to do so, surviving even renunciation and disavowal by its original author, Frank Jackson (1998, reprinted in this volume).

Thus it seems apt to take yet another look at the status of the knowledge argument and the assumptions and intuitions on which it and its critics rely. If it is faulty as so many think it is or must be, one would like to have a good explanation of just where it goes wrong and why it still holds such appeal. Either it is right, in which case it surely deserves our attention, or it is wrong, and we should then like to better understand how it generates such a powerful illusion.

Ten years ago, I (Van Gulick 1993) surveyed the state of play at that time and judged its critics to have gained the upper hand by finding multiple weak points in its argumentative armor. I offered a set of diagnostic questions to sort the various ways in which one might part company with the argument's reasoning, and found several such departure points sufficiently compelling to give one good grounds for rationally resisting its conclusion. That assessment was not universally shared, and even those who might agree in ultimately rejecting the argument and its conclusion might still find the replies that I surveyed not adequate to disarm it or to pinpoint its key defect.

Thus I will begin by briefly reviewing the main lines of response I earlier identified. I believe the questions used ten years ago still distinguish relatively well among the main critical variants, though with a few qualifications that will be noted afterward. Two sorts of revision of the map are needed. On one hand, there seem to be additional ways of disputing the argument and perhaps of "getting off the train" even earlier. On the other hand, by looking further into the details of some of the prior responses we can see some links between them that might not have been obvious before, and as a result some of the original distinctions may begin to blur a bit. Thus I will follow the quick review with the relevant additions and extensions.

As noted above, Jackson himself (1998) has recently come to reject the knowledge argument. In preparing the final draft of this essay, I had the opportunity to read Jackson's explanation of his reasons for doing so (in "Mind and Illusion," this volume), and thus I can now also locate his current view within the space of critical options, which I will do in my final section.

II A Quick Digression on Boomerangs

Before reprising that taxonomy of critical replies, I should note that the knowledge argument is a species of what I have elsewhere (Van Gulick

2003) called "boomerang arguments." (The label is chosen partly in jest of the fact that such arguments have been prominently offered in different forms by Jackson and by David Chalmers, both Australians.) The distinctive feature of a boomerang argument is that it reaches across to the epistemic/cognitive/conceptual domain of facts about our representation of the world, and then swings back to reach a conclusion in the metaphysical/ontological/factual domain about the nature of reality itself. It moves from facts about how we represent or conceptualize the world to supposed results about the necessary nature of the world itself. More specifically, boomerangs often move from supposed gaps or lacks of links in our representations or concepts of the world to conclusions about objective gaps within the world itself and ontological distinctions between the real things in it (ibid.).

The mode of argument has a long but dubious history: there are so many ways in which we might think of, represent, or conceptualize two things as distinct and yet be wrong because they really are the same in ways not apparent to us. The fault or difference often lies not in the world but in our concepts of it. Nonetheless, boomerang arguments have been popular for a long time.

Right at the seventeenth-century start of what we call "modern philosophy," Descartes (1642) attempted in *Meditation VI* to prove the nonidentity of mind and body by appeal to the modal difference in one's supposed ability to imagine one's continued existence in the absence of one's body but not in the absence of one's mind. Of course, as we well know, many things that seem possible or impossible at one stage of scientific knowledge turn out just the opposite with further knowledge of the real structure of the world.

We cannot have water without having H_2O, nor can we have an increase in the heat of a gas without an increase the kinetic energy of its molecules, since, as we have known since the rise of modern chemistry and the demise of caloric theory, these are all that water and the heat of a gas are. The heat of a gas is not some correlate or consequence of its kinetic energy but one and the very same thing. So any attempt to imagine the one without the other is bound to result in a contradiction whether apparent to the earnest imaginer or not. What we imagine at most is a world in which something that is not heat nonetheless shares some of heat's superficial properties. They might be some of those that go to make up what Locke (1689)

called its "nominal" as opposed to its "real" essence, or what in more contemporary two-dimensional semantics might be identified with the primary intension of the term 'heat (of a gas)'. Perhaps we imagine a world in
which something other than molecular kinetic energy affects our thermo-
receptors in a way that mimics heat, as some believe the capsaicin of "hot"
peppers does in this world. That we can do. What we cannot do is imagine
a world in which a gas has an increase of heat (as the kind is picked out by
the secondary or contextually determined intension of 'heat') but has no
increase of molecular kinetic energy.

Prior theories and concepts may not have ruled out their being independent and distinct, but actual empirical discovery reveals that there is
but one thing in the world to which those two concepts both apply in their
partial though effective ways. Thus we now know that real heat and real
kinetic energy—the real things or properties in the world at which our
concepts aim and to which we refer in word and thought—are not capable
of independent existence, because they just are one thing.

Similarly, Descartes's boomerang begs the question against the physicalist. The separate existence of mind without body is conceivable in the
strong sense needed to license a claim of logical possibility and the move to
actual distinctness *only if* mind is in fact distinct from body. If the brain
and mind should be one and the same, then Descartes's attempt to imagine
the one remaining in the absence of the other must lead to a contradiction.
Such a separation would not be logically possible, regardless of how possible it might have *seemed* from his limited conceptual and epistemic perspective. If the lack of entailments between our concepts were sufficient
to validly infer the independence of the items to which they apply, doing
science would be a lot easier. But of course we know it is not. What looked
to Descartes to be an obvious and a priori modal difference need not in
fact reflect any real difference in the world, but merely the limits of his
understanding.

These criticisms are well known, but they have not in themselves sufficed
to prevent new boomerangs from being thrown. Their current wielders are
confident that unlike Descartes's mistaken argument their own attempts to
reach results about reality from mere conceptual and epistemic intuitions
can deflect the sorts of problems that set their predecessors off course, with
various maneuvers including those that invoke two-dimensional semantics
(Chalmers 1996; Jackson 1982). We should remain open to that possibility,

but a fair measure of skepticism about any such attempt would seem to be in order.

The knowledge argument is especially vulnerable and under threat of double faulting in this regard. Not only does it rely on a priori conceptual intuitions to make its case, but the relevant intuitions themselves concern epistemic concepts. It is our supposed intuitions about what would or could (or not) be known in various highly counterfactual situations that lie at the core of the argument. Thus the knowledge argument attempts not only to allow us to infer results about the necessary structure of reality from purely hypothetical reasoning about highly nonactual conditions, it aims to do so by engaging in such reasoning about supposed epistemic facts of what we would or could not know in various situations. Thus we need first to rely on a priori intuitions to reach our supposed epistemic facts and then to infer ontological conclusions from those alleged epistemic limits. If I may push the metaphor a bit, the boomerang has to make a double loop and circle twice within the conceptual epistemic domain before landing back on the real-world, objective side. Again that does not mean the trick cannot be done, but caution and doubt seem justified, as does a high level of critical scrutiny of the argument.

III Resurveying the Range of Replies

The basic structure of the knowledge argument provides the anchor points for the various critical replies I earlier surveyed (1993). The argument, which relies on two main premises and two inferences, might be given in simple form as AK ∼ P:

Argument AK ∼ P

(P1) Mary before her release knows *everything physical* there is to know about seeing red.

(P2) Mary before her release does not know *everything* there is to know about seeing red (because she learns something about it on her release).

Therefore:

(C1) There are some truths about seeing red that escape the physicalist story.

(C2)   Physicalism is false, and phenomenal properties cannot be explained as (or identified with) physical properties.

We can sort most of the critical replies to the argument in terms of the answers they give to a series of successive questions that locate the point at which various critics part company with the original line of argument as shown in figure 17.1.

Q1.   Does Mary learn anything or gain knowledge when she first experiences red?
         //   \\
NO.   (Churchland, Hardin)   YES.
X   Physicalism not refuted. ||
                                                              ||
                                                              \/

Q2.   What sort of knowledge does Mary gain? Is it strictly *know-how*, or does it include new *knowledge of facts or propositions*?
         //   \\
Gains only new know-how.   Gains new knowledge of propositions.
(Lewis, Nemirow) ||
X   Physicalism not refuted. ||
                                                              \/

Q3.   Does Mary upon her release come to know *new facts* and new *propositions*?
         //   \\
NO.   She only comes to know   YES.   She comes to know new propositions.
old propositions in a new way. ||
(Tye, Horgan, Churchland) ||
X   Physicalism not refuted. ||
                                                              \/

Q4.   On what mode of individuation does Mary learn a new proposition?
         //   \\
Only on a fine-grained mode.   On a coarse-grained mode.
(Lycan, Loar)   (Jackson pre-1998)
X   Physicalism not refuted.   Physicalism refuted.

(Each "**X**" marks a point at which the knowledge argument is blocked.)

Figure 17.1
Map of critical options.

Most critics do not take issue with the argument before its second premise. Premise (1) plausibly gets a pass since it functions more or less as a stipulation (though as we will see below in section IV its status as stipulation does not immunize it against all challenge). (P1) provides the key component of the three-part antecedent of the conditional on which the hypothetical reasoning all turns.

If

- Mary were to know everything physical there is to know about seeing red
- while never having herself experienced red, and
- she were then released and allowed to see red,

then what would she learn or come to know?

Different replies to the argument disagree at various points with its story about what comes after the "then." According to the knowledge argument, Mary gains new knowledge of a phenomenal sort, whose existence suffices to refute physicalism. Scope is important here. It is not that Mary comes to know something that suffices to refute physicalism; she has no access to any such proposition, nor does the argument claim she does. What supposedly refutes physicalism is not *what* she learned, but rather the mere fact *that* she learned it. For if physicalism were true, it would seem there could be nothing left for her to learn, given the assumption that she already knew everything physical there was to know. The argument thus might be read as an intended reductio of any physicalist claim to exhaust (factual or knowable) reality as in (PEx).

(PEx)   The physical facts are all the facts there are.

The argument contends that were (PEx) true, there would not have been anything left for Mary to learn upon her release, but since she does (PEx) must be false.

Thus the first obvious point for disagreement is in answer to question (Q1).

(Q1)   Does May learn anything or gain any knowledge when she first experiences red?

The knowledge argument assumes a positive answer, but some critics dispute that (Churchland 1985; Hardin 1988).

The argument appeals to intuitions that are supposed to lead us to imagine a scene in which Mary would express surprise and perhaps say something such as, "At last I really know what it is like to see red." Or if Mary were feeling philosophical she might add, "Now (and only now) do I know the full subjective nature of red experience." That at least is how the argument imagines our intuitions going.

Some critics think otherwise. They fault the argument for underdescribing the hypothetical situation in ways that produce off-target intuitions.

In particular there is the danger that one's intuitions will conflate the stipulated conditions with more normal cases of real knowers, whose physical knowledge is vastly more modest than that which Mary is supposed to have. Indeed we are asked to assume that she knows *everything* physical there is to know about having a red experience. Such absolutely comprehensive physical knowledge—complete knowledge of every physical science detail of the relevant brain states including every aspect, whether microphysical, chemical, physiological, neuroanatomical or neural-network-dynamical, as well as every link and detail in between—is so unlike that which any of us might ever come close to having, that our intuitions in thinking about such an extreme case are easily diverted and led astray.

The cognitive constraints that operate on our epistemic concepts and structure our intuitions about how they might apply in hypothetical situations are conditioned heavily by their operation in their actual domain of application and engagement. We can of course extend our reasoning and thought into counterfactual situations, and try to apply our concepts in nonactual domains. But the farther those contexts diverge from our own, the less likely will those concepts apply unproblematically in the full range of encountered cases. Thus caution is in general prudent when reaching intuitive a priori judgments about highly nonactual hypotheticals.

The general worry clearly applies to the specific case of Mary and especially to the unlimited range of physical knowledge we are asked by assumption to impute to her. As a matter of actual human cognitive limits, it may well be impossible for any real human to know all that Mary is supposed to know. It might simply outrun our human memory capacity, the limits on what we can hold in attention, or our computational and integrative powers; indeed Jackson (this volume) concedes that it would do so. But Jackson and defenders of the knowledge argument regard these as mere "practical limits." They believe what matters is what can be known "in principle." What humans cannot in practice know might still in principle be knowable by our cognitive superiors: supercognitive humans freed from our contingent limitations. And yet even *Super* Mary would not know all there is to know. According to the argument's defenders, Mary's pre-release limits do not derive from any quantitative limits on *how much* she can know but on the fact that everything she knows is *physical*. And so Super Mary's ability to know such things without quantitative limit does not give her any real advantage over Mary in the key respect. More physical knowledge—no matter how extensive or exhaustive—will not do the job. Or so, at least, that is how the argument's defenders imagine our intuitions would play.

Some critics feel otherwise (Churchland 1985; Hardin 1988). They believe that if one describes the hypothetical case fully and emphasizes the highly nonactual and absolutely comprehensive nature of Mary's physical knowledge, then our intuitions will have to be recalibrated, with the result that for many people the mostly likely scenario might become Mary's lack of surprise and her saying something much more like, "Yes, it is just as I knew it would be". Or waxing more philosophical she might declaim, "This experience fully confirms my predictions and prior inferred knowledge of the phenomenal aspect of seeing red as detailed in my physico-neural model of color experience." The fact that in real-world situations any actual and partial physical stories we might get would leave us in the dark about what it is like to be in such a state should not be projected onto the case of Mary or Super Mary without good argument for treating the cases as equivalent.

The hypothetical epistemic situation is so unlike the real-world contexts in which we operate that it is difficult to have uncontroversial intuitions about it. Can the knowledge argument's defenders make the case that their imagined scenario of Mary's postrelease surprise is the only a priori acceptable one? Can they assume that the alternative imagined by its critics—that in which Mary proclaims confirmation of her prior expectations—can be ruled out as impossible by pure a priori reflection on our concepts? It is a big assumption to make, and one can already feel the counterbalancing of plausibility between the argument's assumptions and its radical conclusion. The argument's need for a decisive intuitive judgment in favor of its preferred scenario may seem a thin reed on which to hang so momentous a metaphysical result.

Thus some critics may feel justified in parting company with the argument already at this preliminary stage by simply answering "No" to question (Q1). They may believe that, given a proper appreciation of the extent and comprehensiveness of Mary's prior physical knowledge, the proper reply is, "No, Mary would not learn anything or come to any new knowledge. She would have known it all already."

A negative reply to (Q1) would stop the knowledge argument at the outset; thus it offers a first potential point for parting from its line of reasoning. Since my aim for now is to review my original survey, I will follow it by leaving matters with (Q1) thus unresolved and open to conflicting intuitions. However, when we turn below to amending that review, we will find that there may be ways of departing from the argument even earlier by challenging (P1). Moreover, we will also need to consider ways in which supporters of the argument—though not Jackson himself (1998)—might defend their positive reply to (Q1) and their favored intuitions by appeal to a seemingly plausible empiricist thesis about the necessarily experiential origin of some sorts of knowledge, which we can call in deference to John Locke (1689) "The Pineapple Principle." However, we will put off those matters until later in section IV after we have completed our survey in review.

Most critics of the knowledge argument are willing to concede that Mary learns something upon her release but still deny that its conclusion follows. Their disagreements arise further along in the argument's reasoning, which thus brings us to our second diagnostic question, (Q2).

(Q2)   What sort of knowledge does Mary gain? Is it strictly *know-how* or does it include new *knowledge of facts or propositions?*

One prominent line of reply to the knowledge argument, originally proposed by Lawrence Nemirow (1980, 1990) and supported by the late David Lewis (1988), concedes that Mary gains knowledge upon her release but insists that all she gains is added *know-how*. According to this so-called ability reply Mary gains new skills and abilities to imagine and recognize certain states as red experiences, but she gains no new propositional knowledge. If we follow Lewis in regarding a gain of propositional knowledge as a reduction of uncertainty and a narrowing of one's knowledge of one's location in the space of possibilities, then according to the ability reply Mary gains no such knowledge upon her release. Her exhaustive physical knowledge already suffices to eliminate any uncertainty about the nature of her state or her location in possibility space. If physicalism is true, then once the physical facts are set there are no genuine options or possibilities left open; one's location has been fully determined.

Mary's state is surely different after her release. Her brain has actually now been in the physical state that is identical with seeing red, and as a result of having been in it she may well acquire practical abilities to reproduce that state again in herself through an act of purposeful imagination or to recognize it as the same (or nearly so) should it (or some similar state) reoccur. These skills may well be ones that Mary lacked before. Her mastery of the physical descriptions of such states—no matter how detailed and complete—need not have given her any such abilities to produce or recognize their occurrence in her own brain from the inside. Knowing the physical details of some gastric state does not by itself enable me to produce it in my stomach.

Brains, for obvious reasons, have significant abilities to put themselves back into prior states and to distinguish between various states that they have been in, but many such abilities seem to depend on having been in the relevant state at some prior time. The system's ability to put itself into the state is a matter of its being able to get back to some state that has left a causal imprint on its structure and dynamics. Perhaps the brain's network activity has something to do with it. Networks, like those in the brain that subserve learning, often show a tendency to move back into prior activation patterns. The networks show "biases" in favor of some such past patterns of activity.

Whatever the underlying explanation, the basic facts of memory, imagination, and recognition are obvious from the first-person point of view and accepted as matters of folk psychology. Having seen or heard something novel, one typically gains some ability to call it back through an act of memory or imagination and to recognize like states when they arise on subsequent occasions. So it seems uncontroversial to suppose that Mary upon first seeing red gains some such practical abilities and skills. Thus at least *part* of what she gains is practical know-how, but the key question is whether or not that is *all* that she gains. Advocates of the ability reply say, "Yes, that is all she gains," while others among both the argument's supporters and its critics disagree and claim, "No, she gains more than just new know-how."

Once again we are left with a clash of epistemic intuitions about our highly hypothetical case. Supporters of the ability reply may defend their preferred intuitions by portraying the contrary view as mistaking the mere acquisition of a new mental skill as a gain in factual or propositional knowledge. They will try to get others to see that what looks like new propositional knowledge is just an illusion or confusion about Mary's new abilities. However, they seem unlikely to persuade many of those who disagree to switch their intuitions. The pull of the contrary view, according

to which Mary comes to some new propositional or factual knowledge about the nature of red experience and what it is like, seems too
compelling to dispel by mere appeal to alleged illusions that supposedly
confuse new abilities with gains in propositional knowledge. Nor are
attempts at swaying intuitions in the contrary direction any more likely to
succeed.

Thus we seem left at an impasse of conflicting intuitions with little present hope of decisive resolution. Finding a way around the stalemate will
likely require some rethinking of the issue that places the specific question
asked by (Q2) in a larger context, one that offers a different perspective on
the issue and thus perhaps provides some insights that enable us to see our
way more clearly through the thicket of conflicting intuitions. I will consider some such possibilities below in section IV when we get around to
extending the original survey, but let me first continue my review by sum-
ming the state of play with (Q2) and then moving on to our next diagnostic question.

If we answer (Q2) as the supporters of the ability reply do, then the
knowledge argument is blocked and its antiphysicalist conclusion does not
follow. If all Mary gains is new know-how, then her prior comprehensive
physical knowledge need not have left her with any lack in propositional
or factual knowledge, and the physicalist account of what is real has not
proven incomplete. However, the question of whether that is all she gains
remains open to conflicting intuitions. If one answers (Q2) to the contrary
and holds that Mary gains more than just new know-how, then one will
need to move farther into the argument: either all the way to its conclusion
or to some further point down the line at which one finds some other
reason to depart, which brings us to (Q3).

(Q3)   Does Mary upon her release come to know *new facts* and new
propositions?

(Q3) might seem to be redundant and to be simply reasking that already
posed by (Q2), but there is an important difference indicated by the shift
in what 'new' modifies. (Q2) asks whether Mary gained any *new knowledge*
of a propositional or factual sort, whereas (Q3) inquires as to whether Mary
has gained knowledge of *new propositions or new facts*. In (Q3) the 'new'
applies to the facts and propositions known, whereas (Q2) concerns 'new
knowledge'.

The difference might be significant if one believes that there may be enough of a change in Mary's epistemic state to count it as a new state of knowledge, even if it has the same propositional object as some epistemic state she had already been in before her release. This might be so, for example, if after her release she comes to know a previously known proposition in some quite different way. The newness of the knowledge state might turn on some aspect other than the novelty of its propositional object, perhaps on its affording a new mode of access to it. For example, Mary might come to know directly by introspection or acquaintance some fact or proposition she had previously known only indirectly through theoretical inference. Or perhaps Mary gains the ability to represent the relevant proposition in a new system or medium of representation; she might now be able to use some basic biological system of representation to grasp a proposition that she had previously been able to comprehend only through the medium of scientific theory. Yet if the properties and relations that constitute that fact or proposition are the same as those known before, one might justifiably describe her not as learning a new proposition but only as coming to know an old (i.e., previously known) proposition in a new way.

Indeed this is just the line taken by some critics (Horgan 1984; Churchland 1985; Tye 1986) who concede in reply to (Q2) that Mary gains new propositional knowledge but deny in response to (Q3) that she comes to know any new propositions. That conjunction of replies need not entail a contradiction as long as one is willing to individuate two states of propositional knowledge as distinct on some basis other than their having different propositional objects. If two states of propositional knowledge can share the same propositional object yet count as different, then there is the possibility of conceding that Mary learns more than know-how, but nonetheless the range of propositions that she knows does not increase. One could consistently give a "Yes" to (Q2) and a "No" to (Q3).

A negative answer to (Q3) thus provides an alternative and less obvious way of resisting the knowledge argument. If Mary does not come to know any new propositions, then none need have been left out by the physical story that she knew before release. If the only sense in which she gains new propositional knowledge is that she acquires new ways to access or represent propositions she already knew, then her epistemic change need pose no threat to physicalism. However, it is the innocuous nature of such a change that leads others to reject it as not doing justice to the intuitions that motivate the knowledge argument. David Lewis (1988), for example, argued that it would trivialize the notion of gaining new propositional knowledge. Lewis argued that such an interpretation would lead to the absurd conclusion that one would gain a wealth of new propositional knowledge simply by learning a new language—whether French or Urdu—that allowed one to represent to oneself in a new way facts one already new. That I can now represent the proposition that snow is white to myself by use of the French sentence, "La neige est blanche," or the Urdu sentence, "Barf safed hoti hai," would not seem to add to my stock of propositional knowledge, at least not to that about matters of color or winter precipitation as opposed to any linguistic facts I might have learned about French or Urdu themselves. Such critics dismiss the strategy of drawing the line at (Q3) and argue that nothing should count as a gain in propositional knowledge unless it involves coming to know new propositions and thus adding to the range of propositions that one knows. It would be at best misleading to count anything less as "new propositional knowledge," or so at least they claim.

Once again there is room for disagreement, with proponents of the (Q3) strategy on one side and on the other a mix of those who support the knowledge argument and those like Lewis who wish to reject it but on other grounds. Clearly the supporters of the argument intend for Mary to gain new propositional knowledge in the stronger sense of coming to know new propositions. Nothing less would suffice to secure their antiphysicalist conclusion. Nor is it plausible to read the notion so weakly as to count mere mastery of a foreign language as sufficient for gaining new propositional knowledge of previously known matters, whether about the weather or anything else. However, those who aim to draw their line against the knowledge argument with a positive answer to (Q2) and negative to (Q3) do not seem to be making so simple and obvious an error. Moving from an ability to represent facts about the nature of color experience in the language of theoretical neuroscience to being able to do so through the use of an innate biologically based system of coding seems a far larger and less trivial change than switching from English to French or Urdu in describing facts about snow. Moreover, the change in the system of representation is so much more radical in the former case, that it seems far more likely that one might confusedly regard a new representation of an old fact as a case of actually coming to know a new fact or proposition. Of course those who support the knowledge argument do not intend it in that way, but the aim of its critics is to undermine the argument by showing how the intuition on which it relies might result from error or confusion rather than epistemic reality.

The situation is further complicated by the diversity of ways in which one might individuate propositions. (Q3) asks whether Mary comes to know any new propositions, but there is controversy as well as about what should count as distinct propositions. The issues raised by (Q3) thus run into those in (Q4), the final diagnostic question in our reprised survey:

(Q4)   On what mode of individuating propositions does Mary learn a new proposition?

(Q4) comes into play only if one has given a positive answer to all the prior questions including (Q3). If, on the contrary, one denies that Mary learns any new propositions, (Q4) is moot. (Q4) provides a seemingly final site in our review at which to disagree with the knowledge argument, one that allows the critic to concede the Mary gains knowledge some of which involves learning new propositions, and yet still resist its final antiphysicalist conclusion. Making such a last-minute swerve depends on individuating propositions in a fine-grained intensional way.

Propositions and facts can be individuated in various coarse- or fine-grained ways depending on what range of factors one counts as making propositions the same or distinct. On the coarse side, one might identify propositions with functions from possible worlds to truth-values, or equivalently as the range of worlds in which the function for a given proposition assigns the value True. The proposition that snow is white is defined in terms of the conditions under which it is true; any other proposition true under the same and only the same conditions would count as the same proposition. Thus logically equivalent propositions get collapsed into a single proposition. On such a coarse-grained mode of individuation, the proposition that $5 + 7 = 12$ is the same as the proposition that $\sqrt{63} = 3 \times \sqrt{7}$. They are both necessary mathematical truths and thus both true in every possible world. Since they have the same function from worlds to truth-value, namely the necessary function that assigns the value True to every possible world, they count as the same coarse-grained proposition. Lewis, who often defined propositions as such functions, held as we saw above that an increase in propositional knowledge requires a reduction in uncertainty and a correlated narrowing of one's location in the space of possibilities. In that respect as well the two mathematical propositions are the same. Neither locates me within any subdomain of the space of possible worlds, since both hold in all worlds. Of more direct relevance to the mind–brain case is the fact that the coarse-grained scheme of individuation also counts the propositions "This cup contains water" and "This cup contains H_2O" as the same. Given the scientifically established identity of water with H_2O, whatever is true of water at a world is true there of H_2O as well since they are one and the same substance. Or if one prefers to talk of properties, one can identify the property of "being water" with that of "being H_2O"; they are one and the same real property whatever differences there may be in the two concepts by which we pick it out. Properties as well can thus be defined as functions from worlds, but here they are taken as functions from worlds to sets of objects, those that at that world possess that property. On that scheme as well, water and H_2O everywhere coincide.

Alternatively one might individuate propositions more finely by distinguishing them in terms of their internal intensional structure, most especially in terms of the incorporated concepts by which they respectively determine their coarse-grained functions. $5 + 7 = 12$ might coincide at its world-to-truth-value function with $\sqrt{63} = 3 \times \sqrt{7}$, but still be counted as a different fine-grained proposition on the basis of the difference in the constituent concepts by which they respectively construct the overall world-to-value function that they share.

What then of the proposition that *the cup contains water* and the proposition that *the cup contains H_2O*? Are they the same proposition or not on such a mode of individuation? The overall propositions share the same world-to-truth-value function, and the reference function for 'water' coincides at every world with that for 'H_2O'. They pick out the same property and the same objects, stuff, or regions in every world. They can not diverge since as we said above water just is H_2O; there is only one real property in the world apprehended from two conceptual modes of access. The issue thus is whether or not mere differences in such access or mode of presentation at the conceptual level should lead us to distinguish between two such propositions. Should the differences between our concepts of 'water' and 'H_2O' matter even though they pick out the same real property? Should two propositions that coincide everywhere except that one employs the concept 'water' and the other 'H_2O' be counted as different or the same? The question has no absolute answer. Both modes of individuation are available and well behaved; the issue is which system of categorization and individuation better fits the context at hand. The sorts of situations that we want to model or explain will to a large extent determine which mode of individuation is most apt.

How then should propositions be individuated in the context of the knowledge argument? At a minimum the argument must treat the notion consistently in its various steps to be valid. The claim that Mary learns a new proposition must rely on the same mode of individuation as does the claim that if the complete physicalist story leaves out any true propositions then physicalism is false. The two claims must agree in how they count propositions as the same or different. If they do not, the argument's premises would not connect to support its conclusion.

A coarse-grained mode of individuation, for example, by world-to-truth-value function, would seem to underwrite the latter hypothetical claim about physicalism. Its claim to be a comprehensive account of reality would seem in doubt if it were shown to leave out propositions of the coarse-grained sort (though on this point as well questions will be raised in section IV). But what if all the physical story left out were propositions that differed in only the fine-grained sense from ones that were included? Would physicalism's claim to completeness be undermined by the mere fact that it does not capture or include every variant conceptualization of the real states of affairs and real properties that it nonetheless succeeds in picking out through purely physical concepts?

It would seem not, at least if physicalism is interpreted along the lines of the sort of nonreductive physicalism that has become in one form of another the mainline position in the contemporary philosophy of mind. Nonreductive physicalism combines (or at least aims to combine) a commitment to ontological physicalism with a pluralist attitude about theories, concepts, and modes of representation. Everything that is real is physical in the sense that it is in some way or another realized by underlying physical processes or structures. But that universality of physical realization is compatible with our epistemic and theoretical need for a diversity of means of representing and modeling reality, including many that fall outside the domain of physical theory and the conceptual and representational resources it provides. Every economic transaction may be fully realized by physical events and processes but no one would ever suppose that the physical sciences provide adequate means for describing, modeling, or explaining economic regularities. To think otherwise would be to adopt a form of extreme cognitive or conceptual imperialism about the reach of physical theory. One surely need not buy into such an implausibly strong view about physical theory as a universal cognitive tool in order to count as a physicalist in good standing. Indeed nonreductive physicalists reject that very demand in their commitment to theoretical and conceptual pluralism. So if the only sense in which Mary learns a new proposition is in the fine-grained sense that reflects distinctions of internal conceptual structure, then her acquisition of new knowledge upon release need not conflict with physicalism, at least not if physicalism is interpreted as a basic ontological claim with no pretension that physical science by itself provides all the concepts and modes of representing that we might validly use or require for our diversity of cognitive engagements with the world (Loar 1990; Lycan 1990b; Van Gulick 1985, 1992).

Still, as one of the editors of this volume (D. Stoljar) has advised me, a defender of the knowledge argument might object that Mary prior to release should at least in principle be able to infer every fine-grained proposition true of seeing red from the totality of strictly physical facts. If we let "P" stand for the physical facts and "E" for the experiential facts, does physicalism entail that the conditional P → E is a priori? If it does, then it would seem that Mary should be able to infer the truth of E and thus of any true fine-grained proposition about red experience before her release. Her inability to do so would thus seem to refute any version of physicalism that entails the a prioricity of P → E. I think the right response is to deny that P → E is a priori, at least if E is taken to include every fine-grained proposition true of experiencing red. The physicalist is committed to the necessity of the conditional but not to its being a priori knowable or to Mary's being able to deduce E from P. In particular, there may be good reasons, as I will discuss below in section IV, for believing that Mary prior to her release could not command all of the concepts needed to grasp some of the fine-grained propositions included in E. If she cannot even grasp the relevant fine-grained propositions, she surely is in no position to infer their truth. Though her conceptual limitations might thus deny her cognitive access to some fine-grained proposition E*, she could know some proposition P* that counts as the same as E* on a more coarse-grained mode of individuation. As long as she knows the truth of P* prior to release, her coming to know E* afterward would not involve any reduction in her uncertainty of a sort that would pose a problem for physicalism. Her inability to infer every fine-grained proposition necessitated by the physical facts need pose no problem for the physicalist. Thus the knowledge argument can allow us to deduce the falsity of physicalism from the incompleteness of Mary's propositional knowledge only if incompleteness entails her failing to know some proposition in the coarse-grained sense.

Consistency thus leads us to ask how step (A2) of the argument fares if read as relying on that same coarse-grained mode of individuation. Can Mary be said to learn a new proposition in that sense? Does she learn a proposition in the Lewisian sense of reducing her uncertainty and fixing herself more locally in the space of possibilities? Or is it only in the more fine-grained sense that she comes to know something new that was earlier left out? Does she gain only a new line of conceptual access to the same states of affairs she already knew? Those who wish to use (Q4) to cut the knowledge off late in the game clearly believe that the propositions that Mary learns are new only in the fine-grained sense. However, supporters of the argument think otherwise and claim that what Mary comes to know about the experience of seeing red involves not merely reconceptualization of old facts, but facts not previously known under any conceptualization. Given the highly abstract nature of the matters about which the two sides present their respective intuitions, it is difficult to see what might resolve the conflict. One side sees mere reconceptualization of a coarse fact involving one and the same property apprehended under differing modes of presentation. The other side sees a new fact that picks out a real property not previously included in the physicalist story. So which is it to be: new property and new coarse proposition, or old property grasped through new concept and new fine-grained proposition? How is one to decide? Is mere reflection on what one's introspective experience would be like in such a hypothetical situation supposed to provide all one needs to decide the conflict? That surely seems unlikely, and this may be yet another point at which one may wish to weigh the competing plausibility of the argument's assumptions against that of its radical conclusion.

How should someone who is otherwise disposed toward physicalism on scientific grounds weigh the cost of crediting the argument's intuition that Mary learns a new proposition in the coarse-grained sense against the cost of having to reject physicalism? How much greater weight must we assign to the coarse-grained intuition over the fine-grained one in order for it to outweigh the prior positive value assigned to physicalism? When we have conflicting plausible intuitions, one of whose acceptance would require us to make a major modification in our accepted and otherwise empirically supported theory of reality, it is not irrational to demand that the destructive intuition achieve a clear victory over its competitor in order to win our acceptance of its high cost. The knowledge argument seems unlikely to win any such decisive victory in the conflict of intuitions raised by (Q4). Thus, even those, like nonreductive physicalists, who might follow its line of argument through (Q1), (Q2), and (Q3) will be inclined to disagree at (Q4). They will claim that Mary learns new propositions in only the fine-grained sense, and that no a priori reasoning about our concepts can rule out the possibility that the property of experiencing red that Mary conceptualizes introspectively after her release is just the same as some physico-neural property that she had already earlier grasped through physical concepts. Absent some compelling reason to reject that view in favor of the conflicting intuition, the physicalist can take his stand at the (Q4) point and rationally decline to take the argument's final step. (Q4) thus provides yet one more basis for declining to accept the argument or its conclusion.

Let me sum up my reprise of the critical survey of options. We asked four diagnostic questions, each of which offered the chance of answering in a way that would suffice to stop the argument and block its conclusion. In each case the answers remain open to plausible dispute and contention. Something can always be said on behalf of the answer required by the argument, but plausible reasons can also always be made for the alternative intuition. Going against the argument's preferred option in any of the four cases would by itself suffice to disable the argument. One might deny that Mary would learn anything given her vast physical knowledge (Q1). Second, one might hold that all Mary gains is new *know-how* and new abilities (Q2). A third option would be to claim that Mary comes not to learn any new propositions but only to know old propositions in a new way (Q3). Finally, one might hold that Mary learns new propositions but only in the fine-grained sense (Q4).

To repeat my invitation of a decade ago, "Choose your favorite. Take your pick." Those who find physicalism otherwise plausible have ample options for rationally resisting the knowledge argument and its radical contrary conclusion. Indeed, given that the argument's success requires winning all four contests between conflicting plausible intuitions, it is difficult to understand why physicalists have devoted as much attention to the argument as they have. It would not seem to pose much of a threat. Perhaps, like a porch light pulling moths off-course, it is just too attractive to pass by—even if one is drawn in only to refute it. In fairness, I should note that two editors of this volume (D. Stoljar and Y. Nagasawa) have argued to the contrary that the very disunity of physicalist responses to the knowledge argument suggests that physicalists lack a clear answer to the challenge that it poses. Thus it may be useful at some point in the next section to consider whether the four seemingly incompatible responses I have surveyed might fit together more consistently with a bit of tinkering.

IV Going Farther—New Options and Connections

Having rewalked the previously surveyed terrain, we can turn now to explore a few additional features of the logical geography of critical options. A good point to begin is with the empiricist assumption mentioned above to which supporters of the argument might appeal on behalf of their reply to (Q1). They claim that Mary would learn something new when released, no matter how much physical knowledge she might have had before. That confidence in turn derives largely from the complementary empiricist view that her lack of prerelease red experience guarantees her lack of certain kinds of experiential knowledge. According to what we may call "The Pineapple Principle," in allusion to Locke's original example of the taste of that then-exotic fruit, some knowledge is essentially empathetic or subjective and can be gained only by undergoing the relevant experience. As Locke writes in the *Essay on Human Understanding* (1689):

I think it will be granted easily that if a child were kept in a place where he never saw any other than black and white till he were a man, he would have no more ideas of scarlet or green, than he that from his childhood never tasted an oyster, or a pineapple, would have of those relishes. (Book II, chap. 1, sect 6)

The Pineapple Principle, or something like it, seems to drive the intuition that Mary's prior knowledge would inevitably be incomplete, even though Jackson (1998) himself denies that the knowledge argument relies on it. The relevant assumption is not quite the same as Locke's original, since he was concerned with the necessity of sensation as the means of acquiring certain ideas. Were someone to have induced a red experience in Mary before her release through direct cortical stimulation rather than by holding a red object before her eyes, that would suffice to end her isolation and void the antecedent conditions of the argument's main hypothetical. What is crucial about Mary before her release is not merely that she has never seen actual red objects, but that she has never had a red experience produced in any way, whether by red visual stimuli or otherwise. What matters is the range of her past experiences, and the relevant empiricist assumption concerns the limits on what we can know or understand about experiences of kinds that we have never had. If you have never had a taste of pineapple experience, then there are some real respects in which you lack knowledge about it or about what it is like.

One further qualification may be needed for those who accept some form of physical supervenience: the principle that two beings alike in every physical respect share all their other properties as well. If one accepts such supervenience, a counterexample to the Pineapple Principle might arise if we could imagine constructing a molecular duplicate of someone, call her Ramy, who has had past red experiences but is not having any now (Unger 1966). Since the duplicate DRamy is newly created it has itself never had a red experience. Yet since DRamy is a molecule-for-molecule duplicate of Ramy and Ramy knows what red experiences are like, it would follow by the supervenience thesis that DRamy has such knowledge as well. Thus, given supervenience, the possibility of such duplicates would seem to rule out the strict necessity of actual past experience as a cause of present knowledge of the relevant type of experience.

Thus, if one wants to formulate the empiricist assumption in a way likely to command the widest agreement, it may be necessary to accommodate such cases; but they pose no real problems for the advocates of the knowledge argument. Since its supporters accept its dualist conclusion, many of them might likely reject supervenience as well. Alternatively, if their aim is to construct an argument whose steps will be accepted by those who come to it as physicalists, then a suitably qualified version might be constructed that should still suffice to underwrite the intuition they wish to support. Thus the argument is not affected either way by whether or not molecular duplicates might share a color-experienced person's knowledge of what it's like. Mary is not such a duplicate, and the question is whether or not she lacks such knowledge before her release. All the formulations of the Pineapple Principle, whether qualified or not, would seem to indicate she must. Thus the contest of intuitions moves to the empiricist principle itself: are there forms of knowledge about experience that can be had only by those who have themselves had such experiences (or their duplicates)?

The truth or falsity of the principle is most directly relevant to (Q1). Supporters of the knowledge argument might buttress their intuition that Mary learns something upon her release by appeal to what the principle tells us about what she could not have known earlier. The appeal is not mandated; some supporters of the argument might reject the Pineapple Principle but still give a positive answer to (Q1). One could do so consistently, but at the cost of needing to find other support for one's intuitions about (Q1) and Mary's gain of knowledge. Although the Pineapple Principle seems most directly relevant to (Q1), its overall implications for the knowledge argument are less obvious though perhaps no less important. As we will see below, the principle, or at least a near relative of it framed in terms of the *capacity to have* specific types of experience, may be not only consistent with physicalism but entailed by some plausible versions of it.

The view that lies behind the Pineapple Principle is largely the same as that which leads Thomas Nagel to his claim that it is impossible for humans to fully understand what it is like to have batlike echolocatory perceptual experiences (Nagel 1974). We lack the phenomenal modalities to undergo or project ourselves fully into alien forms of experience that lie outside our phenomenal range. We are thus limited in our ability to know or understand all the subjective phenomenal features that one might come to know or understand from the internal perspective of those who do include them in their experiential repertoire. To state the matter more in Nagel's terms, there are *subjective facts* about experience, where 'subjective' means a fact that can be fully understood only from a specific perspective, namely that associated with the ability to have or undergo such experiences oneself. Only a creature able itself to experience red can fully know or understand the subjective fact of what it is like to have a red experience. If full understanding or knowledge requires empathy, then one can have such projective understanding only for states that are enough like those that we ourselves can be in. Insofar as we can not be experientially like a bat, we have a parallel lack in our ability to know or understand it is like to be conscious in that batlike way. More specifically, insofar as we can not *be* experientially batlike, we cannot fully *understand or know* what it is like to experience batlikely.

Cases like the bat seem to show that there are subjective facts and empathetic ways of knowing that give access to facts that would not otherwise be open to understanding. Some physicalists might challenge the empiricist assumption for reasons like those that lead them to answer "No" to (Q1). They might call into doubt our negative intuitions about what Mary supposedly could not know, by reminding us of the absolutely comprehensive nature of the physical knowledge attributed to her by stipulation. Can the argument's proponents assume that, even given such knowledge on a scale and level so unlike any that we come close to having at present, Mary still would not know or understand the facts about what seeing red is like? Is the intuition that the argument requires about such a radically contrary-to-fact case so obvious that it precludes reasonable doubt to the contrary? My sympathies lie with the Pineapple Principle and the belief in subjective facts, but I must confess that the opposing intuition cannot be readily dismissed as obviously mistaken.

However, the more interesting question is what implications the existence of subjective facts might have for the knowledge argument or for the state of physicalism. Both Nagel (1974) and supporters of the knowledge argument seem to regard subjective facts as incompatible with the truth of physicalism. If one is thinking of physical knowledge as solely third-person knowledge of the sort one might get from studying physical theory, then physicalism's claim to completeness might seem to preclude there being any subjective facts knowable only from a given experiential perspective. Physical science facts are objective facts par excellence; they are of just the sort that might be understood from a plurality of perspectives, for example, by us and by Martian scientists who do not share our sensory modes but who nonetheless accept similar physical theories. Thus if 'physical facts' means 'physical theory facts', then subjective facts—if any exist—would seem to fall outside that range.

However, if one reads 'physical facts' in a broader way to mean all the facts 'that obtain *in virtue of* physical processes' or 'that are *realized by* underlying physical structures', then it is far less clear that no such facts might be subjective in the sense of being perspectivally restricted in their knowability. Nonreductive physicalists in particular will be quick to deny that any such exclusion is entailed. Ontologically reductive physicalism—the metaphysical view that everything real is physically realized—does not entail representationally reductive physicalism or require that the resources of physical theory should suffice for representing and understanding everything that can be known or understood about any feature of the physically realized world. As noted above, nonreductive physicalism rejects conceptual-representational imperialism and the view that physical science gives us all the tools we need for understanding in every context of application, whether it be ecology, economics, or psychology. Ontological realization does not entail that the methods sufficient for modeling the entities and actions at the level of underlying realization must suffice as well for modeling or understanding all the higher-level aspects of the realized systems and their modes of interaction, especially since the relevant modeling needs to be done by particularly structured cognitive agents engaged and situated in a diverse range of contexts of application and interaction. Given the multiple parameters that condition those contexts of understanding and the intentional relations they subserve, it becomes all the less plausible to regard physical theory as a universal tool of understanding or as an all-purpose medium providing commensurable translations of everything that might be validly represented or expressed by any other engaged and situated cognitive system about any aspect of the physically realized world.

This is especially so when the system being understood and the one doing the understanding are one and the same, as they are in consciously self-understanding systems, such as a human or a bat. The nonreductive physicalist should not be at all surprised that such systems are able to understandingly engage their own physically realized dynamic features in ways that cannot be duplicated by any cognitively equivalent external mode of access.

Indeed, I have long argued (1985, 1992) that the existence of subjective facts is not only compatible with physicalism but predicted and entailed by the sort of teleo-pragmatic physicalism that I take to be most plausible. I will not repeat those earlier arguments here in detail, but give just the main idea. According to the teleo-pragmatic view, understanding is always a matter of the potential for successful practical engagement, which often involves mutual reciprocal interaction and perhaps what might be called 'causal resonance' or 'causal harmonic engagement'. The intentional profile or content associated with such understanding is very much a function of the causal profile of their engagement and the sort of access it affords the understander to interact successfully with that which it understands. It is highly unlikely that we could fashion any structure through the use of external third-person physical theory that would allow us to come close to duplicating the causal profile associated with the way in which a complex physically realized self-understanding system, such as a bat or human mind–brain, understands itself.

Nor need the teleo-pragmatic physicalist, or any nonreductive physicalist, think otherwise. The contexts of application for the respective representations are so dissimilar that it is unlikely we can use the one to replicate the causal interactive profile of the other to a degree that would make them intentionally equivalent. That at least is the main idea, and the details can be found elsewhere by those who are interested (Van Gulick 1985, 1992). For present purposes, it should suffice to make at least a prima facie case for the possibility that subjective facts might coexist consistently with some plausible versions of physicalism.

That possibility provides us with an additional option for parting company with the knowledge argument, indeed with an option as promised above for "getting off the train" even earlier, by disputing premise (P1). (P1) is generally conceded by the argument's critics since it functions as a stipulation of the conditions about which we are invited to engage in hypothetical reasoning. Critics may note that no real human could *in practice* command as much as Mary is imagined to do, but the limits would seem to be merely contingent, such as those on memory or attention capacity. Thus there might seem to be no reason why someone could not at least *in principle* know all the physical facts as (P1) supposes Mary does before her release. However, if some physical facts are subjective (in the sense of being understandable only from a specific experiential perspective), then Mary could not even in principle know them given the stipulated restrictions on her past range of experience.

(P1) stipulates a conjunction that might embody a hidden contradiction. Mary is supposed to have never experienced red and yet to know all the physical facts about doing so. Perhaps she could in principle know all the "physical science facts." However, if there are subjective physical facts—facts that are physically realized but cognitively accessible only from the experiential perspective of a certain range of physically realized self-understanding systems (whether bats or normal color-experiencing humans)—then Mary *could not* know all such physical facts about seeing red given her stipulated lack of past experience.

Thus a physicalist critic who believes in the existence of subjective physical facts, as I believe she should, has good grounds for not taking even the argument's first step. (P1) may be intended as a stipulation, but if it ends up specifying a contradiction or a conjunction of conditions that cannot be jointly satisfied, then we are justified in rejecting it, stipulation or not. We can thus add rejecting (P1) on such grounds to our "Take your pick" list of options for resisting the argument. That makes five and counting.

The teleo-pragmatic aspect of self-understanding systems provides the basis as well for the other sort of amendment to the survey that I promised above, that of showing further links among the prior identified options that may end up blurring them a bit, by showing ways in which they overlap or interdepend. (Q2), (Q3), and (Q4) gave critics the options of restricting Mary's gain respectively to know-how, to new ways of knowing old propositions, or to new but merely fine-grained propositions. The three seem to offer distinctive progressively more restricted points at which to draw the line against the argument, and there is some validity to that view.

However, matters get a bit more confused if we push deeper into the details and implications of any of the three. Those, like Lewis, who wish to draw the line at (Q2) will claim that Mary gains only new abilities. But the relevant abilities are highly cognitive in nature and provide mastery of new concepts of the sort required for understanding new fine-grained propositions. Insofar as our grasp of concepts and our ability to deploy them in thought depend on practical intramental skills, real cases in which we gain such skills will be ones as well in which we come to know new fine-grained propositions, ones we previously not only failed to know but could not even have understood or grasped. Thus there is more in common than might at first have seemed between those who aim to draw the line at (Q2) by limiting Mary's gain to know-how and those who part company at (Q4) by crediting her with knowledge of new propositions, but only in the fine-grained sense.

The situation is similar with respect to (Q3). Coming to know an old proposition in a new way will also typically involve both the acquisition of new skills and the mastery of new concepts. For example, if one gains a new mode of direct causal access to some feature of one's mind, one will in the process also likely acquire new skills for recognition and engagement of the sort that would in turn pragmatically anchor one's command of new introspective concepts and thus one's ability to comprehend new fine-grained propositions incorporating those concepts.

Thus what we had earlier identified as three separate options for disputing the intuitions behind the knowledge argument turn out to be at least partly interdependent. Does that fact weaken or strengthen the case against the argument? On one hand it might seem to do the former, insofar as the argument is not forced to prevail in three distinct and completely independent conflicts of intuitions. If the argument's success required adopting its preferred alternative on three separate and controversial issues, that might seem to stack the odds against it, but if those three could be collapsed it might seem more likely to succeed by winning a single clash of intuitions.

On the other hand, the mutually reinforcing links between the various options for disputing the argument might increase their individual plausibility against the competing intuitions required in each case by the argument. Perhaps more important, the three viewed together as a joint but multifaceted option might more effectively explain away the intuition that Mary gains knowledge of new propositions in the coarse-grained sense needed to secure its antiphysicalist conclusion. Any inclination to think of her as doing so might be explained away as merely her gaining new modes of access and associated new skills that give her the mastery of new concepts and thus the ability to comprehend new fine-grained propositions. The unified option might thus provide a more effective counterweight against the epistemic intuitions on which the argument relies. Although the three choice points associated with drawing the line at (Q2), (Q3), and (Q4) may not be fully independent, they nonetheless present three issues on which the argument's intuitions must win against viable competitors, which are made all the more plausible by their mutual incorporation in a consistent alternative view of Mary's epistemic change. In that respect the links between the three options may strengthen the overall case against the knowledge argument and provide a means to answer the disunity challenge raised at the end of section III, about which I will say more after considering one last line of reply.

Our final amendment focuses on the distinction between coarse- and fine-grained propositions and its implications for the argument. As Lewis

(1988) notes, what is needed to defeat physicalism is the conclusion that Mary learns a new proposition in the coarse-grained sense and that she thereby reduces her uncertainty and more narrowly locates herself in logical space. Anything less gets dismissed as mere redescription or translation—like learning to say in Urdu what you were already able to say in English. Your mastery of a new medium of representation in that sense produces no increase in your expressive power or your semantic information, defined as the elimination of epistemic possibilities that thus decreases uncertainty about the nature of the actual world and its location in the space of possible worlds. It may seem that if any matters of fact and actuality are left open in that sense to Mary's state of knowledge until her release, then

- the physical story is incomplete;
- there are truths about the world that fall outside its scope; and
- physicalism is thus false.

However, we must be careful here because many physicalists view those as three different consequences, and nonreductive physicalists in particular would deny that the third follows from the first two. They agree that the *physical science* "story" is not the only valid representation that we need for our successful cognitive engagement with reality, and they also agree that there are true things that can be said, meant, and understood by us that fall outside the expressive range of what we, as the cognitively and causally situated agents that we are, can say within the resources of physical theory. The special sciences give us means of saying, understanding, and knowing facts that are not accessible to us through the structure of physical theory.

However, the nonreductivist aims to hold onto her physicalist credentials insofar as everything real, including everything real described by the special sciences, is physically realized. It is this fact of the physical as the underlying realization base that supposedly anchors its claim of ontological physicalism. Even if there are complex regularities that we cannot apprehend through the medium of physical theory but only through special sciences concepts and modes of access, they too as well are real in virtue of their underlying physical realizations. It would be pointless to try to do biology in the language of microphysics, but that does not undermine the fact that all the properties of biological systems are realized in their underlying physical structure and organization.

The same holds true when the alternative nonmicrophysical system of representation, rather than being that of some higher-level natural science, is instead that embodied in the structure of reciprocal causal engagement that underlies our intramental self-understanding as conscious experiencing physical systems. The relevant modes of access and engagement give us ways of apprehending, recognizing, and, most important, of dynamically interacting with our own mental nature that we could not possibly duplicate through the medium of physical theory. But that is consistent with both sides of the epistemic engagement being physical or physically realized.

Both the understander and what gets understood may owe their reality to the underlying physical structures that realize them, but it does not follow that having a microphysical description of those bases, even a complete microphysical description, would in itself enable us to understand all the real features that we are able to grasp through other systems of representation and engagement such as those associated with our reflexive self-awareness. According to the nonreductive physicalist, realization suffices to ground a claim of ontological physicalism without entailing any claims about the universal adequacy of physical theory as a means of representation and understanding.

Thus two crucial and interdependent issues arise. First, in what sense are the relevant higher-level facts and propositions new and different from those that concern the underlying physical realizations? Second, put in epistemic terms directly relevant to the knowledge argument, would knowing all the facts or true propositions that hold at the microphysical level suffice for knowing all the true facts and propositions that are realized at every level by those underlying microphysical facts? In what sense would knowing the first set settle every question about the latter? Does knowing all the realizer facts guarantee that one also knows all those that are realized? And would knowing all the microphysical facts leave any room to reduce one's semantic uncertainty about one's location in the space of possibilities?

If one accepts a principle of microphysical supervenience, then it may seem that no such room could be left. If all the facts supervene on the microphysical facts, then once the microphysical facts of the actual world are set, so too are all the other facts. There are no subregions left for further information to eliminate. In particular the space specified by the microphysical facts does not divide into distinct subregions that differ from each other with respect to any real nonphysical facts. That is just what supervenience entails: no real difference without a microphysical difference.

Thus if coming to know a new coarse-grained proposition requires locating oneself more narrowly in the logical space of worlds, then being able to locate oneself microphysically might seem to maximize the definiteness of one's location and thus to preclude learning any new coarse propositions. However, one must be careful in moving from matters of metaphysics to epistemological conclusions, just as when one does the converse. In particular we should be cautious in moving from matters of realization and causal determination to conclusions about knowledge and understanding. Just because A-facts supervene on B-facts, it does not follow that knowing the B-facts suffices for knowing, or even for being able to understand, the A-facts. The aesthetic qualities of a painting may supervene on the point-by-point distribution of pigments on its surface, but knowing all the latter facts does not by itself confer knowledge or understanding of its aesthetic qualities.

Perhaps all one lacks in such a case is simply knowledge of some fine-grained propositions and mastery of the concepts they embody. Once we know the full facts about the base, it may seem we could gain at most new ways of redescribing those same facts; there may be no room to gain knowledge of new propositions in the coarse-grained sense of eliminating previously open possibilities.

That intuition has appeal, and in my earlier survey of the argument I did not consider any challenge to it. However, it too may offer options for disagreement. One could perhaps answer (Q4) in the affirmative, conceding that Mary learns a new coarse-grained proposition, and yet still deny that her doing so refutes physicalism. Finding room for such an option requires care in thinking about what counts as knowing one's location in logical space. It's a bit like the old cartoon joke in which a lost visitor confronts an informational display that announces "You are here*" but fails to provide any further map to explain where "here*" is. One might similarly be able to specify a given world as actual and locate it in microphysical space, but still not have a full understanding of the structure of the overall logical space within which it is located. Given supervenience, the microphysical facts may fix its location in that space, but insofar as one does not understand the structure of the containing space, one's knowledge of one's location is incomplete and may leave room for more than notional additions. And insofar as one's cognitive mastery of the structure of the space is incomplete, so too may be the range of propositions one can know or even understand.

In what sense is the complex proposition that specifies the total realization base, RB, for some actual-world object X a different proposition from that which expresses X's having the realized higher-level property, HP? If we think of propositions in the relatively coarse sense as functions from worlds to truth values, it seems that different functions would be associated with propositions that specify objects as having RB or HP, respectively. On the assumption that HP, like most higher-level properties, is open to a diversity of multiple realizations, the two functions will diverge in cases where objects realize HP in virtue of some base other than RB. The function for the HP proposition will assign T in such cases, but that for the RB will assign F. Given supervenience, everything that gets a T from the RB function will also get one from HP, but the converse does not hold because of multiple realization. Thus, even on a coarse mode of individuation, the proposition that X has RB is not the same as the proposition that X has HP.

However, their nonidentity does not by itself guarantee the possibility that Mary could know the first but not the second. Even if the propositions are distinct, it still may be that knowing the first in some way suffices for knowing the latter: either because knowing the realizer facts in general suffices for knowing the realized facts, or because it does so for particular reasons in the Mary case. Supervenience might seem to support such an entailment. As a matter of metaphysics or ontology, X's having RB suffices for X's having HP (or at least does so *modulo* the natural laws of the actual world). So knowing the realizer facts and the relevant laws might seem to guarantee that one should also know the necessarily realized facts as well. One need only draw the consequences.

Of course, we often fail to explicitly recognize many of the less obvious consequences of our beliefs. Knowing Euclid's axioms does not suffice for being able to state or recognize all his theorems; mathematics otherwise would be much easier than it is. However, Mary's problem is not so much a matter of determining which of a given set of propositions are true (or follow as true), but rather a matter of simply being able to grasp or understand them. Consider the analogy with the mathematical case. One might both know the axioms and be able to state some conjectures that one understands, yet still be uncertain as to which if any of them are theorems until one had constructed the required proofs. However, one might be in an even worse epistemic state if one lacked some of the concepts needed to express the relevant propositions. Having mastered the concepts needed to state and understand the basic axioms of number theory does not guarantee that one also has a similar command of those needed to state all its theorems. A mathematical novice might have command of the elementary concepts of arithmetic but lack any concept of imaginary numbers. Before one can know all the propositions that follow from the axioms one must at a minimum be capable of understanding them and having command of all the requisite concepts. Similarly, to get from propositions about the realization base to those about realized higher-order properties, one must have mastered the concepts needed for understanding those latter propositions.

If having a red experience is a higher-order physically realized state, then is there any reason for supposing that the concepts needed for understanding it must be within Mary's grasp prior to her release? Her ability to understand all the propositions about its physical base would not seem to suffice to guarantee her mastery of the requisite higher-order concepts. Indeed her lack is likely to be greater than in the mathematical case. Even if one initially lacks more advanced concepts of number theory, they are at least definable in terms of the elementary concepts that one must master to understand the axioms. Thus those further concepts are cognitively accessible from one's initial epistemic situation even if one lacks practical command of them at the outset.

No similar guarantee need apply in the case of realizer and realized. The concepts needed to grasp propositions about higher-order realized facts need not be definable in terms of those that suffice for grasping propositions about the realization base. Indeed, according to the nonreductive physicalist, we should commonly expect such failures of definability or translatability between the representational systems of the special sciences and those of underlying physical theory. They follow naturally from the pragmatic nature of representation and the way in which representational content depends on the causal structures of both the cognitive agent and the object as well as on the larger dynamic context of engagement within which those representations get applied (Van Gulick 1992). There is little reason to suppose that we can fashion cognitively equivalent higher-level tools out of the resources that suffice for successful engagement at the realization level. As noted above, physics just does not give us the conceptual and representational tools we need for doing economics or introspective psychology.

Returning to Mary, we can now see why prerelease she might lack an adequate understanding of propositions about seeing red, even if such experiences are just higher-order physically realized states. Moreover, we can better appreciate the respect in which she might fail to understand the structure of logical space and thus of her actual location in it. In particular, she may fail to adequately understand the structure of similarity relations that hold between the various situations and worlds in which the higher-order property of seeing red is realized by various underlying physical bases. As noted above, the function from worlds to truth-values associated with the higher-order HP proposition differs from that associated with the proposition about any of its particular realizations RB. Moreover, to understand the HP proposition one must also grasp what it is that makes all the higher-order cases similar despite their diversity of realizations. Indeed, understanding the relevant structure of logical space will require not only that we understand the resemblances between the diversely realized instances of HP, but also the resemblances and differences between them and the equally diversely realized instances of other higher-order, experiential properties HP_i, HP_k, HP_j, ... Without a grasp of those aspects of the structure of the containing logical space, we could not understand the HP proposition or how it figures in the structure of the space within which it allows us to locate ourselves. Lack of such a grasp would put us back in our "You are here*" cartoon predicament.

Thus it seems we have yet another and later option for disagreeing with the knowledge argument and resisting its antiphysicalist conclusion. We might concede that Mary postrelease both learns new coarse-grained propositions and comes to better understand her location in logical space, and yet deny that this refutes or is inconsistent with ontological physicalism understood as the claim that everything real is physically realized. Indeed, nonreductive physicalists may find it the most plausible point at which to draw the line.

A defender of the knowledge argument may object that any such reply relies on shortchanging Mary on her physical knowledge, which by stipulation is complete. He may claim that I have shown at most that Mary might learn something upon release despite having earlier known all the propositions about the *realization base* and all the *microphysical facts and laws*. However, the knowledge argument credits Mary prerelease with complete physical knowledge simpliciter, without any restriction to base or microphysics. Such universal physical knowledge might be taken to include knowledge as well of all the physically realized facts and propositions. However, if real experiences are all physically realized as the physicalist claims, then it would seem Mary would have to have known those realized facts before as well. So there would not be anything left for her to learn, just as the original argument claims.

All parties can agree on the following conditional:

If experiences are physically realized and Mary's knowing all the *physical facts* requires knowing all the *physically realized facts*, then she cannot learn any new coarse fact about experience upon release.

But the critic of the argument will charge the reply with begging the question in assuming that Mary could have known all the physically realized facts prior to release. If there are subjective physically realized facts—as nonreductive physicalism implies—then Mary could not know all the physically realized facts about experiencing red before herself having had the relevant experience.

Thus in a sense our two new critical options interconnect, even though one of them comes before our earlier four questions and the other afterward. The very earliest question of whether it is possible for Mary to know all the physical facts and propositions before her release links up with the new final question of whether her coming to know a new proposition after release would refute physicalism. The answers in both cases may turn on how one defines the range of 'physical facts' and on whether or not there are physical facts that are subjective in the sense of being open to understanding only from a restricted range of experiential perspectives. According to the nonreductive physicalist there are some facts that are physical in the sense of being *physically realized* but are nonetheless *subjective*. If so, then Mary prerelease could not know all the physical facts, if that is meant to include all the physically realized facts. Similarly, Mary postrelease might come to know a new proposition without refuting physicalism, as long as the fact she learns is both physically realized and not able to be adequately grasped or understood nonempathetically through the resources of physical theory.

It is here that the line begins to blur between the fine- and coarse-grained options for resisting the argument. The fourth resistance point in the original survey conceded that Mary learned only a new fine-grained propositions, that is, that she merely came to conceptualize an old fact in a new way but learned no new coarse proposition, nor did she come to locate herself more narrowly in logical space. Our newly added final option turns as well on reconceptualization, but takes a more expansive view of what it involves or makes possible. Mary's acquisition of introspectively anchored concepts, on this latter option, enables her both to understand a new and previously ungraspable proposition and to articulate the structure of logical space in a way that gives her a better understanding of her actual location in it. The two options offer their respective ways of looking at what Mary gains through acquiring such experiential concepts. I tend to prefer the latter, but whichever way one opts the original antiphysicalist conclusion is blocked.

V   A New and Expanded Map of Options

Let me sum up where things stand. The four critical options identified in the original survey all remain. They may be more interdependent than earlier suggested, but that may strengthen rather than weaken the overall case against the knowledge argument. Two new options have been added, one coming before the progression in the original survey and the other coming afterward. We can thus add two new questions to our diagnostic tree to locate these additional ways of parting company with the argument. Let us call them (Q0) and (Q5) to indicate the way in which they bracket our original (Q1) through (Q4).

(Q0)   Is it possible for Mary prior to release to know all the physical facts and propositions about seeing red?

(Q5)   Would Mary's learning after release a new coarse-grained proposition or coming to better understand her location in logical space refute physicalism?

Both questions turn on matters of consistency. (Q0) asks whether it is consistent for Mary to have never experienced red yet know all the physical (or physically realized) facts about such experiences. The believer in subjective physically realized facts will argue that the two conditions are not compossible. (Q5) similarly asks whether physicalism is consistent with the existence of subjective facts, ones that can be learned or understood only by undergoing the relevant sorts of experience. Critics of the argument who are nonreductive physicalists will argue that they are consistent; indeed, nonreductive physicalists will say the existence of such facts is entailed by physicalism properly understood. The equation of the real with the physically realized need not conflict with Mary's learning new propositions postrelease as long as some physically realized facts are subjective.

We can summarize the newly expanded space of critical options for responding to the argument in an enlarged and improved diagnostic tree as in figure 17.2. Once again, I make the same invitation: "Choose your favorite. Take your pick."

What of the disunity concern raised by the editors of this volume (Stoljar and Nagasawa)? As noted at the end of section III, the very diversity of responses to the knowledge argument might be taken to show that physicalists have failed to find a clear answer to its challenge. If they cannot agree about where or how it goes wrong, can they be confident that it does so? This is a serious objection, but as we have just seen the various replies may be less in conflict than they seemed in our original survey. With a bit of tinkering, I think there are plausible ways to consistently combine key elements from multiple replies, especially if one takes a teleo-pragmatic view of the problem. For example, one might argue that prior to release Mary cannot know all the physically realized facts, because her lack of practical intramental abilities prevents her from grasping certain concepts and thus of understanding fine-grained propositions involving those concepts. Indeed her practical limits may even prevent her from comprehending or articulating the structure of logical space in a way that is adequate for understanding some coarse-grained propositions about red experience. There may be not only concepts but properties, physically realized higher-order properties, to which she has no adequate cognitive access prior to release. Unlike Lewis and other supporters of the ability reply, the teleo-pragmatist does not claim Mary lacks only know-how. Rather, the claim is that because she lacks the requisite practical abilities she lacks the ability to grasp various fine- or even coarse-grained propositions about physically realized facts, and thus she could not have complete physical knowledge in her prerelease state, if doing so required knowing all the physically realized facts. Insofar as one can produce such hybrid replies, perhaps I should

Q0. Is it possible for Mary prior to release to know all the physical facts and
propositions about seeing red?

                  //   \\

NO, not if there are physical   YES
<u>subjective facts.</u> ||
X Physicalism not refuted. ||
                                             \/

Q1. Does Mary learn anything or gain knowledge when she first experiences red?

                  //   \\

<u>NO   (Churchland, Hardin)</u>   YES
X Physicalism not refuted. ||
                                           ||
                                         \/

Q2. What sort of knowledge does Mary gain? Is it strictly *know-how*, or does it
include new *knowledge of facts or propositions*?

                  //   \\

Gains only new know-how.   Gains new knowledge of propositions.
<u>(Lewis, Nemirow)</u> ||
X Physicalism not refuted. ||
                                         \/

Q3. Does Mary upon her release come to know *new facts* and *new propositions*?

                  //   \\

NO. She only comes to know   YES. She comes to know new propositions.
old propositions in a new way. ||
<u>(Tye, Horgan, Churchland)</u> ||
X Physicalism not refuted. ||
                                         \/

Q4. On what mode of individuation does Mary learn a new proposition?

                  //   \\

Only on a fine-grained mode.   On a coarse-grained mode.
<u>(Lycan, Loar)</u> ||
X Physicalism not refuted. ||
                                         \/

Q5. Would Mary's learning a new coarse-grained proposition or her coming to
better understand her location in logical space refute physicalism?

                  //   \\

<u>NO   (nonreductive physicalist)</u> <u>YES   (Jackson pre-1998)</u>
X Physicalism not refuted.   Physicalism refuted.

(Each "**X**" marks a point at which the knowledge argument is blocked.)

Figure 17.2
Expanded map of critical options.

amend my invitation: not merely, "Take your pick," but "Take more than one if you like, as long as you do the needed tinkering."

VI   Jackson's Rejection

As a final question, we might ask where we should now locate Frank Jackson in our tree, given his rejection of his own past argument (1998) and his reasons for doing so, which he explains in this volume. Where might those reasons fit in our taxonomy? Does his recent change of mind align with any of the six options we have considered? The answer is both yes and no. He embraces the ability reply and like Lewis and Nemirow views Mary's epistemic gain upon release as merely a gain in know-how. So he might be listed with them as giving an 'only know-how' reply to (Q2). But his reasons for doing so and for denying that Mary lacks any prior propositional knowledge turn crucially on his acceptance of the representational theory of perceptual experience, according to which the phenomenal character of a red experience is exhausted by its representing the world as containing objects with the objective property of redness. Red experiences are not red, and in particular they do not have any property of phenomenal redness (PHRED-ness). Indeed Jackson holds there is no such property as PHRED, and thus Mary cannot be denied access to it prior to her release, nor are there any true propositions about experiences having PHRED that she fails to know or grasp. The property her experience has is not that of *being phenomenally red (PHRED)* but merely that of *phenomenally representing external objects as red*. And that latter property Jackson holds is one that Mary could at least *in principle* deduce from her prior comprehensive physical knowledge. Thus he also aligns with those, like Churchland, who think Mary could infer all there is to know about red experience from her physical knowledge. He fails to give a 'No' to (Q1) only because he regards Mary as gaining know-how.

Jackson attributes his prior acceptance of the knowledge argument to what he now regards as the illusory belief in the property of phenomenal redness (PHRED-ness), and he prescribes the representational theory as the necessary means for dispelling the illusion. Thus, although he ends at the same point as Lewis and Nemirow, he arrives there by an interestingly different route and thereby enriches the critical options.

However, I remain skeptical about his claim that one can defeat the knowledge argument only by accepting the representational theory. Given the diversity of critical alternatives we have surveyed, it is far from obvious that representationalism offers the only viable line of reply. Moreover, I am uneasy about holding rejection of the knowledge argument hostage to the truth of the representational theory, which I am not alone in finding less compelling than does Jackson (Block 1990). To make his solution work Jackson needs to sail a narrow course between two perils. On one hand he must explicate what he means by the representational nature of an experiential state in a way that is rich enough to make plausible his claim that it exhausts its phenomenal character. It must for example include much more that just the state's satisfaction conditions, but also something of how it phenomenally represents those conditions. And what of inverted spectrum cases? If they are possible, should they count as states that are phenomenally different though alike in how they represent the world as being? On the other hand, Jackson must give an account austere enough to support his claim that an experiential state's representational nature can be fully inferred from the physical facts by prerelease Mary. Perhaps he can sail that course, but I think it remains as yet an open question. Jackson himself does not attempt to prove the truth of the representational theory. He defers to other advocates and treats it more as an assumption in offering his diagnosis of where the knowledge argument goes wrong. Nor can I here at the end of this chapter try to disprove the theory. I must content myself with hoping to have shown that those who may have doubts about it still have plausible alternatives for answering the knowledge argument. Please add Jackson's option to the mix, but if you have qualms about the representational theory, you still have lots of others from which to pick.

References

Block, Ned. 1990. "Inverted Earth." In J. Tomberlin, ed., *Philosophical Perspectives*, vol. 4: *Action Theory and Philosophy of Mind*, 52–79. Atascadero, Calif.: Ridgeview.

Chalmers, David. 1996. *The Conscious Mind*. New York: Oxford University Press.

Churchland, Paul. 1985. "Reduction, qualia, and the direct introspection of brain states." *Journal of Philosophy* 82: 2–28.

Descartes, Rene. 1642. *Meditations on First Philosophy*. Paris.

Hardin, C. L. 1988. *Color for Philosophers*. Indianapolis, Ind.: Hackett.

Horgan, Terrence. 1984. "Jackson on physical information." *Philosophical Quarterly* 34: 147–183. Reprinted in this volume.

Jackson, Frank. 1982. "Epiphenomenal qualia." *Philosophical Quarterly* 32: 127–136. Reprinted in this volume.

Jackson, Frank. 1986. "What Mary didn't know." *Journal of Philosophy* 83: 291–295. Reprinted in this volume.

Jackson, Frank. 1998. "Postscript on qualia." In F. Jackson, *Mind, Method, and Conditionals*. London: Routledge. Reprinted in this volume.

Jackson, Frank. 2004. "Mind and illusion." In this volume.

Lewis, David. 1988. "What experience teaches." *Proceedings of the Russellian Society*. Sydney, Australia. Reprinted in this volume.

Loar, Brian. 1990. "Phenomenal states." In *Philosophical Perspectives*, vol. 4: *Action Theory and Philosophy of Mind*. Atascadero, Calif.: Ridgeview.

Locke, John. 1689. *An Essay on Human Understanding*.

Lycan, William, ed. 1990a. *Mind and Cognition: A Reader*. Oxford: Blackwell.

Lycan, William. 1990b. "What is the subjectivity of the mental?" In *Philosophical Perspectives*, vol. 4: *Action Theory and Philosophy of Mind*, 109–130. Atascadero, Calif.: Ridgeview.

Nagel, Thomas. 1974. "What is it like to be a bat?" *Philosophical Review* 83: 435–450.

Nemirow, Lawrence. 1980. "Review of T. Nagel, *Mortal Questions*." *Philosophical Review* 89: 475–476.

Nemirow, Lawrence. 1990. "Physicalism and the cognitive role of acquaintance." In W. Lycan, ed., *Mind and Cognition*. Oxford: Blackwell, 490–499.

Tye, Michael. 1986. "The subjective qualities of experience." *Mind* 95: 1–17.

Unger, Peter. 1966. "On experience and the development of the understanding." *American Philosophical Quarterly* 3: 1–9.

Van Gulick, Robert. 1985. "Physicalism and the subjectivity of the mental." *Philosophical Topics* 13: 51–70.

Van Gulick, Robert. 1992. "Nonreductive materialism and intertheoretical constraint." In A. Beckermann, H. Flohr, and J. Kim, eds., *Reduction and Emergence*. Berlin: DeGruyter.

Van Gulick, Robert. 1993. "Understanding the phenomenal mind: are we all just armadillos?" In M. Davies and G. Humphrey, eds., *Consciousness*. Oxford: Blackwell.

Van Gulick, Robert. 2003. "Maps, gaps, and traps." In Q. Smith and A. Jokic, eds., *Consciousness: New Philosophical Perspectives*. Oxford: Oxford University Press.

Part VII   Postscripts

18   Postscript

Frank Jackson

Materialism is a doctrine in metaphysics. It is a claim about what there is and what it is like. The knowledge argument turns on an epistemological claim, namely, that no story about our world told purely in physical terms—the kind of terms that appear in the materialists' or physicalists' preferred account of the world and its nature—could enable one to deduce the phenomenal nature of psychological states. How is a doctrine in metaphysics supposed to be threatened by a doctrine about the impossibility of a certain sort of deduction?

Many have asked this question, and what follows is the sketch of my reply. (The matter is discussed at much greater length, in the context of a general discussion of the role of conceptual analysis in metaphysics, in "Armchair metaphysics," in *Philosophy in Mind*, ed. John O'Leary Hawthorne and Michaelis Michael, Philosophical Studies, Kluwer, 1994.) My reply comes in three stages. I give the first two stages in outline only, as I take it that they involve by now familiar points. I spend a little more time on the third.

The first point to note is that metaphysical theses that make a claim to completeness commit their holders to supervenience theses. Here is how the point applies in the case of materialism. Consider any possible world that is a minimal physical duplicate of our world. It is, that is, exactly like ours in every physical respect: it is physical individual, property and relation exactly like our world, and moreover it contains nothing extra; it contains nothing more than it has to in order to be physically exactly like our world. (We can count the necessarily existing entities, if there are any, that all worlds have in common as trivially physical for our purposes here.) Materialists who hold that materialism is a complete account of our world, or a complete account of our world as far as the mind is concerned—materialists who are, that is, not some kind of dual attribute dualist—must hold that these minimal physical duplicates are psychological duplicates of our world. They must, that is, hold the following supervenience thesis

(S)   Any world that is a minimal physical duplicate of our world is a psychological duplicate of our world.

For suppose that (S) is false. Then there is a difference in psychological nature between our world and some minimal physical duplicate of it. But then either our world contains some psychological nature that the minimal physical duplicate does not, or the minimal physical duplicate contains some psychological nature that our world does not. The second is impossible because the extra nature would have to be nonphysical (as our world and the duplicate are physically identical), and the minimal physical duplicate contains no nonphysical nature by definition. (Perhaps it will be objected that a minimal physical duplicate contains nothing more than it *has* to in order to be a physical duplicate of our world, and that this allows as a possibility that it has some nonphysical nature provided that that nature is necessitated by its physical nature. But its physical nature is exactly the same as our world's. Hence, if this physical nature necessitates some nonphysical nature, our world must have some nonphysical nature and materialism is false. We could stop right here.) But if our world contains some psychological nature that the duplicate does not, this nature must be nonphysical (as our world and the duplicate are physically identical). But then materialism would be false. For our world would contain some nonphysical psychological nature, and so materialism's claim to completeness concerning at least the psychological nature of our world would be false. Hence, if the supervenience thesis is false, materialism is false—that is to say, materialism is committed to the supervenience thesis.

The second point to note is that supervenience theses expressed in terms of quantifications over possible worlds, as is (S), yield entailment theses. We can think of a statement as telling a story about how things are, and as being true inasmuch as things are the way the story says they are. Let $\emptyset$ be the statement that tells the rich, complex and detailed physical story that is true at the actual world and all and only the minimal physical duplicates of the actual world, and false elsewhere. Let Ω be any true statement entirely about the psychological nature of our world: Ω is true at our world, and every world at which Ω is false differs in some psychological way from our world. If (S) is true, every world at which Ø is true is a psychological duplicate of our world. But then every world at which Ø is true is a world at which Ω is true—that is, Ø entails Ω.

Hence, despite the fact that materialism is a doctrine in metaphysics, it is by virtue of its claim to completeness committed to the entailment of the psychological way things are, including of course the phenomenal way they are, by a rich enough, purely physical story about the way they are.

What has this to do with the possibility of deducing the psychological way things are from the physical way things are? What, that is, has it to do with what I contend that the Mary case shows cannot be done? The answer depends on what should be said about the necessary a posteriori, a controversial matter to which I now turn.

Consider

(A) H_2O covers most of the planet.

Therefore, water covers most of the planet.

Is this argument valid? It is valid in one sense. Every possible world where the premise is true is a world where the conclusion is true. The premise entails the conclusion according to the notion of entailment we presupposed above, the notion of entailment elucidated in terms of being necessarily truth preserving. This is because the conditional 'If H_2O covers most of the planet, then water covers most of the planet' is necessarily true. The argument, though, is invalid in the sense that it is not possible to deduce a priori the conclusion from the premise. This is because 'If H_2O covers most of the planet, then water covers most of the planet' is a posteriori. (The necessary a posteriori status of the conditional follows from the famous necessary a posteriori status of 'Water = H_2O'.) As we might put it: the premise necessitates, logically determines, or strictly implies, the conclusion, but it does not a priori entail it.

It might well be thought (and has been by many) that this argument provides a model for a materialist to view the relationship between the physical way things are and the psychological way things are. A rich enough story about the physical way our world is logically determines the psychological way it is, but does not a priori entail the psychological way it is. The idea is that a view of this kind respects the result that materialists must hold that the psychological way things are supervenes on the physical way they are, without forcing them to admit the possibility of a priori deducing the psychological way things are from the physical way they are. Hence, runs the suggestion, materialists can sidestep the challenge posed by the knowledge argument. What Mary knows logically determines or fixes all there is to know about the psychological way things are, including the sensory or phenomenal way they are, but it does not enable her, even in principle, to deduce the psychological way things are.

I think this suggestion rests on a misunderstanding of what we learned from Saul Kripke about the necessary a posteriori. In a nutshell my reply is that we learnt about *two* things together: the necessary a posteriori, and the contingent a priori, and when we bear this in mind, we see that a *rich enough* story about the H_2O way things are a priori entails the water way things are, despite the fact that 'H_2O covers most of the planet' does not a priori entail that water covers most of the planet. I will make the crucial point with a simple, made-up example.

Suppose that I introduce the word 'Fred' as a (rigid) name for the shape of the largest object next door—that is to say, I explain what the word is to mean in these very terms—and let us suppose that that object is, as it happens, square. The statement (schema) 'If X is square, then X is Fred' will be necessarily true, for it is true in every world by virtue of the fact that 'Fred' is a rigid designator of squareness (together, of course, with the fact that 'square' is a rigid designator). But it will not be a priori. Mere understanding of the words that make it up plus logical acumen cannot by themselves reveal whether the statement is true of false. Hence

(B)   X is square.
      Therefore, X is Fred.

will be valid in the necessarily truth-preserving sense but not in the a priori deducibility sense. This, though, does not mean that there is no argument from the square way things are to the Fred way they are that is valid in the a priori deducibility sense. For 'If X has the shape of the largest object next door, then X is Fred' is contingent a priori. It is contingent because it is false in worlds where the largest object next door is not square. It is a priori because understanding the word 'Fred' is enough to tell you that it is true: the very way I explained the use I was giving the word 'Fred' tells you that any object with the shape of the largest object next door is Fred. Now consider

(B+)   X is square.

The largest object next door is square.

Therefore, X is Fred.

This argument is valid in both the necessarily truth-preserving sense and the a priori deducibility sense. It is necessarily truth preserving because, as already noted, (B) is. It allows an a priori deduction of the conclusion from the premises because the two premises together a priori entail that X has the shape of the largest object next door, and 'If X has the shape of the largest object next door, then X is Fred' is, as already noted, a priori. That is to say, a rich enough story about the square way things are—the story given in the two premises of (B+) taken together—a priori entails the Fred way they are.

The same general picture applies, it seems to me, to the relationship between the H_2O way things are and the water way things are. Our understanding of 'Water' is as a rigid designator whose reference is fixed by 'the stuff that fills the water role', where the water role is spelt out in terms of, say (the details are to some extent controversial and indeterminate, as is inevitable with a real-life example in place of a made-up one), satisfying most of: being an odorless and colorless liquid, falling from the sky, being called 'water' by experts, being necessary to life on the planet, filling the oceans, and so on. The combination of the fact that 'water' and 'H_2O' are rigid designators with its being a posteriori that H_2O fills the water role, explains why statements like 'Water is H_2O' and 'If H_2O covers most of the planet, water covers most of the planet', are necessary a posteriori. The fact that we understand 'water' as being a rigid designator of that which fills the water role means that statements like 'Water = the stuff that fills the water role' and 'If what fills the water role covers most of the planet, water covers most of the planet' are contingent a priori. But then it follows that although argument (A) is not valid in the a priori deducibility sense, the following supplementation of it is valid in both the a priori deducibility sense and the necessarily truth-preserving sense:

(A+) H_2O covers most of the planet.

H_2O fills the water role.

Therefore, water covers most of the planet.

Hence, a *rich enough* story about the H_2O way things are does enable the a priori deduction of the water way things are.

The same goes for the other well-known examples of the necessary a posteriori. As Kripke noted when he argued that 'Heat is molecular motion' is necessary a posteriori, this view goes hand in hand with the view that something like 'Heat causes such and such sensations' is contingent a priori. (Saul Kripke, *Naming and Necessity*, Basil Blackwell, Oxford, 1980, see esp. pp. 132ff. Actually, heat is not always molecular motion, and water is arguably not H_2O so much as sufficiently large aggregations of H_2O molecules; but in the interests of simplicity we fudge.) But then a rich enough story about molecular motion does yield the facts about heat. True, a limited story about molecular motion, one that tells you which substances have a good deal of it but not much else, does not tell you much about heat, despite necessitating the facts about heat. But a story that includes the way molecular motion causes various sensations and whatever else is involved in fixing the reference of 'heat' will tell you all there is to know about heat.

I think that the materialist has to say the same thing about the relationship between the physical way the world is and the psychological way the world is. A partial story about the physical way the world is might logically necessitate the psychological way the world is without enabling an a priori deduction of the psychological way the world is. It might be like the partial stories about H_2O, and squareness encapsulated in the premises of arguments like (A) and (B), above. They necessitate, without a priori entailing, the facts about, respectively, water, and Fred. But the materialist is committed to a complete or near enough complete story about the physical way the world is enabling in principle the a priori deduction of the psychological way the world is. Materialism about the mind is like what we might call 'H_2O-ism' about water. Someone who knows where all the H_2O is *and* enough else about H_2O—that it fills the sea, gets tagged 'water' by experts, its molecules move past each other reasonably freely, and so and so forth—knows all there is to know about water, and this is crucial to H_2O-ism being, as it is, true. There is nothing more to the water way our world is than the H_2O way it is. In the same way, I think it is crucial for the truth of materialism (materialism proper, not some covert form of dual attribute theory of mind) that knowing a rich enough story about the physical nature of our world is tantamount to knowing the psychological story about our world.

Finally, I should point out that there is a much shorter way of making plausible the knowledge argument's presumption that materialism is committed to the a priori deducibility of our psychological nature from our and our environment's physical nature.

It is implausible that there are facts about very simple organisms that cannot be deduced a priori from enough information about their physical nature and how they interact with their environments, physically described. The physical story about amoeba and their interactions with their environments is the whole story about amoeba. Mary would not lack any knowledge about them. But according to materialism, we differ from amoeba essentially only in complexity of ingredients and their arrangement. It is hard to see how that kind of difference could generate important facts about us that in principle defy our powers of deduction, and the fact that we have a phenomenal psychology is certainly an important fact about us. Think of the charts in biology classrooms showing the evolutionary progression from single-celled creatures on the far left to the higher apes and humans on the far right: where in that progression can the materialist plausibly claim that failure of a priori deducibility of important facts about us emerges? Or, if it comes to that, where in the development of each and every one of us from a zygote could the materialist plausibly locate the place where there emerge important facts about us that cannot be deduced from the physical story about us?

19 Postscript on Qualia

Frank Jackson

Suppose I undertook to tell you everything there is to know about where some object is at each and every time. Could you in principle deduce all there is to know about that object's motion? If the at-at theory of motion is true, the answer is yes. But the at-at theory of motion is an empirical claim about the nature of motion in our world. It is not properly a claim about the concept of motion. I argue for this (and for a similar position for a number of other examples) in detail in chapter 10 [of *Mind, Method, and Conditionals*], "Metaphysics by possible cases," but we can put the key point very quickly. The *precise* nature of what we are talking about when we talk about motion is unclear. We are in a kind of 'best candidate situation', to borrow a term from discussions of personal identity. If there is an intrinsic property of objects that genuinely explains, and so is distinct from, their being at different places at different times, and which plays all the roles we centrally associate with motion, then that property *is* motion; but if there is no such property, then an object's being at different places at different times is all that that object's motion comes to.

This means that whether or not we can deduce all there is to know about motion—*our* motion, motion as it is in our world—from all there is to know about positions at times depends on an empirical fact about what our world is like. The deduction is possible just if the at-at theory's candidate for motion is the best candidate for motion in our world. I now think that the same is true for qualia and, more generally, the sensory side of psychology. In some worlds, its nature cannot be deduced in principle from the full account of the physical nature of that world, but in other worlds, including ours, it can. The redness of *our* reds can be deduced in principle from enough about the physical nature of our world despite the manifest appearance to the contrary that the knowledge argument trades on. This is why I now think that the knowledge argument fails.

Why do I think that the sensory side of psychology, as it is constituted in our world, is deducible in principle from enough about the world's physical nature? Our knowledge of the sensory side of psychology has a causal source. Seeing red and feeling pain impact on us, leaving a memory trace which sustains our knowledge of what it is like to see red and feel pain on the many occasions where we are neither seeing red nor feeling pain. This is why it was always a mistake to say that someone could not know what seeing red and feeling pain is like unless they had actually experienced them: false 'memory' traces are enough. This places a constraint on our best opinion about the nature of our sensory states: we had better not have opinions about their nature which cannot be justified by what we know about the causal origin of those opinions. Now the precise connection between causal origin and rational opinion is complex, but for present purposes the following rough maxim will serve: do not have opinions that outrun what is required by the best theory of these opinions' causal origins.[1] Often it will be uncertain what the best theory is, or the question of what it is will be too close to the question under discussion for the maxim to be of much use. But in the case of sensory states, the maxim has obvious bite. We know that our knowledge of what it is like to see red and feel pain has purely physical causes. We know, for example, that Mary's transition from not knowing what it is like to see red to knowing what it is like to see red will have a causal explanation in purely physical terms. (Dualist interactionism is false.) It follows, by the maxim, that what she learns had better not outrun how things are physically.

Toward the end of chapter 5 [of *Mind, Method, and Conditionals*, reprinted as chap. 1 in this vol.], "Epiphenomenal qualia," I point out that a report in one newspaper may be good evidence for a similar report in another newspaper without its being the case that one report causes the other. This is true but, I now think, does not blunt the force of the argument just rehearsed. As noted in that essay, the reason we are entitled to hold that the reports are similar depends on our knowing inter alia that they have a common cause, namely, the event being reported on. But we know this only because of the way reports in newspapers in general impact on us. The fundamental point remains that our entitlement comes back to causal impacts of the right kinds.

I now think that the puzzle posed by the knowledge argument is to explain why we have such a strong intuition that Mary learns something about how things are that outruns what can deduced from the physical account of how things are. I suggest that the answer is the strikingly atypical nature of the way she acquires certain relational and functional information. Suppose that you want to know on landing in Chicago if the weather is typical for this time of year. A good deal of collecting and bringing together of information is required. The same goes for information about functional roles. To know that a certain way of driving is dangerous, or that a certain drug slows the progression of AIDS, requires bringing together information from disparate sources. However, the most plausible approach for physicalists to sensory experience sees it as a striking exception to the rule that acquiring this kind of information requires collation. The most plausible view for physicalists is that sensory experience is putative information about certain highly relational and functional properties of goings on inside us. As it is often put nowadays, its very nature is representational: it represents inter alia certain highly relational and functional facts about what is happening to us. If this is right—and I have nothing to add to the detailed arguments by those physicalists who came to the position decades ahead of me—sensory experience is a quite unusually 'quick and easy' way of acquiring highly relational and functional information. (And evolutionary considerations tell us why we might have acquired this ability to access quickly and easily certain sorts of highly relational and functional information.) Sensory experience is in this regard like the way we acquire information about intrinsic properties—typically, we get the information that something is round more quickly and easily than the information that it is the second largest object in the room. In consequence, sensory experience presents itself to us as if it were the acquisition of information about intrinsic nature. But, very obviously, it is not information about intrinsic *physical* nature, so the information Mary acquires presents itself to us as if it were information about something more than the physical. This is, I now think, the source of the strong but mistaken intuition that Mary learns something new about how things are on her release.

I still think though that we should take seriously the possibility that we know little about the intrinsic nature of our world, that we mostly know its causal cum relational nature as revealed by the physical sciences. I hope and believe (on Occamist grounds) that this kind of 'Kantian' skepticism is mistaken, but I think that the reflections at the end of ["Epiphenomenal Qualia"] have to be taken seriously. But even if a large part of the intrinsic nature of our world is beyond our epistemic reach, the nature we know about supervenes on the mostly functional cum relational nature that the physical sciences tell us about. The considerations at the end of ["Epiphenomenal Qualia"] can be no reason to hold that Mary learns something new about how things are on her release, but rather that there may (*may*) be a lot about fundamental nature that we and she can never know.

Note

1. For something less rough, see Frank Jackson and Robert Pargetter, "Causal Origin and Evidence," *Theoria* 51(1985): 65–76.

20 Mind and Illusion

Frank Jackson

Much of the contemporary debate in the philosophy of mind is concerned with the clash between certain strongly held intuitions and what science tells us about the mind and its relation to the world. What science tells us about the mind points strongly toward some version or other of physicalism. The intuitions, in one way or another, suggest that there is something seriously incomplete about any purely physical story about the mind.

For our purposes, we can be vague about the detail and think broadly of physicalism as the view that the mind is a purely physical part of a purely physical world. Exactly how to delineate the physical will not be crucial: anything of a kind that plays a central role in physics, chemistry, biology, neuroscience, and the like, along with the a priori associated functional and relational properties, count, as far as we are concerned.

Most contemporary philosophers, when given a choice between going with science and going with intuitions, go with science. Although I once dissented from the majority, I have capitulated and now see the interesting issue as being where the arguments from the intuitions against physicalism—the arguments that seem so compelling—go wrong.[1] For some time, I have thought that the case for physicalism is sufficiently strong that we can be confident that the arguments from the intuitions go wrong somewhere—but where is somewhere?

This essay offers an answer to that question for the knowledge argument against physicalism. I start with a reminder about the argument. I then consider one popular way of dismissing it and explain why I am unmoved by it. The discussion of this way delivers a constraint that any satisfying physicalist reply to the knowledge argument should meet. The rest of the essay gives the answer I favor to where the knowledge argument goes wrong. This answer rests on a representationalist account of sensory experience and, as the title of the essay indicates, I say, among other things, that there is a pervasive illusion that conspires to lead us astray when we think about what it is like to have a color experience.

The Knowledge Argument

The epistemic intuition that founds the knowledge argument[2] is that you cannot deduce, from purely physical information about us and our world, all there is to know about the nature of our world, because you cannot deduce how things look to us, especially in regard to color. More general versions of the argument make the same claim for all the mental states with a phenomenology—the states for which there is something it is like to be in them, as it is so often put—and sometimes for consciousness. But we will be almost entirely concerned with color experiences. We will say nothing about consciousness per se; our concern is with the phenomenology of visual experience, and not our consciousness of it or of mental states in general.

The familiar story about Mary is a way to make vivid and appealing the claim about lack of deducibility. To rehearse it ever so briefly: A brilliant scientist, Mary, is confined in a black-and-white room without windows. She herself is painted white all over and dressed in black. All her information about the world and its workings comes from black-and-white sources, like books without colored pictures and black-and-white television. She is, despite these artificial restrictions, extraordinarily knowledgeable about the physical nature of our world, including the neurophysiology of human beings and sentient creatures in general, and how their neurophysiology underpins their interactions with their surroundings. Can she in principle deduce from all this physical information, what it is like to see, say, red?

There is a strong intuition that she cannot. This intuition is reinforced by reflecting on what would happen should she be released from her room. Assuming that there is nothing wrong with her color vision despite its lack of exercise during her incarceration, she would learn what it is like to see red, and it is plausible that this would be learning something about the nature of our world, including especially the nature of the color experiences subjects enjoy. From this it would follow that she did not know beforehand all there was to know about our world.

Moreover, there is a marked contrast with our epistemic relation to properties like solidity, elasticity, boiling, valency, and the like. If I give you enough information about the behavior of a substance's molecules and how they govern the substance's interactions with its environment, you will be able to work out whether it is a liquid, a solid, or a gas. If I tell you about the forces that hold water molecules together and the way increases in the velocity of those molecules as a result of heating can lead to these molecules reaching escape velocity, you will learn about boiling.[3] Likewise for valency and elasticity. But the deduction of what it is like to see red from purely physical information seems a totally different matter.

There are two challenges to physicalism here. One is to explain why there should be a marked apparent difference between the case of seeing red and the case of being liquid or boiling. After all, the phenomena are *alike* in being purely physical ones according to physicalism. The second, more direct challenge is to explain how it can be that Mary's knowledge of our world's nature is, it seems, deficient, despite the fact that she knows all there is to know according to physicalism.

I now turn to the popular response to the knowledge argument that seems to me to fail but which gives us a constraint on any acceptable physicalist response.

The Response That Draws on A Posteriori Necessity

This response[4] on behalf of physicalism to the knowledge argument starts from the point that being necessitated does not imply being a priori derivable. This suggests that although physicalists are committed to the experiential being necessitated by a rich enough physical account of our world—otherwise it would take more than the physical nature of our world to secure its experiential nature, contrary to physicalism—they are not committed to the experiential being a priori derivable from the physical. But the epistemic intuition that lies behind the knowledge argument is, when all is said and done, that Mary cannot carry out an a priori derivation from the physical information imagined to be at her disposal to the phenomenology of color vision. Physicalists should respond to the knowledge argument by adopting a version of physicalism according to which the experiential is necessitated by the physical but is not a priori derivable from the physical.

I have two reasons for rejecting this reply. The first I have given a number of times. It draws on the two-dimensional account of the necessary a posteriori. I will not repeat it here.[5] My second reason can be introduced by reflecting on the famous reduction of the thermodynamic theory of gases to the kinetic theory via statistical mechanics.

Our belief that gases have temperature and pressure is grounded in their behavior. Moreover, we know that their behavior is fully explained by the various features recognized and named in the kinetic theory of gases. There is no need to postulate any extra features of gases in order to explain their behavior. This makes it very hard to hold that no matter how much information we have framed in the terms of the kinetic theory and in terms of the functional roles played by the properties picked out by the terms of that theory, and no matter how confident we are that the kinetic theory and its future developments provide a complete picture in the relevant respects of the essential nature of gases, the passage from this information to whether or not gases are hot and have pressure is a posteriori. What relevant information are we waiting on? We know that all we will get is more of the same. Skepticism about gases having temperature and pressure threatens if we insist that we cannot go a priori from the molecular account of gases and the concomitant functional roles to gases having temperature and pressure.

This point is implicit in the well-known schematic account of why it is right to identify temperature in gases with mean molecular kinetic energy:

Temperature in gases is that which does so and so (a priori premise about the concept of temperature).

That which does so and so is mean molecular kinetic energy (empirical premise).

Therefore, temperature in gases is mean molecular kinetic energy.

The need for the first, a priori premise is sometimes challenged.[6] But unless something like the first premise is a priori, eliminativism about temperature and pressure in gases is inevitable. The right conclusion from the discoveries of the kinetic theory of gases could only be that gases are not hot on the ground that what we needed temperature to explain (their feeling hot and behaving thus and so) is fully explained by their mean molecular kinetic energy. Mutatis mutandis for pressure.

It is sometimes objected to this argument that identities need no explanation. I doubt this doctrine.[7] But the issue is irrelevant. Identities certainly need justification, and the problem is that we have a choice between

(A)   Temperature is not a property of gases, although there is plenty of molecular kinetic energy, and the mean value of that does all the explaining of gas behavior once assigned to having such and such a temperature.

and

(B)   Having such and such a temperature in gases is one and the same property as having so and so a mean molecular kinetic energy, and 'they' do all the needed explaining of gas behavior.

Without the first, a priori premise above, we have no reason to favor (B) over (A).

The considerations that tell us that we had better be able to move a priori from the molecular account of gases to the temperature account can be generalized to the question of all of our empirical beliefs about what our world is like. Physicalists hold (have to hold) that the evidence we have for any of our claims about what our world is like—that England fought two World Wars, that horses eat grass, that Carter was a one-term president of the United States, and so on—is determined without remainder by our world's physical nature. How then can we be justified in holding that we have evidence for what our world is like that outruns what might be inferred in principle from its physical nature alone? It might be objected that this rhetorical question assumes an unduly "causal cum best explanation" view of the relation of evidence to empirical hypothesis. What about simplicity and all that? But physicalists hold that considerations of simplicity, good methodology, and all the rest, favor physicalism. That is why they are physicalists (and rightly so, in my view).

It is this wider consideration that explains my puzzlement over why many hold that the claim that physicalism is committed to the a priori deducibility of the way the world is in all empirical respects from the physical nature of the world is an extreme one.[8] Think of the famous Russell hypothesis. According to it, the world came into existence five minutes ago containing each and every putative 'trace' that might suggest that it has existed since the big bang. As a result, we cannot here and now point to features that distinguish the correct view that our world has existed since the big bang from the Russell hypothesis. What entitles us to reject the Russell hypothesis is that it violates the principles of good theory construction by being *excessively ad hoc*. Now consider the *bare physicalism hypothesis*: the hypothesis that the world is exactly as is required to make the physical account of it true in each and every detail but nothing more is true of this world in the sense that nothing that fails to follow a priori from the physical account is true of it. This hypothesis is not ad hoc and has all the explanatory power and simplicity we can reasonably demand. Ergo, we physicalists can have no reason to go beyond the bare physicalist picture.

It might (will) be objected that bare physicalism is a posteriori impossible, that there are empirical truths about our world, including truths about experiences, that are necessitated by the bare physical account but which do not follow a priori from that account. But that would be to miss the point. The point is that we could not know this. Bare physicalism is a conceptual possibility; the argument is that we have no reason not to allow that it is also a metaphysical possibility. Or, to make the point with a word, recall that many call conceptual possibility *epistemic* possibility. Or, to make the point with an example, those who hold that the existence of God is a posteriori necessary (or a posteriori necessitated by agreed features of our world) are not thereby excused from having to provide reasons for believing in God.

To avoid misunderstanding, I should emphasize that when I talk of being able to move a priori from the physical account to, say, Carter being a one-term president, I do not mean being able to move literally. I mean that there exists an a priori entailment. We cannot derive the gravitational center of the universe from the mass and location of all its parts because, first, we do not and could not know the mass and location of all its parts, and, second, the calculation would be way beyond our powers. All the same, the location of the center of gravity does follow a priori from the physical account of our world, and we know that it does.

This point gives us the following constraint on any physicalist solution to the challenge of the epistemic intuition: it should allow us to see how the passage from the physical to the nature of color experience might possibly be, somehow or other, a priori.

I now come to the positive part of the essay; the part where I explain why physicalists are entitled to reject the epistemic intuition. As heralded, my argument will involve the claim that we are under an illusion about the nature of color experience, an illusion that fuels the epistemic intuition.[9]

Mistaking Intensional Properties for Instantiated Properties

I start with the diaphanousness of experience: G. E. Moore's thesis that the qualitative character of experience is the character of the putative object of experience.[10] The redness of sensings of red is the putative redness of what is seen; when vision is blurred, what is seen appears to be blurred; the location quality of a sound is the putative location of the sound; the experience of movement is the experience of something putatively moving; and so on. Hume observes that the self's experiences always get in the way of experiencing the self.[11] Equally, the putative properties of what is experienced always get in the way of accessing the qualities of experience. I am going to take diaphanousness for granted. The case for it is widely accepted[12] and it is especially appealing in the case of our topic, color experience. Indeed, reservations about it are typically confined to certain bodily sensations where attitudes, pro or con, arguably contribute to the felt quality. The degree to which we dislike a pain is arguably part of its feel.

There are two very different ways to think of the lesson of diaphanousness, corresponding to two very different ways of thinking of the object that putatively has the qualities. On one, Moore's, the object really is an object. It is the object of the act-object theory of experience or the sense datum theory of sensing: experiences are composed of an act of awareness directed toward an object or sense datum that bears the qualities. And the lesson of diaphanousness is that these qualities determine the qualitative nature of the experience. On the other way of thinking, Harman's in "The Intrinsic Quality of Experience," for example, the object is an intensional object. That is to say, 'it' is not an object at all, and our use of verbal constructions that belong in the syntactic category of names is a convenient, if metaphysically misleading, way of talking about how things are being represented to be. We talk of being directly aware of a square shape in our visual fields, but there is no square shape to which we stand in the relation of direct awareness; rather, our visual experience represents that there is something square before us. What makes it right to use the word 'square' in describing our experience is not a relation to something that has the property the word stands for but the fact that the way the experience represents things as being can be correct only if there is something square in existence. Thus on this view the squareness of an experience is an intensional

F. Jackson

property, not an instantiated one. The same goes mutatis mutandis for all the properties we ascribe to what is presented in experience, the properties we have in mind when we talk of the qualities of experience and to which the argument from diaphanousness applies.[13] When we use words like 'square', 'two feet away', and 'red' to characterize our experiences, we pick out intensional properties, not instantiated ones.

I think, with the current majority, that the second is the right way to think of the lesson of diaphanousness. My reason is that perceptual experience *represents*. My experience as of a round, red object in front of me represents that there is a round, red object in front of me. I may or may not accept that things are as they are being represented to be, but I take it as axiomatic that each and every sensory experience represents that things are thus and so.

This line of thought implies that the first way of thinking of the lesson of the argument from diaphanousness, the way that leads to the sense datum theory, must be rejected. We onetime sense datum theorists thought that the requirement that there be something red and round, say, of which the subject is directly aware, automatically captures, or partly captures, the key representational notion.[14] This is a mistake. It is true that I can represent how I am representing something to be by using the actual way something is. For example, I might represent to you the color I remember X to be by holding up an actual sample of the color. Here I would be using the actual color of one thing, the sample, to represent how my memory represents the color of something else to be; a color that X may or may not have. In that sense, we have a model for understanding the sense datum theory. But, and this is the crucial point, the fact that I am using an actual sample of the color cuts no representational ice per se. I could be using the sample to indicate the one color I do *not* think X has. Or I could be following the convention of holding up a sample with the color *complementary* to that I remember X as having. In the same way, standing in a certain direct-awareness relationship to a mental item with such and such properties says nothing, represents nothing per se, about how the world is. The act-object cum sense datum theory leaves out the most important feature of experience: its essentially representational nature. To capture the representational nature of perception, what makes it true that words like 'red' and 'square' apply to our experiences has to be understood on the intensional model.

It might be objected that this argument from the fact that perception represents leaves open the possibility that some but not all of the properties of experience are intensional. Why not hold that experiences have both a representational aspect and a nonrepresentational aspect?[15] In a sense they do. It may be a fact about an experience that it is occurring in Alaska or during the Middle Ages, and neither of these properties is an intensional property of the experience. But the issue for us is whether the aspects that constitute the phenomenal nature of an experience outrun its representational nature, and there are good reasons to deny this.

First, whenever there is a difference in phenomenal character, there is a difference in how things are being represented to be. This follows from diaphanousness. Any change in phenomenal character means a change in the putative character of what is being experienced, and a change in the putative character of what is being experienced *is* a change in how things are being represented to be. Make an experience of red a bit brighter and you make it the case that your experience represents that some object's redness is that much brighter. But if phenomenal character outran representational character, it would be possible to change the former and leave the latter unchanged.

There have, of course, been attempts to describe cases where phenomenal character differs without a difference in representational content, and an important exercise is the critical review of all the cases that might be thought to show the possibility of phenomenal variation without difference in representational content. I am not going to conduct this review, because I think the job has been done well by other supporters of representationalism.[16]

Second, there is a marked contrast between, on the one hand, the way representational devices like maps and sentences represent, and, on the other, the way perceptual experience represents. There is a gap between vehicle of representation and what is represented in the first case that does not exist in the second. In the case of maps and sentences, we can distinguish the features that do the representing—the gap between the isobars on a weather map, the concatenation of the letters 'c', 'a', and 't' in that order in a sentence, the green coloring on parts of a map—from what they represent: a pressure gradient, a cat, areas of high rainfall. We can, for example, describe the gap between the isobars without any reference to what it represents. But, in the case of perceptual experience, we cannot. When I have a visual experience of a roundish, red object in front of me, *that* is what it represents. My very description of the vehicle of representation delivers how it represents things to be. I may or may not accept that things are the way they are being represented to be, but there is just the one way that things are being represented to be, and that way is part and parcel of the quality of the experience. Ergo, we have to understand the qualities of experience in terms of intensional properties.[17]

A major issue for the intensionalist account is how to distinguish sensory representational states from more purely cognitive representational ones like belief. But rather than break the flow of the argument, I postpone my discussion of it. In the next few sections we take the intensionalist picture as a given and note how it allows physicalists to explain away the epistemic intuition.

Explaining Away the Epistemic Intuition

We start by noting how the intensional account undermines the picture of experience that goes with the phrase 'what it is like'.

There is a redness about sensing red (a yellowness about sensing yellow, and so on). We naturally think of the redness as a property we are acquainted with when we sense red and as the property Mary finds out about on her release. We may want to distinguish redness as a property of objects from redness as a property of an area of our visual field, perhaps using 'red*' for the latter. Either way, what it is like is, on this picture, a matter of having redness or redness*, knowing what it is like is knowing about redness or redness*, and the knowledge argument is an argument to the conclusion that Mary does not know about redness or redness*—that is, about the property we are, according to this picture, acquainted with when we sense red.

Intensionalism tells us that there is no such property. To suppose otherwise is to mistake an intensional property for an instantiated one. Of course, when I sense red and you sense red, there is something in common between us that we English speakers report with descriptions that include the word 'red'. But what is in common is not the property tagged with the word 'red' but, first, how things have to be for our experiences to represent correctly, and, second, our both being in states that represent things as being that way.

Intensionalism means that no amount of tub-thumping assertion by dualists (including by myself in the past) that the *redness* of seeing red cannot be accommodated in the austere physicalist picture carries any weight. That striking feature is a feature of how things are being represented to be, and if, as claimed by the tub thumpers, it is transparently a feature that has no place in the physicalist picture, what follows is that physicalists should deny that anything has that striking feature. And this is no argument against physicalism. Physicalists can allow that people are sometimes in states that represent that things have a nonphysical property. Examples are people who believe that there are fairies. What physicalists must deny is that such properties are instantiated.

Moreover, the representationalist-cum-intensionalist approach can explain the origin of the dualist conviction that redness is nonphysical. It is vital for our survival that we are able to pick out recurring patterns. Recognizing your best friend or a hungry tiger requires spotting a commonality. Sometimes these patterns are salient ones. Square tables have an obvious commonality. Sometimes these patterns are not salient. An example is the commonality that unites an acceptable pronunciation of a given word in English. The lack of salience is why it is hard to develop speech-to-text computer programs, though the fact that it is nevertheless possible, that we always knew it was possible in principle and now know that it is possible in practice, reminds us that it is a folk view that there is a commonality. In many cases, the commonality's importance lies in highly relational facts about it. If the theory that color vision evolved as an aid to the detection of food is correct, a series of highly unobvious optical commonalities between edible things and differences from their forest backgrounds are the patterns color vision evolved to detect. Now, highly unobvious commonalities like these normally get detected only after a great deal of collecting and bringing together of information. Color experience is, therefore, a quite unusually 'quick' way of acquiring highly unobvious relational and functional information. It is, in this regard, like the way we acquire information about intrinsic properties: one look at an object tells us that it is more or less round. In consequence, color experience presents to us as if it were the acquisition of information about highly salient, more or less intrinsic features of our surroundings. But there are no physical features fitting this characterization; in consequence, color experience presents itself to us as if it were information about certain nonphysical features. Indeed, we may want to go so far as to say that sensing red *misrepresents* how things are. If this is right, we should say that nothing is red, for nothing would be as our experience of red represents things as being; we should be eliminativists about red and about color in general. A more moderate position is that although our experience of color contains a substantial degree of misrepresentation—the misrepresentation that leads dualists astray—there are complex physical properties 'out there' that stand in relations near enough to those captured by the color solid for us to be able to identify them with the various colors.

Meeting the Constraint

I argued that the physicalist response to the epistemic intuition should allow us to see how the nature of color experience might possibly follow a priori from the physical account of what our world is like. The representationalist account of sensory experience meets this constraint.

Seeing red is being in a certain kind of representational state, on this account. The project of finding an analysis of representation is not an easy one—to put it mildly. But it is a standard item on the philosophical agenda, and the answers that have been, or are likely to be, canvased are all answers that would allow the fact of representation to follow a priori from the physical account of what our world is like. They are accounts that talk of covariation, causal connections of various kinds, selectional histories, and the like, and accounts made from these kinds of ingredients are ones that might be determined a priori by the purely physical.

We will need also an account of how sensing red represents things as being—the content. This would involve, inter alia, making up our mind on whether or not the content of sensing red is such as to imply, given physicalism, eliminativism about redness. Again, this will not be easy—if it were, it would have been done long ago—but there is no reason to think it would be an account that would make being in a state that has that representational content something that could not be derived a priori from the physicalist picture of what our world is like. I know only too well the residual feeling that somehow the *redness* could not be got out of the physical picture alone, but that is nothing more than a holdover from the conflation of instantiated property with intensional property. That 'redness' is not a feature one is acquainted with, but instead is a matter of how things are being represented to be.

What Happens to Mary on Her Release?

The epistemic intuition is that it is impossible to deduce what it is like to sense red from the physical account of our world. In particular, Mary in her room will not be able to do it. I have argued that if 'what it is like' means all the properties of seeing red, it is possible in principle to deduce them all. That follows from representationalism, and the appearance to the contrary arises from the conflation of intensional properties with instantiated ones. But this leaves open what to say of a positive kind about what would happen to Mary on her release. The negative points, that she would not learn about a feature of our world she could not know of while incarcerated, and that tub-thumping convictions to the contrary carry no weight, do not tell us the positive side of the story.

What to say about the relevant change in Mary turns, it seems to me, on what to say about an old, hard issue for representationalist approaches to experience. It is the issue we postponed earlier of how to find the feel in the representationalist picture.

Sensing and Believing

Without having the relevant visual experience, I can believe that there is, here and now, a round, red object in front of me. Perhaps my eyes are shut, but I remember, or perhaps I am being told, that there is such an object here and now in front of me. Or perhaps the thought that there is such an object in front of me has simply 'come into my mind', and I have boldly gone along with it. Or perhaps I am one of the blind-sighted: it seems like guessing, but my success rate shows that I am drawing on a subliminal representational state.

It can be very tempting at this point to try for a mixed theory, according to which sensory experiences have a representational component and a sensory one. The difference between belief per se and sensory experience lies in a sensory addition. But we saw the problems for this earlier. For example, if this is the right view to take, it should be possible to vary the sensory part alone, but for every sensory difference, there is a representational difference. Moreover, it is hard to make sense of a nonrepresentational, sensory core. Any experience with some 'color or shape feel' is putatively of something colored and shaped somewhere, and thereby

represents something about that location.[18] Once there is some phenomenal experiential nature, there is thereby some representation.

Conceptual versus Nonconceptual Content—A Wrong Turn

Many representationalists tackle the problem of finding the 'feel' via a distinction between conceptual and nonconceptual content. The claim is that
belief has conceptual content, whereas experience has nonconceptual content.[19] I think that there are problems for this style of response.

The view that beliefs have conceptual content whereas experiences have
nonconceptual content can be understood in two ways.[20] It can be thought
of as the view that beliefs and experiences have content in different senses
of 'content'; that they have different kinds of content in the strong sense in
which *that there are electrons* and *that there are protons* do *not* automatically
count as different kinds of content. I think this is the wrong way for representationalists to go.[21] Belief is the representational state par excellence.
This means that to hold that experience has content in some sense in
which belief does not is to deny rather than affirm representationalism
about experience. There needs to be an univocal sense of 'content' at work
when we discuss representationalism; a sense on which content is how
things are being represented to be, and on which both beliefs and experiences have (representational) content.

Of course, many say that the content of belief (and thought more generally) is a structured entity containing concepts.[22] But this should not, it
seems to me, be interpreted so as to run counter to what we have just said.
When I believe that things are as my experience represents them to be,
what I believe is precisely that things are as my experience says that they
are, not something else.[23] Alex Byrne says, "that the content of perception
... may outrun the representational capacity of thought ... is surely the
default assumption."[24] But we can *think* that things are *exactly* as our experience represents them to be. What is outrun is our capacity to capture
the content in words; but that is another question. As it happens, my current experience correctly represents that there is something rectangular before me. I also believe that there is. What makes my experience correct and
my belief true is the very same configuration of matter in front of me, and
that configuration contains no concepts. Maybe, in addition, my belief
implies that I stand in some special relation to concepts, but that would be

a reason to acknowledge an additional content to the representational one that belief and experience both possess. And you might, or might not, hold that sensory states also possess that kind of content. But giving belief a possibly extra kind of content is not going to help us with our problem. Our problem is that both belief and experience represent that things are thus and so but only experience has feel—or anyway, has feel to the relevant degree. We are looking for something extra, so to speak, for experience, not a possible extra for belief.

The second way of understanding the view that belief has conceptual content whereas experience has nonconceptual content is as a claim about what it takes to have a belief with (representational) content versus what it takes to have an experience with (representational) content.[25] The kinds of content are the same, but what it takes for the states to have them differs. Experience represents in a way that is independent, or largely independent, of subjects' mastery of concepts, whereas belief does not. For example, it is observed that we can perceptually discriminate many more colors than we have names for or can remember. It is then inferred that I might have a perceptual state that represents that something is, say, red_{17}, without having the concept of red_{17}. But I could not believe that something is red_{17} without having the concept of red_{17}.

I doubt the claim that perceptual representation is nonconceptual in the explained sense. To perceptually represent that things are thus and so essentially involves discrimination and categorization, and that is to place things under concepts.[26] Of course, I agree that when I experience red_{17}, I need not have the term 'red_{17}' in my linguistic repertoire; I need not be representing that the color before me is correctly tagged 'red_{17}'; it need not be the case that before I had the experience, I had the concept of red_{17}; and my ability to remember and identify the precise shade may be very short-lived. But none of these points implies that I do not have the concept of red_{17} at the time I experience it.[27] When I learn the right term for the shade I can see, namely, the term 'red_{17}', it will be very different from learning about momentum, charm in physics or inertial frames, which do involve acquiring new concepts. It will simply be acquiring a term for something I already grasp. My tagging the shade with the word does not create the concept in me, though it does give me the wherewithal to *say* that it applies.[28] Any thought to the contrary would appear to conflate the concept of red_{17}—the shade—with the distinct, relational concept of being indistinguishable from the sample labeled 'red$_{17}$' in some color chart. It might be objected that this latter concept is the one we have in fact been talking about all along. But if this is the case, the initial datum that we experience red$_{17}$ prior to acquaintance with color charts is false. Prior to acquaintance with color charts, we do not experience colors as being the same as such and such a color on a color chart.

The same goes for shapes. It is sometimes suggested that when presented with a highly idiosyncratic shape, you may experience it but not have the concept of it. But we need to distinguish two cases. In one, you see something as having the highly idiosyncratic shape but you lack a word for it. In this case, you do have the concept. All that is lacking is a word for it, which you can remedy by making one up for yourself or by asking around to find out if there is already one in, say, English.[29] In the second kind of case, you do *not* experience the shape prior to having the word and the concept. There are cases where you see that something has some complex shape or other, where that shape is in fact S, but you fail to see it *as S*. You are then told the right word for the shape, acquire the concept it falls under, and thereby acquire the ability to see it *as S*. But then it is false that your experience represented that something is S prior to your mastery of the concept. Your acquisition of the concept changes the perceptual experience.

Of course, what it is to have a concept is disputed territory, and one might define concept possession in terms of having a word for that which falls under the concept. But in that case many beliefs lack conceptual content—animals and people have beliefs for which they do not have words. Or, more generally, one might raise the bar on what it is to possess a given concept in a way that, although it is plausible that anyone who believes that something is K has the concept of K, it is not plausible that anyone whose experience represents that something is K has the concept of K. But it is hard to see how any such reading of what it is to possess a concept could help with our problem. It *adds* to what it takes to believe, and, as we noted earlier, we are looking for something experience has and belief per se lacks.

A Different Way of Finding the Feel

To find the 'feel', I think representationalists should ask what is special about the representation that takes place when something looks or feels a certain way.[30] It seems to me that there are five distinctive features of cases where our sensory experience represents that things are thus and so.

First, such representation is *rich*. Visual experience represents how things are here and now in terms of color, shape, location, extension, orientation, and motion. Tactile experience represents how things are in terms of shape, motion, texture, extension, orientation, and temperature.

Second, it is *inextricably* rich. A sentence that says X is red and round has a part more concerned with redness and a part more concerned with roundness, and we can use sentences to represent something about color while being completely silent about shape or motion or position, and conversely. But you cannot prize the color bit from the shape bit of a visual experience. In representing something about shape, a visual experience ipso facto says something about color (in the wide sense that includes white, black, and gray); and a similar point applies to extension, location, and motion. Equally, you cannot prize the texture and temperature bits from the shape bit of a tactile representation. Something cannot feel to have some shape or other without feeling to have a texture or a temperature (in the wide sense that includes being neither hotter nor colder than one's limb).

Third, the representation is immediate. Reading from a piece of paper that there is something of such and such a color, location, and so on typically induces a belief that represents that there is, but it does so *via* representing that there is a piece of paper with certain marks on it. Of course, immediacy may vary over time. Someone who uses a stick to feel the shape of an object down a hole will start by working from the feel of the end of the stick in his hand, but he typically ends up over time in a state that represents immediately the object's shape. The transition will match the transition from having an experience he characterizes in terms of how his hand is felt to be to one he characterizes in terms of how the object at the end of the stick is being felt to be.

Fourth, there is a causal element in the content. Perception represents the world as interacting with us. When I hear a sound as being, say, behind and to the left, my experience represents the sound as *coming from* this location. To feel something is to feel in part its *contact with* one's body. Vision represents things as being located where we *see* them as being, as being at the location from which they are affecting us via our sense of sight.

Finally, sensory experience plays a distinctive functional role. Many years ago Armstrong analyzed perceptual experience in terms of the acquisition of a disposition to believe as a result of the operation of one's senses.[31] But, as many have objected, the top line in the Müller-Lyer figure looks longer despite the fact that, for experienced customers, there is no tendency whatever to believe that it is. What is, however, true of sensory experience is that it plays a distinctive functional role in mediating between one state of belief and another. It is not itself a state of belief. And it need not move a subject into a state of belief that represents as it does—the subject may know that they are the subject of illusion or hallucination, or may already believe things are as the experience represents them—but it will determine a function that maps states of belief onto states of belief. A subject's posterior state of belief supervenes on her prior state of belief conjoined with her sensory experience.

Obviously, there is much more to say here, both by way of elucidation and by way of defense, but I hope the leading idea is clear. It is that if a representational state's content has inextricably and immediately the requisite richness, and if the state plays the right functional role, we get the phenomenology for free. In such cases, there must be the kind of experience that the blind-sighted, the believers in what is written on notes, and the bold guessers lack.

To give a sense of the intuitive appeal of this approach, think of what happens when you summon up a mental image of an event described in a passage of prose. To make it image-like, you *have* to fill in the gaps; you have to include a red shirt kicking the winning goal from some part of the football field with some given trajectory, you have to make the goal scorer some putative size or other, you have to locate the goal somewhere, and so on. Much can be left indeterminate, but you have to put in lots more detail than is delivered in the passage of prose. Also, you need to create a representation that represents inextricably. The 'part' that delivers the size of the scorer is also the 'part' that delivers the putative location of the scorer and the color of the shirt. And so on. To the extent that you succeed, you create a state with a phenomenology.

Back to Mary on Her Release

So what is the before and after story about Mary? If feel is a matter of immediacy, inextricability, and richness of representational content, and the right kind of functional role, the difference is that, after her release, Mary has representational states with all those properties. If she makes the mistake of conflating intensional properties with instantiated properties, she will think that she has learned something new about how things are, but she'll be wrong. Rather, she is in a new kind of representational state, different from those she was in before. And what is it to know what it is like to be in that kind of state? Presumably, it is to be able to recognize, remember, and imagine the state. Once we turn our back on the idea that there is a new property with which she is directly acquainted, knowing what it is like to sense red can only be something about the new kind of representational state she is in, and the obvious candidates for that 'something about' are her abilities to recognize, imagine, and remember the state. Those who resist accounts in terms of ability acquisition tend to say things like 'Mary acquires a new piece of propositional knowledge, namely, that seeing red is like *this*', but for the representationalist there is nothing suitable to be the referent of the demonstrative.

We have ended up agreeing with Laurence Nemirow and David Lewis on what happens to Mary on her release.[32] But, for the life of me, I cannot see how we could have known they were right without going via representationalism.

Notes

1. Over the years I have received a large number of papers, letters, and e-mails seeking to convince me of the error of my old ways. Much of what I say below was absorbed from, or was a response in one form or another to, this material, but I am now unsure who deserves credit for exactly what. More recently I am indebted to discussions of various presentations of "Representation and Experience" in *Representation in Mind: New Approaches to Mental Representation*, H. Clapin, P. Slezack, and P. Staines (eds.) (Elsevier, 2004).

2. See, e.g., my "Epiphenomenal Qualia," *Philosophical Quarterly* 32 (1982): 127–136, reprinted in this volume. The argument has a long history in one form or another. For an outline version drawn to my attention recently, see J. W. Dunne, *An Experiment with Time* (London: Faber and Faber, 1927), pp. 13–14.

3. This claim is common enough but it has been disputed on the basis of a Twin Earth argument. See Ned Block and Robert Stalnaker, "Conceptual Analysis, Dualism, and the Explanatory Gap," *Philosophical Review* 108 (1999): 1–46. For a response, see David J. Chalmers and Frank Jackson, "Conceptual Analysis and Reductive Explanation," *Philosophical Review* 110 (2001): 315–361.

4. See, e.g., Block and Stalnaker, "Conceptual Analysis," but this is but one example among many.

5. See, e.g., my "Critical Notice of Susan Hurley, *Natural Reasons*," *Australasian Journal of Philosophy* **70** (1992): 475–487, and *From Metaphysics to Ethics: A Defence of Conceptual Analysis* (Oxford: Clarendon Press, 1998).

6. Most recently by Block and Stalnaker, "Conceptual Analysis." For a fuller development of the reply in the text, see my "From H_2O to Water: The Relevance to *A Priori* Passage," in *Real Metaphysics; Papers for D. H. Mellor*, Halvard Lillehammer et al. (eds.) (London: Routledge, 2002). Many once held, and some still hold, that the first premise, suitably fleshed out, is necessarily true as well as a priori. Nothing here turns on this issue. Incidentally, I am following the philosopher's lazy practice of simplifying the science.

7. See David J. Chalmers and Frank Jackson, "Conceptual Analysis and Reductive Explanation."

8. See, e.g., Alex Byrne, "Cosmic Hermeneutics," *Philosophical Perspectives* **13** (1999): 347–383.

9. In my view, the illusion also fuels the modal intuitions encapsulated in the zombie, absent *qualia*, inverted *qualia*, etc. arguments, but I do not argue that here (though it may be clear how the argument would go).

10. G. E. Moore, "The Refutation of Idealism," *Philosophical Studies* (London: Routledge and Kegan Paul, 1922), 1–30.

11. David Hume, *Treatise of Human Nature*, bk. I, pt. IV, sec. VI.

12. See, e.g., Gilbert Harman, "The Intrinsic Quality of Experience," *Philosophical Perspectives* **4** (1990): 31–52.

13. These properties include the usual suspects like extension, color, and shape, but I see no reason not to include, e.g., being a hydrometer. We can see something *as* a hydrometer. The difference between, e.g., being extended and being a hydrometer is that you cannot see something without seeing it as extended, whereas you can see something without seeing it as a hydrometer.

14. See, e.g., my *Perception* (Cambridge: Cambridge University Press, 1977).

15. For a recent view of this kind, see John Foster, *The Nature of Perception* (Oxford: Oxford University Press, 2000), part 3.

16. E.g., recently by Michael Tye, *Consciousness, Color, and Content* (Cambridge, Mass.: The MIT Press, 2000); see also Alex Byrne, "Intentionalism Defended," *Philosophical Review* **110** (2001): 199–240. I should, perhaps, footnote what I think should be said about one example. The very same shape may have a different visual appearance depending on its putative orientation with respect to the subject. This in itself is

no problem for representationalism, as orientation is part of how things are represented to be. However, as Christopher Peacocke points out, e.g., in "Scenarios, Concepts, and Perception" in *The Contents of Experience*, Tim Crane (ed.) (Cambridge: Cambridge University Press, 1992), pp. 105–135, seeing something as a regular diamond and as a square on its side need differ neither in putative shape nor orientation, and yet may still differ experientially. However, when this happens, one figure is being represented to be symmetrical about a line through its corners and the other about a line parallel to its sides.

17. How things are being represented to be need not be determinate. My experience may represent that something is a roundish shape without representing that it is any particular shape—the experience represents that there is some precise shape it has but there is no precise shape that the experience represents it to have. Indeed, it is arguable that all experience has some degree or other of indeterminacy about it. The same goes for maps and most sentences, of course.

18. I am indebted here to a discussion with Ned Block but he will not approve of my conclusion.

19. See, e.g., Michael Tye, *Consciousness, Color, and Content* (Cambridge, Mass.: The MIT Press, 2000) and *Ten Problems of Consciousness* (Cambridge, Mass.: The MIT Press, 1995). Tye's suggestion is *not* that the whole story about where the feel comes from lies in sensory states having nonconceptual content. But it is a key part of the story.

20. As has been widely recognized, most recently in Richard G. Heck, Jr., "Nonconceptual Content and the Space of Reasons," *Philosophical Review* **109** (2000): 483–523; see also Tim Crane, "The Nonconceptual Content of Experience" in *The Contents of Experience*, Tim Crane, (ed.), pp. 136–157.

21. I think it is the way Tye wants to go but I am unsure. But let me say that here, and in the immediately following, I draw on helpful if unresolved discussions with him.

22. For recent example, Richard G. Heck, Jr., "Nonconceptual Content and the Space of Reasons." He is affirming it as an agreed view.

23. I am here agreeing with Tim Crane, "The Nonconceptual Content of Experience," p. 140, but he would not, I think, agree with the use I make of the point on which we agree.

24. Alex Byrne, "Consciousness and Higher-Order Thoughts," *Philosophical Studies* **86** (1997): 103–129, see p. 117.

25. Some argue that the two understandings are connected as follows: the reason for holding that belief contents are special in containing, in some sense, the relevant concepts is that having a belief is special in requiring that one has the relevant concepts.

26. As Christopher Peacocke puts it in *Sense and Content* (Oxford: Oxford University Press, 1983), p. 7: "[experience] can hardly present the world as being [a certain] way if the subject is incapable of appreciating what that way is." Peacocke no longer holds this view.

27. Michael Tye, *Ten Problems of Consciousness*, p. 139, suggests that the key point is that to believe that something is F requires having a stored memory representation of F whereas to experience it as F does not. Thus, belief requires possession of the concept F in a way that experience does not. But one can believe that something is F for the very first time, and if the point is merely that one's system needs to have already in place the capacity to categorize something as F, that is equally plausible for both belief and experience. Christopher Peacocke, "Analogue Content," *Proceedings of the Aristotelian Society*, supp. vol. 15 (1986): 1–17, points out that when we enter a room full of abstract sculptures, we perceive things as having particular shapes but need not have "*in advance* concepts of these particular shapes" (p. 15, my emphasis). This is true, but it does not show that we do not have the concepts at the time we see the things as having the shapes.

28. The talk of tagging the shade should not be understood on the model of a demonstration. According to representationalism, there need be no instance of the color shade to be demonstrated.

29. What drives the idea that the lack of words implies a lack of concepts sometimes seems to be the modal claim that it is impossible to have words for all the shapes and colors we represent in experience, together with the plausible thesis that if I have the concept of, e.g., a certain shape, it must be possible for me to have word for it. However, although it is impossible for me to have a word for every shape I discriminate, for any shape I discriminate, it is possible that I have word for it.

30. I am here following David Armstrong, but he should not be held responsible for the details.

31. D. M. Armstrong, *Perception and the Physical World* (London: Routledge and Kegan Paul, 1961), p. 128.

32. Laurence Nemirow, "Review of T. Nagel, *Mortal Questions*," *Philosophical Review* 89 (1980): 475–476, and "Physicalism and the Cognitive Role of Acquaintance," *Mind and Cognition*, W. G. Lycan (ed.) (Oxford: Basil Blackwell, 1990), 490–499; David Lewis, "What Experience Teaches," reprinted in this vol.

Supplemental Bibliography

This bibliography is divided into four sections. The first section covers books and papers published before 1982, when Jackson's "Epiphenomenal Qualia" was published. Most of the material in this section contains precursors of the knowledge argument. The second section covers books and papers on the knowledge argument published after 1982. We tried to include all materials whose main topic is the knowledge argument. The third part covers selected books and papers on issues of consciousness in general. The fourth part covers other relevant nonphilosophical materials. We would be grateful to be told of errors or omissions.

The latest version of the bibliography is found at ⟨http://philrsss.anu.edu.au/~yujin/ka.html⟩.

1   The Knowledge Argument: Pre-1982

Books

Broad, C. D. 1925. *The Mind and Its Place in Nature*. London: Routledge and Kegan Paul.

Dunne, J. W. 1958 (originally 1927). *An Experiment with Time*. London: Farber and Farber.

Feigl, Herbert. 1967. *The 'Mental' and the 'Physical': The Essay and a Postscript*. Minneapolis: University of Minnesota Press.

Locke, John. 1975 (originally 1689). *An Essay Concerning Human Understanding*. New York: Oxford.

Nagel, Thomas. 1979. *Mortal Questions*. Cambridge: Cambridge University Press.

Robinson, Howard. 1982. *Matter and Sense*. Cambridge: Cambridge University Press.

Russell, Bertrand. 1967 (originally 1912). *Problems of Philosophy*. Oxford: Oxford University Press.

Wittgenstein, Ludwig. 1980. *Remarks on the Philosophy of Psychology*, vol. 1. Chicago: University of Chicago Press.

Papers

Farrell, B. A. 1950. "Experience." *Mind* 59: 170–198.

Feigl, Herbert. 1958. "The 'Mental' and the 'Physical'." In *Minnesota Studies in the Philosophy of Science*, ed. Herbert Feigl, Michael Scriven, and Grover Maxwell, 370–497. Minneapolis: University of Minnesota Press.

Maxwell, Nicholas. 1966. "Physics and Common Sense." *British Journal for the Philosophy of Science* 16: 295–311.

——. 1968. "Understanding Sensations." *Australasian Journal of Philosophy* 46: 127–145.

Meehl, Paul E. 1966. "The Complete Autocerebroscopist." In *Mind, Matter, and Method: Essays in Philosophy and Science in Honor of Herbert Feigl*, ed. by Paul Feyerabend and Grover Maxwell, 103–180. Minneapolis: University of Minnesota Press.

Nagel, Thomas. 1974. "What Is It Like to Be a Bat?" *Philosophical Review* 83: 435–450. Reprinted in his 1979, and Block, Flanagan, and Güzeldere 1997.

Prior, A. N. (1959). "Thank Goodness That's Over." *Philosophy* 34: 12–17.

Prior, A. N. (1962). "The Formalities of Omniscience." *Philosophy* 37: 114–149.

Sprigge, Timothy. 1971. "Final Causes." *Proceeding of the Aristotelian Society*, supplementary volume 45: 149–170.

2 The Knowledge Argument: Post-1982

Books

Braddon-Mitchell, David, and Frank Jackson. 1996. *Philosophy of Mind and Cognition*. Oxford: Blackwell.

Carruthers, Peter. 2000. *Phenomenal Consciousness: A Naturalistic Theory*. Cambridge: Cambridge University Press.

Chalmers, David J. 1996. *The Conscious Mind: In Search of a Fundamental Theory*. New York: Oxford University Press.

——, ed. 2002. *Philosophy of Mind: Classical and Contemporary Readings*. Oxford: Oxford University Press.

Churchland, Paul M. 1989. *A Neurocomputational Perspective*. Cambridge, Mass.: The MIT Press.

Churchland, Paul M., and Patricia S. Churchland. 1998. *On the Contrary: Critical Essays, 1987–1997*. Cambridge, Mass.: The MIT Press.

Crane, Tim. 2001. *Elements of Mind*. Oxford: Oxford University Press.

Davies, Martin, and Glyn W. Humphreys, eds. 1993. *Consciousness: Psychological and Philosophical Essays*. Oxford: Blackwell.

Dennett, Daniel C. 1991. *Consciousness Explained*. Boston: Little Brown and Company. Excerpt reprinted in this volume (chapter 3).

Dretske, Fred. 2000. *Perception, Knowledge, and Belief*. Cambridge: Cambridge University Press.

Flanagan, Owen. 1992. *Consciousness Reconsidered*. Cambridge, Mass.: The MIT Press.

Jackson, Frank, ed. 1998. *Consciousness (The International Research Library of Philosophy)*. Aldershot, Hampshire: Dartmouth Publishing.

———. 1998. *Mind, Method, and Conditionals: Selected Essays*. London: Routledge.

Lycan, William G. 1987. *Consciousness*. Cambridge, Mass.: The MIT Press.

———, ed. 1990. *Mind and Cognition: A Reader*. Oxford: Blackwell.

———. 1996. *Consciousness and Experiences*. Cambridge, Mass.: The MIT Press.

———, ed. 1999. *Mind and Cognition: An Anthology*. Oxford: Blackwell.

Metzinger, Thomas, ed. 1995. *Conscious Experience*. Exeter: Imprint Academics.

Moser, Pual K., and J. D. Trout, eds. 1995. *Contemporary Materialism*. London: Routledge.

Papineau, David. 1993. *Philosophical Naturalism*. Oxford: Blackwell.

Perry, John. 2001. *Knowledge, Possibility, and Consciousness*. Cambridge, Mass.: The MIT Press.

Robinson, Howard, ed. 1993. *Objections to Physicalism*. Oxford: Oxford University Press.

Seager, William. 1991. *Metaphysics of Consciousness*. New York: Routledge.

Shear, Jonathan, ed. 1997. *Explaining Consciousness: The Hard Problem*. Cambridge, Mass.: The MIT Press.

Smith, Quentin, and Aleksandar Jokic, eds. 2003. *Consciousness: New Philosophical Perspectives*. Oxford: Clarendon Press.

Thau, Michael. 2002. *Consciousness and Cognition*. Oxford: Oxford University Press.

Tye, Michael. 1989. *The Metaphysics of Mind*. Cambridge: Cambridge University Press.

———. 2000. *Consciousness, Color, and Content*. Cambridge, Mass.: The MIT Press.

Villanueva, Enrique, ed. 1991. *Consciousness: Philosophical Issues*, vol. 1, Atascedero, Calif.: Ridgeview.

Papers

Alter, Torin. "What a Vulcan Couldn't Know." Unpublished manuscript.

———. 1995. "Knowing What It Is Like." UCLA doctoral dissertaion.

———. 1995. "Mary's New Perspective." *Australasian Journal of Philosophy* 73: 582–584.

———. 1998. "A Limited Defence of the Knowledge Argument." *Philosophical Studies* 90: 35–56.

———. 1999. "The Knowledge Argument (A Field Guide to the Philosophy of Mind)." Available at ⟨http://host.uniroma3.it/progetti/kant/field/ka.html⟩.

———. 2001. "Know-How, Ability, and the Ability Hypothesis." *Theoria* 67: 229–239.

———. 2002. "Implicit Phenomenal Knowledge and the Lewis–Nemirow Ability Hypothesis." Available at ⟨http://www.bama.ua.edu/~talter/Implicit.htm⟩.

Anchustegui, Ann-Marie. 1999. "The Knowledge Argument and the Multiple Route Doctrine." Unpublished paper presented at the American Philosophical Association, Pacific Division.

Beisecker, David. 2000. "There's Something About Mary: Phenomenal Consciousness and Its Attributions." *Southwest Philosophy Review* 16: 143–152.

Bigelow, John, and Robert Pargetter 1990. "Acquaintance with Qualia." *Theoria* 61: 129–147. Reprinted as chapter 8, this volume.

Byeong, Yi. "The Nature of What Mary Didn't Know." Unpublished manuscript.

Byrne, Alex. 2002. "Something About Mary." *Grazer Philosophische Studien* 63: 123–140.

Campbell, Neil. 2003. "An Inconsistency in the Knowledge Argument." *Erkenntnis* 58: 261–266.

Chalmers, David J. 1995. "The Puzzle of Conscious Experience." *Scientific American* (Special Issue: Mysteries of the Mind): 30–37.

———. 2003. "The Content and Epistemology of Phenomenal Belief." In *Consciousness: New Philosophical Perspectives*, ed. by Quentin Smith and Aleksandar Jokic, 220–272. Oxford: Clarendon Press.

———. 2004. "Phenomenal Concepts and the Knowledge Argument." Chapter 13, this volume.

Churchland, Paul M. 1985. "Book Review: *Matter and Sense* by Howard Robinson." *Philosophical Review* 94: 117–120.

———. 1985. "Reduction, Qualia, and the Direct Introspection of Brain States." *Journal of Philosophy* 82: 8–28. Reprinted in Churchland 1989.

———. 1989. "Knowing Qualia: A Reply to Jackson." In his *A Neurocomputational Perspective*, 67–76. Cambridge, Mass.: The MIT Press. Reprinted in Block, Flanagan and Güzeldere 1997 and in chapter 8, this volume.

———. 1998. "Postscript: 1997." In his *On the Contrary: Critical Essays, 1987–1997*, 153–157. Cambridge, Mass.: The MIT Press. Reprinted in chapter 8, this volume.

Conee, Earl. 1985. "Physicalism and Phenomenal Properties." *Philosophical Quarterly* 35: 296–302.

———. 1994. "Phenomenal Knowledge." *Australasian Journal of Philosophy* 72: 136–150. Reprinted as chapter 10, this volume.

Crane, Tim. 2003. "Subjective Facts." In *Real Metaphysics: Essays in honour of D. H. Mellor*, ed. by Hallvard Lillehammer and Gonzalo Rodriguez-Pereyra. London: Routlege.

Dennett, Daniel C. 1994. "Get Real." *Philosophical Topics* 22: 505–568.

Dretske, Fred. 1999. "The Mind's Awareness of Itself." *Philosophical Studies* 95: 103–124. Reprinted in Dretske 2000.

Endicott, Ronald P. 1995. "The Refutation by Analogous Ectoqualia." *Southern Journal of Philosophy* 33: 19–30.

Foss, Jeff. 1989. "On the Logic of What It Is Like to Be a Conscious Subject." *Australasian Journal of Philosophy* 67: 205–220.

Furash, Gary. 1989. "Frank Jackson's Knowledge Argument against Materialism." *Dialogue* 32: 1–6.

Gertler, Brie. 1999. "A Defence of the Knowledge Argument." *Philosophical Studies* 93: 317–336.

Graham, George, and Terence Horgan. 2000. "Mary, Mary, Quite Contrary." *Philosophical Studies* 99: 59–87.

Grahek, Nikola. 1986. "The Limit of Functional and Physicalistic Knowledge of Mental States." (In Serbo-Croatian.) *Filozofska Istrazivanja* 18: 703–712.

Hellie, Benj. 2004. "Inexpressible Truth and the Allure of the Knowledge Argument." Chapter 16, this volume.

Harman, Gilbert. 1990. "The Intrinsic Quality of Experience." In *Philosophical Perspectives*, vol. 4, 31–52. Atascadero: Ridgeview. Reprinted in Block, Flangan, and Güzeldere 1997.

Horgan, Terence. 1984. "Jackson on Physical Information and *Qualia*." *Philosophical Quaterly* 34: 147–152. Reprinted as chapter 14, this volume.

Huang, Yih-mei. 1990. "Physicalism and Qualia." (In Chinese.) *Philosophical Review (Taiwan)* 13: 161–184.

Jackson, Frank. 1982. "Epiphenomenal Qualia." *Philosophical Quaterly* 32: 127–136. Reprinted in Lycan 1999; Chalmers 2002; and as chapter 1, this volume.

———. 1986. "What Mary Didn't Know." *Journal of Philosophy* 83: 291–295. Reprinted in Block, Flanagan, and Güzeldere 1997; Moser and Trout 1995; and as chapter 2, this volume.

———. 1995. "Postscript." In *Contemporary Materialism*, ed. by Paul K. Moser and J. D. Trout, 184–189. New York: Routledge. Reprinted as chapter 18, this volume.

———. 1998. "Postscript on Qualia." In his *Mind, Method, and Conditionals*, 76–79. London: Routledge. Reprinted as chapter 19, this volume.

———. 2000. "Some Reflections on Representationalism." Available at ⟨http://www. nyu.edu/gsas/dept/philo/courses/consciousness/papers/RepresentationalismNYU5 April00.PDF⟩.

———. 2002. "Mind and Illusion." Paper presented at the Royal Institute of Philosophy. Chapter 20, this volume.

———. 2004. "Looking Back on the Knowledge Argument." Foreword, this volume.

———. 2003. "Knowledge Argument." *Richmond Journal of Philosophy* 1: 6–10.

Jacquette, Dale. 1995. "The Blue Banana Trick: Dennett on Jackson's Color Scientist." *Theoria* 61: 217–230.

Kiernan-Lewis, Delmas. 1991. "Not Over Yet: Prior's 'Thank Goodness' Argument." *Philosophy* 66: 241–243.

Levine, Joseph. 1993. "On Leaving Out What It's Like." In *Consciousness: Psychological and Philosophical Essays*, ed. by M. Davies and Glyn W. Humphreys, 121–136. Oxford: Blackwell. Reprinted in Block, Flanagan, and Güzeldere 1997.

Lewis, David. 1988. "What Experience Teaches." In *Proceedings of Russellian Society* 13: 29–57. Reprinted in Lycan 1999; Block, Flanagan, and Güzeldere 1997; Chalmers 2002; and as chapter 5, this volume.

Loar, Brian. 1990. "Phenomenal States." In *Philosophical Perspectives IV: Action Theory and the Philosophy of Mind*, ed. by James Tomberlin, 81–108. Atascadero: Ridgeview.

———. 1997. "Phenomenal States (Revised Version)." In Block, Flanagan, and Güzeldere (1997), 597–616. Cambridge, Mass.: The MIT Press. Reprinted in Chalmers 2002; excerpt reprinted in this volume (chapter 11).

Lycan, William G. 1990. "What Is the 'Subjectivity' of the Mental?" In *Philosophical Perspectives IV: Action Theory and the Philosophy of Mind*, 109–130. Atascadero: Ridgeview.

———. 1995. "A Limited Defence of Phenomenal Information." In *Conscious Experience*, ed. by Thomas Metzinger, 243–258. Exeter: Imprint Academic.

———. 2003. "Perspectival Representation and the Knowledge Argument." In *Consciousness: New Philosophical Perspectives*, ed. by Quentin Smith and Aleksandar Jokic, 384–395. Oxford: Clarendon Press.

McConnell, Jeff. 1995. "In Defence of the Knowledge Argument." *Philosophical Topics* 22: 157–187.

McDonald, Cynthia. "Mary Meets Molyneux: The Explanatory Gap and the Individuation of Phenomenal Concepts." Unpublished paper.

McGeer, Victoria. 2003. "The Trouble with Mary." *Pacific Philosophical Quarterly* 84: 384–393.

McMullen, Carolyn. 1985. "'Knowing What It's Like' and the Essential Indexicals." *Philosophical Studies* 48: 211–233.

Mellor, D. H. 1993. "Nothing Like Experience." *Proceedings of the Aristotelian Society* 93: 1–16.

Meyer, Uwe. 2001. "The Knowledge Argument, Abilities, and Metalinguistic Beliefs." *Erkenntnis* 55: 325–347.

Montero, Barbara. 1999. "Frank Jackson Changed His Mind." *Philosophy News Service*.

Moreland, J. P. 2003. "The Knowledge Argument Revisited." *International Philosophical Quarterly* 43: 219–228.

Nagasawa, Yujin. 2002. "The Knowledge Argument against Dualism." *Theoria* 68: 205–223.

Nemirow, Lawrence. 1990. "Physicalism and the Cognitive Role of Acquaintance." In *Mind and Cognition: A Reader*, ed. by William G. Lycan, 490–499. Oxford: Blackwell.

Newton, Natika. 1986. "Churchland on Direct Introspection of Brain States." *Analysis* 46: 97–102.

Nida-Rümelin, Martine. 1995. "What Mary Couldn't Know: Belief About Phenomenal States." In *Conscious Experience*, ed. by Thomas Metzinger, 219–241. Exeter: Imprint Academic. Reprinted as chapter 12, this volume.

———. 1998. "On Belief About Experiences: An Epistemological Distinction Applied to the Knowledge Argument against Physicalism." *Philosophy and Phenomenological Research* 58: 51–73.

———. 2002. "Knowledge Argument." In the *Stanford Encyclopedia of Philosophy*, available at ⟨http://plato.stanford.edu/entries/qualia-knowledge/⟩.

Noordhof, Paul. 2003. "Something Like Ability." *Australasian Journal of Philosophy* 81: 21–40.

Papineau, David. 1993. "Physicalism, Consciousness, and the Antipathetic Fallacy." *Australasian Journal of Philosophy* 71: 169–183.

———. 1995. "The Antipathetic Fallacy and the Boundaries of Consciousness." In *Conscious Experience*, ed. by Thomas Metzinger, 259–270. Exeter: Imprint Academic.

———. 2003. "Theories of Consciousness." In *Consciousness: New Philosophical Perspectives*, ed. by Quentin Smith and Aleksandar Jokic, 353–383. Oxford: Clarendon Press.

Pereboom, Derek. 1994. "Bats, Brain Scientists, and the Limitations of Introspection." *Philosophy and Phenomenological Research* 54: 315–329.

Pettit, Philip. 2004. "Motion Blindness and the Knowledge Argument." Chapter 6, this volume.

Ravenscroft, Ian. 1998. "What Is It Like to be Someone Else?" *Ratio* 11: 170–185.

Raymont, Paul. 1995. "Tye's Criticism of the Knowledge Argument." *Dialogue* 34: 713–726.

———. 1999. "The Know-How Response to Jackson's Knowledge Argument." *Journal of Philosophical Research* 24: 113–126.

Robinson, Howard. 1993. "The Anti-Materialist Strategy and the 'Knowledge Argument'." In his 1993, 159–183.

———. 1993. "Dennett on the Knowledge Argument." *Analysis* 53: 174–177. Reprinted as chapter 4, this volume.

Sommers, Tamler. 2002. "Of Zombies, Color Scientists, and Floating Iron Bars." *Psyche* 8. Available at ⟨http://psyche.cs.monash.edu.au/v8/psyche-8-22-sommers.html⟩.

Stemmer, Nathan. 1989. "Physicalism and the Argument from Knowledge." *Australasian Journal of Philosophy* 67: 84–91.

Stjernberg, Fredrik. 1999. "Not So Epiphenomenal Qualia, or, How Much of a Mystery Is the Mind?" Available at ⟨http://www.lucs.lu.se/spinning/categories/language/Stjernberg/index.html⟩.

Stoljar, Daniel. 2000. "Physicalism and the Necessary A Posteriori." *Journal of Philosophy* 97: 33–54.

———. 2001. "Two Conceptions of the Physical." *Philosophy and Phenomenological Research* 62: 253–281. Reprinted in Chalmers (2002); excerpt reprinted in this volume (chapter 15).

———. "Physicalism and Phenomenal Concepts." Unpublished manuscript.

Thomas, Nigel J. T. 1998. "Mary Doesn't Know Science: On Misconceiving a Science of Consciousness." Paper presented at the American Philosophical Association, Pacific Division.

Thompson, Evan. 1992. "Novel Colors." *Philosophical Studies* 68: 321–349.

Tye, Michael. 1986. "The Subjective Qualities of Experience." *Mind* 95: 1–17. Reprinted in his 1989.

———. 1997. "Qualia." In *Stanford Encyclopedia of Philosophy*, available at ⟨http://plato.stanford.edu/entries/qualia/⟩.

———. 1998. "Knowing What It Is Like: The Ability Hypothesis and the Knowledge Argument." In *Reality and Humean Supervenience: Essays on the Philosophy of David Lewis*, ed. by Gerhard Preyer and Frank Siebelt. Frankfurt: Proto Sociology. Reprinted in his 2000; and as chapter 7, this volume.

Van Gulick, Robert. 1993. "Understanding the Phenomenal Mind: Are We All just Armadillos?" In *Consciousness: Psychological and Philosophical Essays*, ed. by Martin Davies and Glyn W. Humphreys, 137–154. Oxford: Balckwell. Reprinted in Lycan 1999; Block, Flanagan, and Güzeldere 1997.

———. 2003. "Maps, Gaps, and Traps." In *Consciousness: New Philosophical Perspectives*, ed. by Quentin Smith and Aleksandar Jokic, 323–352. Oxford: Clarendon Press.

———. 2004. "So Many Ways of Saying No to Mary." Chapter 17, this volume.

Vierkant, Tillmann. 2002. "Zombie-Mary and the Blue Banana: On the Compatibility of the 'Knowledge Argument' with the Argument from Modality." *Psyche* 8. Available at ⟨http://psyche.cs.monash.edu.au/v8/psyche-8-19-vierkant.html⟩.

Vinueza, Adam. "The Knowledge Argument." In the *Dictionary of Philosophy of Mind*, available at ⟨http://www.artsci.wustl.edu/~philos/MindDict/knowledgeargument.html⟩.

———. 2002. "Knowledge Argument." In *Encyclopedia of Cognitive Science*, ed. by Lynn Nadel. New York: Grove's Dictionaries.

Walter, Sven. 2002. "Terry, Terry, Quite Contrary." *Grazer Philosophische Studien* 63: 103–122.

Waner, Richard. 1986. "A Challenge to Physicalism." *Australasian Journal of Philosophy* 64: 249–265.

Watkins, Michael. 1989. "The Knowledge Argument against the Knowledge Argument." *Analysis* 49: 158–160.

3 Consciousness in General

Books
Beakley, Brian, and Peter Ludlow, eds. 1994. *Philosophy of Mind: Classical Problems and Contempoary Issues*. Cambridge, Mass.: The MIT Press.

Block, Ned, Owen Flanagan, and Güven Güzeldere, eds. 1997. *The Nature of Consciousness: Philosophical Debates.* Cambridge, Mass.: The MIT Press.

Brown, Warren S., Nancy Murphy, and H. Newton Malony, eds. 1998. *Whatever Happened to the Soul? Scientific and Theological Portraits of Human Nature.* Minneapolis: Fortress Press.

Chomsky, Noam. 1980. *Rules and Representations.* New York: Columbia University Press.

———. 1988. *Language and Problem of Knowledge.* Cambridge, Mass.: The MIT Press. Excerpt reprinted in Beakley and Ludlow 1994.

———. 1988. *Language and Problems of Knowledge: The Managua Lectures.* Cambridge, Mass.: The MIT Press.

Dretske, Fred. 1988. *Explaining Behavior: Reasons in a World of Causes.* Cambridge, Mass.: The MIT Press.

Foster, John. 1991. *Immaterial Self.* London: Routledge.

Hardin, C. L. 1988. *Color for Philosophers.* Indianapolis: Hackett.

Jackson, Frank. 1977. *Perception: A Representative Theory.* Cambridge: Cambridge University Press.

———. 1998. *From Metaphysics to Ethics.* Oxford: Oxford University Press.

Levine, Joseph. 2001. *Purple Haze: The Puzzle of Consciousness.* New York: Oxford University Press.

Lewis, David. 1999. *Papers in Metaphysics and Epistemology.* Cambridge: Cambridge University Press.

Lillehammer, Hallvard, and Gonzalo Rodriguez-Pereyra, eds. 2003. *Real Metaphysics: Essays in honour of D. H. Mellor.* London: Routledge.

McGinn, Colin. 1991. *The Problem of Consciousness.* Oxford: Blackwell.

Pinker, Steven. 1997. *How the Mind Works.* New York: W. W. Norton.

Ryle, Gilbert. 1949. *The Concept of Mind.* London: Hutchinson.

Searle, John R. 1992. *The Rediscovery of the Mind.* Cambridge, Mass.: The MIT Press.

Strawson, Galen. 1994. *Mental Reality.* Cambridge, Mass.: The MIT Press.

Tye, Michael. 1995. *Ten Problems of Consciousness: A Representational Theory of the Phenomenal Mind.* Cambridge, Mass.: The MIT Press.

White, Alan R. 1982. *The Nature of Knowledge.* Totowa, N.J.: Rowman and Littlefield.

Papers

Akins, Kathleen A. 1993. "A Bat without Qualities?" in *Consciousness: Psychological and Philosophical Essays*, ed. by Martin Davies and Glyn W. Humphreys, 258–273. Oxford: Blackwell.

Alter, Torin. 2002. "Qualia." In *Encyclopedia of Cognitive Science*, ed. by Lynn Nadel. New York: Grove's Dictionaries.

———. 2002. "On Two Alleged Conflicts between Divine Attributes." *Faith and Philosophy* 19: 47–57.

Bachrach, J. E. 1990. "Qualia and Theory of Reduction: A Criticism of Paul Churchland." *Iyyun* 39: 281–294.

Bealer, George. 1994. "Mental Properties." *Journal of Philosophy* 91: 185–208.

Biro, John. 1993. "Consciousness and Objectivity." In *Consciousness: Psychological and Philosophical Essays*, ed. by M. Davies and Glyn W. Humphreys, 178–196. Oxford: Blackwell.

Block, Ned. 1990. "Inverted Earth." In *Philosophical Perspectives*, vol. 4, ed. by James Tomberlin, 52–79. Atascadero: Ridgeview. Reprinted in Block, Flanagan, and Güzeldere 1997.

———. 1995. "On a Confusion About a Function of Consciousness." *Behavioral and Brain Sciences* 18: 227–247. Reprinted in Block, Flanagan, and Güzeldere 1997.

Boltuc, Piotr. 1998. "Reductionism and Qualia." *Epistemologia* 21: 111–130.

———. 1999. "Qualia, Robots, and Complementarity of Subject and Object." Available at ⟨http://www.bu.edu/wcp/Papers/Mind/MindBolt.htm⟩.

BonJour, Laurence. "What Is It Like to Be a Human (Instead of a Bat)?" Available at ⟨http://faculty.washington.edu/bonjour/Unpublished%20articles/MARTIAN.html⟩.

Byrne, Alex. 1999. "Cosmic Hermeneutics." In *Philosophical Perspectives, 13: Epistemology*, ed. by James Tomberlin. Atascadero, Calif.: Ridgeview.

Campbell, Keith. 1983. "Abstract Particulars and the Philosophy of Mind." *Australasian Journal of Philosophy* 61: 129–141.

Chalmers, David J. 1990. "Consciousness and Cognition." Available at ⟨http://www.u.arizona.edu/~chalmers/papers/c-and-c.html⟩.

———. 1995. "Facing Up to the Problem of Consciousness." *Journal of Consciousness Studies* 2: 200–219. Reprinted in Shear 1997.

———. 2003. "Consciousness and Its Place in Nature." In *Blackwell Guide to Philosophy of Mind*, ed. by Stephen P. Stich and Ted A. Warfield, 102–142. Oxford: Blackwell.

Chomsky, Noam. 1975. "Knowledge of Language." In *Minnesota Studies in the Philosophy of Science*, vol. 7: *Language, Mind, and Knowledge*, ed. by Keith Gunderson, 299–320. Minneapolis: University of Minnesota Press.

———. 1988. "Language and Problems of Knowledge." *Synthesis Philosophica* 5: 1–25.

———. 1992. "Language and Interpretation: Philosophical Reflections and Empirical Inquiry." In *Inference, Explanation, and Other Frustrations: Essays in the Philosophy of Science*, ed. by John Earman, 99–128. Los Angeles and Berkeley: University of California Press.

———. 1994. "Naturalism and Dualism." *International Journal of Philosophical Studies* 2: 181–209.

Churchland, Paul M. 1996. "The Rediscovery of Light." *Journal of Philosophy* 93: 211–228.

Crane, Tim, and D. H. Mellor 1990. "There Is No Question of Physicalism." *Mind* 99: 185–206.

Crane, Tim. 1993. "A Definition of Physicalism: Reply to Pettit." *Analysis* 53: 224–227.

Daly, Chris. 1998. "Modality and Acquaintance with Properties." *Monist*, 81: 44–68.

Ellis, Ralph D. 1999. "Why Isn't Consciousness Empirically Observable? Emotion, Self-organization, and Nonreductive Physicalism." *Journal of Mind and Behavior* 20: 391–402.

Gertler, Brie. 2001. "Introspecting Phenomenal States." *Philosophy and Phenomenological Research* 63: 305–328.

Hershfield, Jeffrey. 1998. "Lycan on the Subjectivity of the Mental." *Philosophical Psychology* 11: 229–238.

Howthorne, John. 2002. "Advice for Physicalists." *Philosophical Studies* 109: 17–52.

Hyslop, Alec. 1998. "Methodological Epiphenomenalism." *Australasian Journal of Philosophy* 76: 61–70.

Jackson, Frank. 1994. "Finding the Mind in the Natural World." In *Philosophy and the Cognitive Sciences: Proceeding of the 16th International Wittgenstein Symposium*, ed. by Roberto Csati, Barry Smith and Graham White, 101–112. Vienna: Verlag Holder-Pichler-Tempsky. Reprinted in Block, Flanagan, and Güzeldere 1997.

———. 1994. "Armchair Metaphysics." *Philosophy in Mind*, ed. by John O'Leary Hawthorne and Michaelis Michael, 23–42. Dordrecht: Kluwer.

———. 2003. "From H$_2$O to Water: The Relevance to A Priori Passage." In *Real Metaphysics: Essays in Honour of D. H. Mellor*, ed. by Hallvard Lillehammer and Gonzalo Rodriguez-Pereyra. London: Routledge.

Johnston, Mark. 1997. "Manifest Kinds." *Journal of Philosophy* 94: 564–583.

Jolley, Kelly Dean, and Michael Watkins. 1998. "What Is It Like to Be a Phenomenologist?" *Philosophical Quarterly* 48: 204–209.

Lahav, Ran. 1994. "A New Challenge for the Physicalist: Phenomenological Indistinguishability." *Philosophia* 24: 77–104.

Levin, Janet. 1986. "Could Love Be Like A Heatwave? Physicalism and the Subjective Character of Experience." *Philosophical Studies* 49: 245–261. Reprinted in Lycan 1990.

Levine, Joseph. 1983. "Materialism and Qualia: The Explanatory Gap." *Pacific Philosophical Quarterly* 64: 354–361.

Lewis, David. 1983. "Postscript to 'Mad Pain and Martian Pain'." In his *Philosophical Papers*, vol. 1, 130–132. New York: Oxford University Press.

———. 1995. "Should a Materialist Believe in Qualia?" *Australasian Journal of Philosophy* 73: 140–144. Reprinted in his *Papers in Metaphysics and Epistemology*, 325–331 (Cambridge: Cambridge University Press).

Lyons, William. 2001. *Matters of Mind*. Edinburgh: Edinburgh University Press.

Mander, William J. 2002. "Does God Know What It Is Like to Be Me?" *Heythrop Journal* 43: 430–443.

Maxwell, Nicholas. 2000. "The Mind–Body Problem and Explanatory Dualism." *Philosophy* 75: 49–71.

———. 2001. *The Human World in the Physical Universe*. Lanham, Maryland: Rowman and Littlefield.

———. 2002. "Three Philosophical Problems About Consciousness and Their Possible Solution." Unpublished manuscript.

McCulloch, Gregory. 1988. "What It Is Like." *Philosophical Quarterly* 38: 1–19.

McGinn, C. 1989. "Can We Solve the Mind–Body Problem?" *Mind* 98: 349–366.

Nagasawa, Yujin. 2002. "Review of *Purple Haze* by Joseph Levine." *Australasian Journal of Philosophy* 80: 245–247.

———. 2003. "God's Point of View: A Reply to Mander." *Heythrop Journal* 44: 60–63.

———. 2003. "Divine Omniscience and Experience: A Reply to Alter." *Ars Disputandi*. Available at ⟨http://www.arsdisputandi.org/publish/articles/000098/index.html⟩.

———. 2003. "Thomas vs. Thomas: A New Approach to Nagel's Bat Argument." *Inquiry* 46: 377–394.

Nagel, Thomas. 1979. "Subjective and Objective." In his *Mortal Questions*. Cambridge: Cambridge University Press.

Nemirow, Lawrence. 1980. "Review of *Mortal Questions* by Thomas Nagel." *Philosophical Review* 89: 473–477.

———. 1995. "Understanding Rules." *Journal of Philosophy* 92: 28–43.

Pettit, Philip. 1993. "A Definition of Physicalism." *Analysis* 53: 213–223.

Robinson, Denis. 1993. "Epiphenomenalism, Laws, and Properties." *Philosophical Studies* 69: 1–34.

Robinson, Willam S. "Qualia Realism (A Field Guide to The Philosophy of Mind)." Available at ⟨http://www.uniroma3.it/kant/field/qr.htm⟩.

———. 1999. "Epiphenomenalism." In *Stanford Encyclopedia of Philosophy*, available at ⟨http://plato.stanford.edu/entries/epiphenomenalism/⟩.

Shoemaker, Sydney. 1982. "The Inverted Spectrum." *Journal of Philosophy* 79: 357–381. Reprinted in Block, Flanagan, and Güzeldere 1997.

Stanley, Jason, and Timothy Williamson. 2001. "Knowing How." *Journal of Philosophy* 98: 411–444.

Stoljar, Daniel. "An Argument for Neutral Monism." Unpublished manuscript.

———. 2001. "Physicalism." In *Stanford Encyclopedia of Philosophy*, available at ⟨http://plato.stanford.edu/entries/physicalism/⟩.

Van Gulick, Robert. 1985. "Physicalism and the Subjectivity of the Mental." *Philosophical Topics* 22: 51–70.

Zemach, Eddy. 1990. "Churchland, Introspection, and Dualism." *Philosophia* 20: 3–13.

4 Some Relevant Nonphilosophical Reading

Lodge, David. 2001. *Thinks...*. London: Secker and Warburg Random House.

Nordby, Knut. 1996. "Vision in a Complete Achromat: A Personal Account." Available at ⟨http://www.u.arizona.edu/~chalmers/misc/achromat.html⟩.

Sacks, Oliver. 1985. *An Anthropologist on Mars*. New York: Alfred K. Knopf.

———. 1996. *The Island of the Colorblind*. New York: Alfred K. Knopf.

Wells, H. G. 2000 (originally written in 1904 and published in 1911). *The Country of the Blind*. London: Travelman.

Index